THE CAMPAIGN MANUAL

A Definitive Study of the Modern Political Campaign Process

6th Edition, 2002

by

S. J. Guzzetta
Political Campaign Consultant
American Association of Political Consultants

6th Edition Designed & Edited by
R. Authur Murray and Jean D. Justus

LIBRARY OF CONGRESS CARD CATALOG NO.: 81-67615

ISBN: 0-942805-09-7

Published and Distributed by:

AmeriCan GOTV Enterprises, LLC
and
Political Publications
425 Howard Gap Loop Rd.
Flat Rock, NC 28731

www.AmeriCanGOTV.com
info@AmeriCanGOTV.com

DEDICATION

Dedicated to my friend and partner,

Carole Seminara Guzzetta

and our daughter

Joanna Seminara Guzzetta

for their unfailing love and support.

Also

to my friend

Abe S. Ashcanase

for his inspiration, encouragement, and assistance.

ACKNOWLEDGMENTS

The author gratefully acknowledges the guidance and assistance provided him throughout his career by his mentor and friend, Dr. Joel Fisher, Ph.D., J.D. of Los Angeles, California, a noted authority on the American political process and the two-party system.

And to the many others, both in and out of the field of politics, who contributed so much to his education and training, especially Joe Cerrell, George Young, Eddie Mahe, Ronn Campbell, H. Fletcher Reynolds, Carol Allen, March Miller, Craig Markva, Angela Reese, Abe Ashcanase, Tom Edmonds, and Dr. Walt DeVries.

About the Author

Sal Guzzetta is a veteran Political Campaign Consultant who is considered to be among the top ten of his field. He has managed over 35 campaigns during the past 30 years and consulted on an additional 200 throughout the United States, at all levels of government.

A graduate of California State University, Fullerton, he holds a bachelor's degree in political science, the American Political Process, with minors in Economics, Communications, and Human Services. His graduate fields were in the American Political Process and International Relations. In addition to graduating with honors, he has the distinction of being one of the few individuals in this country to have completed all of his undergraduate work in 18 months.

After ten years as an insurance and business consultant, during which time he was also an active volunteer on numerous political campaigns in New York and California, he entered college with the deliberate intention of becoming a Political Campaign Consultant. Under the guidance of Dr. Joel Fisher, he developed a curriculum of studies designed to provide him with the foundation for this new career. He is, therefore, the first professional political campaign consultant in the industry. At that time, no other college or university offered a program for Political Campaign Consultants or managers.

Following his academic training, he apprenticed for a year with Joe Cerrell, Cerrell Associates, Inc., Los Angeles, California, working on campaigns in Beverly Hills and Los Angeles. This experience provided valuable "on the job" training in campaign techniques, especially fund-raising, public relations, and free media communications. Later, he continued his apprenticeship with George Young, George Young and Associates, Inc., Los Angeles, California. For two years, he managed campaigns in California, Michigan, and Pennsylvania. While with Mr. Young he developed an in depth knowledge of media production and placement, direct mail campaigns, and the dynamics of campaign management.

In 1975, he founded Campaign Management Associates, Inc. (CMA), a non-partisan political consulting and management firm in Los Angeles, California. Determined to provide a "one stop shop" for candidates in order to help reduce a campaign's overhead costs, he continually expanded the range of services provided. For four years, he continued to work on various campaigns around the country in Washington State, Iowa, Wisconsin, Florida, California, and other parts of the country.

It was during this period that Mr. Guzzetta developed and produced VERITAS, an integrated, voter identification and targeting program. VERITAS assisted candidates and Party Committees with the coordination of poll results, verifying data input, generating useful reports, maximizing the value of direct mailings, the management of phone bank and precinct operations, fund-raising, and with the development of appropriate manuals for campaign staff and volunteers.

In 1979 Mr. Guzzetta moved to the Washington, D.C. area and formed the political consulting firm of S. J. Guzzetta and Associates in Alexandria, Virginia. During this period, he consulted on campaigns in Maryland, Virginia, Delaware, Indiana, Texas, Louisiana, North Carolina, Illinois, California, Guam, and Michigan. In addition to his campaign consulting, he lectured, conducted campaign seminars, and did research and analysis in a constant effort to improve and refine the basic techniques and procedures used in campaign management. In 1988, in addition to his other activities, Mr. Guzzetta became the publisher of Political Publications and was responsible for developing its marketing and administrative program.

Mr. Guzzetta has been a frequent lecturer at the North Carolina Institute of Political Leadership, the Ted Sorensen Institute of Political Leadership in Virginia, the National Campaign Institute, Campaigns and Elections Seminars, Florida State University, the Graduate School of Political Management in New York City, the Campaign Management College, numerous national, and state party seminars, the American Association of Political Consultants, the American Medical Political Action Committee, and the Indiana Chamber of Commerce. He has participated as a co-sponsor and lecturer at the Campaigns and Elections Seminars in Hungary, Czechoslovakia, and Poland. He has also done lectures and provided political assistance to political parties in Taiwan and Brazil.

He wrote the 1st edition of *The Campaign Manual* in 1981. Later he wrote two companion books called *The Campaign Strategy* and *The Finance Manual*. *The Campaign Manual 6th Edition*, is an updated and revised composite of all three books.

Today, Salvatore (Sal) J. Guzzetta is semi-retired and lives in Alexandria, VA. He continues to lecture and to write on the development and management of political campaigns.

PREFACE

When I first wrote *The Campaign Manual* in 1981, I attempted to provide the reader with a basic guide to the fundamentals of the political campaign process. In fact, it was originally written as an internal manual for campaigns on which I was consulting. Later, I was encouraged to develop it into a book that could be used by candidates who, in all probability, could not afford to hire a Political Campaign Consultant, nonetheless, still needed basic guidance in the fundamentals of managing a well organized and effective political campaign. I have shown the concepts, methods, and techniques that are a part of the foundation of political campaigning and that would be of value and interest to not only candidates, but to individuals with a general knowledge and interest in the political campaign process.

I have been pleasantly surprised since writing the manual, at the broad spectrum of users who have found *The Campaign Manual* to be interesting and educational. Candidates at all levels, challengers and incumbents alike, have used the book. Directors of political action committees, associations, unions, and staff members of the national, state, and local political parties are among the list of users. Libraries, colleges, and universities throughout the country were quick to put the manual on their shelves. Many professors have made it a standard in their political science classes in spite of the fact that *The Campaign Manual* was never intended to be the campaign management textbook in the scholastic sense that it has become. Most of all, I have been especially pleased by the number of my fellow Political Campaign Consultants, both here and in Canada, who have used *The Campaign Manual*. Many of them have used the book as it was originally intended, i.e. to train campaign staff on "how to" operate a successful political campaign. Some have used it as a selection tool by lending it to prospective clients with the understanding that, if after reading it they were still determined to run for office, then they would talk further about getting together. Finally, some have paid the highest compliment of all by taking the time to let me know that they too gained knowledge for having read it. My sincerest thanks to all.

In this revised and updated 6th Edition, I have combined the relevant material from *The Campaign Strategy* and *The Finance Manual* into a single book. I have also updated relevant data in all areas of campaign management in the Millenium. I have responded to suggestions to elaborate on job descriptions, computerizing the campaign, campaign management software, the use of the Internet, and the campaigning process in general. I have spent more time discussing the variables in campaigning situations. You will also find some new material about the changes that have occurred as a result of new technology developed since earlier editions. In addition, we have invested much time and energy into making the reference aspects of the manual much more "user friendly."

I would appreciate reading your comments about the value of this Manual to you, and, as always would enjoy your suggestions on how I might continue to improve future editions. Keep in mind that *The Campaign Manual* is a general guideline on the development, finance, organization, and management of a winning campaign. It is by no means intended to cover every possible campaign situation. It will, however, assist you in understanding the process, and enable you to make the necessary extensions into your own specific campaign.

The Campaign Manual is also qualified as applicable for the democratic process in the international arena. It can be used with cultural adaptations, in the promotion of the democratic political and electoral process in emerging societies. It is being used in 33 countries throughout the world.

Finally, it is with pride and pleasure that I am able to announce the release of the initial version of our campaign management software application, GOTV *Campaign Optimizer*.

GOTV *Campaign Optimizer* has been written and programmed to mirror the logic and strategy taught in *The Campaign Manual*. To my knowledge, it is the first campaign management software that has been written and produced by a professional campaign management consultant, specifically for campaign management.

Sal Guzzetta

Table of Contents

Chapter 1
The Development of Campaign Strategy

A Definition of Campaign Strategy

Definition
The campaign strategy is the science or art of political command as applied to the overall planning and conduct of political campaigns. The maneuvers designed to frustrate, surprise, or overcome an opponent in order to secure a victory in an election. The plan of action that results from the practice of this science.

The development of a political campaign strategy is probably the most difficult, and yet a necessary part of the campaign process. The variables involved are almost countless. The number of possible solutions, alternatives, and responses are less numerous.

Consider the word *opponent* in the definition of campaign strategy. Is the *opponent* referred to the individual (or individuals, if a primary election) that you, as a candidate are attempting to defeat, or should the *opponent* be extended to encompass the electorate as well? Certainly, an obvious case exists that the term *opponent* applies to those individuals within the electorate who are working, actively or passively, for your *opponent*. It could also be extended to those people who have already made up their mind to vote for your *opponent* simply because he or she is *your opponent*. For example, they vote a straight party ticket no matter what either candidate's positions are on the issues. Voters using this strategy are sometimes referred to as "knee jerk" or "partisan" voters.

Who are your opponents? Until they prove otherwise, any voter that through uncertainty, indifference or carelessness can cause you to lose the election.

If we take as a given that your workers and the people who are going to vote for you regardless of your stand on the issues are your supporters, then they are clearly not your *opponents*. Sometimes their actions or words can be as devastating to you as those of your opponent. We will cover this later. For now, we will classify them as supporters and study the two groups in the middle. Those who plan on voting but are undecided as to whom they are going to vote for and those who will fail to vote, whether intentionally or not. Are these people your opponents? Probably not in a technical sense, but in the very real world of political campaigns they should be treated initially as though they are your *opponents*, until they prove otherwise, as their uncertainty, indifference or carelessness can cause you to lose the election. In any event, the campaign strategy must encompass these individuals and methods must be devised to encourage them to become active supporters. In a relatively close election, that is, in elections where the electorate is considered equal among partisan voters, the individuals in the middle usually decide the outcome. Therefore, whoever develops and successively implements a strategy designed to win over both the undecided voters and those who might not otherwise vote will in all likelihood win the election.

Candidates failing to clearly identify their real *opponents* rarely win the election.

In the real world of politics, the majority of candidates fail to identify these individuals, much less develop, and carry out a strategic plan for winning them over. The results are obvious. Candidates failing to clearly identify their real *opponents* rarely win the election. If they should win under these circumstances, it is likely another case of their *opponent* losing, or figuratively speaking their *opponent* has beaten themselves with a very poorly developed strategy and/or an over-confident attitude interfering with a winning strategy.

Returning to the definition, notice the sentence that refers to *maneuvers designed to frustrate, surprise or overcome an opponent*. If we include the middle groups of potential voters in the definition of opponents, does it follow that frustration is a legitimate tool that can be used against the middle groups by a candidate in order to win? To go a step further, is it even necessary? Some would probably say YES to both questions, and others an emphatic NO! I choose not to embroil myself in this philosophical argument. It is clear that some degree of finesse is certainly an integral part of virtually every political campaign. I would suggest that you have never read a candidate's campaign literature listing his or her faults or weaknesses.

The technique of frustration as a political tool is practiced by omission as well as commission and I should point out here, before anyone starts feeling too self-righteous, that the same questions could be raised about the last resume or employment application you read. We take it as a given in our method of campaigning that it is the responsibility of the opponent to point out these omissions. Whether we approve of it or not, our society accepts a certain degree of *maneuvering*. As with most values, what may be acceptable at one time may not be acceptable at another.

The next word used in our definition is *surprise*. Doing or saying something, that is so unexpected that your opponent will find it difficult to overcome, if it can be overcome at all. By its very nature, this tactic involves deception. Another negative word in some people's definition of politics, but in the real world, a necessary ingredient in most campaigns. Be advised that sometimes it can backfire as Walter Mondale discovered following his now infamous pledge to raise taxes when elected. An argument could easily be made that Mondale should have used a little ambiguity in that circumstance. The element of *surprise* in the strategic plan finds application in all three major parts of a campaign (*field operations, media, and candidate activities*). Its use is also an integral focus of *The Campaign Manual*.

The next word defining purpose is *overcome*. In military terms, the word 'blitzkrieg' probably describes it best. Loosely, it means to develop an assault, or an attack, so overpowering that your opponent is unable to stop it or recover from it. It can involve an intensive media campaign that so greatly dominates the consciousness of the middle ground opponents that they are persuaded to join your camp. It might even be so drastic that it encourages defections from your opponent's camp a la the Reagan Democrats. It could involve an intensive well organized Field Operation program designed to ensure a well-coordinated and effective Get-Out-The-Vote (GOTV) effort on Election Day. It might have a persuasive method of communication unused or unavailable to the opponent. This tactic is probably the most socially acceptable of the three, but it has its counterproductive side as well. Most students of political campaigns can recount any number of elections where the charge was made that a candidate was trying to "buy the election" by spending massive sums of money. In some cases, the charge sticks and produces a backlash effect. We will be discussing this tactic throughout *The Campaign Manual*.

It is, however, my opinion that the most important word in the sentence (and not by coincidence, the purpose of this book) is, *designed*. All of these tactics and the legions of variables that they employ must be *designed* or carefully planned. It should be pointed out that even the decision not to have a strategic *design* (plan) *is a strategic design.*

Be mindful, that every tactic has its downside and must be considered and evaluated. We will discuss how to do that in each of the early chapters in this Manual. In the later chapters, we will deal primarily with organization and implementation of the campaign *design* (plan). We will, as well, concentrate on fund-raising as a campaigning issue.

In the strategic planning process, the most important element is information. There is a direct, emphatic correlation between the amount and quality of the information used in the development of any campaign strategy and the outcome of that campaign.

In *The Campaign Manual*, I have drawn on my many years of experience as a political campaign consultant involved in campaigns throughout the country at all levels. I have categorized the major elements in the strategic planning process as I have used them over the years. In the strategic planning process, the most important element is information. In the military, it is called intelligence. "Intelligence" or "information gathering" refers to the acquisition of all pertinent data available that might affect the outcome of a campaign, either positively or negatively.

There is a direct, emphatic correlation between the amount and quality of the information used in the development of any campaign strategy and the outcome of that campaign. While reading *The Campaign Manual* you must be mindful of the amount of research called for prior to your ability to call the strategic planning process completed. If you are in a political campaign as a candidate, manager, or planner, do not become discouraged with the quantity of research warranted. Forever, keep this assertion in mind, as there are few truer. In each of the following sections, the subject of *information gathering* as it pertains to a particular factor will be addressed. Keep in mind, however, that most of this process takes place before the campaign formally begins.

The next sections cover the factors that I have used in the development of campaign strategy. Not all campaigns will have to use all of them. To the extent that they do, the methodology applies to all campaigns, regardless of level. Whether a candidate is running for a school board seat or U.S. Senate, the methods used in each campaign are essentially the same.

In order to simplify matters, I use the term District in reference to all campaigns, throughout the Manual. The term is applicable to any geopolitical area whether it is a Ward, City, County, State, or Congressional District. The term precinct is universal throughout the United States when referring to the smallest geopolitical unit. In *The Campaign Manual*, a District is defined as one or more precincts within the confines of a particular campaign. This is done without regard to other designations. In addition, in the interest of keeping things simple, I am generally referring to a two-candidate campaign environment. If you are in a Primary election with multiple candidates, the same guidelines will apply to all serious opponents.

As you read some of this material, my remarks may appear to be blunt, or insensitive. Please be assured no personal offense is intended. This is a Manual written to provide guidelines on how to develop and carry out campaign strategy. In the course of doing this, it is necessary to examine and deal with the realities a political candidate faces during the campaign process. This should not be construed as my approving, or necessarily disapproving of these realities. Short of suggesting or recommending anything illegal, I have avoided placing my values into this discussion.

Chapter 1 - The Development of Campaign Strategy

Except where specified, the terms, "candidate" and "opponent" can be either male or female. To keep with a conversational style, you, the reader, are referred to as the candidate. I will occasionally break away from this style to distinguish between an incumbent and a challenger. In most cases, whether the candidate is an incumbent or a challenger running for the first, second or third time, it is not important enough to be considered a factor by itself. The strategic planning process outlined here must be followed. The status of the candidate might affect some of the factors and we will cover them when it does.

Wherever possible, I have tried to show how the information gathering can be done by the candidate or by staff members without professional assistance. However, every effort should be made to have professional assistance whenever possible. This is especially true in the area of polling. At the very least, the candidate should obtain a copy of a previous poll, recently completed, covering the district. Usually, these can be obtained from the local, state, or national Party committees, or from a candidate who ran for a higher race that covered your district. Another possible source is the local Chamber of Commerce. Usually they will have conducted polls to determine the demographic makeup of the district for commercial purposes. This data is especially helpful in the application of your limited resources. Rarely is there a campaign that can afford to do everything that should be done to assure victory. Usually, it is a matter of degree. Since the average campaign has limited resources, it is urgent that they be spent prudently in order to achieve maximum impact.

A candidate with a low name ID defeating a candidate with a high name ID is equal to .22 caliber rifle defeating a tank. Short of a miracle, you have no chance of winning with either the rifle or the low name ID.

After all the information necessary is gathered and analyzed, you must then make a combination of objective and subjective decisions as to deployment of your resources. Some of these decisions will be relatively obvious; I refer to these as the *objective decisions*. We know for example, it is extremely rare for a candidate with low name identification (Name ID), to beat an opponent with high name identification. It does not require a professional to figure out that unless there is name ID parity, the campaign will not be won.

However, there are many decisions to be made that are far from so clear cut. How, for example, do you achieve parity in name identification within a 12, 8, 6, or 4-month period? What if your maximum budget for this objective is $54,000 and you find yourself in a geopolitical district with 300,000 voters. In some cases, the circumstances will dictate the answers. In others, common sense or intuition will have to suffice. The best method is to have a professional campaign consultant who, by virtue of education and experience, knows how to allocate these resources in the most effective manner. In the absence of professional experience, *The Campaign Manual* will provide the guidance for your independent action.

Throughout *The Campaign Manual*, you will find references to different tools, vendors, and products that will assist you in your campaign. In most cases, these are tools, vendors, and products which I have used in the past, and found them to be reliable and effective. In a few cases, I have not personally used the item but have researched it. I am satisfied that it deserves my recommendation.

Chapter 1 - Word Index

Chapter 2
Characteristics of the Candidates

Physical Characteristics

Definition
Physical characteristic definition covers not only height, weight, race, and gender, it refers to factors such as marital status and observable personal mannerisms such as the style of walking or talking as well.

For the most part, physical characteristics are factors that we attach to an individual without knowing anything about that individual from an emotional or intellectual point of view. In other words, the person who others would perceive us to be, after excluding education, work history, personal interests, and habits. To a certain extent the examination and impact of these physical characteristics in the strategic planning process, applies to a candidate's spouse, children, and close family members. To a lesser extent, they apply to the circle of friends, associates, supporters, and staff members of a candidate.

Check List - Physical Characteristics

Review the comparative checklist of many of the physical characteristics that are used to help focus your attention on this factor. An identical comparison checklist would be completed for the respective spouses as well.

Physical Characteristics	Candidate	Opponent
Gender		
Race		
Nationality		
Age		
Marital Status		
Height		
Weight		
Color of Hair		
Color of Eyes		

Complete version in *Appendix A.*

Resources

Now that we know what information we need, the next step is gathering it. For this, it is relatively easy. Much of it can be determined by personal observation or obtained from your opponent's campaign literature.

Most of the literature about your opponent is relatively objective. You may want others to determine those characteristics that are more subjective. Modesty might prevent you from a clearly subjective assessment of your own physical appearance. Assessments such as these might result in more accuracy, if done by a third party.

Candidates should include a biographic profile (Bio) in their initial press kits

If information is not readily available in published sources, then call and ask for it. Rarely will individuals, or their staff members, be reticent about sharing this information. In fact, candidates should include a biographic profile (Bio) in their initial press kits to be given out at the time of their announcement of candidacy. A signal that your opponent has something potentially damaging to hide, would be if he or she did not make information available on any of the characteristics listed (for example, condition of health).

Individual Analysis

Positive and negative characteristics as defined by the electorate are normally referred to as electoral pluses or minuses. Many times a difficult strategic decision is made based on the pluses exceeding the minuses. In other words, the decision would enable you to gain more favor than you would lose.

After the information has been gathered you and your advisors must critically analyze the results. The difficult part is the accurate analysis. If it is to have a high degree of validity, it must be analyzed from the perspective of the electorate, the voting public. This may or may not parallel with your perspective. In addition, it must be done without regard to personal value judgments. Positive and negative values as used hereafter only refer to the impact on an individual's voting pattern, not necessarily on the candidate. To complicate this further, the electorate is rarely uniform in its evaluation of these characteristics. What might be significant in a positive sense in one group, could well be a negative factor in another, or relatively neutral in a third group. For example, if you were a Caucasian it would probably be a positive factor if running for political office in Newport Beach, CA. However, it could be a negative factor in Detroit, MI. In like fashion, an Italian-American might find an ethnic sounding name ending in a vowel an over all positive factor in Buffalo, NY, but have a real problem with it in Macon, GA.

To help with the strategic decision making process, we need to first segment the electorate within our district into manageable groups that are relatively easy to identify. The two most common groups that are usually found on most voter registration files are gender and party. There could be many more groupings and, as a rule, the more levels segmented, the more precise is the analysis. When doing polls, for example, we might try to determine age groups, education levels, income levels, marital status, religious preference, nationality, party affiliation, and occupation. We would then compare the ratio of these groups to the census data information and determine the appropriate percentages. We could then interview representative samples of each group to determine their feelings about a particular position on an issue, or the personal characteristics of the candidate.

In this manner, we can test what percentage of a particular group is favorable, unfavorable, or undecided about personal characteristics, candidates, or issues. If, for example, 75% of all Caucasian females and 60% of all Caucasian males in a district comprised of 90% Caucasian voters, felt that beards created a negative image and you have one, you might want to think about changing that aspect of your physical appearance. In these early stages of a campaign, most candidates do not have the resources to make available the services of a professional polling firm. Therefore, we can improvise. The following chart is a simple guideline to illustrate this process. It will focus attention on the impact these characteristics will likely have on the electorate.

Analysis Chart - Physical Characteristics

Characteristic	Codes	Caucasian Male	African American Female	Hispanic Male
Gender	+ -			
Race	+ -			
Nationality	+ -			
Age	+ -			
Marital Status	+ -			
Height	+ -			
Weight	+ -			

Complete version in *Appendix B.*

Assignment of Values

The next step is to assign the positive or negative value for each item in each grouping. In polling, they would use percentages of the whole sample to determine these values. The sample drawn is a microscopic representation of the whole electorate within a specific district and is usually referred to as a "representative sample." The size of the sample required to validate in any given district is somewhat debatable. Usually the larger the sample, the less the margin of error. This is normally referred to in terms of plus or minus percentage points. In an average Congressional District of 500,000 people a sample size of 500 people, corresponding to the major demographic groupings, is considered valid within + or - 3%. Lately, I have noticed national polls conducted with a sample of 500 people and claiming validity within + or - 3%. Frankly, I have a hard time accepting their validity.

One way is to consider each item, and intuitively assign a value. For example, you could presume that being an African American candidate among African American male voters would be a positive and put an X in that block. You could then presume that having a mustache would be a positive among all-female voters and put X's in those blocks. You could then presume that being 5'2" and weighing 250 lbs. would be a negative for most voters and put an X in the negative blocks for all voters. Of course, you are extending your own prejudices and impressions onto each of these groups. You might be correct in your assessment, but you could as easily be wrong. Keep in mind that this stage continues to be part of the *information gathering process*.

Strategy should be developed around a negative characteristic that can not be changed. For example if being overweight was considered a negative, an overweight candidate should concentrate on radio commercials only. Your opponent would probably include you in at least half of his/her TV commercials to visualize the negative.

You could improve this process slightly by having a disinterested person make these assessments, but you would be receiving an extension of his or her prejudices and impressions. A better way would be to ask a friend to form what is referred to as a "focus group." A group of individuals usually about 15, who are roughly proportional to the breakout of groupings chosen within your district. For example, if your district consisted of 52% females, 48%

The quality of the information has a direct bearing on the soundness of your strategy and the outcome of the election.

males, and 82% Caucasian, 12% African American, and 6% Hispanic, then your focus group might consist of eight women and seven men, with six Caucasian women, six Caucasian men, an African American man, an African American woman, and an Hispanic woman.

The interviewer, your friend, would then ask the focus group to give their reaction to the various characteristics as stated, or they could be in print form, eliciting a written response. To preserve some degree of integrity, neither the candidate, nor the opponent can be identified. By recording the number of responses indicating a positive or negative reaction, you can quantify the positive and negative characteristics in your district. A majority of positive responses to a characteristic cause an X to be placed in the particular block, vice-versa for the negative responses.

Professional polling firms attempt to hire individuals disinterested in the outcome in order to avoid an extension of the polling person's prejudices and impressions.

The problems with this method are obvious. Finding a friend and fifteen people willing to go through this exercise can be very difficult. Although it may be difficult, it is considered more accurate as an information gathering exercise and is usually preferable to the first option. Incidentally, focus groups are used throughout the country by major political candidates and in the worlds of commerce and industry. It is considered one, and I stress one, of several information gathering techniques found effective. Normally though, the results are correlated with other information gathering techniques before major decisions are made. In addition, professionals conduct the focus groups and they are usually larger and more representative of various levels of groupings. Beyond this, as stated before, you could have a professional poll taken. However they are expensive and the more factors tested, the more expensive they become. In most campaigns, the intuitive feelings of the candidate, and maybe the closest advisors are going to be used. It is important to understand that even this is far more preferable than doing nothing.

A benchmark poll consisting of 500 interviews and 35 to 40 questions can be expensive and will average $35,000.00

If you are able to put together a focus group, be sure to expose them to your characteristics, as well as your opponent's. It is critical that you be as realistic about your own positives and negatives as you are about those of your opponent. If you, or an advisor are managing the focus group, be as brutally honest as possible. You should presume your opponent is doing an analysis on you and this is no time to let your ego manifest itself.

Analysis of the Data

You have reached the point now, where, for this factor (physical characteristics) you should have two sets of data. The raw factual data about the physical characteristics of you and your opponent, and possibly spouses, and the impact value data that is showing how the electorate might perceive these characteristics.

Put the charts side by side and study them. Add up the pluses or minuses, either the number of Xs or the numeric values if you used those, and see how each of you come out over all. Are the ratios relatively equal? Has a pattern emerged, which reasoning would suggest might be significant? Characteristics such as gender, race, or age that cannot be altered and are especially negative or positive should be noted. What about those characteristics which could be altered or modified, such as height, weight, or facial hair? Are there significant differences between the perceptions of the men or women, Caucasian or Hispanic? Be analytical, but not judgmental.

Now do a comparative analysis, item by item, between you and your opponent. Be critical and not wishful. If being an African American candidate is a definite negative in the district, acknowledge it, and move on to the next characteristic. Make up a list showing, in one column, those characteristics that were perceived as positives, and in another column, the negatives. In a third column, show your opponent's positives, and the negatives in a fourth column. Study this page and put an X through those same characteristics that rated positive responses for both of you. Next, circle the same characteristics that rated negative responses. Consider the remaining characteristics, if any, in each column for each of you. Who has the most uniquely positive characteristics, and the most negative? Are they fixed characteristics, or modifiable?

Developing the Strategy

In developing campaign strategy, you stress your positives and ignore or downplay your negatives, while stressing your opponent's negatives and ignoring or downplaying his or her positives.

As a general rule of thumb, in developing campaign strategy, you stress the positives and ignore or downplay the negatives. However, you should always presume your opponent will not be so accommodating and be prepared to offset, to the extent possible, the revelation of your negatives.

Simultaneously, you might directly or indirectly expose your opponent's negatives, while ignoring his or her positives. While direct exposure risks the charge of negative campaigning, it can be very effective. Indirect exposure is subtler, but risks being missed altogether by the electorate.

A classic example of both of these rules involves the various campaigns of the late Tom Bradley, Mayor of Los Angeles. Mayor Bradley was an African American candidate in a city that had an 18% African American population base when he first ran. Realizing that his race was then a negative factor among the electorate, his campaign drew minimal attention to this characteristic. Most print advertising featured his name, his accomplishments, and the office he was seeking, but not his picture. The few pole signs that did have his picture were strategically placed in the African American and Hispanic neighborhoods of Los Angeles. Even these pictorials did not immediately identify him as African American. In addition, most of the electronic commercials were on radio, while the TV commercials were kept to a minimum. This was a definite case and an excellent illustration of ignoring, or under-playing a perceived negative.

Conversely, his opponent, former Mayor Sam Yorty, taking his re-election for granted, did not do anything to directly, or indirectly expose this characteristic. The rest as they say, is history. Tom Bradley beat Sam Yorty in one of the closest elections in Los Angeles' history. A sizable percentage of the people, who were polled after the election did not know that Tom Bradley was an African American when they voted for him.

Four years later when Mayor Bradley ran for re-election, that particular characteristic was no longer a negative factor in the city of Los Angeles, because the good job Mr. Bradley did as Mayor had neutralized it. However, it did re-surface when Mayor Bradley entered the race to become the governor of

California. This time, his opponent was not so accommodating or complacent. The research indicated that the race characteristic was a statewide negative, so the decision was made by the Bradley campaign to downplay his race.

Governor Deukmejian's campaign was not about to allow Bradley to underplay this perceived negative. His camp realized a direct exposure would produce a backlash effect, so they decided on an indirect approach. Under normal circumstances, the last thing a candidate would do is "feature" the opponent in his or her commercials, in effect awarding your opponent with free public exposure and increasing Name ID. However, in this case, they felt that it was to the Governor's advantage to make sure that the entire electorate realized that Bradley was an African American. So they featured pictures of Tom Bradley in most of their commercials and saturated the airwaves throughout the state. It worked. Gov. Deukmejian won handily. As a footnote, the last time these two ran against each other, it was almost a dead heat. Other factors had taken center stage.

There are many ways to successfully handle negative physical characteristics regardless of their nature, if you know what they are and strategize on how to use them.

There are many ways to handle the positive and negatives of physical characteristics if you know what they are and how to use them. This is usually true regardless of their nature. As another example, I know of one candidate who had two physical characteristics which among some voters, produced laughable results. This is one of the worst kind of negative reactions. He was decidedly bow-legged with a slight waddle to his walk. He was relatively short, 5'8", and had a buxom wife who stood at 5'10", without shoes. The sight of the two of them walking together was reminiscent of a keystone comedy. While these were negative characteristics, his face and bearing conveyed a positive image and his status as a husband and father were definite positive ratings against the opponent's negative ratings in both of these areas. This dilemma was resolved by filming him from the waist up when walking, unless it was a long shot. In one scene they used a telephoto lens to shoot him coming down the courthouse steps, then zoomed in quickly to pick him up from the waist up. The viewer saw him in motion but was unable to detect the awkward walk. Except for a family portrait arranged with his wife sitting, flanked by the children, and the candidate standing behind her, his campaign never took other pictures of them together.

Again, in this instance, his opponent, a long-term incumbent, was complacent and did not know of this negative physical characteristic, or if he did, chose not to use it.

Review the list of physical characteristics. Is your age a positive and your opponent's a negative? For example, are you 55 and your opponent, 32? Consider how you can capitalize on it and turn it to your advantage. First, make sure your picture is on all visual campaign material. Use the word "experience" as often as possible, not only in listing your accomplishments, but also in relating your life experiences, both happy and sad. Experience usually equates with competency, trustworthiness, and efficiency. All are desirable traits in a leader. To point out your opponent's lack of experience, without appearing to be negative, envelope the attack in a compliment. Praise your opponent for being a bright, *young* person and express how proud you are to see such bright, *young* people getting involved in politics. The day will come when your opponent and those like him will *become* fine leaders.

Comment on how similar he or she is to your son, or daughter, and then recount an experience you had with your child when he or she was a youngster. The point will be made. This is sometimes referred to as putting a silk glove on an iron fist.

We could go through the entire list and develop a method to handle each of them, in the same way, if you are aware of them and willing to use them. Remember that we are not discussing relevance here or values. Note also, I have not in any way suggested the fabrication of any physical characteristic. We are concerned here with the method used to develop a strategy to win. I leave it to the individual and the electorate to decide the issues of relevance and values.

Intellectual Characteristics

Definition
Intellectual characteristics include intelligence levels, education, philosophical disposition, mental stability, and one's general thought processes.

Unlike the physical characteristics, intellectual characteristics are not so readily apparent. The definitions can be statistical, objective or subjective in nature. While we may be born with some (a basic IQ or a propensity to mental stability), others are usually acquired. These characteristics, though not visible to the naked eye, become clear through the achievement of certain scores on tests throughout one's life, in the manifestation of one's ability to cope with problems without resorting to drugs or alcohol, the spoken or written pronunciations made about the legal, moral, or social issues facing society, and in how one conducts his or her daily life.

Accurate or not, all of these elements provide us with clues about the intellectual characteristics of an individual. The examination and impact of the *intellectual characteristics* in the strategic planning process apply not only to a candidate's spouse, children, and family members, but also to a lesser extent to his/her circle of friends, associates, supporters, and staff members.

Check List - Intellectual Characteristics

The following comparative checklist includes intellectual characteristics and should be examined regarding the Candidate, Opponent, and both spouses.

Intellectual Characteristic	Candidate	Opponent
Highest Education Level		
G.P.A. / SAT Scores		
Profession / Title		
Associations (Present)		
Economic Philosophy (L,M,C)		
Political Philosophy (L,M,C)		
Alcoholic (Y/N)		

L = Liberal M = Moderate C = Conservative

Complete version in *Appendix C*.

Regarding alcohol, drugs, and neurosis, you will have to rely on reputation as a guide in answering them as they apply to your opponent and opponent's family. Avoid becoming clinical about the word neurotic. Consider, for example, if there are any phobias that might be significant. It might be strategically important, for instance, if you are running for Congress in Alaska and your opponent has a fear of flying.

I placed articulate in this list because in the collective mind of the electorate, unless there is a physical impediment, there is usually a direct correlation between a person's intellectual capability and their ability to express themselves clearly about their thoughts and ideas.

Resources

Some of this information should be available from the same sources mentioned previously. Items such as education level, university or college attended, special academic honors, profession, and title, plus past and present associations are usually featured in a candidate's campaign literature, or on their Web site, if they have one. If not, the direct approach will generally be successful. If your opponent has ever been in public life, the local newspaper will likely have a file on him or her with much of this information in it. Normally these files are available to the public.

In *The Campaign Manual,* most references to national campaigns are pre-Clinton. Neither of President Clinton's campaigns were exclusive contests between him and a major opponent, since the inclusion of the Ross Perot factor in both campaigns created such an alteration that I do not believe either of his campaigns can provide significant examples on how to run an effective campaign.

The additional characteristics might be more difficult to determine and you may have to estimate some. IQ levels, for example, are rarely published, so you might have to talk to some individuals who personally know your opponent to see if he or she, in their opinion, is of average intelligence, above average, or highly intelligent. The philosophical leanings of an individual can usually be inferred from their position on various issues, either in writings or in speeches. Their known associates or people whom they have previously supported might also provide an opinion. Most people usually follow set patterns. If they are conservative in their personal life style, they are usually conservative in the other areas of philosophy. Observe where they live, the type of house and neighborhood that they live in, the kind of car that they drive, the manner of dress that they have chosen, and the way that they wear their hair. All are clues regarding a person's intellectual characteristics. I doubt that a social liberal will be seen leaving the hair salon wearing a three-piece suit, wing tip shoes, and showing off his latest crew cut. Occasionally, you will find people who are moderate on social matters, but conservative on economic ones. However, rarely will you find someone who goes from one extreme in one area to another in a different area.

Since these labels tend to be confusing, I will list some of the stereotypical tendencies, as I see them. You can add more if you like. The list, and granted some of the personal traits are tongue-in-cheek, does help to establish, which ones can be linked to previously known biases of the electorate. Reference the campaign between George Bush and Michael Dukakis and the strong attempts made by the Bush campaign to make Dukakis synonymous with liberal. In that campaign they were dealing with national research which indicated the majority of the electorate considered themselves moderate or conservative. Notice on my list how moderates tend to identify with conservatives on more issues than they do with liberals. This might not be the case in your district and this is why our research will attempt to make this determination.

Philosophy	Conservative	Moderate	Liberal
Economic	Less taxes Free market Free trade Anti-union Balanced budget	Less taxes Mixed market Some restricted Trade Indifferent to unions Balanced budget	More taxes Government control Protectionism Pro-union Balance unnecessary
Political	Republican Less government Votes regularly Strong defense Favors SDI	Repub./Democrat Moderate government Usually votes Strong defense Not certain re: SDI	Democrat More government Sometimes votes Some defense Against SDI
Social	Anti-abortion Prayer in school Death penalty Anti-drugs Against ERA	Qualified abortion Prayer in school Some death penalty Anti-drugs Favors ERA	Pro-choice No prayer No death penalty Some drugs (pot maybe) Favors ERA
Personal	Buick Wool Shaves daily Libertarian Church regularly Cocktails	Chevrolet Wool/Cotton Skips shaving Soft Determinist Church sometimes Beer/Wine	Toyota Polyester Likes beard Determinist Church rarely attends Wine

L = Liberal   M = Moderate   C = Conservative

SDI
Strategic Defense Initiative

ERA
Equal Rights Amendment

Individual Analysis

After you have gathered your data, a critical analysis of the results must be made from the perspective of the electorate. Again, the electorate may or may not be synchronized with your own analysis. As with the physical characteristics, the electorate is rarely uniform in its evaluation of these characteristics.

Demographic characteristics include race, gender, age, education levels, income levels, occupation, religion, party affiliation, marital status, locale, and nationality.

I have already alluded to some of the problems regarding philosophical differences. These problems are further complicated because the segmentation necessary to develop valid intelligence goes deeper than the two levels, race and gender that we used in the previous analysis. Some of the other factors that must be considered are age, education levels, income levels, occupation, religion, party affiliation, marital status, locale, and nationality. These factors are referred to as the demographics of a given area. As with race and gender, you can usually find out how your district is divided among these various groupings, in terms of raw numbers or percentages, by checking the census tract data available. You can obtain this information at your main public library, Chamber of Commerce, over the Internet, or sometimes at your U.S. Representative's district office. You might also check with your local university or college in the Research Science Department or your local radio or TV station, since they often do demographic analyses for their clients.

You can also check if a previous candidate had a recent professional poll taken covering your district. The pollster will have checked the census tract data in preparing their sampling and the demographic breakout they arrived at should be adequate for your analysis. To include all the possible variables on this chart would be impractical. Therefore, I am going to illustrate only two in order to demonstrate how it is to be done. Usually you would "pick and choose" certain demographic breakouts based on availability and significant percentages. For example, married and unmarried would produce large percentages when applied to the electorate, as would male and female. Race as well as nationality could also be significant in some districts. Income could be incrementally divided by $10,000 levels. Alternatively, you could simplify the analysis by considering increments of over and under $50,000 annual income only. Education could be categorized as more than high school graduate, high school graduate, or less than high school graduate. Remember that the more closely defined your analysis; the more valuable are the results.

The specific percentage to use when determining significance, is a debatable point among professionals. In most races below U.S. Senate in large states, I use 10% as my cut off point, unless a particular demographic characteristic makes up at least 10% of the whole electorate. In that case, I do not single out that grouping for impact analysis based on that characteristic.

When making these determinations the basic consideration should always be gender. Build the other demographic considerations from that starting point. There is a greater propensity for men earning $50,000 per year to vote alike among themselves as a group, than there is *between* men and women earning $50,000 per year. As Walter Mondale's campaign found (to their chagrin), there was a vast difference between the way Italian-American men reacted to an Italian-American woman running for vice-president (candidate, Geraldine Ferraro), than in the way that Italian-American women reacted towards the female candidate.

The following will usually be the hierarchical order of demographic variables that are used (in ascending order):

1. Gender
2. Race
3. Marital Status
4. Age Levels
5. Party Affiliation
6. Income Levels
7. Education Levels
8. Nationality
9. Religion
10. Occupation Groups
11. Locale
12. Other

In some cases, a lower variable is so dominant it can take precedence over any variable or variables that are usually ranked higher. For example, the feelings between Arab-Americans and Jewish-Americans are usually very intense and will often override the variables of gender, race marital status, age, and perhaps even more.

Analysis Chart - Intellectual Characteristics

Items	Values	Caucasian Male	African American Female	Hispanic Male
Education	+ -			
Honors	+ -			
Profession	+ -			
Associations	+ -			
Economic Philosophy	+ -			
Alcohol Use	+ -			
Neurotic	+ -			

Complete version in *Appendix D.*

Assignment of Values

As in the previous section, you have three choices in determining the relative values for each of these intellectual characteristics. You can use your intuitive feelings or those of your advisors, a focus group, or a professional poll.

If you use intuitive feelings, remember to be as critical as possible in assigning values to yourself and your opponent. If you are able to assemble a focus group, try to define the composition of the group along the lines of the demographic variables corresponding to your district. Similar to our previous discussion, if for example, 30% of your district is made up of Polish-Americans, then 30% of your focus group, 4-5 should be of Polish descent. If the educational breakout of your district is 30% less than high school, 60% high school graduates, and 10% some college or higher, then your focus group should reflect this breakout as well. Obviously, we all have multiple characteristics. Therefore, the same people in your focus group can encompass several of your focus group requirements. This does not necessarily bias the validity of the responses.

Pollsters and political consultants prefer to conduct a series of polls throughout a given period. They can then observe averages and trends that add considerable validity to the results. You can follow the same procedure with your focus group/s by conducting several meetings over a longer period.

Rarely do people approach a problem, or have a reaction to a characteristic from the same reference or starting point. For that matter, even the starting reference point can be a function of timing. How a person reacts to a perceived problem at the age of 50 is not necessarily the same as they would at age 30, even with all other factors being relatively equal. Outside stimulus can also be a mitigating factor. Times of war or social or economic crisis can also affect a person's reference point. Frankly, an individual's mood at any given point in time, even on the same day, might also be a factor.

Analysis of Data

As with the physical characteristics, you now have two sets of data to consider. Again, look at them side by side and add up the pluses and minuses. Consider any pattern that has emerged? Analyze the considerations regarding the relativity of the ratios?

In the analysis chart of intellectual characteristics, most characteristics are fixed. They cannot be significantly altered by choice. Major exceptions would be the philosophical characteristics regarding economics, political, social, and personal.

Are there any significant differences between the perceptions of the men and women, the Caucasians, the African Americans, or the Hispanics? Be analytical, not judgmental.

Do your comparative analysis, item by item, between you and your opponent. Be critical, not wishful. If being an economic liberal is a definite negative in the district, acknowledge it and move on to the next characteristic. Make up a list showing in one column those characteristics that were perceived as positive, and in another, the negatives. In a third column, show your opponent's positives and in a fourth column your opponent's negatives.

When you are finished, study the chart and put an X through those same characteristics that rated positive responses for both of you. Next, circle the same characteristics that rated negative responses. Consider what remains, if any, in each column. Who has the most uniquely positive characteristics and the most uniquely negative? Are they fixed characteristics or modifiable?

Developing the Strategy

Developing strategy based on this set of characteristics is analogous to going through a minefield. You must maneuver very carefully. The wrong decision can be very explosive and very costly.

After studying the results, the first seven items could be very significant if there is a strong differential between you and your opponent. If you are a Princeton graduate, with an above average IQ, who made the Dean's list with a GPA of 3.95 and your opponent found it difficult to graduate from high school, there is a real differential. Should you make this an issue in the campaign? In my opinion, very definitely. The correct strategy though would be to do it by accentuating the positive. If you blatantly call attention to the difference with the electorate, you run the risk of being labeled an elitist and will produce a backlash effect. This would be a case of the minuses exceeding the pluses.

On the other hand, include in your brochure and biographic data handouts a listing of your academic accomplishments. Stress the value of education in the decision making process. Share some of the personal experiences you had while attending college, in working to get there, and the meaning it had in your life. The electorate will get the message. Whatever you do, do not engage in the intellectual snobbery manifested by George Bush's attempt to put down Mike Dukakis's tenure at Harvard. Coming from a Yale graduate, this tactic was sure to explode.

If you were an alcoholic, but a member of Alcoholics Anonymous or some other rehabilitation program, you would want to bring this fact out in the open at the start of the campaign. Phrase it in terms that describe it as a personal victory over a serious disease.

Other delicate areas in this analysis chart could be alcohol use, drug use, and/or neurosis. If you were an alcoholic, but a member of Alcoholics Anonymous or some other rehabilitation program, you would want to bring this fact out in the open at the start of the campaign. Phrase it in terms that describe it as a personal victory over a serious disease. The same would apply to drugs or any neurosis that you had overcome. If you fail to acknowledge the issue early on, it will give your opponent the opportunity to expose the information, leaving you in the position of defending yourself. If, on the other hand, you are using these substances and are not receiving treatment, you should seriously reconsider your decision to run for public office. Your use of drugs, or excessive use of alcohol, is bound to surface sooner, or later, and the political results would be disastrous, not to mention the legal implications.

If you have absolute proof that these characteristics apply to your opponent and he or she is not receiving treatment, you should handle this issue carefully. First, send your opponent a certified letter asking him or her to withdraw from the race in view of these facts. State that he or she, in your opinion, is not qualified to hold public office for this reason. Enclose supporting documentation and indicate this information will be made public unless a withdrawal is forthcoming within one week. If your opponent does not withdraw, call a press conference and disclose the information you have obtained. Advise the media of the actions you have taken as far as notifying your opponent. Be sure to indicate this action is being taken with the deepest regrets. Stress that the citizens of your district deserve the best representation possible and your opponent would simply be unable to provide it.

The candidate should be isolated from exposing very negative factors. Use a third party to expose scandalous or improper behavior by an opponent.

Previously, I gave an example of neurotic behavior regarding a fear of flying as being an impediment to effective service in public office. Of course, other types of neurosis can be burdensome as well. A fear of crowds would certainly be a handicap. This very often, very personal information regarding any neurosis should not (if possible) be exploited publicly, directly by the candidate. If it does apply, it is a far more successful strategy to have this divulged by a third person. Direct use would likely produce a backlash effect. As with alcoholism or drug use, much depends on the particulars. Is treatment being received? How debilitating is it and under what specific circumstances does the neurosis manifest itself? How will it adversely affect the office being sought and/or the district?

Associations, past and present provide clues to possible areas of criticism. George Bush made much of Mike Dukakis' membership in the American Civil Liberties Union. It was offered as proof of Mr. Dukakis' liberal philosophy and an attempt was made to prove guilt by association. Regardless of the merits, in the electorate's collective mind, or at least in the minds of the majority of them, the ACLU is considered an extremely liberal organization. Similarly, membership in Posse Comitatus or the Ku Klux Klan would be generally construed as an indication of extreme conservatism. If your opponent belongs to an organization about which you are uncertain, investigate.

Hobbies also provide clues to intellectual characteristics. It is commonly presumed that reading, playing chess, or solving math problems as a hobby is an indication of a high intellectual capability. Normally the electorate will respond favorably to these hobbies and most involving the pursuit of better health, such as tennis, jogging, golf, and swimming. If however, there is a pattern of high-risk hobbies such as sky diving, mountain climbing, scuba diving, and racing, the inference could be made that the person might be reckless with government responsibilities.

The most politically volatile intellectual characteristics are those dealing with philosophy. People are usually divergent within a specific area of philosophy.

When developing strategy you must be specific about which area of philosophy that you are addressing. I have broken these characteristics into four areas: economic, political, social, and personal. As stated previously, it is far from unusual for an individual to be conservative in one area and moderate in another. What is true of the individual is also true of the electorate. This is why using a simplistic label to describe yourself, or your opponent, as a liberal, moderate, or conservative, is usually ineffective.

In the beginning of the Bush / Dukakis campaign for President, the Bush campaign referred to Mike Dukakis as a liberal. The assertion simply did not stick. The electorate looked at Mike Dukakis and the visual images that they received were of a conservative. The early polls indicated a majority of the electorate actually believed he was more conservative than George Bush. It was not until the Bush campaign began *qualifying* the liberal characteristic (that they were pinning on Dukakis), that their assertions gained success. When they began attacking him as a social liberal, citing his stand on abortion and referring to the convicted murderer's weekend leave policy that the polls began to change. The Bush camp followed up with Dukakis' stance on the Pledge of Allegiance in school and his membership in the ACLU. Soon enough, the electorate could identify the meaning of the liberal label, and it stuck. The majority of the electorate was not comfortable with it and by September 1988, the polls indicated that George Bush had taken a significant lead.

In his personal lifestyle, Mr. Dukakis' philosophy would probably fall into the moderate category.

Determining the philosophy of a majority of the electorate at a given time and in a given locale is difficult, but so very necessary. Since many factors can exert influence on these areas of philosophy, it is only by regular monitoring that a candidate can pinpoint the popular philosophy of the majority of the electorate accurately. Unless you have access to extensive polling data, you will have to turn again to your focus group as an alternative. Incidentally, the national political parties do extensive polling in these areas. Usually their research divisions will share this information upon request. In addition, several of the national polling firms and newspaper publications provide a subscriber service that shares the results of their constant polling. These services tend to be expensive, generally costing anywhere from $800 to $2,000 per year. Check with your main public library or the Political Science Department of your local university to see if they are subscribers to any of these subscriber services and if they make the data available over the Internet or elsewhere.

In philosophy, there are three basic tenets, i.e. *libertarians, determinists,* and *soft determinists.*

One guideline I use in trying to make these determinations is to apply the tenets of the basic schools of philosophy. Essentially, in philosophy, there are three, i.e. *libertarians, determinists,* and *soft determinists*. *Libertarians* (not to be confused with the political party of the same name) are those who believe that all humans have a free will and are totally responsible for their actions as adults. At the opposite end of the philosophical spectrum are the *determinists* who believe our actions as adults are determined by education and cultural values imposed on us from birth through adolescence and are subsequently reinforced by society. In the middle, we find those referred to as the *soft determinists* who believe that humans are born with a free will and are ultimately responsible for their actions as adults. They do, however, allow for the mitigating circumstances of one's culture and make some allowances for the resulting behavior.

In political terms, I usually think of Republican/Conservative as a modern extension of the libertarian philosophy. The Democrat/Liberal is an extension of determinism. The moderates of both parties are the soft determinists.

In deference to the philosophers, I am the first to admit that this is a very simplistic explanation of the different philosophies. However, it has worked well for me over the years and I suggest it here as a possible guide for you in the strategy making process. As you apply this guide, you will find it is very helpful in predicting the reference point, and therefore the subsequent solution being proposed by your opponent to the economic, political, and social issues currently prevalent.

Libertarians tend to think in terms of, "the government that governs least, governs best." The determinists believe in "government direction over our lives from the cradle to the grave." The soft determinists float on differing positions in between those views. Since the soft determinists are usually in the majority, they are constantly being pushed or pulled by one faction or the other.

This poses an interesting question regarding the development of campaign strategy. As a candidate for public office (by definition), your strategy must be to win the election. To do this you must reflect the will of the majority of the electorate or at least appear to do so. If you are a conservative or liberal, do you stick to your principles and publicly espouse them? On the other hand, do you shift your position on the issues to the moderate school of thought that is currently prevalent?

In 1964, Barry Goldwater went with his principles and lost to Lyndon Johnson. In 1972, George McGovern went with his and lost to Richard Nixon. In 1984, Walter Mondale went with his principles and lost to Ronald Reagan.

Never accuse your opponent of flip-flopping if you have flip-flopped as well. Referring to the Bush/Dukakis campaign, Mike Dukakis accused Bush of having voted once to limit an increase in Social Security benefits. What he failed to point out was he also voted against that particular increase. The charge of hypocrisy raised by the media caused Dukakis a greater backlash effect, than any benefit he gained from his original charge against George Bush.

The expression "flip-flopping on the issues" refers to the tendency of political candidates to find the current middle ground and then move to use it. Winning the battle is the critical factor. The usual justification is that once the power of office is achieved, they can then *lead* the electorate to their way of thinking. Is this what your opponent is doing? Is this what you plan to do? If you have reason to believe that your opponent is flip-flopping on the issues, you can make it a major issue during the campaign by documenting it and then exposing it. In your exposition make it clear that your opponent is doing this to "get elected." It is your belief that once in office your opponents hidden agenda will surface, to the regret of the electorate, making it an issue of integrity.

If you are accused of flip-flopping and you are guilty, you might respond by admitting to the error of your ways, explaining how or why you changed your position, and finish with how you are a stronger person for having gone through the process. The cliché, "I didn't leave the Party, the Party left me," still works.

The final characteristic in this section is *"articulate."* Previously, I referred to how the electorate perceives a correlation between intellectual capability and the ability to *articulate your position*. Consider this seriously as a strength or weakness, along with that of your opponent when developing the campaign strategy. If your opponent has difficulty articulating well, possibly due to a lack of formal training, you could challenge him or her to as many public debates as is reasonably possible. This would work to your advantage if by virtue of your training, you were clearly superior to your opponent in this regard. If, on the other hand, you know that your opponent articulates far better than you do, it would be wise to stay away from as many public debates as possible, without creating an atmosphere of obvious avoidance.

In any event, keep in mind this characteristic is modifiable. I remember one very intensive campaign for a city council seat in a major city. Two weeks before the election, the polls showed that the race remained extremely close, in fact too close to call and the trend was going in the direction of the challenger. The city council member was very bright and had a firm grip on the issues. However, due to his background, he really lacked debating skills. His opponent on the other hand was very experienced in debating and believed the election would be secured after the final debate. It was to be a televised debate and the viewing audience was expected to be high. The Councilman's campaign called in a speech communications specialist during the week before the debate and they worked together intensively.

The Councilman did not win the debate, but neither did his opponent. The long anticipated knockout punch was never landed and the Councilman went on to win a week later by less than 200 votes.

Here, the opponent's strategy was sound. Exploit the incumbent on an obvious weakness to win over the undecided among the electorate. The Councilman's strategy was also sound. Recognize the weakness, shore up your defense, and neutralize the attack.

Emotional Characteristics

Definition
Emotional characteristics are those we normally associate with behavioral traits. These traits help define our personality and character. They are the feelings that shape or influence our intellectual and physical capabilities.

Emotional characteristics are difficult to define. They are even more difficult to research. You are almost totally dependent on the impressions of others, and this impression is affected by their own definition.

Occasionally, emotional characteristics become public knowledge through personal exposure. Former Senator Ed Muskie shedding tears in New Hampshire gave the electorate insight into one of his emotional characteristics. The Watergate tapes enlightened many about former President Richard Nixon. Chappaquidick provided several clues about some of Senator Ted Kennedy's emotional characteristics. Most of us, however, become very adept at hiding our emotional characteristics, especially so in the public eye. Those who wish to know one's emotional characteristics usually have to learn them through observation alone.

When we think of emotions, words like joy, anger, hate, happy, sad, and love come to mind. Emotional characteristics are the manifestations of these feelings. They are measured in degrees of relativity. All humans experience them, some experience more than others. You must focus on this differential to be successful with this issue regarding the strategy making process.

In a similar way, the impact of these emotional characteristics applies to a candidate's spouse as well. The following checklist includes many of these characteristics. Although arbitrary, I have included sexual orientation and religion on this list.

Checklist - Emotional Characteristics

Characteristic (y/n)	Candidate	Opponent
Arrogant		
Belligerent		
Charismatic		
Confident		
Courageous		
Dynamic		
Honest		
Integrity		
Modest		
Sexual Orientation		

Complete version in *Appendix E.*

Resources

Refer to the previous sources of information you have acquired. They will assist in providing you with some insight into the emotional characteristics of your opponent. Study the adjectives and adverbs used to describe words or deeds. You can very often draw conclusions from actions that have been taken in past situations. As previously indicated, you will have to depend heavily on hearsay evidence. Talk to people who know your opponent personally, socially, or professionally.

You could do an extensive credit check. Politically, however, this could be dangerous and tempt a backlash. It would also be illegal unless authorized by your opponent.

If the opportunity presents itself to observe your opponent in a social setting, you should take advantage of it as often as possible. Pay close attention to the interaction that takes place between your opponent and the people present. When your opponent is speaking publicly, go and listen. Pay close attention to *how* he or she is expressing himself or herself. Listen for tone, cadence, and modulation. Watch the eyes, they are, as the saying goes, the "windows of the soul." Take notice of your opponent's body language, and that of his spouse and family. If sitting, are the arms and/or legs crossed? If standing, is your opponent leaning forward slightly or rigid? Are the hand gestures impulsive or deliberate? Is eye contact direct or evasive? Is the over all composure stern or relaxed? Is your opponent humorous or dour? Does your opponent greet others confidently, or with temerity? Does the handshake appear to be firm, or limp? Is your opponent attentive to others? Who is the center of conversation? Observe personal mannerisms. Engage your opponent in conversation and try to determine his or her reaction to you. Analyze the choice of language used. Your most accurate opinions will be formed through a personal assessment by you and by those close to you.

If your opponent is an incumbent, check the voting record and arguments made before any vote. If active in the community, check the type of civic and social activities he or she has done. These would generally appear in a biographic sketch.

Be very careful and cautious if you complete the analysis on your own. Your own insights may be helpful, but they are likely biased. Remember that the objective here is to determine how others perceive you. *Truth* is what people perceive.

Ask your spouse or someone very close to you to complete the checklist regarding you. Then give copies to close friends and relatives and ask them to be candid in their observations. Assure them the checklist may be sent back in a plain white envelope with no indication of the source. This needs to be carefully done so that information does not leak and so that your questionnaire does not create personal issues between yourself and those whom you choose to involve.

Compile the results and consider each item based on an opinion of the majority. If it contradicts your own impressions, analyze why this difference exists.

Individual Analysis

Politically, we are concerned with the impact these emotional characteristics will have on a person as a candidate or as an elected leader. Remember that we all have these emotional characteristics to some degree or another. If you were to measure these characteristics on a scale of 1 to 10, with 10 signifying the strongest impact on our decision making process, it might look like this:

Low Impact - Predictable	1 2 3
Medium Impact - Possible	4 5 6 7
High Impact - Probable	8 9 10

At the lower end of the scale, the results are predictable. As a rule, they will not affect the decision making process adversely. At the higher end of the scale, there is a high degree of probability that emotional characteristics will affect the decision making process. Those characteristics that fall in the middle present the most problems strategically speaking. Since the impact will likely be unpredictable, they are difficult to attack or defend.

In doing this analysis, assign a numeric value of 1 to 10 to each item. You can base this value on empirical evidence, hearsay, majority opinion, or intuitive feelings. As you go through the items assign an impact value for what would be considered the positive characteristics as well as the negative ones.

Be very objective and critical in this preliminary analysis. The emotional characteristics play a pivotal role in the electorate's perception of a candidate. It is well documented that in politics *perception is reality*.

Unlike your analysis of physical and intellectual characteristics, this analysis is not concerned with the perception of the electorate at this point. Before you can proceed to consider the perception of the electorate, you must narrow the list to only those characteristics that will have a probable impact on your opponent, as a candidate or elected official. The others will have only an affect on his or her campaigning style, so do not ignore them from that perspective.

Analysis Chart - Emotional Characteristics

Caution must be used in the preparation of this chart. By their very nature, some of the words used to describe certain emotional characteristics are strongly negative. Their use in a focus group or poll could bias the responses. Few people would give a positive response to a characteristic like cruel, volatile, or belligerent.

Conversely, few would give a negative response to integrity, honest, or caring. If any of these characteristics are in the probable range, try to rephrase them on the analysis chart. Use your thesaurus to find a synonym or antonym that will effect the same result. For example, contentious is a weaker term for belligerent and would not evoke a knee jerk negative response. A positive response to the word pacifist would indicate a valid presumption of a negative rating for belligerent.

Take notice that those emotional characteristics that are in the low range have their value as well. They will round out your impression of your opponent, despite the narrow testing procedure. In debates or other types of campaign activity, this information could prove vital. As the saying goes, "leave no stone unturned."

Characteristics that fall in the medium range should be included in the testing when enough characteristics are not found to be in the high range. You probably will not be able to use them in a direct sense. However, they will give you an indication of potential "hot buttons" that may trigger a public reaction.

To illustrate the development of the analysis chart, I have randomly picked some emotional characteristics for illustrative purposes only. You need to consider emotional characteristics in their entirety and implement the previous step determining their relevance to your situation.

Characteristic	Values	Caucasian Male	African American Female	Hispanic Male
Courage	+ -			
Honest	+ -			
Introvert	+ -			
Optimistic	+ -			
Moralistic	+ -			
Sexual Orientation	+ -			

Complete version in *Appendix F.*

Assignment of Values

Assigning values for emotional characteristics differ from those usually used for physical and intellectual characteristics. The standard demographic patterns do not apply in most cases.

The purpose of assigning values to emotional characteristics is to determine the relative importance attached to them by the electorate.

Virtually all groupings place a relatively high value on integrity, honesty, compassion, courage, and sexual preference. Conversely, characteristics like cruel, belligerent, miserly, insecure, and volatile usually bring negative responses. The purpose of assigning values to emotional characteristics is to determine the relative importance attached to them by the electorate. Placing an X in the respective blocks will not be of much help. In this case, you need to use the actual numeric answers generated by your focus group.

The interviewer should prepare a list of characteristics to be tested. A copy of the list should be given to each person in the focus group. Ask them to assign a value of 1 to 10 for each item. One being the least desirable characteristic and ten being the most desirable. After this is done, add the results for each item and divide by the number in each grouping to obtain the average rating. This value is then placed in the respective block for each item.

For example, if there are seven Caucasian females in the focus group and they assign values for sensitivity as follows: 10, 10, 9, 8, 8, 6, 6, adding the numbers equals 57. Then divide 57 by 7 for an average value of 8.1. Place this value in the block for Caucasian females. Complete this procedure for each of the specific characteristics being tested for you and your opponent.

Analysis of Data

You should now have two sets of data; an emotional profile of you and your opponent (and spouses) and an analysis of how this profile could influence the electorate.

Study them carefully and continue with your analysis. Which candidate appears to have the most positive values over all? Are there any characteristics, which are modifiable? Are there characteristics that you need to modify?

Make a list of your opponent's characteristics that are considered by the electorate to be least desirable. Do the same for yours. Then make a third list of your characteristics, which are considered most desirable. Do the same for your opponent. Which characteristics for both of you fall into the median range?

Now compare these charts with the ones done for physical and intellectual characteristics. See if there are any apparent inconsistencies or variations from a stereotypical norm.

Complete this process by summarizing, for you and your opponent, all the data collected. Develop a biographic profile for each of you. List all the positives and negatives. Make a special note of which items are fixed and which are modifiable. Think in terms of offensive and defensive maneuvers.

The Candidate should choose to be involved in the campaign activities that best suit his characteristics. Activities are varied and include debates, door-to-door campaigning, plant gate introductions, shopping center meet and greet, public forums, fund-raising, media events, coffee klatches, or press conferences.

Now, analyze the emotional characteristic data from the perspective of predisposition. Try to determine how you and your opponent would react to various attacks and circumstances. What type of campaign activity is best suited for each of you? There are numerous types, as pointed out in *The Campaign Manual*. Be sure to also consider your spouse's characteristics and the best campaign activities that she will be suited for as well.

Do not miss the opportunity to extend this analysis past the election and into the future. Try to project how these characteristics would affect you and your opponent's performance as an elected official. Based on the analysis, what type of image could be projected? Can you capitalize on this projection?

Remember to be objective and critical throughout this process. If you believe you are unable to do this, ask a trusted friend or advisor to do it for you. Preferably, it should be someone with political campaign experience, or advertising and public relations skills.

Developing the Strategy

In developing a strategy based on the personal (physical) characteristics, you would normally consider two basic objectives. First, how can you accentuate your positives, while down playing your negatives? Second, how can you accentuate your opponent's negatives, while ignoring his or her positives? In addition to these objectives, you will need to consider two more when dealing with emotional characteristics. How can you cause your opponent to make a serious tactical error and how can your opponent cause you to make one?

Challengers usually have an edge over incumbents in relation to this second set of objectives. I have noticed, over the years, that some incumbents develop a propensity to be arrogant. The longer they are in office, the more arrogant they seem to become.

This characteristic played a major role in a campaign I observed a few years ago. The opponent was a U.S. Representative who had held the office for 26 years. The research indicated a high rating for the characteristic trait of arrogance. However, when measured against the electorate, it did not produce much negative impact value. It almost seemed to be interpreted as a macho value or a show of confidence, especially among men. It was obvious that any attempt to exploit this characteristic directly would backfire. The campaign decided to use this knowledge to cause the incumbent to make a tactical error.

In this case, they developed two game plans and deliberately fueled the incumbent's arrogance. One plan laid out a strategy that was very similar to those previously used in previous campaigns against the incumbent. They would make sure this plan became public and then rely on the incumbent taking the Challenger's campaign for granted. After all, the Candidate had seen it before, and would likely presume that the incumbent would not need to do anything different from previous campaigns.

The second plan, that is, the real plan called for a radical departure from previous campaigns. Only six people knew of this plan. Essentially, it called for the development of a communications technique that had never before been used in that district. They planned to coordinate the new activity with the more traditional methods to develop a fast moving attack.

It worked. It was mid-September before the incumbent realized what was being done. It was too late to respond. Throughout the campaign, the challenger controlled the playing field and, subsequently, the outcome of the election.

In the 1988 presidential race, George Bush's campaign made skillful use of their evaluation of Mike Dukakis' emotional characteristics. Their attacks on his patriotism sent him scurrying for the infamous ride in the tank. This gave the political cartoonists a field day. Pressing his emotional hot buttons, they caused him to flip flop on one position after another. By mid-campaign, many of his own supporters were uncertain about where he really stood on any issue.

The use of still graphics accentuate your positives and say more than words about emotional characteristics on signs, logos, billboards, and brochures.

Consider the use of still graphics to accentuate your positives when developing a strategy based on the first set of objectives. Still graphics, such as signs, logos, billboards, and brochures can say more than words about emotional characteristics. As a rule, a picture is worth a thousand words. Pictures tend to illustrate the type of person that you are and strengthen that image in the mind of the electorate. Bold lettering and colors communicate one impression. Script lettering and pastel colors communicate a completely different message. Never loose sight of the value that the abstract will play. If the still graphic is wordy or cluttered, it will communicate that message in addition to what you are actually saying in your words.

Whether or not you should feature your picture depends still further on the message that this will communicate. Assuming there are no physical characteristics that would have a negative impact, you can communicate several emotional characteristics with facial and body expressions. Refer back to your analytic data and see which characteristics have the highest positive impact among the electorate. Then, include in your brochure, pictures of you in settings that visually communicate those characteristics. If for example, compassion has a high positive rating, have a picture included showing you listening intently to some senior citizens. Leaning over a hospital bed talking to a patient or distributing food to the needy will also make the point. If sensitivity is a major impact value, make a picture of you dressed casually playing with your children on the living room floor, or playing ball or some sporting activity with children. Talking with a farmer in a cornfield or a disabled person sitting in a wheelchair is also very effective.

When doing action graphics, whether commercials or events for free media coverage, use the background and sound to either reinforce the point you are trying to make or to add a secondary message.

We can assume that your campaign has decided to make a biographic commercial to improve your *Favorability* rating with the electorate. By itself, this could communicate several emotional characteristics like loving, caring, happy, affectionate, protective, and heterosexual. Secondary characteristics could be added by enveloping them in a unique setting. For example, if religion has a high positive impact rating, the graphic could show the family coming down the steps of a church, while a voice over does an introduction of each member. In the background could be the strains of an appropriate religious melody recognizable by the primary target group.

Communicating a positive message is vital. For many years, I have been advising candidates to frame their message around the three C's - Concern, Compassion, and Common sense. It has been and I suspect always will be, a very positive message that every voter can relate to.

If you need to make a point about the quality of education, go to a high school and film a teacher standing in front of the class lecturing. While he or she is talking, fade out several of the students, so only empty seats are seen. You do the voice-over talking about the results of a poor education system and what it really means in terms of the dropout rate. Close with a visual of you sitting on the corner of the teacher's desk, blackboard in the background, saying how if elected you will make a difference. In the background, a haunting melody gives way to musical sounds of hope and resolve. You have now communicated concern, compassion, caring, and have added strength to your primary message about the quality of education.

Did you ever wonder why so many political commercials pan the audience while a candidate is speaking? They are trying to attach a charismatic characteristic to the candidate. They do this by focusing on the eyes and facial expressions of the audience as they listen, in rapt attention. Virtually every graphic, whether still or in motion, can be enhanced, maximizing its value, by these means. The costs increase slightly, but the strategic benefits increase greatly. The same is usually true when emphasizing your opponent's negative emotional characteristics. Rarely will your opponent oblige you by posing for a negative photo or commercial. However, with the use of well-chosen graphics, one can make the point.

Rarely will your opponent oblige you by posing for a negative photo or commercial.

The little girl and the daisy in the bomb commercial used by Lyndon Johnson's campaign against Barry Goldwater has become a classic on how to accomplish this objective. In one 30 second spot millions of the electorate were convinced that Barry Goldwater was volatile, belligerent, cruel, and demagogic. Actually, they never once saw a picture of Barry Goldwater.

Another classic example was the Tip O'Neill look-alike commercial produced by the National Republican Congressional Committee. For those of you who do not recall the commercial, the Republicans wanted to convey what they perceived as the pompous, arrogant, calculating, and insensitive characteristics of the then Speaker of the House, Tip O'Neill. Through him, they wanted to extend to the electorate those characteristics as applicable to all the Democratic members of the Congress. There was also an OPEC oil embargo against the United States and austerity measures were being imposed on the American people. To make their point, the Republicans used a portly actor who looked remarkably like Representative O'Neill. They filmed him with a cigar in his mouth, driving a large gas-guzzling auto, while a voice over poked fun at the average American waiting in gas lines. They certainly made their point and Republican congressional candidates enjoyed one of their most successful years.

In modern times, a commercial used by the Bush campaign was very effective in communicating a perceived weakness in Michael Dukakis. Wanting to characterize him as being irresponsible, insensitive, and uncaring, they seized on a furlough policy in Massachusetts which enabled persons convicted of 1st degree murder who were not eligible for parole to have weekend passes from prison. While a voice over deplored the ramifications of this policy by Gov. Dukakis, the visual showed prisoners going through a turnstile at the entrance of a prison, one right after the other, going in and coming out. A graphic overlay pointed out that 286 never returned. The spot was very effective.

Most campaigns cannot afford the luxury of even a limited number of TV commercials. Many must rely on free media coverage or still graphics to make their points.

How much free media coverage is available depends on the level of the office being sought and the locale. As a rule, the larger the community, the greater the campaign is covered by the press. Unless a candidate for a lower level race does something newsworthy, on its own merits, the local media will virtually ignore the campaign. Unfortunately, it seems sometimes that the only activities the media considers newsworthy are those involving criminal or tragic circumstances. I do remember one rather innovative campaign that drew attention not normally given to a campaign of its size. A candidate running for state representative, in order to make a point about high taxes, dressed up in a Minuteman costume and dropped tea bags from a bridge into a river.

As a rule, the larger the community, the greater the campaign is covered by the press.

In this case, the stunt paid off dramatically and the candidate received a considerable amount of free media coverage and subsequently won the election. Most candidates, however, have to content themselves with the limited amount of still graphics they can purchase to highlight their positive characteristics and their opponent's negatives.

One of the most cost-effective ways to highlight the candidate's positive characteristics against the opponent's negatives is to make use of a comparative analysis sheet or tabloid, showing where you and your opponent stand on ten or twelve comparative issues.

This being the case, one of the most cost-effective ways to do this is by using a comparative analysis sheet or tabloid, showing where you and your opponent stand on ten or twelve comparative issues. You further focus the comparison by adding a third column asking the voters to list their preference on each issue. This method not only focuses attention on the intellectual characteristics but, by inference, can highlight several emotional characteristics as well. Other than this piece, your campaign might be limited to a brochure and a tabloid. If this is the case, focus on your most positive characteristics. Be sure to follow the previously stated advice regarding use of color, typeface, and background.

A winning strategy is not necessarily predicated on what you want to project or accomplish. It is based on what will win the election.

Remember that emotions are characteristics that we feel. They are not necessarily what we are. However, as stated, in politics perception is usually the reality. How the electorate perceives a candidate is, as far as they are concerned, how he or she is in reality. A winning strategy is not necessarily predicated on what you want to project or accomplish. It is based on what will win the election. When a conflict arises, unless there is a valid reason not to, go with the percentages.

Name ID Rating

Definition
The name identification rating (name ID rating) is an indication of how many people recognize a candidate's name.

The name ID rating is expressed in terms of a percentile, 30% name ID rating, 50% name ID rating. Further, the name ID rating is defined as being "soft" or "hard." A soft name ID rating is one that has been established after a prompt has been given by an interviewer. A hard name ID rating is one established without any prompting.

For example, if you asked 100 people who the Republican candidate for president was during the 1988 campaign and 65 answered George Bush, then George Bush's hard name ID rating would be 65%. If you asked who the Democratic candidate was and 44 answered Mike Dukakis, then his *hard name ID rating* would be 44%. Conversely, if you ask 100 people who the Republican candidate was in 1988, George Bush or Mike Dukakis (in fact, mentioning their names as choices) and 90 answered George Bush. Since you have prompted a response by mentioning the name, his name ID rating of 90% would be considered a *soft name ID rating*.

Some pollsters use another variation of this prompt. They tell the interviewee they are going to mention several names. They then ask if the name is familiar to them. Usually they will go through six to eight names. Included among them will be two fictitious names. The results of this method are also considered *soft ID name ratings*. It is interesting to note and should be kept in mind as a clear reference point that the fictitious names will usually receive between 10 and 15% name ID ratings. In fact, almost any name will realize those percentages.

Relevance

A candidate's name ID rating is critically important in the development of campaign strategy. One of the few truisms in politics, all things being equal, is that the candidate with the highest name ID rating will inevitably win.

Name ID parity is normally achieved very quickly between the major party presidential candidates, which results from the extensive media coverage that they both receive. However, as you go down the ticket, the media exposure decreases proportionately. Achieving parity, or greater, then becomes a direct function of campaign strategy. *You* must make it happen.

How high your name ID rating must be is conditioned by two factors: your opponent's name ID rating and the level of the race in which you are running. As a rule of thumb, I use the following guide as a *minimum* objective:

How high your name ID rating must be is conditioned by two factors: your opponent's name ID rating and the level of the race in which you are running.

U.S. Senate	90% soft name ID rating
U.S. Representative	80% soft name ID rating
Governor	90% soft name ID rating
Other statewide office	80% soft name ID rating
State Senator	60% soft name ID rating
State Representative	50% soft name ID rating
County Supervisor	70% soft name ID rating
Mayor	80% soft name ID rating
City Council	70% soft name ID rating

...continued

Other city office	50% soft name ID rating
School Board	40% soft name ID rating
Sheriff	50% soft name ID rating
Judge	40% soft name ID rating

To understand more fully the relevance of this factor, you need to analyze the voting habits of the electorate, remembering that for the sake of our discussion, we are defining the electorate as all those who can vote, excluding strictly partisan voters. At the Presidential, U.S. Senatorial, U.S. Representative, and Gubernatorial levels most voters have a sense of which candidate they are voting for beyond the party label. It is then usual to see voters split their ticket. As you will see in the next section, *Favorability* ratings combine with the name ID rating to make this determination.

When you consider political offices below these levels, most voters will tend to cast their votes along party lines, unless they have a sense of familiarity with a particular name. In that case, they might deviate from their norm. This sense of familiarity can be a result of a candidate having a famous surname like Kennedy, Roosevelt, or Reagan. It could also be the result of a common name like Smith, Jones, or Brown.

Nationality has a tendency toward playing a strong role as well. There may be an affinity for Italian, Irish, Polish, Hispanic, or other ethnic surnames. Gender is also becoming a strong factor. The issue of Name ID can be very persuasive and sometimes, as poorly justified as a simple case of having known someone with that particular surname. All of these situations are relatively passive. That is, little can be done to change the situation that exists. However, you can plan activities that will make your name become more familiar to the electorate, thereby increasing your hard and soft name ID rating.

Significance

Name ID is a significant factor. It is usual for the name ID rating factor to transcend most of the other factors among the electorate.

High name ID gives you credibility in the mind of the electorate. Until you have it, they simply will not be receptive to your message.

The high importance of name ID sometimes explains the election, or re-election, of a person from one party in an area where the other party tends to dominate. This factor is so significant that local and state party chairpersons will often try to recruit candidates for races simply because they have a high name ID rating as a result of nonpolitical activities such as sports, acting, or broadcasting.

Its significance can also be measured by the amount a candidate must spend just to improve it. I recall one race involving a challenger for a U.S. Representative's seat. The challenger started a year before the election with a statistically insignificant name ID rating of 12%. The incumbent had a hard name ID rating of 90%. Two weeks before the election, the challenger's hard name ID rating was 92%. To accomplish this, the campaign had spent 40%, or $168,000, of its $420,000 budget strictly for building name ID. The candidate went on to win by the largest margin of any challenger that year.

Resources

You can determine your name ID rating, and your opponent's, through polling.

You can determine your name ID rating, and your opponent's, through polling. Focus groups do not work well for this purpose. If you cannot afford to have a poll taken, see if previous poll data exists and is available to you. If unsuccessful in getting the information from existing sources, conduct your own poll. The easiest way to do this is to develop a basic questionnaire. Include a list of five to seven names. One should be your name and one the name of your opponent. Two should be the names of elected officials within your district who might possibly endorse your candidacy. One should be the name of a person whom you know to be relatively popular. Make up one or two others and include them on your list.

To make your poll more authentic add an open ended issue question when calling. For example, "What do you think are the two most serious problems facing our community?" You could also include a couple of relevant close-ended questions like, "Are you satisfied, or dissatisfied, with the efforts of our police to control crime in our community?" or "Would you support increasing taxes in order to build a new school in our area?" Then explain your list of names and your need to record their reaction to the list by saying, "I'm going to read several names to you now. Please tell me if you have heard of the name, as I read each one."

Since the poll is being done before the campaign has actually begun a ballot question between you and your opponent would not be too meaningful. Also since you are really trying to determine name ID, it may not be necessary to ask a number of demographic questions. Later, I will discuss how to do polling that is more extensive.

The standard size of the polling sample size (one-tenth of one percent of the district) decreases in districts with more than 500,000 residents and increases slightly for districts with less than 50,000.

At this point, you should expect a relatively high degree of validity by simply calling every 10th name in the telephone book. Since the voice of the respondent will usually indicate gender, you can balance your respondents on that characteristic. Most districts breakout 52% female and 48% male. The number of interviews you need depends on the population of your district. Generally, the size of your sample should be equal to one-tenth of one percent of the district.

When you have finished, compile the results and divide each number by the total number of completed interviews. The resulting percentage will provide an indication of each person's *name ID rating*. For example, if your district has a population of 250,000 you should interview 250 people. If 100 say they have heard of your opponent, divide 100 by 250. Your opponent's soft name ID rating would be 40%.

Polling Tips

Some tips regarding polling.

a) Ask several female volunteers to do the telephone interviewing. An unknown female voice is less threatening than a male's voice over the telephone.

b) The best time for calling is between 7:00 and 9:00 P.M., Monday through Friday, and 10:00 A.M. to 5:00 P.M. on Saturday. Do not call on Sundays. Be sure to investigate state and local laws to verify legally acceptable telemarketing and polling times allowed in your district.
c) The interviewer should always be pleasant and speak slowly.
d) Do not waste time. If resistance is encountered, go on to the next person.

Sample Questionnaire - Name ID

Person called: ______________________________ Phone #: ____________________

"Good evening, this is Mary Smith. We are conducting a short poll this evening and wonder if you would take a few moments to help us. The few questions will take less than three minutes."

Note - wait for their response. If their response is no, thank the party immediately and say good night, if their response is positive, continue:

"Thank you for your assistance,

First, what do you think are the two most serious problems facing our community today?"

(Note Response) ____

"Thank you. Next, would you say you are satisfied, or dissatisfied, with the efforts of our police to control crime in our community?"

(Circle one) SATISFIED DISSATISFIED

"Fine, thank you. Now, would you favor, or oppose, an increase in taxes to build a new school in our area?"

(Circle one) FAVOR OPPOSE

"Thank you. Finally, I will read several names to you. Please tell me if you have heard, or not heard of the person's name before. OK."

(Prompt, if necessary)		(Circle one)
"Michael Jackson"	"Have you heard before?"	YES NO
"Tom Jones"	"Have you heard before?"	YES NO
"Margaret Thatcher"	"Have you heard before?"	YES NO
"Tom Sellick"	"Have you heard before?"	YES NO
"Sal Guzzetta"	"Have you heard before?"	YES NO
"Helen Hayes"	"Have you heard before?"	YES NO

"Okay, great. Thank you very much for your assistance. I really appreciate your help. Goodnight."

MALE FEMALE (Circle one)

Name of Interviewer: ____

Analysis of Data

After compiling the results by gender and combined totals you should have an objective picture of your respective *name ID ratings*. You will also have an indication of where the electorate stands on some issues. In a later chapter, I will discuss the relevance of this information. For now, we will focus on the *name ID factor:*

1) Look at the results for your fictitious names. How do the other ratings match up with them? Are they higher or lower?

2) Look at the results for the popular name. How do the other ratings match up with them? Are they higher or lower?

3) Study the differentials between you and your opponent.

4) Take your study to the next level and consider if the differentials are consistent between men and women. This could have a bearing on the design of your graphics.

5) Note the differentials that exist between you, your opponent, and the other elected officials. Would their endorsement or signature on a fund-raising letter be helpful to you?

6) How do the percentages compare to the previously stated objectives for the level of office being sought? Compare them for you and your opponent. If there is a significant negative difference, this might be an indication of real vulnerability.

Developing the Strategy

If your *name ID* is higher than your opponent's *name ID* and as high as the objective for the office being sought, you are in good shape. Your strategy for this factor would be to sustain the rating. Usually this can be accomplished in the normal course of your other campaign activities. You would not want to spend significant amounts of your resources for this specific purpose. Doing so would be non-productive and to the extent that it takes funds away from other objectives, it would be counter-productive.

If these two conditions are not the case, then you must develop a strategy to realize your objectives. While it is true any physical campaign activity builds *name ID*, some activities work more effectively than others. If you had unlimited resources, you could saturate the media with commercials featuring your name and the office being sought. In most campaigns, this would be unrealistic. The amount of saturation required would be extremely expensive.

Most of us have a built in or psychological resistance to the introduction of new names or new products. By the time we are adults, our memories are filled with so many items to remember that we become very selective about what we will retain. In order to overcome this resistance, manufacturers will often spend millions of dollars in advertising to introduce a new product line.

Unfortunately, almost any product or idea will be accepted by the public more quickly than the public will accept a politician and his or her ideas. Built in resistance can be likened to a steel door when it comes to acceptance of a new politician. In order to penetrate the door, your strategy must include continuing saturation over a relatively long period of time.

Today the Ford Taurus is as well recognized as the Honda Civic. When it was first introduced, the media campaign was massive by any definition, and sustained for over two years. During any given evening of prime time television, Ford ran six 30 second spots on all three major networks. Within each spot, the name Taurus was seen or heard at least 4 times. This assault was designed to penetrate our consciousness with the name of a new car.

In advertising, there is a measurement device that is used to indicate what percentile of the people will see a particular advertisement in any given place, at any given time. The advertising outlets are able to determine this by means of their own polling, which they pay independent firms to do for them. They ultimately base their advertising rates on this data. This device is referred to as a GRP rating (gross rating points). It is important for you to understand the significance of this system. Essentially, the GRP rating tells the advertisers how many people on a given day will see or hear a particular advertisement. In the case of radio and TV, they can also tell the demographic make up of the audience. This broader system is referred to as the Arbitron ratings.

GRP Rating
Gross Rating Points is a measurement device that is used to indicate what percentile of the people will see a particular advertisement in any given place, at any given time.

In the case of the GRP ratings, the number given indicates what percentage of the people will see or hear that advertisement under certain specified conditions. For example, you could buy enough TV time to virtually guarantee 50% of the people who turn on a TV on any given day will see your commercial. This would be referred to as a 50% GRP rating. Alternatively, with a 30% GRP rating, you could virtually guarantee 30% of the people who go beyond their property on any given day, will see a specific billboard advertisement. Since high saturation, over a long period of time, is the objective with regard to this characteristic, most candidates will find the cost of achieving the highest GRP rating to be the determining factor.

Arbitron Ratings
Indicate not only what percentile of the people will see a particular advertisement, but also the demographic make up of that audience.

For this reason, signs become the "weapon of choice" for most campaigns in order to realize this objective. A combination of billboards and bus signs, having a 50% GRP rating over a seven or eight month period, would make anyone's name as well known as Ronald Reagan's. To realize the same results using TV and radio would cost 15 to 20 times the amount you would have to spend on signage.

Nonetheless, in order to check your progress you would conduct your poll every 30 to 45 days and do your comparison and analysis of *name ID ratings*. You should begin to see positive results within 60 days after starting this program.

The high cost of TV airtime renders campaign signs as the "weapon of choice" for most campaigns in order to realize high saturation regarding name ID.

The problem with signs is that they are rather limited in their ability to communicate a message. Essentially, they can be used for little else than building *name ID*. They contribute little toward building your *Favorability rating* or adding any substance to your campaign. People have only about 4 seconds to read them. Therefore, be cautious about attempting to communicate much more than your name and the office being sought, the longer the message, the greater the waste.

We should take a moment here to recall the previous references to still graphics. The use of lettering and colors are extremely important when designing your signs. Their use can help communicate a secondary message that says

In the second or third stage of your campaign, you might improve your Favorability rating by adding your picture.

something about the type of person you are trying to project. Keep your signage clean and simple displaying your name, your party if a partisan race, and the office being sought. A bar can be used for emphasis, but avoid excessive graphics and always keep the short exposure time (4 seconds) and therefore, readability in mind. Bus signs, billboards, yard signs, window signs, pole signs, and corrugated 4 x 8 signs should all look alike, displaying an identical message, if any. To illustrate my point, consider the last time you saw a McDonald's Restaurant decorated differently than all the rest. Your campaign has much less time to build *name ID*. Never waste time, money, and effort on a variety of signs and messages as it will be totally counter productive.

Campaign yard signs should be double sided signs made of lightweight plastic that is almost impervious to weather. They should fit over a metal frame, be printed on both sides and easy to install. One national supplier of campaign signs is Patriot Signage, Inc., Phone: 800-777-7446; E-mail: sales@patriotsigns.com or www.patriotsigns.com

Regardless of the level of office being sought, your strategy must include a plan to build up your *name ID rating*. As you build your *name ID*, you are establishing your credentials with the electorate as a viable candidate. Until you have done this, they will not be receptive to positive messages about your candidacy. Of even greater significance, they will not find your criticism of your opponent to be credible. To go on the attack before generating a sufficient name ID rating would be counter-productive as well. Often candidates are so eager to begin criticizing their opponent that they begin their campaigns on the attack. This strategy generally backfires and they are labeled as negative candidates.

The Dukakis campaign for president in 1988 has become a classic example for this failed strategy. Right from the opening round of the Democratic convention, the Dukakis campaign attacked George Bush. A month later they added Dan Quayle to their attack. They were so eager to tear down George Bush that they failed to remember to build up Mike Dukakis. Whether it was arrogance or naivete is unimportant. They seemed to believe that simply by securing the nomination, Mike Dukakis' *hard name ID rating* was on a par with George Bush's rating. This was simply not the case. Even without a poll to prove otherwise, they should have realized this would be an impossible situation. No governor of a medium sized state is going to have parity with a person who has been Vice-President for eight years (having been nationally elected twice). Conversely, because George Bush's *name ID rating* was so high, his campaign was able to go on the attack right after their convention and make it stick.

By mid October, the Dukakis campaign appeared to realize their error, withdrew all of their negative commercials, and began a series of positive ones about Mike Dukakis. Signs and bumper stickers began to appear throughout the country, but it was too late. They had put the cart before the horse, and their campaign was doomed to go nowhere.

Definition
The Favorability rating is a method of measuring the positive or negative impressions the electorate has in association with a candidate's name.

Favorability Rating

The Favorability rating is stated in terms of a percentage of the electorate as a whole. That is, a candidate may have a 52% *Favorability rating*, or a 60% *Favorability rating*. This means 52%, or 60%, of the electorate has a favorable impression of that candidate. It is sometimes referred to as the job approval rating. However, this is restrictive. The measurement goes beyond these criteria. When the *Favorability rating* drops below 50%, it is referred to as a

Despite the remarkable job President Clinton's consultants did by convincing the American people and the media that his high job approval rating was all that mattered during the Lewinsky scandal, his personal *Favorability rating* did decline steadily.

negative rating, if over 50%, it is referred to as a positive rating. Essentially, the *Favorability rating* goes together with the *name ID rating* and should not be measured alone.

The *Favorability rating* is normally determined by polling. However, in the latter stages of the campaign, focus groups can be used effectively. Pollsters will use questions like, "Thinking about Senator Bob Smith, do you approve, or disapprove of the way he is doing his job in the U.S. Senate?" or, "Thinking about Mary Jones, the Republican candidate for U.S. Congress which word would most accurately reflect your impression of her? Would you describe your feelings as favorable, or unfavorable?"

Relevance

The *Favorability rating* goes together with the *name ID rating* and should not be measured alone.

Depending on the level of the campaign, the *Favorability rating* can be of critical importance in the development of a campaign strategy. At lower levels, all things being relatively equal a relatively *high name ID rating* is usually sufficient to win. As a rule of thumb, the higher the campaigning level, the more critical is the *Favorability rating* in the campaign. This is especially true from the perspective of a challenger. ***Another of the few truisms in politics is that the electorate does <u>not</u> vote a candidate out of office, if the candidate's Favorability rating is over 50%.*** Challengers, therefore, usually have to develop a strategy that will generate a *Favorability rating* of more than 50%, while causing the opponent's rating to drop below 50%. Incumbents do not usually have this problem. Though the electorate gives low *Favorability ratings* to politicians as a whole, they tend to exclude their own legislators.

One of the few exceptions I am aware of occurred several years ago in the celebrated race between Sen. Ken Keating of New York and Robert Kennedy. Both men had Favorability ratings well over 50%. It just came down to one having to be the winner.

It is difficult to be specific about the time this factor becomes relevant in a campaign. A city clerk's race in a medium sized metropolitan area during a presidential campaign year, would not, in all probability, receive much attention. A city clerk's race in a small town in Iowa, during an off-year election, could be a highly visible race that would prompt the *Favorability rating* to be a critical factor. In this way, the same might be true of state legislative races or city council races. In most cases, you should consider it highly relevant in federal races, statewide races, and races in districts with a population of 50,000 or greater.

Significance

In tandem with the name ID rating, it is usual for the Favorability rating to overwhelm all other factors in the campaign.

A classic example is the presidential race between Ronald Reagan and Jimmy Carter. President Carter had all the advantages of incumbency. Virtually all other factors were in Carter's favor, except for the *Favorability rating*. Because of his handling of the Iran hostage crisis and the oil embargo by the OPEC nations, Carter's *Favorability rating* had dropped below 40%. The Reagan campaign, by constantly reinforcing a negative feeling in the mind of the electorate, kept the Carter campaign on the defensive. By linking the creation of a high inflation rate, high interest rates, and high unemployment rates to the oil embargo and President Carter's policies, they actually caused the *Favorability rating* to drop even lower during the course of the campaign. The Reagan campaign strategy worked very effectively, despite the fact that Reagan's own *Favorability rating* never exceeded 50% during the course of the campaign.

Reagan of course won in the campaign that ABC dubbed as the "anyone but Carter" campaign.

Contrary to the popular wisdom of the time, I do not believe there was a Reagan mandate, nor were there any significant coattails. In fact, a rare phenomenon in American national politics occurred. In numerous congressional and senatorial races throughout the country, Republican candidates received a higher percentage of the vote than did Reagan. It was an unusual case of reverse coattails.

The Bush / Dukakis presidential campaign followed a more traditional strategy. At least it did from the perspective of the Bush campaign. The Bush campaign built George Bush's *Favorability rating* from 40% before the Republican convention to 56% by mid-October. At the same time, their strategy helped push Governor Dukakis' *Favorability rating* of 54% following the Democratic convention, to below 40% by mid-October. In an unusual manner, the Dukakis campaign and the Democratic Party assisted the Bush campaign. At the Democratic convention in Atlanta, GA, the Democrats, instead of using the occasion to project a positive image of their party, its platform, and Governor Dukakis, took an almost perverse delight in the ridiculing of George Bush. The scorn displayed took on a decidedly personal tone and definitely started the downward trend in the Dukakis' Favorability rating. As previously mentioned (and worth repeating), the problem was the Dukakis campaign had not yet solidified their own base, nor established a solid positive *Favorability rating*. Consequently the attacks were deemed negative, arrogant, and out of line. This set the stage for what is now history.

The Dukakis campaign continued their strategy to belittle George Bush in a very personal manner. By the time the Republican convention took place in New Orleans, LA, the following month, they had failed to establish any identification for Governor Dukakis. The electorate knew little about him as a person and even less about where he stood on the issues. Even more significant, they had not established positive feelings for him nor his vision for the future of America, before attacking his opponent.

The Bush campaign, following a strong presentation at the Republican convention, embarked on a dual strategy of building George Bush's *Favorability rating* while attacking Mike Dukakis. Since the Dukakis campaign was still pursuing a unilateral strategy of trying to undermine Bush's *Favorability rating*, the Bush campaign was able to define Mike Dukakis according to its terms. The electorate, not having anything to weigh against this definition, accepted it.

In an ironic twist to the Dukakis campaign strategy, around October 15th, they changed to a series of very positive commercials defining Mike Dukakis. These were designed to improve his *Favorability rating*. This would have been an appropriate strategy earlier (in July and August). In retrospect, the irony was that they should have done just the opposite. Since it was far too late to undo the damage done to Mike Dukakis' *Favorability rating*, or even significantly improve it, they should have adopted the strategy of the Reagan campaign. That strategy called for a strategy to force George Bush's *Favorability rating* below that of Dukakis'. This would not be accomplished by continuing to

When negative campaigning is used as an effective strategy, if nothing else, it may well get attention. Nonetheless, to be successful, it must be followed with the implementation of a winning strategy to capitalize on the attention gained.

attack him personally, but rather by focusing on 2 or 3 issues that the electorate could relate to, such as housing, education, and government waste.

There is an old joke about a mule and a carrot. It seems that a farmer was trying without success to get a mule off his haunches and moving. He finally tried waving a carrot a few feet in front of the mule, but the mule ignored it. A stranger who happened upon the scene told the farmer he knew how to get the mule moving. He told the farmer to stand several feet in front of the mule holding out the carrot. Then before the farmer could react, he picked up a 2 X 4 and whacked the mule right across the forehead. The mule quickly got up and began to follow the farmer. When the farmer objected to the stranger's rough handling of his mule, the stranger explained that while the carrot was a good idea, you first had to get the mule's attention.

Resources

You can determine your *Favorability rating*, and your opponent's, by having a poll taken. As with the previously discussed factors, check to see if a recent poll exists that might be available to you. If you cannot afford a professional poll, conduct your own following the suggested outline in the previous section. If your opponent is an incumbent, you can test his or her *Favorability* rating in the first poll taken. If you are not the incumbent and your *name ID rating* is expected to be very low, wait until your campaign has been in progress for at least two months before testing your *Favorability rating*.

If your campaign is a low level race, in a community with a population of 100,000 or less, basing your poll on the demographic characteristics of race and gender should be valid enough for this purpose. However, if your race involves a larger geopolitical district you should obtain information that is more specific. You will need this detail in order to design a more highly targeted media campaign. This means that you will need to develop demographic information about the respondents. In order to do this, you first need to know the demographic makeup of your district. Review the sources previously mentioned for this information, i.e. a recent poll taken by your party or another candidate, the local Chamber of Commerce, or U.S. census data available over the Internet, at your local library, university, or U.S. Representative's office. In addition, this data will be available from commercial sources.

Once you have this data, you can build your own demographic profile for your district. Base your profile on five to seven demographic characteristics that you believe would be most significant for your district and race. At the core, be sure to include income levels, education levels, race, marital status, and gender. If your race is a partisan race, include party. Since gender is a basic demographic characteristic, it helps to divide the data into two sets, one for male and the other for female. The sets would look like this:

Chapter 2 - Characteristics of the Candidates

1. Female

2. Income Levels
   - A. Under 20M
   - B. 20 - 30M
   - C. 30 - 50M
   - D. Over 50M

3. Educational Levels
   - A. Less than H.S.
   - B. H.S. Graduate
   - C. Some College
   - D. College Graduate

4. Marital Status
   - A. Married
   - B. Single
   - C. Divorced
   - D. Widowed

5. Race
   - A. Caucasian
   - B. African American
   - C. Hispanic
   - D. Asian
   - E. Native American

6.* Ethnic Origin
   - A. Italian
   - B. Irish
   - C. German
   - D. Polish
   - E. Slavic
   - F. Mexican
   - G. Puerto Rican
   - H. English

7.* Religion
   - A. Protestant
   - B. Catholic
   - C. Jewish
   - D. Moslem

8.* Voter Type
   - A. Republican
   - B. Democrat
   - C. Independent

1. Male

2. Income Levels
   - A. Under 20M
   - B. 20 - 30M
   - C. 30 - 50M
   - D. Over 50M

3. Educational Levels
   - A. Less than H.S.
   - B. H.S. Graduate
   - C. Some College
   - D. College Graduate

4. Marital Status
   - A. Married
   - B. Single
   - C. Divorced
   - D. Widowed

5. Race
   - A. Caucasian
   - B. African American
   - C. Hispanic
   - D. Asian
   - E. Native American

6.* Ethnic Origin
   - A. Italian
   - B. Irish
   - C. German
   - D. Polish
   - E. Slavic
   - F. Mexican
   - G. Puerto Rican
   - H. English

7.* Religion
   - A. Protestant
   - B. Catholic
   - C. Jewish
   - D. Moslem

8.* Voter Type
   - A. Republican
   - B. Democrat
   - C. Independent

* Optional - For illustrative purposes only.

If you used all of these demographic characteristics you would have 34 sets of sub data times 2 equaling 68 tabulations for each question in your poll. In a poll, these demographic headings are usually listed across the top of the page and referred to as "the banner." They establish the columns going down the page.

The questions and the potential responses are listed in the far-left column of the page. The responses shown numerically and as a percentile of the whole sample are then posted in the box, called a cell, which is found where the answer meets the appropriate demographic. The tables thus generated are referred to as cross tabulations, or cross tabs for short.

Doing these cross tabs involves a significant amount of work. Polling firms make extensive use of today's computer power and sophisticated software to do these calculations and print the results.

Obviously, doing these cross tabs involves a significant amount of work. Polling firms make extensive use of today's computer power and sophisticated software to do these calculations and print the results. If you are going to do your own, you have three options. You can do them manually. Another way would be to ask the computer science department of your local college if they could assist you, assuming they are allowed to help political candidates. Finally, you can obtain a software program for your personal computer that has been designed to do cross tabulations. Presently, I am aware of only one company that markets a program that can do cross tabulations and is relatively easy to use. The program is called *Survey-Pro* by Apian Software, 800.237.4565 or at www.apian.com. If you plan to do a number of detailed polls, it will be worth the investment.

As you will see in later sections, these polls can become very extensive. For example, a benchmark or base poll will usually have 25 to 30 questions, plus the demographic qualifiers. Even if you use only three or four main demographic groupings, plus their sub groups, the number of calculations could run into the thousands. Also, keep in mind that when doing this type of poll involving the demographic qualifiers, not only does the length of time for each interview increase significantly, but the number of interviews required also increases. In the previous section, we were measuring name ID and the only demographic qualifier was gender. If a poll is to have a high degree of validity, then it must correspond to the demographic makeup of the target district.

People will rarely answer qualifying demographic questions until they have heard the polling questions. The exception being whether or not they are registered to vote.

Since the qualifying demographic questions are not asked until the end of the survey, you will not know whether that particular respondent fits your sample requirements. Most pollsters need to conduct two to three times the number of interviews required for the sample while discarding those that are superfluous. You, on the other hand, can shortcut this somewhat by making a demographic predetermination, using the first three digits of the telephone number as a guide. The digits are like zip codes in that they identify a specific geographic area. If you know certain sections of your district have a preponderance of people fitting one of your demographic characteristics, like race or income levels, you would randomly select a group of telephone numbers from that area equal to your criteria requirements.

For example, if your demographic profile requires that 18% of your respondents have income levels over $50,000 and the size of your sample is 200, you would need 36 respondents who make more than $50,000 per year. People in that income bracket tend to live in the same area. Find out which telephone number prefix covers the area and then select every 10th name until you have 36 numbers to call. This prefix information is listed in the front of your telephone book.

You will need to select about 100 numbers to complete the calls to this grouping since a number of calls will be unanswered or answered by the growing number of voice mail systems and because only 60% of those who do answer will take the time to respond. As you can see, even with this predetermination exercise, you will need to select about 3 persons to call for every planned interview, resulting in a need to select about 600 persons in order to do 200 interviews for your sample.

Political action committees (PACs), party committees, and major contributors will rarely give funds to a candidate based on in-house poll results, or on polls done by unknown pollsters.

The validity of a professional poll and the reputation of a pollster are built on several criteria, not the least of which is the degree of attention given to this type of detail. This is the reason that political action committees (PACs), party committees, and major contributors will rarely give funds to a candidate based on in-house poll results, or on polls done by unknown pollsters. This fact needs to be considered when making your decisions regarding the cost of polling.

Sample Questionnaire with Demographics

Person called: ______________________________

Phone: ____________________

Date called: __________________

Male Female (Circle One)

"Good evening, this is Mary Smith. We are conducting a brief poll of registered voters this evening. Are you registered to vote?"
If YES - Continue. If NO, say thank you and goodnight.

"That's great. I wonder if you would mind taking a few moments to help us by answering a few questions. It should not take more than 10 minutes. Thank you."

(Q1) "First. Of the following five issues, which one do you think needs the greatest attention from the city government?

(Randomize) (Record Answer)

A. Reducing crime.
B. Holding down taxes and spending.
C. Reducing unemployment.
D. Improving public transportation.
E. Improving trash collection.
F. None of the above.

Chapter 2 - Characteristics of the Candidates

(Q2) Next, which one is your second choice?

(Randomize) (Record Answer)

A. Reducing crime.
B. Holding down taxes and spending.
C. Reducing unemployment.
D. Improving public transportation.
E. Improving trash collection.
F. No second choice.

(Q3) OK, that is fine. Now for our third question. Here are the names of some people active in local politics. For each one, please tell me if you are aware of him or her. If aware, ask, Is your general impression of him or her favorable or unfavorable?

(Rotate Names) (Record Answer)

A. Bob Michaels
(1) Aware, favorable
(2) Aware, unfavorable
(3) Not aware

B. Mary Kowalski
(1) Aware, favorable
(2) Aware, unfavorable
(3) Not aware

C. George Adams
(1) Aware, favorable
(2) Aware, unfavorable
(3) Not aware

(Q4) OK, thank you. Next. Do you approve or disapprove of the way Bob Michaels is handling his job as mayor?

(Record Answer)

A. Approve
B. Disapprove
C. No opinion

(Q5) Regarding this fall's election for mayor, if the election were being held today, would you be voting for:

(Rotate Names) (Record Answer)

A. Bob Michaels
B. Mary Kowalski
C. George Adams

OK, thank you. Now I would like to ask a few questions for statistical purposes.

(Q6) What is your approximate age?

(Range) (Record Answer)

A. 18 - 35
B. 36 - 50
C. 51 - 65
D. 66 over

(Q7) Thank you. What is the last grade of school you completed?

(Range) (Record Answer)

A. 11th grade or less
B. H.S. graduate (12th grade)
C. Some college
D. College graduate
E. Post-graduate work

(Q8) Thank you. What is your present marital status?

(Options) (Record Answer)

A. Married
B. Single
C. Divorced
D. Separated
E. Widow/Widower

(Q9) OK. Which of the following income groups includes your total family income last year before taxes?

(Range) (Record answer)

A. Under $20,000
B. $20,000 - $30,000
C. $30,000 - $50,000
D. $50,000 - $70,000
E. Over $70,000

(Q10) Thank you. One final question and we will be done. Is your racial or ethnic heritage Caucasian, African American, Hispanic, Asian, American Indian, or other?

(Options) (Record Answer)

A. Caucasian
B. African American
C. Hispanic
D. Asian
E. American Indian
F. Other

Thank you very much for your time and assistance. You have been very patient and I really appreciate your help. Goodnight."

Analysis of Data

If you are not using a program like *Survey-Pro* to do your computations, you should develop a worksheet to facilitate this process. You will need one for each demographic heading. Following are two examples of what they might look like. List the actual numbers, the percentile of the total for each response, and the percentile of the whole sample for each total figure.

Tabulation Work Sheet #1

Total Sample: No. | %

Response	Totals		Male		Female	
Q1, A						
Q1, B						
Q1, C						
Q1, D						
Q1, E						
Q1, F						

Complete version in *Appendix G.*

Tabulation Work Sheet #2

Total Sample: No. | %

Response Response	Totals		Causian Male		African American Female		Hispanic Male	
Q1, A								
Q1, B								
Q1, C								
Q1, D								
Q1, E								
Q1, F								

Complete version in *Appendix H.*

Study the work sheets carefully. Focus especially on discernible patterns. Are there groups that appear to be stronger for you than for your opponent? If, for example, you have more potential votes among Caucasian males over 50, try to determine why. Refer back to your analysis of the personal characteristics. See if you can find the cause for this factor.

Analyze your opponent's strengths and weaknesses. Why do they exist? A more detailed poll could probe for the reasons. However, if time and the amount of effort required preclude this, then you will have to make this determination subjectively.

Do not take anything for granted. In order to develop a sound strategy you need to know why a positive or negative impression exists. Correlate the information about you and your opponent with the issue oriented data. See if there is a pattern. Do those people who tend to feel a certain way about a specific issue also feel the same way about you or your opponent? Is there an apparent contradiction in this comparison?

Remember that it was this kind of analysis that provided the critical clue in the development of the Bush campaign strategy against Michael Dukakis. Following the Democratic convention, the polls indicated that people who tended to be conservative on the issues favored Mike Dukakis. The polls actually indicated that they thought that Dukakis was more conservative than George Bush. This insight was what prompted the Bush camp to launch its vigorous campaign to expose Mike Dukakis as a liberal. It was this kind of detailed analysis that focused the Bush camp strategy and changed the expected course of that campaign.

Developing the Strategy

Given the importance of building your *Favorability rating* to over 50%, this objective should be your first priority. *After* this has been accomplished, if it is necessary, then focus on bringing your opponent's *Favorability rating* down.

Our sample survey tested *the name ID* and *Favorability ratings* simultaneously. If the percentile of the respondents indicating that they were aware of you is below the criteria required for name ID regarding the office being pursued (Q3), your strategy must be the same as that outlined previously. If your *Favorability rating* is below 50%, your strategy must be designed to bring it above that percentile. Conversely, if your opponent is above 50%, your strategy must be designed to bring it below that percentile.

As stated, where still graphics are well suited to improving *name ID rating*, they are of minimal value in affecting *Favorability ratings*. To accomplish this objective live graphics are superior. Live graphics encompass the mediums of television, video, and radio. In television and radio, they are usually referred to as free or paid. Paid for radio and television times are called commercials. Time that is provided by the station is referred to as free time. Videos are tapes developed for playing on a VCR machine on a home television set.

Of all the communication mediums available to political candidates today, none are more effective than commercials and videos in communicating feelings. These feelings, or impressions, can be positive or negative. They can improve your *Favorability rating* if done well or actually create negative feelings about you if done poorly. If directed against your opponent, they can create negative feelings about him or her, if done properly and at the appropriate time. If not, they can boomerang and cause positive feelings for your opponent and a backlash toward you.

Your situation determines the best strategy for your campaign.

Your situation determines the best strategy for your campaign. This can not be stressed enough. Numerous campaigns have failed because they lacked the patience to wait until *name ID* and *Favorability rating* objectives were

There is a strong tendency in politics to mimic what others have done in their campaigns. This is generally a serious mistake. Your strategy should be custom made to the particular needs of your campaign.

You should never focus on more than two or three issues during the campaign.

The video presentation is also a great opportunity to make your appeal for campaign volunteer assistance and to seek campaign donations.

achieved before going on the attack. Sometimes, this is caused by getting a late start in the campaign. More often though, it is the candidate's supporters who, in their eagerness to attack the opponent, force the campaign into making this error.

You build a positive Favorability rating by accentuating those personal characteristics which your research indicated provoked a positive response from the electorate. You reinforce it with positive statements about those issues that were of the greatest concern to the electorate, as determined by your poll.

Depending on the level of campaign you are involved in, and the locale, your campaign strategy should include using varying degrees of the commercial mediums available. In a later section, I will discuss the impact that the commercial media will have on your strategy based on level and locale. However, even a low budget campaign that is not targeted by the local media outlets to donate free coverage, can make effective use of videos. Today over 90% of all households have a VCR and for a few thousand dollars you could produce and distribute 1,000's of videos throughout your district.

The videos can be easily self produced with the help of some of your associates and then sent to a video duplication firm for reproduction. First, develop your script. Start with an opening scene by placing the candidate in a comfortable setting, introducing him or her and what the video the viewers are about to see is all about. Tell the viewer a little about the candidate, his or her education, profession, and service to the community. Begin to talk about the family and pan to scenes of the spouse and the children. Preferably, this should be in an outdoor setting, with the family interacting. Make the introductions conversational, as though talking with a new neighbor.

As narrator, you should begin to talk about the issues, pan to scenes of the candidate in a setting relating to the subject matter. For example, if schools are the issue, he or she could be walking down the corridor of a local school, or in the playground area. Make the backdrop fit the issue. If the issue is community crime, you might include the city jail. If the issue is neighborhood blight, you might include a walk through an area of abandoned and neglected housing.

Finish the video back in the original setting. Looking directly into the camera, the candidate should express concern about these issues and what he or she will do, if elected, to help resolve them. Ask the viewer for their help and their vote on Election Day. Close the video with a shot of your campaign yard sign, preferably located on an appropriate district property.

The whole video presentation should not last more than 30 minutes. In your close, ask the viewer to pass the video on to a neighbor and urge them to view it. This is also a great opportunity to make your appeal for campaign volunteer assistance and to seek campaign donations. Short and to the point, solicit a contribution to offset the cost of the video. In fact, you should always enclose a business return envelope (BRE).

BRE
Business Return Envelope

There are several ways you can distribute the video. As you are walking your precincts, if you encounter someone who expresses support for you and offers to help your campaign, give them a copy and ask them to circulate it in their neighborhood. If you have specific groups or organizations supporting your candidacy, ask their members to take copies and circulate them. In addition, you can tie them into discussions at any coffee klatch that you plan to do. You could also spot mail them around the district with a cover letter asking voters to take a few minutes to view the video and pass it on to a family member or neighbor. Finally, send a copy to your local television stations in the hope that they use clips of it on a quiet news day.

Begin to circulate these videos at least 120 days before the election. All of them should be in circulation at least 90 days before the election. This is true whether it is a primary or a general election period. If it is a primary period, target the videos to households with a member of your party in it. Then, redirect the videos to the "undecideds" in the general campaign period.

If your campaign cannot afford the self-production of a live video, or there is some other reason precluding its utilization, then you will have to rely on your still graphics strategy. In any case, they should be designed to improve *Favorability rating* as well as building your *name ID rating*. As mentioned previously, the colors you choose and the typeface used will help. In your brochure and tabloids, use pictures that reinforce the message in the copy. The graphic design, layout, paper stock, and printing should always combine to create a quality product.

If you can develop a brief theme for the campaign that is relevant to the major issue, use it in your graphics. If it is not relevant, then do not use it just for the sake of having one.

Personal History

Definition
Personal history is defined as the accumulation of a candidate's life experiences, other than those related to professional or civic experiences. More specifically, those experiences which can shape or influence a person's character and values.

The Personal History Checklist should be completed on the Spouses of both the Candidate and the Opponent.

Personal history would include date and place of birth, early, primary, and extended family information, primary, secondary, and post-secondary education, athletics, military service, awards and decorations, personal family information, and religious background. To some extent this information can provide clues to a person's judgement and be a predictor of future behavior.

Checklist - Personal History

Personal History	Candidate	Opponent
Place of Birth (City, State)		
Date of Birth		
Father's Name		
Mother's Maiden Name		
Father's Occupation		
Mother's Occupation		

Complete version in *Appendix I.*

Resources

Most of this information is available from sources previously listed. Since most of this data is objective, it should be readily available in your opponent's biographic material, yearbooks, newspaper articles, or by direct interviewing. Your research should also include an analysis of the institutions, organizations, activities, and localities involved.

Look well beyond the obvious in order to add depth to the responses.

For example, what are the rankings of the schools attended? What is their orientation? How would you categorize the religious preference indicated? Some like the Catholics, Mormons, Christian Scientists, and Pentecostals can have a profound impact on an individuals early life, while others like Episcopalian, Presbyterian, or Unitarians may have less impact. What general category would the service organizations fall into? Community service, personal gratification, or political. How would you classify the localities lived in? Blue collar, white collar, professional, rural, or urban. Are the fraternities or sororities academic or social? Consider any physical impairments and/or traumatic experiences that may be uncovered? Are they impediments to the strain of campaigning and/or public office?

Individual Analysis

Historical data cannot be altered to accommodate the norms or preferences of the electorate.

Analyzing this data from the perspective of the electorate is a bit more difficult than the characteristics referred to previously. Since this data is historical, it cannot be changed or altered to accommodate the norms or preferences of the electorate. However, it might be useful to test certain items with a focus group, or poll to see if they merit emphasis in your campaign literature or commercials. This would be particularly true if there are significant differences between you and your opponent.

Given the time constraints of a poll, we normally would not test any of these factors using that device. If something appears especially significant, we might occasionally include it to see if there are any demographic variations. Usually, a focus group analysis is adequate for most campaigns below the national level and major statewide races.

Build your focus group using the same considerations discussed previously regarding gender, race, or economic levels. Using the + and - system, have the focus group interviewer ask the members to rate each characteristic if it would have a positive or negative impact on their voting. Ask them to leave it blank if it is neutral. For example, if a candidate had prior military service, would that be a positive or negative influence on voting for him or her? Continue along this line with all the characteristics listed.

Analysis Chart - Personal History

The following chart illustrates some of the personal history characteristics that may warrant the consideration of a focus group or poll. The district's demographic definition will assist in deciding whether or not this time and expense will be invested wisely. For example, if your opponent is an Italian American, has recently moved to the area from NY State, is a non-practicing

Catholic and divorced several times, these characteristics may well deserve focus if the election district is in a "Bible Belt" center of any southern state.

Items	Values	Caucasian Female	African American Male	Hispanic Female
College	+ -			
Occupation	+ -			
Religion	+ -			
Military Service	+ -			
Impairments	+ -			
Divorced	+ -			
Children	+ -			
Social Organizations	+ -			

Complete version in *Appendix J.*

Assignment of Values

Since we are using a plus / minus system for this analysis, add the number of pluses across each row to determine relative impact. Divide the total number by the number of individuals in the focus group to arrive at an average. For example, 10 individuals in the focus group said it would be a positive factor if a candidate had prior military service. If there are 15 individuals in the focus group, divide 10 by 15 to arrive at an average of 67%. Continue these calculations for the total in each category and then do them for each demographic grouping.

After calculating the positive responses, the same process should be followed for the negative responses. The differential between the two figures, the positive percentages and the negative percentages, would indicate the percentage that is relatively neutral about the political influence of each item in their voting process.

Analysis of Data

There are several analyses that need to be made from this data. First, you need to study the objective data listed for both you and your opponent. As you study your data, analyze it from the perspective of your opponent.

What does the data say about you? Is there anything that your opponent can use against you, either directly or indirectly, by emphasizing characteristics that he or she has, which you do not? For example, your age differential could be a factor in certain areas of the country. The number of times you have divorced could be a factor. Your ethnic origin could be a factor in some sections of the country. The reputation of your parents could be a factor. Conversely, can these factors be positive for you? Now reverse the process and analyze your opponent's data using the same criteria. Keep in mind, your opponent is probably going through this same exercise. Analyze each item by itself and then in relation to the other items that might interact to produce certain results. For example, are there brothers and/or sisters? If so, where does your opponent fit into the family structure? What relevance might this have in relation to the cultural background that he or she was raised in? The American generation that he or she is associated with could be significant. In certain cultures, whether you are the first born or the last born can have a decided affect on the way you were raised. Did your opponent attend private, public, or parochial schools during the formative years? There can be a significant difference in the quality of education and the levels of discipline between different school systems and this could have a bearing on personality, intellect, and character.

Be critical and objective in your analysis. Do not make the mistake so many candidates do by only seeing what you want to see.

Next, analyze the responses of the focus group to the various items tested. Consider any significant differences between the demographic groups that might indicate a specific strategy for that group. Compare the number of positives each has over all and by line item. If either of you have a positive percentage of 50% or more for any item, this item should be emphasized during the campaign. Conversely, any negative percentage of 50% or more is a definite weak point that should in all likelihood be exploited by you, and conversely, will in all likelihood be exploited by your opponent. If in fact, you have one or more weak points (ratings less than 50%), you should immediately develop a response to that weakness, turning it into a positive. For example, if you have recently moved into the area and this is considered a negative by the focus group, your strategy would be to emphasize that you have chosen this area because of your complete love and devotion to the area, stating reasons. In addition, you believe that the diversity of your experience will make you the stronger candidate. That was one of the mistakes Mike Dukakis made and look what happened to his campaign. Remember that negatives do not necessarily make you lose the election. We would all have negatives if subjected to an in-depth analysis of our lives. What is important, is our response to these negative considerations. Your ability to identify negatives, coupled with your ability to develop a strategic response turning those negatives into a positive is the very essence of a strategic plan that will push your campaign ahead of your opponent.

Do not fear your negatives, but rather embrace them. With consideration and planning, any negative can be reversed and turned into a "win - win situation."

A negative characteristic can be your only downfall in the final analysis. Your true failure can only be associated with a complete lack of preparedness to handle the negative attack. If need be, review my earlier reference to the mule and the 2" x 4". The attack on your negatives will undoubtedly get the attention of the electorate. This attention will increase your name ID rating (and it will be *free*). If you have prepared yourself properly to successfully handle the negative, your prepared response will not only increase your Favorability rating, it will lower the Favorability rating of your opponent. If handled successfully, your opponent will be thought of as not only negative him/herself, but as "just plain wrong" about you.

Developing the Strategy

Use personal history to build your positive ratings

In most situations, you would use personal history to build your positive ratings. In the early stages of the campaign, you should develop what is referred to as a bio (biographical) brochure.

This brochure would normally feature a picture of yourself, one of your family, including your parents, brothers, and sisters. The family picture should be in an outdoor setting, showing everyone in a relaxed, natural pose. A caption below the photo should identify everyone in it. Your picture should be a head and shoulders shot in a 3/4 pose. All pictures should be arranged with a professional photographer.

The copy in the brochure should emphasize your personal, business, and civic history. Do not discuss issues directly, as that will come later. Rather, create an impression of who you are and where you stand by featuring the highlights of your general history.

Write your bio in a narrative style rather than just listing each event. Make it interesting to read, but be brief. Instead of just listing organizations to which you belong, state how long you have been associated with the organization and indicate if you have held any office. Be sure to feature the office that you are running for. Give each item a little depth. Use color and graphics to create a positive feeling about you. The brochure should be printed on 60 #, glossy paper, and folded to fit a #10 envelope. Whether you are graphically inclined or not, listen to the suggestions of your printer. The printer's advice will be invaluable in sending the right message on your printed materials. The printer will also have suggestions regarding the best value for your dollar. For example, when deciding size and definition, it will make a major difference to the cost of your brochure if you realize two brochures from a single sheet of paper, rather than one (final dimensions will be the critical criteria).

Shortly after you announce your candidacy, saturate your district. In your letter, introduce yourself, explain in one or two brief paragraphs the reasons that you are running for office and close with an appeal for their support and for a campaign contribution. The letter should be on a single sheet. Make it a "Dear Friend" letter on your campaign stationery. Nowhere in the bio brochure or letter should you refer to your opponent by name. In your letter, you can refer by inference to your opponent, if you feel it is necessary, but never by name.

In a normal campaign, you would announce near the 1st of February, put up billboards by The 15th of February, and send off this mailer about the 1st of April.

Along with your letter of introduction, enclose your brochure and a wallet style, self-addressed, return envelope and mail your introduction to every registered voter in your district who has voted in at least two of the last three elections. If your campaign can not afford this, mail it to every registered voter of your party. It would be very unusual if you did not receive sufficient contributions to pay for the mailer. This bio mailer should be sent out 45 days after your billboards and/or 4 X 8 signs go up throughout the district. During these early stages, pass out this biographical brochure wherever you and your volunteers campaign. Include it in all your press kits, PAC kits, and fund-raising letters.

Since we have touched on the subject of direct mailing, I will briefly address the issue now. We will discuss mailings in detail throughout the manual. There are two main issues involved, that is, after you take for granted that communication with the voters is without any doubt a campaigning necessity. The first issue is targeting your constituents with the appropriate message; the second is keeping costs in line. To my knowledge, there are only two ways to accomplish these goals successfully.

If you re-read the paragraph before last, you will note that I have directed you to create a letter of introduction, not only address it, but target that address in order to keep costs in line with your campaign budget. How then, will you best accomplish this goal?

You will be unable to campaign with any real level of effectiveness if you do not obtain a list of the registered voters in your district.

Let me point out that you will be unable to campaign with any real level of effectiveness if you do not obtain a list of the registered voters in your district and all of the data collected that is associated with them. This information is available in a number of places, including your local Election Board office. It will be available in both electronic format and printed hard copies. You will be able to arrange for these voter lists sorted, including or excluding, any category of information that has been collected that you may have interest in (to simplify this choice take all information associated with your voters, as knowledge is your best weapon). There will be a charge for this service each time you arrange for a targeted list. In addition, you will be able to arrange for mailing labels at the Board for an additional fee. Alternatively, you can take the electronic file to a service bureau that will be able to create your mailing labels, likely at a cost per thousand labels.

Target your introduction letter to a name and address

Now, armed with this registered voter information, you can target your introduction letter to a name and address. In this way, you can get the most "bang for your buck." You can save the expense of letter creation and postage of letters sent needlessly to unsorted addresses. In this case, I have suggested sending the letter to only those voters that are:

a) in your district,
b) registered,
c) have voted in two of the last three elections.
d) alternatively, only the registered voters, in your district, affiliated with your party.

The need to target voter groups will only intensify as your research develops a number of groups in your district, with different issues personal to them.

If there was an issue regarding a proposed highway, you will want to target those in the direct path of the highway with one message, while your campaign would be better served by targeting those in the surrounding areas, with a different focus (regarding the proposed highway), or even a different issue altogether. This would be especially true, if your district was so large that those in the east had completely different issues than those to the north and west.

Ultimately, a decision must be made. Will you pay an outside service to manage the communication needs of your campaign or will you outfit your campaign management team with the tools necessary to run this aspect of your campaign in-house? It is my personal opinion that the answer to this

Whether you are an incumbent or a challenger, you must first establish your credibility as a candidate and solidify your base. It is imperative that you do not take this strategy for granted.

question is buried in that old adage, "Pay me now or pay me later." In other words, will you invest the available funds in the technology to do this voter communication within your campaign team, or will you contract an outside service bureau to communicate on your behalf. In either case, it will be expensive to communicate with the electorate.

By way of a quick review, the reason for communicating at this point was to implement your strategy to focus on building a *positive name ID rating*. There will be plenty of time later in the campaign to focus on both the issues and your opponent. First, you must establish your credibility as a candidate and solidify your base. Whether you are an incumbent or a challenger do not take this strategy for granted. It is imperative that you do not.

Career History

Definition
Career history is defined as the cumulative employment experiences a candidate has had throughout his or her life.

Career history includes the details of any employment for financial compensation from childhood up to the present time. It also includes a description of each job and the reasons for any change in employment.

In effect, you build a resume of yourself and your opponent, just as you would if you were applying for a new position. This is essentially what you and your opponent will be doing. Just as with any other position, your qualifications and experiences are relevant factors in an employer's decision to hire you. In this case, your employers are the electorate. Not only is your career history an indication of your ability to perform the specific duties required for an elected official, it is also another clue to predicting future behavior.

Checklist - Career History

The Career History Checklist should be completed on the Spouses of both the Candidate and the Opponent.

Career History	Candidate	Opponent
Present Employer Approx. Date of Employment Recent Position or Title Approx. Annual Earnings Type of Work Preformed Number of People Supervised Noteworthy Accomplishments		
Past Employer Period of Employment Position or Title Reason(s) for Leaving		

Complete version in *Appendix K*.

Resources

Your research should also include an analysis of the companies involved and their primary activities.

Most of this information should be available from the same sources previously discussed. This data is also objective and should be available in your opponent's biographic material. If not, ask directly, or have someone do that for you. This is a reasonable request; it would be unusual for any candidate to object to responding positively.

Analyze the results of your research and look for any pattern in the employment history and/or companies worked for. For example, are they service oriented, manufacturing, professional, construction oriented, sales, or financial? What categories would they fall into?

Since elected officials at almost every level, not only have responsibility for making, defining, and/or enforcing laws, they also have the responsibility to supervise and direct the activities of public servants within their specific areas of concern, is there evidence of experience that suggests the ability to perform these duties? As any management expert will tell you, there is a direct correlation between an employee's productivity and the managerial skills of their supervisor.

Individual Analysis

Your analysis of this data can be made from several sources. Obviously, your own intuitive assessment is a factor. You can also incorporate a business profile of yourself and your opponent within your focus group. Do not identify the profiles. Have the focus group interviewer ask the members to evaluate, in general terms, one profile compared to the other. If there is a noticeable preference for one over the other, probe as to the specifics causing this differential.

In a polling environment, pick two or three specific characteristics to test. Usually this is done with questions that start with "How important is this *characteristic* to you in helping you to decide whom to vote for? Is it very important, important, not very important, or makes no difference?" Do not underestimate the value of this data. One of the major factors in George Bush's win over Michael Dukakis was the job experience factor. It consistently showed up on almost every poll taken as one of the primary reasons people were voting for Bush. This factor was also tested in a highly sophisticated modeling program written by a Mr. Jim Merritt of Phoenix, Arizona. When various business characteristics were changed while all other factors were held constant, there were significant shifts in vote results.

Incidentally, Mr. Merritt's model was so incredibly accurate that a major party paid Mr. Merritt a substantial amount of money for exclusivity, in a critical election year. As I have said, being unable to match your opponent weapon for weapon can be fatal.

Analysis Chart - Career History

Due to the nature of a career history, analysis can be best accomplished by creating your focus group as previously discussed, imitating as closely as possible, the demographics of the electoral district. The interviewer will then ask the group a series of career related questions comparing candidate to opponent. A similar process can be expanded to include the spouses. Naturally, the profiles that the focus group is analyzing are unidentified.

Sample questions regarding career history:

1) How important is a candidate's profession in your voting decision?
2) Which profession do you believe best prepares a candidate for public office?
3) Do you believe prior management experience is an asset for public office?
4) Do you believe an attorney is better qualified than a businessperson to be an elected official?
5) If a person had been in business and went bankrupt, would that affect whether or not you would vote for that person?

Assignment of Values

As before, use the plus / minus system to assign value to the assessment categories. Add the pluses and minuses by your demographic groupings within the focus group.

If you are using a poll, indicate in your cross-tabs the results by demographic groups. This is another situation where having a program like Survey Pro would be extremely beneficial. Since doing cross-tabs manually is such an exhaustive undertaking, chances are you, or your staff, will become very discouraged at the thought of doing one.

Nonetheless, one of the primary functions of polling is to plot a graph using the results from various polls taken over a defined time. This enables you to determine shifts in attitude in a timely manner and enables you to adjust your strategy accordingly. Unless you poll at regular intervals, you have lost one of your primary weapons in the strategic decision making process. You will find it difficult enough just keeping volunteers doing interviews much less doing the tedious work in the tabulations of these results. Programs like Survey pro relieve your staff of this major chore and considerably improve your chances of doing regularly scheduled polls during the course of the campaign.

Analysis of Data

As with the other groupings of characteristics that you have analyzed, you must first study the data that you have accumulated as objectively as possible. What does the data say about each of you? Is there a pattern of accomplishment in each of these profiles? Of industriousness? Of integrity? Of management experience and/or leadership? Are there stereotypical negative factors, such as high job turnover or an indication of failing to achieve steady growth? Is the primary occupation professional, white collar, skilled, semi-skilled, or laborer?

Have you or your opponents ever been in a managerial position? Quantify the supervisory experience and depth of responsibility that each of you has over your working careers? Have either of you been in a position which required the development of communication skills? A political leader must, almost by necessity, be able to effectively articulate ideas and positions.

Politics is one of the most stressful jobs in our society. What factors in each of your business backgrounds demonstrate an ability to withstand this intense pressure?

Without these skills, their ability to perform their responsibilities is significantly diminished. One of the reasons we have so many attorneys in public office is because they receive extensive training in this area. Conversely, there are very few accountants and engineers in public office because they receive very little training in the communications area, unless they pursue it on their own.

Again, analyze each factor by itself, and in relation to the others. Coupled with the other characteristics we have already discussed, a pattern should be developing. Do the business characteristics appear to be consistent with the other groups of characteristics? If not, why?

Most of us are creatures of habit. We tend to develop some consistency in all the facets of our lives. If a characteristic or group of characteristics appears to be inconsistent with the others, there must be a reason for it. Find out why. It could be strategically important.

Developing the Strategy

If your analysis, based on the focus group, polls, or your own intuitive feelings, indicates a strong Favorability rating for your business background, then emphasize it during the early stages of the campaign.

Some candidates I have known over the years have felt it would be immodest to stress their business accomplishments. I suggest this is false modesty. Given that your business experience is a significant factor in the electorate's decision making process, you have an obligation to be as complete and candid about your business background as possible. Outline your career history and business accomplishments and accolades in your campaign bio without modesty. This should be a very positive piece without reference to your opponent. If you use print graphics, photos of you in these settings would assist you in making your point.

On the other hand, if you are able to get early access to electronic media, carry this message into that as well. If doing television spots, go on site to reinforce your message. For example, if you are an attorney, film yourself in an empty courtroom as you discuss your concerns about justice and how hard you have worked to assure that every person gets fair treatment. This should prove very effective. If you are the owner of a business, a setting inside your place of business, or at the outside entrance as employees go in or out, would make your point.

Present your profile as often as you can by repeatedly stressing it in your campaign media and press releases. With this strategy, you will gradually cause a comparison between you and your opponent. Let others make the comparisons between your business background and your opponent's background. If your focus group or polling analysis indicates a negative reaction to certain characteristics in your opponent's background, be careful about the development of your strategy regarding your use of your career history advantage. Be patient and develop both your name ID and Favorability rating before any attempt is made to capitalize on any negative characteristic of your opponent. Your strategy should be to emphasize your positive characteristics. In so doing, you will force the natural comparison between candidates, and expose the negative characteristics of your opponent. This strategy will enable you to avoid any possibility of being accused of the negative campaigning label that can be so devastating to any campaign.

The *reverse gambit* strategy will emphasize your positive characteristics. In so doing, you will force the natural comparison between candidates and expose the negative characteristics of your opponent, avoiding any possibility of being accused of the negative campaigning label.

Often referred to as the *reverse gambit*, what political strategist could ever forget President Reagan's famous line in his debate with Walter Mondale when he assured the country that he would never make an issue out of age? Reagan then referred to Mondale's youth and inexperience. It was a classic *reverse gambit*. In this instance, Reagan eluded to Mondale's youth and inexperience in order to negate Mondale's opportunity to make an issue of Reagan's age. By acknowledging his negative characteristics and developing a strategy to deal with them in the face of the electorate, Reagan completely eliminated any chance Walter Mondale had of making Reagan's advanced age an issue in the campaign.

This strategy, especially when done with a touch of humor (as President Reagan did), can be very devastating. Consider the *reverse gambit* the next time you want to call attention to a negative characteristic in your opponent's background. If done with care and planning, you can make your point, devastate your opponent, and avoid even the hint of a negative campaigning accusation.

Civic History

Definition
Civic history is defined as the accumulated experience a candidate has in volunteer service to his or her community prior to becoming formally involved in the political process.

Civic history can be under the auspices of church, school, charity, social, athletic, community, or as a personal activity. Any type of involvement that demonstrates a willingness to serve others without financial gain can be considered as a civic contribution.

Since generally speaking, most individuals seeking public office have previously demonstrated a willingness to serve their community, a failure to have done so might be indicative of other motivating factors that could be strategically significant.

There are many reasons why individuals enter public life, but historically our most successful politicians, regardless of party, are those who have viewed public life as a continuation of their service to the community.

Checklist - Civic History

Civic History	Candidate	Opponent
Boy/Girl Scout Leader		
Little League Coach		
PTA Activist		
Homeowners Association		
Youth Activity		
Veteran's Activities		
Sr. Citizen Activities		
Organized Charities		

Complete version in *Appendix L*.

Resources

This information may not be as readily available as previously discussed data. Normally, if it exists, it will be in your opponent's bio. On the other hand, do not be fooled, the absence of information does not necessarily mean that none exists. Occasionally a sense of modesty might preclude a candidate's calling attention to this part of their history.

Here again, the direct approach might work best. Call or write your opponent and ask him or her what groups or activities he or she has been involved in, if any. A refusal to provide a direct answer, or evasiveness, *could* be a further indication of no activity in this regard.

Check further with your resources in the community, especially any Centers of Influence that you know, to see if they are aware of any activity of this type done by your opponent.

Think about your own experiences along these lines and write them down. If there are none, be prepared to explain why not when the issue arises during the course of the campaign. Remember that your opponent is probably doing this same analysis of you.

Individual Analysis

After accumulating this data, look at it from the perspective of the voter. Has there been a significant commitment of time, energy, and/or resources devoted to the betterment of the community?

Again, consider any patterns that have evolved? For example, have most of the activities been centered on social organizations, like the Elk, Moose, Lions, Junior Chamber of Commerce, or is the pattern almost exclusively church oriented? Are the activities generally very public or very private commitments?

Except for testing, the question of whether or not a history of civic involvement is an important factor in helping a voter to decide whom they are going to vote for, you really can not determine effectively the relative merits of one type of activity over the other.

This intelligence has value primarily in its relationship to the pattern developed by the other groupings of characteristics. To repeat what was stated in the previous section, we are creatures of habit. To presume that a person suddenly develops a sense of civic responsibility when they decide to run for office is a bit incredulous for most people. If a person has not demonstrated this sense of responsibility heretofore, it certainly exposes them to a legitimate questioning of motivation now.

I do not mean to imply that this would be in and of itself a negative factor. However, it would certainly raise a question worth pursuing. In politics, we would refer to it as a "red flag," a warning signal of a possible vulnerability.

Since it is not practical to test the specifics of this data with a focus group or poll, I will skip the Analysis Chart and Assignment of Values subsections we used with the previous groupings of characteristics.

Analysis of Data

First, study the data developed in the checklist. Referring to the patterns previously discussed, what pattern would your opponent infer about you?

Be especially critical about what the data is saying about you.

Are you actively involved? Is there a special interest in one group, or one type of activity? Does one exist? Why? For example, if all or most of the activity centers on youth activities, is it only because your child or children were involved? Could this be construed as much more of a parental responsibility than a civic one? If the pattern centers heavily on benevolent organizations, like the social lodges, could this be construed more as a social activity than a civic duty? Does a pattern develop which is centered around organizations like the Junior Chamber of Commerce, where their charitable activity does provide meaningful service to the community, nonetheless, it is also quite often a means to foster one's business career.

Alternatively, is there a true pattern that shows genuine concern and compassion for the well-being of others and the community at large. Is the motive the self-satisfaction, which comes from helping others through civic responsibilities performed for one's community or are there ulterior motives?

These are all clues, or intelligence gathering, that will help to develop the profile of your opponent, and illustrate how your opponent might see you.

Developing the Strategy

Your strategy in using this set of characteristics must be subtle. Regarding your own activities, state them without overemphasizing them. Demonstrate that your concern for people is genuine and that you view this step into politics as an extension of that concern. Express your frustration at being unable to accomplish those things you believe need to be done to improve the quality of life in the community unless you are in a position to change the laws, or funding, or direction of leadership.

Never attack your opponent for being uninvolved or for being involved only for ulterior motives.

Never attack your opponent for being uninvolved or for being involved only for ulterior motives. Rather, stress your belief that only an individual who has been truly involved in helping to solve the community's problems could understand the pain and suffering caused by those problems and help to define their solutions. It is one thing to read about the plight of the homeless; it is quite another, to go into the streets to help them.

Summarizing Personal Characteristics

This is a good place to briefly review our analysis of the strategic process up to this point. In subsequent sections, we will analyze how strategy is developed and how it is dependent on all of the extraneous factors that exist within the campaign environment. It is critically important to realize that these other factors do not exist in a vacuum. They are all impacted by the profiles developed in this and the preceding sections. I have deliberately discussed these characteristics first because too many politicians and consultants, in my opinion, place an inordinate amount of attention and emphasis on the other factors in the strategic decision making process.

It is only by going through the steps outlined in the previous sections that you will gather valuable information, not only about your opponent, but about yourself. You will learn to view your opponent, and of equal importance, you will learn to view yourself, not only as you perceive one another, but in addition, as the electorate perceives each of you. Given the nature of a large majority of the voting public, these factors are of paramount importance in the development of a campaign strategy.

Over the years, I have seen too many campaigns use "boiler plate" campaign plans and copycat commercials that had little or no relevance to the particulars of the campaign that they were being used in at the time. In almost all cases, the results were disastrous. I suspect, in most of these campaigns, the reason "boiler plate" campaign plans and copycat commercials were used was due to either ignorance or expediency, or both. Unfortunately, all too often the people who are responsible for developing strategy simply have no real idea of how to develop it. It is, as I hope I have illustrated thus far, a scientific and painstaking process.

It should be obvious by now that a considerable amount of hard work and expense is involved in the intelligence gathering process. It is *always* easier to copy a plan or commercial that worked for someone, somewhere, sometime, and use it in your own campaign. Unfortunately, the results attained by this ignorance and expedience is rarely success. Just as no two people are completely alike, no two campaigns are completely alike. Consequently, no two-campaign plans should be completely alike.

There are many constant values within a campaign environment. At least 85% of the campaign is or should be made up of constants having almost universal application in American style campaigning. These, however, are tactical considerations. *Strategic considerations* simply do not fall into neat patterns, yet both are vital ingredients to the successful campaign. A candidate cannot win with only one and not the other.

The very essence of developing your strategy is to develop *your strategy*.

According to numerous studies done by the University of Michigan over the last fifty years, less than 15% of the electorate vote for an individual based on that individual's position on the issues. This percentage actually *declines* the lower down the ticket you go. Unfortunately, we become so mesmerized by the presidential, major senatorial, and gubernatorial races that capture the media's interest and attention that it becomes easy to presume or extend their considerations into all other campaigns. However, by sheer virtue of the massive amounts of money spent and media attention received, those races are unique in their own right. Be mindful of the fact that these unique races comprise less than 100 of the 425,000 elections that take place in our country every two years. This represents an insignificant one-quarter of one tenth of one percent (.000236%). To base your strategy on what worked in these races is almost certain to be a fatal mistake. I have often used the comparison of football to baseball. They are both games played with a ball and that is where the comparison ends.

A very wise person said, "if you want to be victorious in battle, know your enemy as you know yourself." This is as true today as it was hundreds of years ago.

Know your relative strengths and weaknesses as well as your opponent's. Then, armed with this knowledge, begin to examine their relevance within the constraints of the following considerations and factors. Carefully study all the groupings of individual characteristics developed and combine them to develop a realistic profile of yourself and your opponent.

Chapter 2 - Word Index

Chapter 3 Additional Characteristics

Financial Resources

Definition
Financial resources are the sources of funds available to the campaign from which to solicit operating capital. A considerable number of political campaigns fail simply because they are undercapitalized.

When starting a political campaign, similar to starting a new business, the funding available is extremely critical. Many businesses fail, not because they were lacking a great plan, a great product, or a great management team, but rather they lacked the necessary capital to translate those resources into a successful enterprise. In like manner, a considerable number of political campaigns fail simply because they are undercapitalized.

A candidate who can not successfully communicate to the electorate and build name ID and Favorability rating will lose.

Marketing is another term for communicating. Unless a candidate can successfully communicate to the electorate and build name ID and Favorability rating, the campaign will be lost. Unless the candidate can communicate ideas and solutions, and be convincing as to why the electorate should vote for him or her over the opponent, the campaign will fall short of its objective to secure a seat in public office. Almost the entire campaign budget will be devoted to marketing the candidate and his or her ideas and solutions to the electorate.

Since marketing a candidate requires money, a winning strategy must include the means to acquire enough money for your campaign marketing plan.

Since marketing a candidate requires money, a winning strategy must include the means to acquire enough money to complete your campaign marketing plan. In the initial stages, there must be enough funds available to start the campaign. This is referred to as start-up capital. In later chapters, we will discuss the techniques that can be used to acquire the funds necessary to market your campaign. Immediately, we must turn our attention to the start-up capital that must be provided by the candidate and/or the candidate's closest supporters.

For discussion purposes, we will assume that your opponent has access to, or the ability to acquire financing for his or her campaign. If this were not the case, your strategy could then be modified accordingly.

Available Options

Your first option, of course, is to look at your own ability to provide the necessary start-up capital to finance your campaign. If you do not believe enough in the efficacy of your own candidacy to invest in it, why should others do so? In any event, you must be prepared to answer this question to the satisfaction of prospective campaign contributors.

As a rule of thumb, the necessary start up capital or seed money as it is sometimes referred to, is between 10% and 20% of the campaign's budget. The less known a candidate is at the start of the campaign, the more money required at start-up. For example, a candidate running for Congress for the first time and starting with a relatively low name ID rating would need 10% of the anticipated campaign budget in seed money. The average congressional campaign budget in 1998 was $700,000.00. This candidate would need at least $70,000.00 to begin the campaign.

As unfair as this may seem, the incumbent officeholder, with a proven record of accomplishments, will find it relatively easy to raise funds from other sources.

If you do not have this amount to invest personally in your campaign, you would normally turn to friends and family who believe not only in you, but also in the possibility that your campaign can be successful. Realistically, your political party, PACs, strangers, or banks will not assist you at this stage. To them, you are an unknown entity, at least as a campaigner. The banks might make an exception if you have enough personal collateral to secure a loan.

Depending on your status, your strategy is dictated by your options.

Legal Restrictions and Time Constraints

State or Federal legal restrictions on candidate financing further restrict your options.

State and Federal finance regulations may further restrict your options. Federal regulations for federal offices will not permit you to accept corporate contributions. Personal contributions are limited to a maximum of $1,000 per person in each election period. Some states are somewhat less restrictive for non-federal candidates. On the other hand, some are even more restrictive. Arizona, for example, once limited personal contributions to $100. Obviously, one of the first things you should do is research the laws applicable to the office you are seeking. You would then develop your strategy within the framework of those laws.

Research the contribution restrictions for your office and district. Your campaign management software should monitor the contributions against these restrictions. Record all contributions in order to file federal and/or state financial reports as required.

Timing is also an important consideration when planning the strategic decision making process. Consider your status at the outset of the campaign, including your name ID rating, your Favorability rating, your position as an incumbent or first or second-time challenger, and plan your start date for fund-raising activities accordingly. Generally, the lower the name ID rating, the earlier you must begin. I strongly advise first time challengers to start activity at least one full year before the primary or general election. Candidates, who have run before, can usually start 2 months later, or ten month before the election. Incumbents, depending upon how long they have been in office, can start 6 to 9 months before the election.

Developing the Strategy

If one candidate can afford a weapon that the other can not then the one affording the weapon has a considerable advantage. The one with the superior firepower inevitably wins.

After you have analyzed your financial resources, do the same regarding your opponent. As you will see later, the campaign tactics available are conditional on the availability of financial resources. In other words, if neither you nor your opponent can afford to buy a particular campaigning "weapon," such as television commercials, then neither of you would have to factor in a defense against that weapon. If on the other hand, one candidate can afford a weapon that the other can not, then the one affording the weapon has a considerable advantage. I use the analogy of a chess game to make this point. If your chess opponent has a Queen on the board, and for whatever reason you do not, barring an incredible mistake by your opponent, you will lose.

In campaigns, as in battles, the one with the superior firepower inevitably wins. There are exceptions, of course, but they are rare, and will not be without specific reasons to explain the unusual results. As a rule, you must match your opponent's ability to communicate to the electorate, weapon for weapon. If not always in quantity, at least in quality.

The skillful deployment of assets as communication weapons will become the determining factor in winning or losing the election.

Another caution worth mentioning here is "overkill." If you are in the enviable position of having a major communication tool (weapon) at your disposal that your opponent does not have, use it sparingly or not at all, unless your tracking polls indicate that your position is slipping against the position held by your opponent. By not using it, you can counter the "unexpected," and be at the ready to deal out some "unexpected" of your own. By using it sparingly, especially once you have taken a lead in the polls, you can avoid provoking a backlash effect among the electorate if they perceive that your tactics are "overkill." That is, you are using your financial superiority to decimate your opponent, not simply win the election.

If you and your opponent have relatively equal strength in this regard, then the skillful deployment of these assets as communication weapons will become the determining factor.

Personnel Resources

Definition
Personnel resources are assets available from the campaign management team to be deployed throughout the implementation of the strategic campaign plan.

Campaign resources are both tangible and intangible assets and would include, but not be limited to finances, management team, party support, and list of capable volunteers. Someone once noted that there would be no wars if generals alone fought all the battles. The reality is that many people fight in a battle and the same holds true for a campaign. Although the candidate is the focal point, there are usually scores of people, depending upon the size of the campaign, who are behind the scenes making the strategic plan happen.

At the point that you are campaigning to an electorate of over 5,000 voters, you must depend upon volunteers or paid staff members to help you implement your strategy. Whether it is putting up signs, walking precincts, or working in a telephone bank, you need people to support and assist you as much as you need financial resources to support the implementation of the strategic plan.

The campaign should seek a volunteer force based on one volunteer for every 250 district voters. A statement that should never, ever be heard before or during any campaign, "I have enough volunteers, but thanks for asking."

Just as there is a direct correlation between the amount of money needed and the size of the campaign, there is also a direct correlation regarding the number of people that you will need working day in and day out on your behalf. Speaking generally, you will need one volunteer for every 250 people in your district. If there are 10,000 people in your district, you will need 40 volunteers. If there are 50,000, you will need 200. It is only at the higher offices (major U. S. Senate, Gubernatorial, or Presidential campaigns) that this ratio is not relevant, as an army of this magnitude could never be assembled. This is not to be confused with whether or not an army of that magnitude is necessary. Obviously, the larger the army, the greater the chance for victory. A statement that should never, ever be heard before or during any campaign, "I have enough volunteers, but thanks for asking." This circumstance is not possible.

Available Options

If you are a first time candidate, the first place to look for help is to your friends and relatives. If an incumbent, in addition to the established list of volunteers already at the ready, they can appeal for volunteers from the people who have benefited from their term in office and will find it much easier to produce the desired results. A software application like GOTV *Campaign*

Another advantage that those who ran previously, winning or not, will enjoy is the position to draw from an already established volunteer list, many of which will have campaigning experience. An incumbent, in addition, can draw on the support of those he or she has assisted during the term in office.

Optimizer will allow you to accumulate a list of actual and prospective volunteers and their skills. It will track what they have done and what they have committed to do. This data can be accumulated before an election, during a campaign, and throughout your term in office. In so doing, you can have a decisive advantage, having your volunteers ready to do battle at all times.

The organizations you belong to, whether professional or social, are also excellent resources. Political organizations that are sympathetic to your stand on major issues will also provide assistance. Usually, this takes the form of research assistance, but occasionally they can provide volunteer help and sometimes even monetary assistance. Your local party organization may be of assistance. However, in most locales this assistance is very limited but is worth checking into. In some cases, your national party can also provide limited assistance. Both major parties have a local elections division to assist non-Federal candidates and a Congressional and Senatorial divisions to assist Federal candidates.

In most campaigns, you will need at least one full time staff person to assist in the day to day management of the campaign. Whether volunteer, or paid, this person should be someone with proven managerial skills.

Regardless of the sources, you must be able to recruit these individuals before the start of campaign activities. You will find job descriptions and duties for the various positions on a campaign team throughout *The Campaign Manual*.

Legal Restrictions and Time Constraints

There are no legal restrictions regarding the use of genuine volunteers.

Legal restrictions regarding volunteers are dependent on the definition of a "genuine" volunteer. If an organization pays for the services of an individual to work on your campaign, this individual, although not paid by the campaign, is not a volunteer and the payment to the individual represents a contribution and is subject to the same restrictions that apply to financial contributions. In a like manner, the use of an incumbent's staff is prohibited unless their time on the campaign is spent after normal working hours.

The Campaign Manual is sold in a work book edition. It is produced for staff and volunteer training (among other things). It is essential that everyone involved understand their role and the role of fellow campaigners. For further information, or to order your copies visit: www.AmeriCanGOTV.com or e-mail: info@americangotv.com

The time constraints are similar to those discussed in the previous section. Usually, volunteers need to be trained if they are to perform effectively. Materials have to be prepared. At least one person should be designated as the volunteer coordinator, with the responsibility for providing this training and assistance. When you have completed your study of this manual, you will have an excellent idea of the training requirements. The average amount of time a volunteer will spend on a campaign is about 20 hours. Therefore, constant recruiting is necessary to replace volunteers. Your strategy should include a plan to accomplish this on an ongoing basis. Volunteer management can be very time consuming. Many hours can be saved if this is managed by a capable campaign management software application capable of tracking volunteers and activities.

Sound strategy dictates that the first group of volunteers you recruit should be the members of your finance and steering committees. These are the two core committees in every campaign. They are your senior staff officers, to use

The average amount of time a volunteer will spend on a campaign is about 20 hours. Therefore, constant recruiting is necessary to replace volunteers.

the military analogy. The caliber and experience of these people becomes an integral part of the strategic decision making process.

Remember that the best strategy in the world is worthless unless you have the financial and personnel resources available to implement it.

Developing the Strategy

Develop a plan to actively recruit the type of people who can successfully fulfill the responsibilities associated with each role.

Carefully analyze your personnel resources. Do the finance committee members have the ability to raise the funds necessary to finance your campaign? Are they truly dedicated to your candidacy and are they willing to make the necessary sacrifices in time, energy, and money to help you win?

The same questions must be asked of your steering committee members. Your political future depends on these people. Do you honestly believe they are capable of fulfilling their obligations? You must be honest and tough when answering these questions. You are about to do battle and the weak link is the one that will hurt you the most. One of the best sources is a center of influence within your district. *Centers of Influence* are defined as community leaders such as religious leaders, elected officials, former candidates, heads of service organizations, business leaders, and party chairpersons.

Centers of Influence are defined as community leaders.

Once you have critically analyzed your resources, study your opponent's. Given your information regarding the financial and personnel resources of your opponent, are there any types of campaign activity that your opponent's campaign plan would not be able to implement? If they lack the resources to staff a phone bank, it would be a safe presumption that they would not be using that particular tool during the campaign. What about their ability to canvass the precincts, or do an intensive Get-Out-The-Vote (GOTV) effort on Election Day? Are there weak links in their campaign based on these restrictions? If so, how can you exploit them?

If there are weak spots, you can take advantage of them by implementing a plan that focuses a significant percentage of your campaign's resources in those areas. As important as it is to match the communication tools that your opponent is using, it is even more important to emphasize those that your opponent is not using. I recall a campaign where the district's voter registration data was not computerized. It was available only in a printed format. This being the case, the candidate in that district, historically, placed little emphasis on precinct, phone bank, and direct mail operations. The amount of work required was simply too great to do those things manually.

Remember - ***there is nothing onerous about taking advantage of an opponent's weakness. The very nature of a strategic plan demands that you do.***

With this potential weak link in his opponent's campaign, the candidate, in concert with his party's county committee, keyed into a computer the data on every registered voter in the district. This was a very expensive and tedious undertaking which took three months to accomplish. When finished, the candidate was able to do an extensive precinct, phone bank and direct mail campaign in the district, virtually unopposed by his opponent. By the time his opponent fully realized the significant impact this was having on the campaign it was too late to counter. The candidate won in one of the most stunning upsets in the country that year.

The need to have an efficient communication link to the voters in your district can not be emphasized enough. Your best link will be through a campaign management application that is able to sort, categorize, and mail merge targeted information to sections of the electorate.

There are a limited number of communication tools available to most candidates. They are:

1. Precinct operations, canvassing
2. Phone Bank operations
3. Print graphics
4. Stationary and mobile signs
5. Direct mail
6. Radio ads
7. Television ads
8. Newspaper ads
9. Campaign web site
10. Candidate's personal appearances
11. Free media

Some of these tools require financial resources, while some require people. Analyze carefully which you can employ based on your financial resources, and which you can employ based on your personnel resources. Analyze the same characteristics of your opponent's campaign. If there are any disparities, plan to exploit them as a part of your strategy. If there are none, then skill and intensity become the next criteria to consider. However, before we can discuss these factors you need to analyze the district or battlefield as carefully as you have analyzed yourself and your opponent.

District Demographics

Definition
District demographics are the characteristics that describe the district by certain categories, i.e., gender, race, marital status, income levels, party affiliation, age, and occupations.

As we have already seen, demographics are the characteristics that describe individuals by certain categories. Gender, race, marital status, occupation, income levels, religious affiliation, party affiliation, age, and nationality are the most commonly used in the political process. There are considerably more categories than this. As a rule however, their value for political campaign analysis is limited. The extra work and cost involved does not justify their inclusion.

The most relevant scale used for the greatest value regarding demographic characteristics is usually prioritized as follows:

1. Gender
2. Race
3. Age
4. Marital Status
5. Party Affiliation
6. Religious Affiliation
7. Occupation
8. Income Levels

Numbers 4 through 8 will shift in priority depending on which issues are of the greatest concern in your district at any given time. In addition, occupation in some districts, especially in the Northeast and upper Midwest areas of the country, might have a subcategory of union or non-union member.

Relative Value

It is difficult to believe that one could over state the need to be able to target any given voter grouping with the appropriate message. Here again, I encourage you to employ the use of capable software to sort and target voting groups.

Demographic groupings tend to share common concerns, values, and perspectives. If you are to effectively communicate your message to these groups, you must know what they are and how they are perceived. In addition, you need to know what percentile of the whole electorate each grouping constitutes. Your campaign has limited resources and if you are going to use them for maximum effectiveness you cannot afford to waste them on groups that are not receptive. Ideally, you should be a leader who would be able to convince all of the groups to follow your direction all of the time. The reality however, is that a political campaign is not a pulpit. Unless you win, thereby acquiring the ability to provide your solutions to the problems, your campaign becomes virtually meaningless.

I am aware of the historical significance minor parties and their candidates have had on our public policy. Some have been effective in causing the national parties to shift their positions on major issues. Nonetheless, whether or not these shifts would have been more purposeful and comprehensive had they won office, is a debatable question that can truly never be answered. As pointed out early, the presumption of a good campaign strategy is that one enters a political campaign to win.

A winning strategy dictates an emphasis on those issues that you share with a majority of the electorate, and demands that you place less importance on those issues that you do not share with a majority of the electorate.

In order to do this you must identify the major concerns of a majority of the people in your district who are going to vote and develop your strategy accordingly. I do not mean to imply or suggest that you espouse positions that are alien to your philosophy. It is a matter of philosophical prioritization.

A winning strategy dictates an emphasis on those issues that you share with a majority of the electorate and demands that you place less importance on those issues that you do not share with a majority of the electorate. Conversely, if you were aware of a contradictory position that is held by your opponent with a majority of the electorate, your strategy would be to expose that differential.

Again, unless you have done the research necessary to determine all of this, you will be unable to implement either of these strategies.

Available Resources

The U.S. Census Bureau can be found at www.census.gov

To obtain a general overview of the demographic make up of your district, look first at the U.S. Census data. This information is normally available in major public and/or university libraries and over the Internet. This data is categorized by most of the major groupings with which you would be concerned. Unfortunately, depending on the timing of the last census, this data can be rather dated. However, in any event, the information should be current enough for your purpose. Updated census information will be available in 2001.

This data is broken down into what are called census tracts. These are geographic areas designated by a number covering every square inch of the country. Since many political district boundaries are configured along census tract boundaries, it is relatively easy to acquire specific data for your district. It is helpful in your planning if you superimpose the census tract boundaries

The Campaign Manual recommends the use of the 5 on 5 organization plan to be studied later. This is a method of dividing the District into 5 Regions and then sub-dividing each Region into 5 Areas, since the concerns of geopolitical divisions of your district will not be completely similar.

and numbers over your precinct or zip code map of the district. If your game plan is using the 5 on 5 organization plan recommended (later) in *The Campaign Manual*, you would also try to draw your Region and Area boundary lines based, in part, on major demographic groupings.

After you have obtained the census data, select the demographic groupings that are most relevant to your district and campaign. Then, when drawing your sample for polling or focus group purposes, try to match as closely as possible the percentages based on the census data. For example, if the census data indicates 53% of the people in your district who are of voting age are female, then 53% of your polling sample or focus group should be female.

Once you have determined the percentiles for the groupings you have chosen and drawn your sample, you can then proceed to poll or conduct the focus group sessions in order to determine the issues of greatest concern to those individuals. If there are a number of issues of concern, your poll or focus group should attempt to rank them in order of relative importance.

Developing the Strategy

Once you have identified the major concerns of the electorate, broken down by geopolitical division, you are ready to proceed. Armed with this insight, you can now develop your position papers, basic speech, press releases, and the advertising campaign that will emphasize your position on those issues. Your strategy should be to focus on a maximum of 2 or 3 issues during the campaign. If you attempt to concentrate on more, you will dilute your message and fail to identify yourself with a theme that the electorate can relate to during their decision-making process. Be always mindful, that a critical part of your strategy must be, to build a high name ID rating and a high Favorability rating as well.

Focus on selling yourself based on the resources that you have, not on the ones that you wish that you had.

You should always sell your ability to be compassionate, even when an unpopular choice must be considered.

Consideration can now be given to how to best convey your message. To a great degree, the methods of communication will be determined by the financing available. Whether you can afford television commercials or a limited direct mail campaign, convey the image that will best resolve the concerns of the electorate. The electorate wants their leaders to be compassionate, even if they themselves have no immediate problem that calls for that compassion. I can remember a campaign in which a major highway had been proposed, cutting through only one neighborhood of a rather large electoral district. It was only a concern for a small area. The incumbent ignored the small group immediately affected by the highway and devoted himself to other issues. The challenger focused on the issue from the viewpoint of the need for another highway, the huge expense on the taxpayers, the environmental concerns, and the hardships imposed on the neighborhood by a seemingly uncompassionate city council. It was not long before the majority of the city had been captured by the compassion expressed by the challenger for the families in the targeted neighborhood. The challenger's message was simple, "If they can do it to them, they may do it to you!" By adopting this strategy, the challenger was able to focus his limited resources on a single issue, but do it well. He gained the reputation of being tough, since he stood alone in opposition to the highway, and compassionate toward the electorate, a characteristic that everyone can appreciate whether affected by the issue or not. All voters would like to think that (when the time comes) they have someone in power in their corner. The majority bought into the compassionate message and the incumbent never recovered. This example teaches us two principles. You should always sell your ability to be compassionate, even when an unpopular choice must be considered, and you should focus on selling yourself based on the resources that you have not the ones that you wish that you had.

As for selling your message, take the advice of those that know. Your printer for example has years of experience in assisting firms with marketing ideas. Ask for, and consider that advice. Solicit the opinions of those close to you. Your focus group can also play their role here. Remember that no thought should go unexplored. Even your choice of campaign colors can reinforce these messages. Certain groupings tend to favor certain colors and combinations. Once you have decided which group/s you are going to focus on, research their predominant color preferences. You will find, for example, that Caucasian (adult) males tend to prefer blue.

Concentrate the greatest percentage of your campaign activities (therefore funding), on those groups that can provide you with the most votes. This is especially true in the early stages of the campaign. Though the old cliché is true, that every vote you take away from your opponent is worth two, it is usually not worth the cost and effort that it takes in the early stages of the campaign. It will deplete your funding, as the cost per vote gained will be very high in the initial stages of campaigning, since usually the *"decideds"* are the voters paying attention in the early stages and it will be expensive to change their mind, if you can at all. I say this assuming a campaign with limited resources. It may be good public relations to announce that you are going to take your campaign to all of the people, but the fact of the matter is, if you do, and can not afford to, you will probably lose.

In other words, until your polling indicates that you have a viable opportunity to influence a specific group for which previous research indicated that you had a low Favorability rating, do not waste valuable resources chasing expensive votes. Secure your base first. In so doing, your signs, introductory letter and bio, general ads, and free press coverage will give you some exposure and at least, improve your name ID rating. This must be done before attempting to win over any *"decideds."* If, toward the latter stages of your campaign, you have totally secured your base and maximized your vote opportunities among the *"undecideds and ticket-splitters,"* then, and only then, you might make overtures to other groups, if resources permit.

PIPS Analysis
The Precinct Index Prioritization Schedule was first developed at Claremont University in California in 1972.

In a later chapter in *The Campaign Manual*, I will explain a very precise method of determining where your campaign is in relation to your planned objectives, known as the PIPS analysis. If you follow this procedure throughout the campaign, you will know, at any given time if and when to make those overtures.

As mentioned previously, if your opponent's position on one or more of the major issues is out of touch with a majority of the electorate, it is sound strategy to expose this during the campaign. If you do however, remember the timing factor. Until your Favorability rating is greater than 50%, you should focus your strategy on a positive campaign that will build your name ID and Favorability rating to that level. Once you have achieved credibility as a candidate, the electorate will accept your criticism of your opponent. If you criticize your opponent before gaining credibility, you run a high risk of being dismissed as a negative candidate with no program of your own.

Once you have reached this plateau in the campaign, you should evaluate your opponent's Favorability rating. If it is well below 50%, stay the course and avoid criticizing. If it is above 50%, then you have no choice but to pursue this differential aggressively in order to bring your opponent's rating down below 50%.

Not only does sound strategy dictate this course of action, but an argument could be made that if your opponent is so effectively out of touch with a majority of the electorate, you have an obligation to bring this out into the open and to their attention.

Definition
Geographic characteristics are the physical characteristics of the geopolitical district in which you are seeking elected office.

District Geographic Characteristics

When considering the geopolitical characteristics, the size and topography of your district are primary considerations, followed by accessibility to various points within the district and the modes of transportation required accessing each area.

Relevant Factors

Time is one of the major considerations in political campaigns.

Many candidates start their campaign with the mistaken notion that they will be able to personally make contact with all or most of the registered voters in their district. They soon find out that this is not possible. The best you can hope to do is to maximize the percentage you can make contact with. In an average congressional campaign lasting nine months, the candidate can usually arrange contact with 20% of the electorate. A very well planned strategy might improve this to 30%. A very well planned strategy with a ton of good fortune may reach 40%.

Regrettably, media coverage has become a substitute for candidate contact.

Since the candidate's personal contact with the electorate is one of the most powerful weapons in use during a campaign, time spent on personal campaigning and the length of the campaign are serious considerations. This is one of the reasons why the media has become such a dominant factor in many campaigns. Essentially, it is a communication device that sometimes substitutes for personal contact. Originally, media coverage was used to supplement the candidate's activities. Regrettably, during the past twenty years media coverage has become a substitute for candidate contact. I use the word, regrettably, because it remains a poor substitute, at best. People still want to meet the candidate face to face, even if it is just a quick handshake and a few words, they will remember the experience and it can be a very persuasive factor.

There is no substitute for personal contact. It simply works.

Numerous polls taken after a candidate has walked a precinct show a marked improvement in the Favorability rating and voter preference for the candidate. In other words, there is no substitute for personal contact. It simply works.

Campaign management software should have a capable activity scheduler, including an ability to record the particulars of the event, a master campaign calendar and day timer functions.

Rather than finding substitutions for candidate activity, a good campaign should continue to seek ways to increase the candidate's exposure with as many activities as the maximum usage of time will allow. When events conflict, the candidate should be sent to the event with the higher expectancy of personal contact, while a substitute handles the second event with the candidate's sincere apology. Better yet, despite the hard work involved, try to find some compromise so that the candidate can at least make a short appearance at the second event. It is a known fact that personal attendance sometimes subjects the candidate to rejection, but this is not a valid reason to prefer sending the substitute.

Analysis of the District

What are the physical characteristics of your district? How large is it? Is it urban, suburban, rural, or a combination of some or all? Is it flat, mountainous, or assorted terrain? Are there physical barriers that will delay or even prevent travel from precinct to precinct?

Consider this, if you are in districts around the Puget Sound in Washington State, you have to consider boat travel as well.

Consider the highway system and conditions. How long does it take to travel from one point to another at various times of the day and evening? Can it be traveled comfortably by car, bus, or train, or will you be forced to use air travel? Are the homes relatively close together so that you can walk the precinct, or do you need to drive from one home to another?

What impact does the local weather have on this activity at any given time of the campaign? A precinct in Minnesota that might be walked in June would probably be improbable in February.

What other campaign activities besides the candidate's might be affected by these geographic considerations? Think not only in terms of the candidate, but also in terms of how conditions will affect the attitude of your volunteers.

Is the district so large that long distance telephone charges would make a centralized phone bank economically unsound? What impact does the size of the district or other physical barriers have on scheduling regular meetings with essential volunteer personnel, or on planning campaign events? Does the size of the district have an impact on the electorate's primary issue concerns from one area to another? In other words, are those voters in the east, concerned about the same issues as the voters in the west and south? What effect does the size of the district have on the availability and type of media and media coverage?

These are the kinds of questions that must be asked and answered in the strategic decision making process. The size and physical characteristics of your district will dictate the time necessary to make contact with the electorate. Since contact with the electorate is a function of time, how the physical characteristics affect this important element must be considered, analyzed, and factored into time's equation.

Developing the Strategy

It has been said that the way to solve a big problem is to break it up into smaller parts, enabling one to solve each of these smaller problems individually. It is for this reason that the *5 on 5 plan* divides a political district into 5 Regions, and then subdivides each Region into 5 Areas.

In developing this aspect of campaign strategy, *The Campaign Manual* will discuss the advantages of a campaign structural plan that I call *the 5 on 5 plan*. This plan is very effective in facilitating the administration of the campaign and its communication structure. In addition, *the 5 on 5 plan* is an effective resolution to most of the problems that are imposed by the geographical characteristics that we have been discussing in this section. Essentially, *the 5 on 5 plan* divides a political district into 5 Regions, and then subdivides each Region into 5 Areas. Each Area is comprised of precincts, depending on the number in the district. Ideally, there is an equitable distribution of the electorate in each of the Regions and Areas. However, when the geographic considerations are factored in, and they present serious problems to the ideal division, then every effort should be made to accommodate those geographic considerations. In other words, Region and Area lines should be drawn with the geographic constraints in mind. For example, if possible, you would not configure a Region or Area crossing any major river or freeway.

The 5 on 5 plan will facilitate a focused campaign message on the issues that are of primary concern to the electorate within each of the Regions, or Areas for that matter. It significantly increases the productive value of one of your campaign's strongest assets, candidate activities.

If you have a number of counties in your district, you should attempt to keep county lines intact and cluster them within the same Region. In doing this, you solve several problems. When campaigning, with proper scheduling, you can focus your activity in a single day within a specific Region. This cuts down considerably on travel time and maximizes your more productive efforts in seeing voters. If the Regions are spread over a large geographic area, you might want to establish more than one Regional office, with phone banks in each in order to reduce telephone costs.

Your strategy would entail scheduling your events and appearances within a specific Region or Area, after your voter analysis indicates where the greatest opportunity to obtain votes is in relation to the other areas. That is, where the greatest number, in relative terms, of undecided voters reside. Once you have secured your base of support, your next level of activity should be to focus on those voters who are traditionally "ticket-splitters" or "undecideds." *The 5 on 5 plan* of organization enables you to focus your campaign activities on these voter groups in an efficient and productive manner. Instead of working against the geographic characteristics of your district, you work within them. This results in a maximum use of your time and effort.

As to the style of your campaign activity, in regards to door to door campaigning, there are a few basic rules to follow. When canvassing, you should always attempt to have someone with you. If you have a precinct captain, or representative, that person would be the ideal one to accompany you. Ensure that a sufficient quantity of literature is available to distribute to the planned campaigning area. Some should be stamped with, "I was campaigning in your neighborhood today and had hoped to meet you. Sorry I missed you. If you have any questions about me or my campaign, please do not hesitate to give me a call at ______." Leave these in the door or someplace obvious when no one is at home. Be certain however, that volunteer canvassers do not leave campaign literature if it can not be securely fixed to a visible location. If the literature blows away, it will be a neighborhood annoyance viewed with a negative response and result in a waste of campaign assets. Federal regulations prohibit the use of U.S. mailboxes for the delivery of campaign literature. It is also imperative that you check on local solicitation regulations. In any event, most people will appreciate your thoughtfulness and respond favorably. Do not canvas neighborhoods that post signs forbidding solicitation, as this privilege will not be appreciated. Make a note of these neighborhoods and insure that they are covered by direct mail. In addition, private neighborhoods will likely have a neighborhood committee that may give the candidate permission to canvas the neighborhood, or can assist in arranging candidate contact with the neighborhood.

If you use a computer program, it should prepare a printout of the precinct you will be walking, in street order. That is, with the names and houses listed in sequential order so you can walk one side of the street and then the other. Some election board offices can supply walk sheets and will do so for a fee.

Keep your visit brief. A simple hello and short introduction followed by a request for their support in the upcoming election is all that is necessary. Hand the person a brochure and say goodbye. If the resident attempts to engage you in conversation be polite but brief, you have many potential supporters to visit.

Sometimes a little gimmick can be very effective. I recall one race where the candidate, who was running on an environmental issue, obtained thousands of little pine tree seedlings, about an inch and a half high. He had a tag put on them with his name and the office he was seeking. It stated simply, "With his compliments, the candidate." If a resident was out, he left the tree on their doorstep. The impact was almost unbelievable. He won that state legislative race and went on to become a U. S. Congressman. People are still talking about those little pine trees, many of which were planted and are thriving to this day.

As with all other characteristics that we have discussed thus far, the geographic characteristics are integral parts of the strategic decision making process. They too must be given full consideration when developing your strategy.

District Economic Characteristics

Definition
The economic characteristics of a district can be defined by the per capita income of the people living in the district.

The economic characteristics of a district include factors such as the unemployment rate, the average price of a house, the relative economic stability of the district during the past ten years, and its projected growth rate. The most specific data involved here is available at your local Chamber of Commerce, from current census reports, the local Board of Realtors Association, local investment counselors, the local library, and depending on the size of the district, the Internet.

Relevant Factors

Politics affects economics, and economics affects politics.

Politics affects economics, and economics affects politics. In fact, the two are so inter-related and inter-dependent that you cannot discuss the problems and/or solutions of one without the other.

It has never ceased to amaze me how many universities attempt to study one discipline without a detailed study of the other. It is as though they believe that in the real world each discipline exists in a vacuum independent of the other. Unfortunately, in the real world, this could not be further from the truth. Many Political Science majors who go on to become politicians or Political Consultants are poorly prepared to deal with the economic characteristics in a campaign, or as officeholders themselves.

The inter-relationship in this area is so strong that unless you fully understand the ramifications of your decisions as an elected official, or of your opponent's if you are a challenger, you cannot fully evaluate the economic characteristics of your district, as they pertain to the strategic decision making process. When taken collectively, Federal, State, and local taxes account for approximately 43% of the American wage earner's budget. In other words, $.43 out of every dollar earned is spent on government services of one kind or another. This is a larger percentage then the amounts spent on food, housing, or transportation. For the voter whose per capita income is $25,000 per year, there is a significantly greater appreciation of the 43% tax factor than for the voter whose per capita income is $50,000 per year.

A study of the economic characteristics of your district is a very important step in the development of your campaign strategy.

In addition, if the average price of a home is $102,000, this too is of greater significance to the voter averaging $25,000 per year than it will be to the voter earning $50,000. Conversely, if the average price drops to $72,000 then the degree of differential, as it relates to significance, is not as great.

Analysis of the District

The 5 on 5 plan is also effective in addressing the economic characteristics of your district. You are now able to study the economic characteristics of each Region separately from those of the whole district.

Since you have divided your district along the geographic and demographic lines, you are now able to study the economic characteristics of each Region separately from those of the whole district. In many districts, you will find significant differences between them. An old adage reminds us that birds of a feather flock together. This tends to be true in our society, though not always by choice. More often than not, where we live is dictated by economic considerations. Overall, in order to increase your support, the issues you would stress, and the solutions proposed, should be tailored to the specifics of each Region, as opposed to a generic message delivered district-wide. Additionally, wherever possible, your style of campaigning and fund-raising should be tailored to the economic considerations of each Region.

Using the criteria established in our definition, develop an economic profile for each Region. What is the per capita income, the unemployment rate, the average price of a home, the 10-year stability rate, and the projected growth rate of each Region?

Developing the Strategy

Throughout the district your campaign message should focus on the two most important factors that determine the outcome of an election, increasing your name ID and Favorability ratings. The next step involves the development of specific messages to the electorate that demonstrate both your interest and involvement in the issues of primary concern to them, and your solutions to the extent that you can affect them in the office for which you are running.

In many cases, you will find that two or more Regions share the same concerns and the messages can then be consistent. However, where there is a difference, your message must be tuned to this difference. Primarily, your strategy should be designed to accomplish this through targeted direct mail and personal campaigning. In most campaigns, these two methods of communication are the most effective and the most economically viable.

Earlier, we discussed tailoring your direct mail to the primary concerns of various demographic groups. As you will recall, you were shown how you could determine what these concerns were through focus groups and polling. Through the same methods, and at the same time, you can identify these concerns based on economic characteristics. Then, by developing what are called variable paragraphs, you can tailor your direct mail to address the greatest possible majority of these concerns.

Microsoft Works, *Microsoft Word*, or *Corel Word Perfect* are examples of capable word processing software. GOTV *Campaign Optimizer* has its own word processor integrated within the program.

To implement this process, you will need a computer and one of the many word processing software programs that have the capability of generating personalized letters. The impact of these personal letters, targeted to the appropriate group of voters, can alter the outcome of the campaign significantly.

The methodology involved requires the development of at least thirty or forty paragraphs of three or four sentences each, differing in content, style, and readability levels. The number of demographic and/or economic characteristics that you wish to address will dictate the number of variable paragraphs that you will need. By interchanging these paragraphs between the first and last paragraphs of a five or six paragraph letter, you can create an incredible number of personalized letters in virtually the same amount of time it takes to generate a single generic letter.

Remember that the letter should be no more than one page in length and consist of five or six paragraphs. The first and last paragraphs are constants and the middle three or four are variables. Each variable paragraph should deal with a specific issue and be written in different styles and readability levels.

Different writers have different methods and styles of accomplishing this objective. Personally, I find that numbering the paragraphs by related categories and subcategories is most effective. A system using 1A, 1B, 1C, with 1 identifying the major grouping and the letters identifying the sub-groupings works well for me. For example 1A would be the primary paragraph, 1B would be essentially the same paragraph but written in a different style and level of readability and 1C would be different still. 1A in this example might be for Caucasian males 18 to 30 years of age, 1B could be for Caucasian males 30 to 50, and 1C would be for Caucasian males, 50 years and over.

After I had written a number of paragraphs covering these types of groupings, I would then begin a series combining a different set of groups prevalent in the district. The content, or message, of each paragraph is, of course, tailored to the primary concerns of that specific group. Again, this is determined from your focus groups and polling.

When all of the letters are done and the voter registration files are sorted and selected based on the same criteria, for example, males 18-30, the software will merge the text file with the data file and generate a targeted letter as quickly as it would a generic letter. The result is that you could, conceivably have twenty different houses on the same street receiving twenty different personalized letters. Each one addresses their specific concerns and your proposed solutions. The results are dramatic, to say the least. Consider the consequences, if your opponent can accomplish this and you are not able.

Candidates should consider taking at least one course in Oral Communications at their local college. It is, without question, the best training I am aware of to help develop these skills. Even if you are skilled in this area, a refresher can never hurt.

When it comes to writing in a different style and readability level, I find it helps considerably to visualize someone you know in that particular group. Then use the same words in writing that you would use verbally in discussing the issue. Most of us, consciously or unconsciously, tailor our speech to our audience. Do the same with your letter writing. Avoid stilted language. Be personal and informal. Write as much from the heart as the head. A letter is a very personal means of communication, unlike television or radio, which can be so impersonal.

Write your appeal directly to the reader. Think of the people you are writing to as your friends and share with them your common concerns and solutions. Show the reader you are a real person just like them, with feelings and concerns. Be sincere and always close with an appeal for their vote, their help, and a contribution to help finance your campaign.

These letters should be positive in nature. Avoid saying anything about your opponent, except by inference. Later, we will discuss doing comparative pieces in mailings that are less personal. A letter should be a sharing experience and not be used as an opportunity to bludgeon your opponent. A letter like this should be mailed at least twice during the course of the campaign.

As your polling indicates shifts in the electorate by groupings that are for or against you, you can design your mail program accordingly. As the old political saying goes, "it doesn't make sense to preach to the saved or the damned." Focus your resources on those groupings that are most consistently ranking as "undecideds" or "ticket-splitters". This is especially true in the latter stages of the campaign.

In your personal campaigning and fund-raising, tailor your style to the group's economic characteristics. This does not mean you should pander to the particular group with whom you are campaigning. It does mean finding a common ground in style of speech and conversation with those groups. It means being aware of local colloquialisms and how to use them when speaking. It also means communicating through your speech and body language that you are able to relate to them as individuals.

Customize your fund-raising activity in a particular Region based on its economic characteristics. Later, we will discuss various types of fund-raising events that are productive and tailored to those economic characteristics.

Remember that, as an officeholder, at any level from local to national, you are going to make decisions that will affect the economics of every person in your district. A major part of your strategy, therefore, should be to demonstrate to the electorate that you have an awareness of this responsibility and the determination to exercise it prudently. Keep the discussion focused on you and your solutions. Remember that, if the electorate were completely satisfied with your opponent's understanding and solutions, they would not be listening to you.

Definition
The voting characteristics of the district are defined as the makeup of the electorate by party identification, i.e. Republicans, Democrats, or non-aligned with one of the two major parties.

District Voting Characteristics

Aside from the makeup of the electorate by party identification, the voting characteristics of the district include the voting results of the district over the last three election cycles, that is the past six years, and the percentage of voter turnout in each of those election periods. These figures are available at your County Registrar's office, the Secretary of States' office, your political party's headquarters, and in quality political almanacs.

Relevant Factors

Since voting history is likely to repeat itself in any given geopolitical district, you must analyze the previous results of campaigns for the office for which you are running.

In developing your campaign strategy, you must analyze the previous results of campaigns for the office for which you are running. You will also need to analyze these results in relation to other campaigns taking place at the same time and covering the same geopolitical area. In addition, you must determine, as closely as possible, the expected turnout of voters in your election, i.e. the actual number of votes expected to be cast. In a later section, we will be discussing the impact of other races on your campaign. In this section, we will focus more on historical patterns and their relevance to your campaign.

Barring a major calamity or issue, there is a strong tendency for voting history to repeat itself in any given geopolitical district. If the voter turnout in the previous off year election, a non-Presidential election year, has been 42% of the electorate, the odds are it will remain about 42% in your campaign, if it is occurring in a non-Presidential election year. If it goes up to 54% in a presidential election year, the odds are it will go to about 54% in your campaign, if it is occurring in a presidential election year.

Unless you have an accurate projection of the number of votes that you must receive in order to win, you have no firm basis for determining your objectives.

Nevertheless, you must go a step further. There is a propensity for the percentile to drop as you go down the ballot. In other words, it might be 54% for the presidential campaign, hold around that percentile for the statewide races, and then gradually drop for the Congressional, state representative or senator, and local races. Be mindful that this is a general statement and that I have seen some campaigns at the lower levels draw a higher percentile than the higher races. If this has occurred in previous campaigns for the office for which you are running, it is critically important that you analyze the reasons for this unusual occurrence. The important point is that you need to know what the expected turnout will be for your specific race in the year you are running.

The relevance of party registration in a particular district becomes more significant the lower down the ballot you go. Most "ticket splitting" occurs at the Presidential, Gubernatorial, U. S. Senate, and Congressional levels. If you are running for other than those offices, but in a year in which one of those races is taking place, then there is a strong tendency for people to revert to party lines when casting their vote. If it is an odd year election, the tendency is clearly not so strong. Consequently, the voter registration breakdown in your district will be extremely important in the strategic decision making process, since even in non-partisan races, there is a tendency for the votes to fall along party lines.

Analysis of the District

The *PIPS Analysis* developed at Claremont University in California in 1972 has proven to be a very scientific method for determining specific precinct objectives.

The most popular tool political campaign consultants use to do this type of analysis is called a *PIPS analysis*. PIPS (Precinct Index Prioritization Schedule) was first developed at Claremont University in California in 1972 and has proven to be a very scientific method for determining specific objectives. Nonetheless, its accuracy depends on your skill in picking the right campaigns to factor into the formula.

Normally, you would take the voting results for three races in at least the last two cycles. It becomes even more accurate if you use three, but two will normally suffice. The races chosen are referred to as the high, the low, and the median. Some people use a Presidential campaign as the high race. I consider this a mistake. Resulting from the aforementioned propensity for "ticket splitting" at that level, the results tend to be skewed when applied against lower levels.

I find that a closely contested race for Governor or U. S. Senate provides a more realistic measurement. For the low race, pick one of the more non-controversial statewide races like Secretary of State or State Controller. Usually, the votes drawn by these races are strictly along party lines. They also tend to draw the lowest turnout percentage.

For the median race, you should use the previous results of the campaigns for the office you are seeking.

Once you have decided on the three races you will be using in your analysis, the rest is simple arithmetic. On a precinct by precinct basis, add the total number of votes cast for each year's race and divide the sum by three. The result will be a very accurate prediction of the total number of votes that will likely be cast in a like year. Most campaigns will indicate a differential between the two years you have used in your analysis. You can add the two sets of figures and divide them by two, or to give yourself a margin for error, use the higher figure.

Once you have arrived at this result, study the voter registration figures for that precinct by party affiliation. Even in states that do not register by party, this percentile can be determined by analyzing the primary election results of a partisan race. For example, assume Precinct 347 has 420 registered voters. Your PIPS analysis indicates the voter turnout in this precinct will be 46%, or 193 votes. A further analysis of Precinct 347 indicates that 32% of the voters are registered Republican, 38% are Democrat, and the remaining 30% are non-aligned. Applying these percentages to the expected voter turnout of 193 would produce the following results:

62 Republican voters
73 Democratic voters
58 independent voters

Assuming your campaign has secured your base of support, you could plan to receive 90% of your partisan vote. If you were a Republican candidate, this would equal 56 votes. Since your minimal objective for this precinct is 50% + 1, you would need 98 votes to win. Subtracting the partisan vote of 56 from 98 leaves 42 additional votes needed. Generally, you could expect to receive 10% of the Democratic votes, or 7. Subtracting 7 from 42 equals 35 votes to secure. Therefore, of the 58 independent voters, you must receive 60% of those votes, i.e. you need to secure 35 additional votes in order to win. Obviously, this is a clear indication of where and how to focus your campaign activity.

Precinct 347 - 420 Voters	**Race A**	**Race B**
Governor - High	295	224
Office Vied For - Median	180	164
State Controller - Low	161	134
Average Votes Cast	212	174
Average Votes Cast in last two Election Periods	**193**	**46%**

Votes by Party	
Republican - 32%	62
Democrat - 38%	73
Non-Aligned - 30%	58
Votes Needed To Win (50% + 1)	**98**

Candidate	**Based 90%**	**Switched Allegiance 10%**	**Additional Votes Required To Win**	**Percentage of Non-Aligned Votes Needed**
Republican Candidate	56	7	**35**	**60%**
Democrat Candidate	66	6	**26**	**45%**
Non-Aligned Votes Available	58			

If you use a campaign management program, you would post these results in the appropriate section for each precinct. The numbers would then print at the top of each phone bank and precinct walk sheet printout as a constant reminder of that precinct's objectives. If your program does not do this, add the information manually.

Prepare a wall chart listing all of the precincts and their respective objectives. Post this in your phone bank and campaign headquarters.

Developing the Strategy

Later in *The Campaign Manual*, there is a detailed plan of operations divided into the five stages of the campaign (seven, if there is a contested primary election), which is designed to focus not only your campaign's activities on those objectives, but also to monitor the campaign's progress in achieving them.

Here, I will address a plan that involves a concerted effort at various levels to secure your base of support in the early stages and then directing your efforts toward the independent voters. It enables you to know with a high degree of certainty, at any given stage of the campaign, whether or not you are realizing your objectives. It then enables your campaign to achieve its objectives by focusing its energies Election Day on your Get-Out-The-Vote drive (GOTV).

If you really wish to be elected, hard work can not be avoided, only targeted for success.

Regrettably, doing all of this, from the PIPS analysis to conducting the campaign management style that I teach requires a considerable amount of hard work and effort. All too many candidates, especially challengers, try to take more expedient routes, and fail. Too often, they prefer to rely on intuition or the advice of others who actually have no more experience than does the challenger, or worse, stand to profit by their advice.

Thus far, we have spent the better part of this book, discussing the necessity for developing demographic profiles of yourself, your opponent, and most importantly, of the electorate. We have pointed out the necessity of sound information gathering as a major factor in the strategic decision making process. If you were to do all of this and then fail to capitalize on that information, clearly you would have wasted a lot of valuable time and hard work. On the other hand, if you couple that information with a plan of action, the results will be compelling.

By cross referencing the demographic information developed in the previous sections with the results of your PIPS analysis, you will have a precise analysis of those groups of individuals you must convince to vote for you in order to win.

If you cross reference the demographic information developed in the previous sections with the results of your PIPS analysis, you will have a precise analysis of those groups of individuals you must convince to vote for you in order to win. Once this is done you can target your media campaign, including the direct mail program discussed in the previous section, with an incredibly high degree of accuracy. This will result in maximizing the campaign's efforts, including your own activities.

Rather than scheduling your candidate's activities in a reactive manner, you are able to reinforce your other campaign activities in a very precise and deliberate manner. Instead of wasting large sums of money shot-gunning your campaign's message, you can conserve (often) all too limited resources and focus them on gaining maximum effectiveness.

In thirty years, I have never managed an easy campaign or found an easy way to win an election.

Over the years, I have become very suspicious of political consultants and campaigners who say they know an easy way to win an election. I realize, of course, that occasionally something happens quite by chance and a challenger wins without going through this process. Believe me, the odds of that happening are very low and extremely rare in the approximately 750,000 campaigns conducted every two years in this country.

If you are a serious candidate for public office, and I presume you are just by virtue of having read *The Campaign Manual* to this point, you must develop a strategy that is sound and reasonably certain of victory if followed precisely. You owe it not only to yourself for the sacrifices you are making as a candidate, but to your family and the hundreds, if not thousands, of people who are supporting your campaign.

Definition
The media characteristics of the district are defined as commercially available methods of communicating with the electorate.

Media Characteristics of the District

The media characteristics of the district include television, radio, newspapers, the Internet, magazines, newsletters, tabloids, direct mail, stationary signs, mobile signs (including airplane banners and blimps), sound trucks, print material, and novelty items.

Relevant Factors

The primary weapons of your campaign are the various types of communication.

As with weapons in battle, each one has its primary function and effectiveness. A well-developed campaign strategy requires a detailed knowledge of each of those weapons and their proper utilization within a campaigning atmosphere. Which one to use, how to use it, and when to use it for maximum effectiveness are all relevant factors in the strategic decision making process. Having a precise knowledge of which methods are readily available to your campaign and those that are most cost effective in realizing your objectives is also critically important. For instance, you can use television commercials to build up your name ID rating, but for most campaigns, this is a very inefficient use of this means of communication. Knowing which alternative methods of communication are both effective, and more importantly, are more reasonably priced, is a critical element of your intelligence gathering process.

Your name ID rating is the first criteria to be met.

As indicated previously, your name ID rating is the first criteria to be met. In building name ID, for example, you need to know something about the psychology of people as it pertains to the introduction of a new product or idea. In our society we are being bombarded daily with new products and ideas. Most of us have built up a relatively high resistance to the introduction of these new ideas and products. Consider children on the other hand, they have not yet developed this resistance and are much more likely to accept change. Ordinarily, when presented with a new political candidate, the public's resistance reaches its maximum level. I often refer to this as a "steel door" mind. Keep in mind that all methods will work if given enough time and resources. The relevancy issue is which method of communication will work best within the campaigning constraints of time spent and resources utilized. Most people not only resist the introduction of a new candidate, they actually repel it. In order to batter down this steel door, you must use a method of communication that is not only persuasive but also highly repetitive. The message must be seen at least every other day over a period of six or more months, by a majority of the electorate in your district. To sustain this kind of penetration using television, radio, or newspapers would be well beyond the reach of most candidates. Alternate methods must be utilized, unless of course you have an unlimited campaign budget. By the way, this also is extremely rare.

Keep in mind that all methods will work if given enough time and resources. The relevancy issue is which method of communication will work best within the campaigning constraints of time spent and resources utilized.

Analysis of the District

Before you can make these determinations and develop your strategy, you need to do an analysis of the available media outlets within your district.

Run of the Station (ROS)
This enables radio and television stations to place commercials whenever they want to fill open time. It is usually much less expensive than scheduled time since you have no choice regarding viewing time and no assurances of when your commercials will be aired.

Television and Radio

Television and radio stations should be analyzed based on similar criteria. Are there one, or more stations located within your district, or are they located outside of it and covering a much broader area? Stations have different rate schedules for different times of the day. What are the average costs for a 30-second television or radio spot in news and prime time? What does the station charge for ROS (run of the station)? The most expensive time on radio is called "drive time." Those times are in the morning and evening when most of the audience is commuting in cars. Radio stations sell ROS time and will usually guarantee a number of drive time spots with the ROS purchase.

In television and radio, the Arbitron ratings provide a breakdown of the demographic groups that watch each show, in each period. What policies do the stations have regarding the allocation of time to all candidates? Federal law requires television and radio stations to make an equal amount of time available to each candidate. However, some stations limit the total amount of time to be divided among the candidates.

Newspapers

How many are available in your district? Are they daily, weekly, monthly? Do they endorse candidates, and if so, what is their history in this regard? If weekly, what are their deadline days for ads and articles? What is the rate schedule for various size ads? How do they vary the cost in consideration of the length of the run, i.e. if you plan to repeat the ad? Newspapers are not subjected to the same Federal regulations regarding political candidates as radio and television. What are their policies regarding space allocation? Do they have special rates for political candidates?

If a daily, what are the circulation rates for each day of the week? Based on their research, which sections are the most widely read? Which demographic groups read which sections? Newspapers also use the same type of research as supplied by the Arbitron ratings.

Signs

Does your district permit billboards? Are there buses that use side and rear signs that travel your district on a regularly scheduled basis? What about taxis and bus waiting bench signs? Is there a metro rail system in your district that sells sign space in the cars?

What are your local restrictions regarding the use of lawn, window, and pole signs? Are there any restrictions regarding the use of bumper stickers or signs in public places? What about the use of signs near polling places?

The Internet is the fastest growing communication media in the world today.

Web Sites

The Internet is the fastest growing communication media in the world today. It has nowhere to go but up, straight up. According to surveys, in the 1996 Elections, only 3% of the public used the Internet to gather political information to assist them in voting decisions. This figure doubled during the 2000 Elections. It is predicted that this rate will more than double by 2004 and more than double again by 2008. If this happens, within 10 years, over 50% of registered voters will turn to the Internet to analyze their candidate choices.

In the 2000 Elections, over 50% of candidates employed the use of a web site, if for no other reason than one of their opponents did, proving again, if nothing else, that you cannot afford to ignore a weapon used by any other candidate. All this being the case, the Internet, and the use of candidate web sites is not only here, it is here to stay.

Keep these points in mind regarding this relatively new campaign communication technique. All styles of communication discussed are possible on a web site and much care and planning should be taken to use the appropriate style at the appropriate stage. An amateurish web page design is worse than no page at all. Use a professional. The initial site should concentrate on building name ID. As your campaign develops, the site can be built from position papers, press releases, and assorted campaign data to increase voter awareness and favorability. Polls indicate that the viewing public want to see the web sites change regularly, keeping them interesting, and making it worth their while to return to the site as the campaign progresses to Election Day. In this atmosphere, a majority has responded favorably to the comparative piece, but I still caution you against its use until the final stages of the campaign. After the election, the web site will serve as a valuable tool to stay connected to the constituents.

Sound trucks or other vehicles

What are the local restrictions regarding the use of sound vehicles in residential neighborhoods? Can they be used in commercial areas? Are blimps or airplane sign towing services available in your district? What are the local restrictions regarding their use? What are their hourly rates?

The other methods of communication can be addressed in the same manner. Usually, there are no restrictions regarding campaign novelty items, though an argument could be made about their cost effectiveness in a campaign.

Developing the Strategy

After you have completed this analysis, study the results. If a particular method of communication is not readily available to you, or is not economically viable, discard it. There is no sense considering television, for example, if you are running for a state representative's office in a major metropolitan area. Not only, would it be cost prohibitive, the overflow would be too great to justify the expenditure. The coverage would greatly exceed the boundary limits of your district.

Apply this test to the other methods of communication you research. Through this process of elimination, many candidates will find their viable options severely limited and this will dictate the strategy to be used. If your race has all or most of these methods available to it, then you should develop your strategy based on your primary objectives in each stage of the campaign

The GRP rating (gross rating points) is used to determine how many people on any given day, over a given period, will see or hear a particular message.

In advertising, one of the methods used to evaluate the efficiency of each communication method is the GRP (gross rating points) rating. As pointed out, research is done to determine how many people on any given day and at any time will see or hear a particular message. In some cases, this is broken down even further by demographic classifications.

In the initial stage, since your primary objective is to build name ID, you would use stationary signs as the most cost-effective manner to accomplish this. If for example a certain number of billboards, strategically placed around your district, have a 50% GRP rating on any given day, this means that 50% of the people that leave their home each day would see at least one of the billboards. Billboards and corrugated 4 X 8 signs strategically placed throughout the district, over a period of at least six months, are extremely effective in building name ID rating. A 50% GRP rating over this period would usually result in at least a 50 point increase in name ID (on a scale of 1 - 100).

The most common and cost effective stationary sign is the neighborhood lawn sign. These, depending on use, can be both effective and ineffective. Coverage is the key. There is no value in 5 or six of these small signs on the same property. Used in this manner, they will create a negative response. By coverage, I mean systematically, get volunteers to allow you to place lawn signs at strategic locations. Near corners is best, to catch the slowing traffic. One or two small signs on every street are far more successful than 20 signs on one street and none on four others. Never place lawn signs on private property without permission. Never tamper with another candidate's signs. Be certain that your volunteers understand the negative response that would come of this action becoming public.

There are several things to consider when designing and using stationary signs for communication. First, keep the message simple. Remember that the average motorist has only 4 seconds to read a sign or billboard. If it takes longer to assimilate your message, they may ignore it and drive by without focusing on it (remember the steel door). Always emphasize your name and the office for which you are running. Have your graphics prepared professionally. It does not make sense to spend thousands of dollars for signs and billboard rental to have your message lost because of a poorly designed message. Use at least two colors and keep it consistent with your campaign's colors. Be sure to rotate signs, especially billboards during longer campaigns (every two months in a six-month cycle). Finally, change both the location and the paper to keep the message looking fresh. This will make it more persuasive.

When considering the use of personal portraits, there is a wide spread difference of opinion in professional circles on the effectiveness of this technique. I am on the side that prefers their use. A professional portrait adds depth to the message and increases the Favorability rating by illustrating personal appeal.

During the middle stages of the campaign, use direct mail and tabloids to build your Favorability rating. This will also reinforce the message being sent from the campaign by your phone bank, precinct captains, press releases, and your own activities.

We have already discussed how to use direct mail for maximum effectiveness. Tabloids are a very inexpensive means of communicating your message. If done well, they enable you to tell a story, primarily with pictures, about the type of person you are and why the electorate should want you to be elected.

There are several styles used to direct the effectiveness of tabloids. One is designed to build your Favorability rating, using pictures and captions, leaving a great deal of open space between the pictures will accomplish this goal. Another type is more issue oriented. In this style, you reprint all of your press releases, as though they were news stories. It gives those people, who are genuinely concerned about the issues and your position on them, an opportunity to evaluate you. It is usually very effective to mail this tabloid style selectively to those people who indicate to your phone bank callers or precinct captains that they are undecided.

The tabloid is the general style used when doing a comparative piece. Some consider, even refer to it as the negative or attack piece.

The tabloid style is used when doing a comparative piece, which should be reserved for the latter stages of the campaign. Some consider it a negative or attack piece. In essence, you take 10 or 12 essential issues as determined by your focus group or polling as being of primary concern to the electorate. You list these very prominently in the left column. Your heading asks the readers to take a brief test to decide for themselves, which candidate best represents their views and interests.

In the second column from the left, you would list your opponent's position on each issue based upon either votes taken or positions stated in speeches and campaign material. In the next column from the left, you list your positions. In the fourth and final column, you ask the readers to list their positions and then make the comparison.

This comparative piece can be as effective done in a tabloid, a single page supplement, in a letter, or as a full page ad in the newspaper. A word of caution; be certain of your facts regarding your opponent's positions on the issues. As a rule of thumb, if you can not verify it to an impartial observer's satisfaction, do not use it. Never use a comparative piece until the final stages of the campaign and not until you have significantly raised your ID name rating.

Radio and television, if available and usable by your campaign, should also be used during the final stages of the campaign. The particular messages communicated should be based on the results of your polling. If your polling indicates you are ahead, keep your commercials low key. Use POS (Person on the Street) types focusing on a cross section of the district, i.e. older person, young person, or blue collar. These are interviews of people on the street who say positive things about you.

Follow up this series with spots portraying you talking with people in your district, from your backyard, in front of a plant, or in a cornfield. Show your concern for their problems and your determination to do something about solving them.

If the polling shows you leading, keep the spots positive and avoid any reference to your opponent, except by inference. Protect your position and reinforce it.

On the other hand, if the polls show you trailing, you must go on the attack. Remembering that the second criteria essential to victory is Favorability rating, if your opponent's rating is above 50%, you must bring it down in order to win. Your strategy should always be to attack only from a position of strength. If you were to attempt this type of attack strategy before achieving this position, it would almost certainly boomerang and result in a negative Favorability rating for you. If your campaign has successfully implemented its strategy in the early and middle stages of the campaign, your name ID and Favorability ratings should be high enough by this stage to attack (only if necessary) without hurting your credibility as a viable candidate.

Summary

1) Always analyze the media characteristics of your district. Discard those that are not viable for your campaign and focus on maximum utilization of those that are available to you. Proper utilization of appropriate methods will accomplish all your objectives successfully.

2) In each stage of the campaign, use your media campaign to supplement and reinforce your campaign's objectives. Make sure all of your media activity is working together in a concerted effort with your other campaign activity to accomplish each stage's objectives.

3) Stationary and mobile signs are most effective in building name ID, and to a lesser degree, your Favorability rating.

4) Direct mail, tabloids, radio, and television are the best tools to both, increase your Favorability rating, and to use when it is necessary to attack.

5) Web sites are the fastest growing communication technique in use today. Their multi-use can employ every style of communication. They allow you to publicly report on the development of your campaign. They allow voters to communicate directly with your campaign. Comparative pieces should always be reserved for the later stages of the campaign.

6) Anything that relates to the issues or addresses the candidate's qualifications to hold a particular office is fair game. Normally, disparaging attacks are considered by the electorate to be out of order, and unless there is a major case of moral turpitude involved, should remain off limits.

7) The use of frequent polling is the best intelligence-gathering device to help you make these determinations.

Note: Although it has not been used extensively to date, I believe that e-mail campaigns will become a relevant method of mass campaign communication by the next major election cycle. Its usage would parallel the direct mail campaign. The growth of its use will be unavoidable due to its very low cost per contact and growing ability to communicate with a very large segment of the public. In addition, it has been recently proved as a virtually untapped fund-raising tool.

Definition
Other races are defined as those campaigns that occurred or are occurring among the same electorate.

Impact of Other Races

All campaigns, even some past campaigns can affect your campaign. They can be fought at the Federal, State, and local levels. They can be individual campaign items such as ballot propositions or initiatives.

Relevant Factors

The relevancy of this factor depends on several conditions. The level of office you are campaigning for, its relationship to the other campaigns with the potential of impacting your campaign, and your status as an incumbent or challenger. If your campaign were relatively close to the top of the ticket, the impact would not be as great as if you were running for a lower level office. If you are an incumbent, your status makes your campaign less vulnerable than if you are a challenger.

As discussed earlier and worth repeating, as a rule the top of the ticket tends to draw the highest percentile of voters. There are exceptions, but usually, the lower on the ballot you go, the stronger is the tendency for an increase in the drop off rate. It is not unusual to see 52% of the electorate in a district cast a vote for the Presidential race, while only 40-42% cast a vote for a state representative's race on the same ticket. Drop off rates will usually go from 5% to as much as 50% of the number of votes cast at the top of the ballot.

Although there are a number of reasons why this occurs, the most common reason is a lack of awareness and/or interest in the races other than those at the top of the ticket. Your analysis should have indicated if this happened in your district's previous campaigns. In an off year election the drop off rate is not as pronounced at the lower end of the ballot. The voter turnout rate, in itself, is usually 10-20% lower than in a Presidential year. In an odd year election, the turnout rate is usually a couple of points less than in an off year election. When doing your PIPS analysis, these differentials should be taken into account. In developing your strategy, you must take into account the potential impact of these other races, whether positive or negative.

Analysis of the District

It is wise to do your analysis of the impact of other races in your district, if not before you decide to run, at least in the earliest stages of the campaign. If the candidate's party registration is in the minority in the district, they might decide to wait until a Presidential election year in the hope of picking up a potential coattail effect, i.e., capitalizing on the higher turnout rates and the popularity of the Presidential or major state-wide candidate.

Your political party committee, whether Federal, State, or local, will want you to run an integrated campaign. However, this is a decision you will have to make based on the best interests of your candidacy.

When doing this analysis be critical in your assessments. Your ability to control this factor is very limited and could influence the development of your game plan. Whether to run a completely independent campaign, or integrate certain activities with the top of the ticket campaign, would be your primary consideration.

Developing the Strategy

As a rule of thumb, you should always operate your campaign plan independently of any other campaign. Your strategy should be designed to ensure your chances of receiving the number of votes necessary for you to win. To the extent that alliances with other campaigns are of demonstrable value to your campaign, you might factor them into your plans. However, be aware that you risk a backlash from any negatives that campaign has, or may develop.

Many democratic candidates were forced to distance themselves from presidential candidate, Governor Dukakis, in the latter stages of his campaign when his negative ratings began to rise and the polls showed him losing decisively. This may appear to be cruel and disloyal, but in politics, this may well be the nature of the business. You must be prepared to make tough decisions in order to win. A candidate's first loyalty should be to the people of the district, the campaign contributors, and the volunteers. Party loyalty should take a back seat to these other considerations.

Frankly, it is for this reason that candidates tend to be suspicious of the advice given by party staff workers and campaign consultants who have come from their ranks. There is always the fear of divided loyalties. When the interests of your party and/or the candidates at the upper levels on the ballot coincide with yours, then it is mutually advantageous to develop alliances. If they do not, you should not allow your campaign to be pressured into developing alliances that are the least bit detrimental to your campaign. Consider where their loyalties would lie if the situation was reversed and your campaign was perceived to be a liability to their campaign. Be clear on this point, they would not associate with you, or your campaign.

On the other hand, when they are mutually advantageous, despite the risks involved, the union can be very successful. You might consider joint literature drops in your precincts, tying them into your phone bank operations, and participating in joint appearances. Occasionally, one campaign might want to sponsor joint rallies and/or fund-raising events. It is also relatively standard practice to develop a joint sample ballot mailer, for the final week of the campaign, which lists all of the party's candidates.

In my opinion, the coattail factor is more of a legend than a reality. The media, in general, persists in perpetuating this myth although the statistical evidence does not support the claims.

I previously referred to coattail effects and the impact this might have on your race. Unfortunately, coattails are more of a legend than a reality. Many years ago when machine politics dominated our political process, there was a real value to the top of the tickets' ability to bring other candidates of their party with them into office. Those days are long gone. Today, with candidates running their own independent campaigns, it is usual to see reverse coattails, with the lower level candidates carrying the top of the ticket. In fact, as previously stated, in recent years we have begun to see cases of a reverse drop off rate with more people in a district voting for the lower level candidates and/or initiatives than for the top of the ticket.

The media, in general, persists in perpetuating this myth although the statistical evidence does not support the claims. There are few reporters today who have the ability or inclination to do their own research. They find it expedient to simply regurgitate the "conventional wisdom" and pass it on to their readers or viewers as fact. This, of course, influences the people with whom they are talking and the myth goes on.

As a bottom line here, you must factor into your strategic decision making process the impact of other races regarding the effect they might have on voter turnout. All other considerations must be weighed carefully on an individual basis.

Definition
Election regulations refer to all local, State, and Federal ordinances, laws, or regulations that affect the political process.

Impact of Election Regulations

The list of regulations collectively covers from A to Z including the likes of, local sign ordinances, financial disclosure reports, or providing access to radio and television advertising. Candidates and political campaigns at all levels are affected in some way.

Relevant Factors

Since it is the Candidate who is legally responsible, it is the Candidate who must research laws and regulations that affect his or her campaign.

Before developing your strategy, you must research which set of laws and regulations affect your specific campaign. Nothing would be more devastating than having a civil or criminal complaint filed against a candidate during the course of a campaign. Even the filing of a complaint would usually be enough to cause irreparable harm to your campaign. Whether you are guilty or not would have little relevancy to the outcome. In some cases, a violation can be a criminal offense subject to fines, imprisonment, or a combination of both. Thus, in addition to the political consequences, there could be serious personal ones as well. **For this reason, you as the candidate must make yourself familiar with these regulations and make it your responsibility to comply with them all.**

Analyzing the District

Most state regulatory information is available and can be downloaded from most state web sites.

In analyzing your district, in this regard, the analysis really begins with the level of office you are seeking. If it is a local or state office, you should immediately contact your Secretary of State's office or State Board of Elections and obtain a copy of your state's regulations regarding filing as a candidate and a set of the appropriate campaign financial disclosure report forms. In most states, these parallel the Federal regulations and forms. Every candidate for political office, political action committee, party committee, or independent committee must file these reports several times during the election cycle. The reports detail all contributions received by the campaign and in most cases, all its expenditures. They also list loans, debts, and obligations.

Federal regulations and reports are available at the FEC web site www.fec.gov.

The Federal forms, known as FEC reports, are available from the Federal Election Commission in Washington, D. C. January 2001, it became mandatory to file FEC reports electronically. Although, it is not mandatory at the state level, many states now offer this convenience, with the likelihood that mandatory electronic filing at the state level will follow the Federal lead in the near future. This is simply one more strong reason to computerize your campaign. A program like GOTV *Campaign Optimizer* has been approved to meet the mandatory Federal and, where available, state electronic filing procedures.

Once you have copies of the appropriate forms, you should study them and whatever supporting documentation is sent with them. Note especially, what restrictions are placed on the type and amount of contributions you may receive. The Federal government currently places a limit on the maximum contribution amount at $1,000 per individual per election period. The time before the primary election (whether or not you are in a contested primary) is considered one period. The time before the general election date is considered another.

Since the Candidate is ultimately responsible to insure that the campaign complies with every regulation, it is then his or her responsibility to be knowledgeable regarding not only the laws and regulations as written, but also their possible interpretation.

One of the difficulties with laws and regulations is that they are always subject to interpretation. Election regulations are by no means exempt. For example, be careful about staying on the company payroll if you are an employee of a corporation or a partnership. There is no problem, of course, if the Candidate is a sole owner. Since it is illegal for a corporation to contribute to a Federal Candidate and in many states to any other type of Candidate, the continuation of the Candidate's financial remuneration arrangement while campaigning full time could very well be defined as an illegal corporate contribution. In the case of a partnership, each individual is presently allowed to contribute up to $1,000 in the Primary and General campaign period. Any amount over that, directly or in salary, could also be defined as an illegal contribution, i.e. the partner's portion of the candidate's salary can not exceed the contribution limit of $1,000 per period.

To avoid any breach of the regulation, a Candidate should consider an arrangement with his or her employer or partner spelling out the services he or she will provide in exchange for salary during the time being spent as a Candidate, perhaps providing consulting services on an as needed basis. By rule of thumb, if you are not sure of the interpretation of circumstances involving the possible breach of any law or regulation, arrange for the governing agency involved, to provide you with a written opinion.

Political Action Committees (PACs) are (at this writing) limited to contributing $5,000 to one individual in each period and your party's limits are determined by each cycle. Corporate contributions are (at this writing) strictly forbidden.

States have similar restrictions for non-Federal candidates. However, many vary as to maximum amounts and some do permit corporate contributions. In some cases, you must file duplicate sets of these reports with another agency, such as your county registrar of voters, if a local candidate, or your Secretary of State, if a Federal candidate. The reports are normally filed about six times during the campaign year and twice during the off year. They must be filed indefinitely if any transaction is still pending, such as the campaign's bank account remaining open.

Other possible election restrictions that must be taken into account are local laws concerning the placement and size of signs and areas in which campaigning is not allowed. Each municipality and county will normally have its own laws regulating these two activities. If your district covers more than one municipality or county, you will have to research all of them. Once learned, factor them into your strategic decision making process.

You should also check the Federal Communications Commission (FCC) regulations regarding your rights as a candidate regarding radio and television even when you do not actively plan to use either. Since the airwaves are technically public property, the Federal Government does mandate or restrict their usage and if your situation changes, you will want to know what your options are.

Another frequently unknown provision mandated by Congress is that stations must sell time to candidates at their lowest commercial rates. This is the discount rate reserved for major advertisers like the auto companies.

Violations of these regulations are usually criminal offenses subject to fines and/or jail terms.

Since the various reports that are filed are public records carefully study your opponent's reports and determine the plan of attack and implement counter measures.

Currently, regulations state that radio and television stations may not discriminate among candidates regarding the purchase of airtime. Whatever time they sell to one, they must make available to another. This applies not just to the quantity of time, but to the quality of time as well. In order to ensure compliance the regulations state that you may request, at any time, the advance buy schedule of your opponent and give you the opportunity to match it. As a minimum, you should request this schedule, since it will outline a part of your opponent's campaign plan and you must at least attempt to counter (communication) weapon for weapon.

When developing your strategy and budget, obtain a listing of these rates before making your decisions as to the amount you may use them. A campaign plan must be knowledgeable enough and flexible enough to take advantage of every weapon. *"Be Prepared"* is a great motto for all to aspire to.

Developing the Strategy

The various reports that are filed are public records and of course, anyone can request access to them. Since the source and amount of contributions provide not only valuable intelligence about your opponent's base of support and the amounts that can be spent on various types of campaign activity, your plan must entail a careful review of his or her reports as soon as they are filed. By carefully studying your opponent's reports, you can determine your opponent's plan of attack and implement counter measures. It will also enable you to ascertain whether your opponent has the resources to mount an all out offensive during the final stages of the campaign.

Sometimes, the sources of the contributions alone can be a campaign issue. If your opponent is drawing an inordinate amount of contributions from one segment of the community or industry, the charge can be made that your opponent is not representative of all the people.

Depending on the district, this type of an attack can be very effective, especially at times when the ethics of public officials are so much in question. At the very least, it usually forces your opponent onto the defensive and a good campaign will always try to keep an opponent in that position. Remember the caution regarding securing your own support base before going on the attack.

If you are running against an incumbent be sure to study their financial reports over the past two elections. Try to discern a pattern of campaigning based on their expenditures. What types of communication they favored? Does your opponent take advantage of the latest techniques and technology available in modern campaigning? We all tend to be creatures of habit. Once politicians find a formula that works, they are reluctant to change it. Knowing this can result in a real advantage.

Try to determine not only the types of communication tools used, but the timing as well. Plan your activities accordingly. A sound principle in campaign strategy is to defeat an opponent in a skirmish or at the very least, neutralize the impact of his or her activity. If your opponent is an incumbent and consistently drops a mailer in the final stage of the campaign lauding accomplishments during the previous term, it would be a good time to drop your comparative piece. Alternatively, if the polls warrant an attack, drop a direct attack piece on your opponent's record.

Plan your strategy regarding sign and campaign restrictions carefully. Do not order the corrugated 4 X 8 signs if local ordinances restrict the size to something smaller. However, if they do, check to see if the ordinance restricts only signs on public property or a right of way. Normally they do restrict signs on a right of way. Nevertheless, private property remains available. In this case, find supporters who live near major roads who are willing to display your signs for the duration of the campaign. If this is prohibited, use magnetic or roof car signs. I have never seen an ordinance restricting their use. Plan a campaign with as many volunteers as possible displaying them on their cars. The point is, if local ordinances restrict an activity, you must find alternative ways to accomplish your objective.

Be innovative about restrictions that might curtail your plans.

I once managed a campaign in a district that restricted the use of large campaign signs. After analyzing our situation, we realized two things. The bordering counties had no such restrictions, and several major employers were located in the bordering counties. This reality meant that a major segment of the voting public traveled across county lines to and from work each day. By placing large campaign signs across county lines on the travel routes to and from these employment sites, we avoided any breach of local sign restrictions and communicated our message to a large segment of the voting public traveling to and from our campaign district. A clear example of employing an innovative way to accomplish our objective despite local restrictions and in addition, made use of a means of communication that our opponent failed to consider.

I will speak here for a moment on what is often referred to as the domino effect of a decision or plan. The example above is a very good example of the greater value created from an isolated incident because of the domino effect. In that case, the opponent, who had the ear of the local media, complained bitterly about the breach of the local campaign sign restriction by our candidate. This negative attack became a front-page story and was published before anyone realized that the sign locations were across county lines, where in fact, no restrictions were breached at all. My point here is the domino effect of the innovative signs, hitting the front page and creating a major news splash and a major increase in my candidate's name ID rating. The domino effect continued when it was published days later that the signs were in fact legal. Since it was the opponent who was wrong in unloading his negative attack, especially without checking the facts, my candidate dramatically increased his name ID rating and Favorability rating. In addition, the positive result from a single idea, coupled with its domino effect, was entirely at the expense of the opponent. From that point on the dominos continued to fall, my candidate was off to a running start and the opponent never recovered from his defensive position.

During the final four weeks of the campaign, assign a responsible volunteer the job of calling all the radio and TV stations, on a daily basis, to monitor your opponent's media buy. Plan your campaign budget so that you will have the reserves available to match these buys in the final weeks. In the event that your opponent attempts a last minute negative attack, be prepared to cut a spot within hours, and be on the air with a countering strategy within twenty-four hours.

Never let a serious attack go unanswered.

The electorate expects you to defend yourself. An attack unanswered is, in their minds, true until denied. Your message can be a clear denial, coupled with an expression of regret that your opponent would stoop to such low gutter tactics in a last minute effort and desperate attempt to salvage a losing campaign. You know the voters of your district are honorable people and will repudiate such shoddy tactics at the polls on Election Day.

In this day of high-speed technology, you could cut and air a commercial like this within 3 or 4 hours of the attack. You would simply substitute it for the spots you had already planned to run for two days after the attack. To obtain even more coverage, go to a central location, while a staff person is calling all the TV and radio stations to announce an emergency press conference to answer the charges.

As irritating as many of these restrictions can be, a sound strategy will provide a sound way to capitalize on the situation in a positive manner. You must first have a thorough understanding of the circumstances and an awareness of the alternative methods available, within the scope of the restrictions, in order to enable you to still accomplish your primary objectives.

Definition
The impact of time constraints refers to all the elements of the campaign that involve functions of timing.

Impact of Time Constraints

The impact of time constraints includes the planning phase, the announcement date, the duration of the campaign, the beginning and end of each stage of the campaign, and the time requirements involved for each component of the campaign.

Relevant Factors

In political campaigns, **timing is crucial.** There is no substitute for time.

In most business enterprises, timing is a critical consideration. In political campaigns, it is crucial. Since campaigns operate for a limited duration and climax on a single day with decisive consequences, each hour of every day takes on critical proportions. In business, there is always tomorrow, in campaigns, tomorrow may be inconsequential.

I have already referenced the function of time in building name ID and Favorability ratings. I have referred, throughout this book, to almost every element of the strategic decision making process within the context of time. Yet, I feel this section is one of the most important because, next to financing, timing is so essential and yet so neglected by candidates, especially by challengers.

A sound campaign strategy implies the time necessary to achieve your objectives.

One of the reasons many incumbents remain in office so long is because they have learned the value of timing. One campaign ends and within days they are planning the next. There is no substitute for time. No amount of money will recapture it once it is gone. The physical constraints of man and machines are unalterable. Both have definite limits and must have time to carry out their responsibilities. By definition, a sound campaign strategy implies the time necessary to achieve your objectives.

In order to incorporate this crucial factor into the development of your strategy, you must have a thorough understanding of the time requirements of every component of the campaign. If your strategy calls for using a phone bank staffed by volunteers, you must know how to calculate the number of volunteers and telephone units required to accomplish your objectives within the precise time constraints of the campaign. You must know the lead-time required to plan and execute a major fund-raising event, a press conference, rally, or generate a mailing. Later, we will discuss precise formulas for making these calculations. If you are going to be a candidate or a campaign manager, study them in detail.

There is much more to being a candidate than having a loyal group of supporters and being on the right side of the issues.

There is so much for you to learn and so relatively little time to learn it. If you have an opportunity to attend a campaign training school or seminar, do so. As I personally learned the hard way thirty-two years ago, there is much more to being a candidate than having a loyal group of supporters and being on the right side of the issues.

Analysis of the District

In the section, Geographic Characteristics of the District, we covered the time constraints imposed by this particular factor on campaigning. You must now analyze your district in relation to all of the other factors that affect timing. What is the availability within your district of the goods and services necessary to implement your planned activities? Graphic shops, printers, and mail-processing shops are just part of what is needed. What facilities are available to hold different size fund-raising events, debates, or rallies? If there are choices, what are their respective costs and other requirements?

Once you have outlined your basic strategy, you must then prepare a timeline. Working backwards from the date of the election, set the date for each planned activity. Then continue working backward from that date and indicate the time requirements necessary for each component of that activity. In order to do this accurately, you will need to know the lead time requirements of the various suppliers who will be involved. This means more research. Continue in this manner back to the date that you decided officially to become a candidate.

In analyzing your district, you should find and record the names of individuals or companies whose services you might need for each activity. To facilitate the budget process, you could then obtain estimates and costs for those services or products. A campaign management application such as GOTV *Campaign Optimizer* has the ability to record vendors, their products, and notes on their offerings.

Developing the Strategy

In a political campaign, time can be your ally or your foe.

By using time more effectively and efficiently than your opponent, it can influence the outcome of your campaign. Your strategy should take advantage of every hour, from the day you decide to become a candidate, to the day of the election. If you are financially able, you should plan on campaigning full time from the day you publicly announce your candidacy. If you are unable to do this, develop a strategy that relies on surrogates to represent you at events that you will be unable to attend personally. Maximize the impact of your scheduling during those hours when you are able to campaign personally. This means focusing on events that have the greatest exposure to the electorate.

Develop within your staff and volunteers an appreciation of time. Little things like putting a count down calendar on a wall in the campaign headquarters helps to reinforce this concern. Plan events for staff and key volunteers at the beginning of each new stage to keep everyone conscious of the passage of time.

Ideally, you should begin your campaign planning at least one full year before the election.

Begin planning the campaign at least one year before the election. Devote the first 3 months to doing the necessary information gathering, or research, outlined in this manual. At the same time, organize your basic committees, especially, your fund-raising committee. Recruit your staff members, if your plan calls for them and identify your essential volunteers. Secure and outfit your campaign headquarters.

Focus on the reasons why people should vote for you, *NOT* why they should not vote for your opponent.

Pick a day in February to announce your candidacy and plan a major press conference for it. Have as many of your supporters and family members in attendance as possible. Have a press kit ready for distribution and be prepared to answer questions from the reporters and attendees. The number one question is usually, "Why are you running?" Have a well-prepared answer based on positive reasons.

It is said there are only two times in a politician's career when the press is nice to him or her. The day he or she announces their candidacy and the day they announce their retirement. In-between, you are fair game. Take advantage of this one "free" day. If handled well, it will set the stage for your campaign.

Impact of Financial Constraints

Definition
The financial constraints within a campaign are defined as the limitations imposed by the cost of the various elements necessary to accomplish the campaign objectives.

The financial constraints include not only the cost of goods and services, but in addition, the candidate's ability to finance his or her living expenses throughout the campaign as well.

Relevant Factors

The weapons of a modern campaign are the various types of communication mediums, or devices, available at any time. How effectively you use them is certainly a primary factor in the ultimate outcome of the campaign. A simple concept but so true, you must have them to use them. Even so-called *free media* communication takes money to generate, that is, the cost of issuing press releases and holding news conferences. Until the day comes, if ever,

Regardless of what particular strategy is developed to accomplish your objectives, unless you can raise the finances necessary to implement that strategy, it will fail.

There is a direct correlation between the amount of money raised and spent in a campaign and the campaign's outcome.

when there is public financing for campaigns at all levels, your strategy must include a plan to raise the funds necessary to communicate your message.

Keep in mind, that there is a direct correlation between the amount of money raised and spent in a campaign and the campaign's outcome. Unless a case of scandalous behavior is involved by one of the candidates in the race or the campaign funds are seriously misspent, the candidate with the most money will invariably win. Cynics refer to this truism as "buying the election." In most cases, this is absurd. In the vast majority of districts, the days of "walk around" or "street" money are long gone.

Simply said, money buys communications, and that is that. Without the ability to communicate, you cannot win. Unless of course, something extraordinary happens to your opponent and you win by default. This is an extremely rare occurrence.

Ironically, there is a strong self fulfilling prophecy factor at work in many campaigns. The conventional wisdom believes that a certain incumbent can not be beaten. Consequently, people do not contribute the necessary funds to the challenger. Sure enough, without those funds, the challenger loses and the conventional wisdom is proven right, i.e. the incumbent can not be beaten.

Analysis of the District

Before deciding to run for political office, you need to realistically assess your chances of raising the necessary funds to finance a winning campaign.

Starting with yourself, assess you own resources. Do you have the ability to provide the seed money necessary to finance a fund-raising campaign? Are you prepared to commit those resources without hesitation? Do you have the ability to survive financially during the campaign without working?

Study the fund-raising results of previous campaigns. How successful were previous candidates in raising funds within the district? There are relatively few prospects outside the district that will contribute funds, until you have demonstrated your ability to raise funds inside your district. The theory being, if members of your community are not prepared to support your candidacy, indicating their confidence in you and your ability to win, why should they?

This theory will apply even to your own political party. They too have limited resources to distribute among many candidates. Within the framework of their responsibility, they cannot squander campaign contributions on a losing cause.

Developing the Strategy

Political campaign consultants know that every campaign requires the development of two game plans. One is called *The Finance Plan*, and is the operative plan designed to implement your strategy for raising funds. The other is your *Campaign Plan*, which details the implementation strategy of your campaign. By using the exact same care you did in developing your campaign strategy, you must now develop your finance strategy. Not only must you have a plan to raise the necessary funds; your plan must incorporate the campaign's timeline, so that the funds are available when they are needed.

Before you can develop this strategy, you need to know the budget requirements for implementing your total campaign strategy. In other words, your budget should be conditioned on your campaign strategy and not the other way around. Few candidates are able to finance their campaigns with their own resources. The vast majority must develop a plan that involves the support and assistance of others. A sound strategy involves breaking the big problem down into a series of little problems and then developing a plan to solve them.

The most effective way is to develop a three-tiered fund-raising plan. Level 1 involves a finance committee whose responsibility it is to focus on large donors and major fund-raising events. Level 2 involves the community through a direct mail appeal and minor fund-raising events. Level three focuses on raising funds outside the district from individuals, PACs, and party committees.

Once you have established your budget, divide the amount among the three levels. A typical division would be 50% raised by level one, 35% by level 2, and 15% by level 3. Be mindful that the candidates own contribution to financing is regarded as part of level one.

Summary - A Fable

Once Upon a Time....

....in a far off land, there lived a noble Baron in a castle made of stone. He was the lord and master of all in the land. His subjects were fond of him. However, like most subjects, they had their concerns and certainly their complaints.

In a far off corner of the Baron's land lived a young nobleman. He did not like the Baron. It apparently had something to do with the tax rates he was levying against the noblemen and his middle class subjects.

One day, the nobleman decided that he could do a better job of managing things. As he would need to be Baron to do so, he decided to defeat the Baron in combat and become the new Baron. The way he figured things, it would not be so difficult. After all, the subjects were bound to be on his side. They did not like the tax rates any more than he did.

So he threw down the gauntlet, announced his campaign to defeat the Baron, and with a small group of loyal followers he set off for the castle. Unfortunately, he forgot his map. Along the way, he ran into all kinds of nasty obstacles that slowed him down and caused him to detour. Much valuable time was lost and his supplies rapidly dwindled.

As he passed through one village after another, he would raise the cry, "Down with the Baron and his oppressive taxes. Follow me to the castle and we shall defeat him and then I'll become the Baron."

As it turned out, the further away from his little corner of the Baron's land he got, the more the Baron's subjects cried, "Who are you?" and "Why should we follow you?" "How can you be so sure you will beat the Baron," or "The Baron is so powerful, he will wipe you out, and then make our lives even more miserable. Besides, he isn't that bad." The nobleman was unprepared and did not know what to say to all of this. He repeated his criticisms of the Baron and asked the subjects to follow his lead. Only a few did, and his army marched on.

As more and more obstacles were encountered, many of the subjects became disillusioned and left the nobleman's army to return home to their warm and comfortable cottages. As the date for the battle approached, the nobleman was still struggling to get there. Realizing he was way behind schedule, he ordered his troops into a forced march, causing even more to drop out and leave.

Finally, he arrived at the Baron's castle just in time. His troops were exhausted and undernourished. He was low on supplies and weapons. Many loyal subjects that had started the journey at his side had abandoned him along the way, taking supplies with them.

He marched up to the castle gates and demanded the Baron surrender to him. The Baron responded by daring him to continue his campaign. The battle began. All day long, it waged on. Repelled by the Baron's defenses, the nobleman's forces were gradually defeated. The nobleman tried desperately to force the Baron into the open so they could fight man to man, but the Baron merely laughed and stayed secure behind the castle walls. Finally, in desperation, the nobleman demanded that his supporters charge the castle. What happened next is too gruesome to recount. Whatever was left of the nobleman's strength was destroyed and the campaign went down to certain defeat.

The Baron survived and became stronger than ever. No one seriously challenged his rule for many long years. The nobleman survived and made it home. When he was last heard from, he was sitting in front of his warm fireplace telling stories to his grandchildren about the time he stormed the castle gates with only his bare hands to defeat the Baron. Each time he told the story he made himself sound braver and more heroic.

One day, his 6 year old grandson looked lovingly up to him, and said, "But grandpa, wasn't it a big mistake to attack a castle with just your fists?" The nobleman, at first taken aback, could only nod his head.

Several years later, another nobleman from a different village decided that he would make a better leader than the old Baron. Fed up with high taxes and concerned about the laws and treaties that the Baron was enforcing, he resolved to challenge the Baron's leadership. Unsure of how he would go about this, he began by studying everything he could concerning the Baron, his habits, and his fortifications.

Back and forth he went across the land, talking with people, exploring the routes, and even getting himself invited to the castle for a party. While inside the castle, he noted how he could penetrate the castle and the strength of the Baron's army.

He called together some loyal friends swearing them to secrecy and explained what he had in mind. They resolved to join with him and help him raise the gold necessary to finance what could be a long campaign.

The nobleman sent couriers to all the towns and counties of the Barony. At each church site or market, the couriers would tack up flyers that had a sketch of the nobleman, a brief description of his background, and a statement about the way he thought things could be better in the Barony.

After the nobleman finished his research, he developed a plan. He planned to lay siege to the castle and taunt the Baron until his pride forced him to come out and fight. He kept studying the Baron and learned everything he could about him.

Realizing he had to have a reserve plan in case the first plan failed, he decided to investigate a new weapon he had heard about from a traveling minstrel. It seems this new weapon could be fired from a safe distance and had the ability to break down stone. Investigating further, he discovered that the story was true and arranged to secretly obtain one.

While these preparations were going on, he sent his supporters to all of the villages inquiring of the people, as to who was loyal to the Baron, who opposed him and who hadn't quite made up their mind. The volunteers explained the nobleman's ideas and how much better off they would be if the nobleman were the new Baron.

Little by little, the volunteers managed to convince more of the undecided subjects to support the nobleman. The next day they returned with a copy of the nobleman's battle plan and the subjects were very impressed. Little did they know that this was not actually the real battle plan. The nobleman knew that the Baron would have a copy soon enough and plan to defend against it.

Finally, the nobleman was ready to advance on the castle. They knew precisely where and when they would attack the Baron since the route had been well scouted and the advance well planned. The nobleman's scouts put up markers along the way so that they could make sure that all were on the right path and the same schedule.

Just as the plan anticipated, the Baron's army came out of the castle and the battle was fought. When it was over, the majority of subjects remaining supported the nobleman and he was declared the new Baron. He occupied the castle, sending the Baron into retirement with a generous pension.

The new Baron continued his rule, until one day, word came of this nobleman in a far off village......

Moral of the Story

For literally thousands of years, there have been noblemen, barons, and every other political designate alike fighting for control of the loyal subjects. Nothing has changed except the weapons used to do the fighting. In essence, what took place in the Barony, takes place in political campaigns all over the country at every level each geopolitical division.

Regrettably, the vast majority of candidates are like the first nobleman. In fact, over 95% of challengers are exactly like him, and do exactly as he did, as they attempt to overcome the systematic hurtles that impede their progress toward elected office. I say, regrettably, not because I have anything against the incumbents who inhabit these offices, but rather because I believe any system that establishes an incumbent so permanently in office, must necessarily, by virtue of it's own self generation, be deemed unresponsive to the will and needs of the people.

The development of campaign strategy is not a hit or miss proposition. It is not an intuitive process. Rather, it is a scientific process built upon hard work and solid research, with a small amount of luck thrown in for good measure.

Frequently Asked Questions on Strategy

1. **Can every candidate be beaten?**

A. Theoretically, yes. Realistically, not really. If a candidate is an incumbent with a high Favorability rating and a shrewd campaigner, the odds of a challenger beating that person are extremely low. The challenger would continue to work towards catching up in a campaign that is rarely long enough to do so. By definition, a shrewd campaigner never takes an opponent for granted. They are campaigning every day they are in office, reinforcing their name ID and Favorability rating through direct mail and constituent service. If an incumbent becomes complacent and predictable, or if the Favorability rating drops below 50%, he or she becomes vulnerable. Another vulnerability presents itself when an incumbent takes a very unfavorable position on a district issue and the challenger is in line with public sentiment.

2. **How should a candidate handle a past indiscretion?**

A. Honesty remains the best policy. The electorate is very fair minded. They can understand and excuse a past indiscretion, especially one that occurred at a young age. What they are very intolerant of is deceit or hypocrisy. You can be assured that whatever happened in your past will surface during the campaign. It is far better if you expose the indiscretion at the beginning and put it behind you before you start campaigning.

3. **Should a candidate take campaign contributions from any legitimate source?**

A. Opponents, and often the media, will attempt to make a case of guilt by association. This can be a real political liability if the individual or organization involved is perceived to be a negative factor in your district. Refer back to the discussion on the advantages of political alliances. By rule of thumb, if you are not sure of the impact, do not take the contribution. It could well become a liability.

4. **What should a candidate do about all the "good" advice received from supporters?**

A. This is a difficult situation, especially, if the advisor has given or has the potential to make a major contribution. If you have done your research thoroughly and developed a sound strategy based on that research, you are the one who is in the best position to judge the merits of any advice and its inclusion in your game plan. Remember a good executive is able to "pick and choose" from the many good ideas expressed to him or her, then incorporate only those which fit into a long range program to reach an objective. Unless the individual giving the advice has done the same research, he or she sees only a part of the whole picture. As has already been pointed out, no segment of the campaign exists in a vacuum. An individual that looks at only one problem or one part of the whole picture could be doing a real disservice to your campaign, when trying to apply a generic solution. Thank them for their advice, tell them you will consider it and then analyze its impact on the *"whole"* campaign.

5. **What should a candidate do if repeatedly misquoted in the press?**

A. Do not make a public accusation against the media or even the reporter in question. First call the reporter and ask for a face to face meeting to discuss the situation. If unsuccessful, call the editor or publisher and again have a private discussion to try to resolve the issue. If this still fails, ignore the reporter and avoid giving him or her any further interviews unless other members of the press are present.

6. **What should a candidate do if unsuccessful in the campaign?**

A. Run again. Even a losing candidate has built a formidable base of support. It is much easier the next time to build on that base. The name ID and Favorability ratings are considerably higher at the onset. In addition, the experience gained during the first attempt at campaigning is invaluable. Study your previous campaign. Determine precisely what worked and what did not. Concern yourself with not repeating earlier mistakes. Rarely is a loss a result of only one or two factors. Usually, it is a series of small things that did not occur as planned and might have seemed inconsequential at the time. However, when added together they adversely affected your game plan. Studying carefully will uncover these issues. Focus on what you did not do as much as on what you did do. The methodology used within this manual can be applied to solving even the unique problems.

7. **Is there a first consideration when deciding whether to run for office?**

A. Perhaps. The acquisition of power is a driving, passionate force, more so, than even the acquisition of money. It is neither acquired, nor given up easily. As President Truman so aptly put it, "If you can't stand the heat, get out of the kitchen." If you are not prepared to fight, using all your energy and resources, from beginning to end, do not run.

Chapter 3 - Word Index

Chapter 4
Development of the Game Plan
Introduction to the Study of a Candidate's Campaign

The modern American political campaign is a dynamic process subject to an almost unlimited number of variables. Consequently, it is impossible to develop a manual that can be used for all types of campaigns, at all times. However, after thirty years of professional experience as a Political Campaign Consultant and Campaign Manager, I have found there are a substantial number of activities that are relatively constant throughout the campaign process.

In my opinion, the few manuals that are available for those interested in the political process deal too much with the general theory regarding the variables, while failing to emphasize the constants. In addition, the author attempts to provide guidance without reference to the type of campaign involved, i.e., Federal, State, or local races. *The Campaign Manual* corrects these deficiencies by centering its basis on a Congressional campaign, which my experience has shown uses the same type of activity as most other campaign types, insofar as the constants are concerned.

The prototype plan that will be developed is based on a Congressional Candidate's campaign in an urban/suburban district. Each candidate will have to make the necessary adjustments if his or her election district, the geographic area in which they are running, is different. For example, the use of volunteers for precinct canvassing is severely restricted in a heavily rural district. However, since the objectives of that activity must still be realized, another method must be developed and substituted by the Candidate and/or campaign committee.

Hard work is a necessary ingredient to success in general and without a doubt, political campaigns are no exception.

As you study this Manual, you will notice the enormous amount of work involved and its relatively high cost. Generally, the immediate reaction is "Is all this really necessary to win?" The answer is an *emphatic* YES. The dollars involved really translate into communications designed to inform and motivate the voter. Unless a Candidate is able to effectively communicate his or her message to the electorate the chances of winning are slim. It is true that some candidates occasionally win with budgets substantially less than the recommendation here. However, these are the exceptions and not the rule. The hard work speaks for itself. We have no shortage of cliches to express our general belief in that concept. "Nothing ventured, nothing gained," "Anything worth doing, is worth doing right" or my personal favorite, "If you can't take the heat, get out of the kitchen." Hard work is a necessary ingredient to success in general and without a doubt, political campaigns are no exception.

Occasionally there are outside factors that help low-budget candidates win "in spite of themselves." It does happen, albeit infrequently.

Occasionally there are outside factors that help low-budget candidates win "in spite of themselves." It does happen, albeit infrequently. A "coattail" effect from a Candidate for President or statewide office, involvement of an opponent in a scandal, an incumbent who refuses to take a challenger seriously and does little to ensure re-election, the death or major disability of an opponent during the election cycle, or an unusually low voter turnout are isolated circumstances that can skew the expected results of a low-budget campaign.

The question every Candidate must ask and answer is whether he or she wants to risk the outcome of the election on one or more of these outside factors. Approximately 95% of all incumbents win re-election and better than two-thirds of those who are beaten lose to a challenger running a well financed, professionally managed campaign. The few congressional challengers who win as a result of an outside factor usually number less than three in any given election year.

Most serious candidates and Political Campaign Consultants find these odds unacceptable. In fact, many consultants have reached a point where they will no longer take a client who does not have a realistic attitude concerning the odds and is committed to "do it right." The candidate must have a reasonable likelihood of raising 50% of the necessary dollars within their own district. It is simply unreasonable to venture hundreds of thousands of dollars and thousands of volunteer hours, ignoring the odds, in the hope that lightning will strike.

Definition
The "franking" privilege enables an incumbent to send most mail to constituents postage free.

One of the reasons that "doing it right" is especially important in a challenger's situation is that an incumbent has a number of built-in advantages. One such advantage is the "franking" privilege, that is, free postage on most mail to constituents. This is more often than not worth over $100,000 a year before even beginning to spend a dime on the re-election effort. When you add the benefits of being able to use their staff, many of whom have campaign experience, plus their ability to command the attention of the "free" media, i.e. media coverage not paid for, we have probably added another $100,000 to the total. In reality, the incumbent starts with a $200,000 advantage. When you add another $600,000+, which most incumbents can raise handily, you begin to understand why consultants are so skeptical about the successful outcome of low budget campaigns.

However, on the other hand, the challenger has three built-in advantages of his or her own. First is simply time. Often the challenger is able to campaign full time while the incumbent is required to stay focused on their elected duties in a state capital or perhaps even in Washington. The second is a clean slate. Challengers can create their records; incumbents must live with theirs. If the incumbent's record is out of step with the majority or even certain segments of the electorate, when exposed appropriately, it can be a major advantage and a decisive factor. The third is the volunteer organization and is generally a result of the first and second advantages. When the incumbent's record is unpopular with a percentage of the public, creating a pre-motivated pool, and the challenger has more time to devote to volunteer development, the volunteer organization can become quite extensive, even overwhelming to the incumbents campaign effort.

If a challenger develops an intensive well organized and adequately financed campaign at all levels of the process the odds of winning can be improved to at least a 50/50 chance for success. I am convinced that challengers with a well organized and adequately financed campaign can win at least 60 percent of the time. This being true, it is worth stating that more often than not, challengers lose because they fail to develop an intensive well organized and adequately financed campaign at all levels of the process. It is analogous to a person starting a new business when ill prepared because of not knowing the market, how to manage, or because of under capitalization.

In the following sections, we will discuss the basic tactics that must be employed if a strong assault is to be mounted on all fronts, creating an intense pressure on the opponent, at all levels and in all areas during the various stages of the campaign. We will also discuss the various functions, objectives, and responsibilities of each member of the campaign team, along with specific suggestions on how to accomplish them.

One of the purposes of studying this manual is to assist the candidate to identify if there is a need for professional assistance.

Please note that although I believe this manual to be comprehensive, I do not consider it a substitute for professional help and guidance. Operating a campaign for Congress or a comparably sized voting district of 500,000+ people is equivalent to operating a small company with an annual budget of $1.2 million. To attempt to manage such a company without experienced help is foolish. In over 30 years in politics, I have never seen a campaign managed by volunteers win over one that was managed by experienced, professionals, except perhaps in instances when outside factors were dominant. One of the purposes of studying this manual is to assist the candidate to identify if there is a need for professional assistance.

The campaign is a game of physical endurance, skill, and determination.

Throughout *The Campaign Manual,* you will find constant references to the game of chess. Disrespect is not intended by these references to a campaign as a game. A campaign, nonetheless, is a very serious game, a strategic contest between two adversaries. The campaign is a game of physical endurance, skill, and determination. As in chess, there is a need to develop a winning strategy that, by its very nature, must include defeating the opponent. I have never seen a volunteer grassroots campaign beat an opponent who could afford to use media effectively. To use the chess analogy, dependence entirely on a volunteer grassroots campaign is like trying to beat the incumbent with just pawns on the board. Think of the volunteers as the pawns and the major pieces (queen, bishop, knight, and castle) as the various media elements in the campaign. The Candidate is the king. The player moving the pieces is the Political Campaign Consultant, adviser, or strategist.

It becomes more understandable why so many candidates with barely any volunteers (pawns) but a full "backboard" can wipe out the most aggressive grassroots campaign. Good intentions and the "righteousness of your cause" are simply not enough. Unless the opponent has at least an equal number of major pieces in the backboard, the result of the game is usually a foregone conclusion. On the other hand, if a challenger can match the incumbent piece for piece on the backboard and put more pawns on the board than the incumbent, the odds can improve considerably. Now the game is relatively equal. Playing skill becomes the next dominant factor and, as so often happens, a forced mistake made by the incumbent can help determine the outcome. I often find it amusing when those who purport to report on and analyze election results fail to take into account such basic differentials within a particular campaign. Oftentimes, political analysts infer profound reasons such as the popularity of a particular Party's program or an incumbent President's program or a shift in the prevalent political philosophy of the electorate to explain the outcome of a particular campaign. This is not to say these can not be critical factors in the political process, but rather that they are often greatly overrated.

Throughout *The Campaign Manual,* I will be referring to stages and levels. There are three levels of activity within the normal campaign: the Candidate, field operations, and free or paid media. There are also five major stages, or seven, if there is a contested primary election. I refer to them as:

Stage 1 - Pre-announcement
Stage 2 - Voter ID
Stage 3 - Positive Advocacy
Stage 4 - Negative Advocacy and
Stage 5 - GOTV (Get Out The Vote)

At any given time during the campaign all three levels and the five stages should be working in conjunction. This might seem obvious to some, but you would be amazed at how many campaigns I have witnessed headed in three different directions at the same time.

I also refer throughout *The Campaign Manual* to Regions and Areas. I have developed a basic district organizational structure that I have since used in all of my campaigns. It has been copied by many other campaigns over the years and is in wide use today. Called the 5 on 5 Organization Plan, it is a proven method for efficiently administering the field operations program and implementing the precinct and voter objective strategy. It also facilitates communications within the campaign structure.

Definition
The Field Operations Committee is responsible for the voter objectives in each respective Region and Area.

The basis of the 5 on 5 Organization Plan consists of dividing the electoral district into five Regions based on a combination of factors, such as the number of voters, number of precincts, demographic similarities, natural geographic lines, and zip code boundaries. Each Region is then sub-divided into five Areas using the same criteria. A chairperson is assigned to be responsible for the voter objectives in each respective Region and Area. These 30 chairpersons in conjunction with the phone bank supervisors make up the campaign's Field Operations Committee. If possible, it is very important not to split zip codes when creating these Regions and Areas. Once established, these Region and Area designations remain constant throughout the campaign and are used for all campaign activities such as direct mail, both political and fund-raising, phone bank operations, scheduling, and special events.

In addition to the Field Operations Committee, every campaign must have three other basic committees. There is the Finance Committee, which will be discussed later, the Advisory or Steering Committee, and the Research Committee.

Definition
The Advisory Committee is responsible for overseeing the campaign and providing the Candidate and Political Campaign Consultant with information and progress reports.

The Advisory Committee has the responsibility of overseeing the campaign and providing the Candidate and Political Campaign Consultant with information and progress reports on the various activities within their specific area of responsibility. It is usually comprised of the Candidate, the Candidate's Spouse, the Campaign Chairperson(s), the Treasurer, the Regional Chairpersons, the Research Committee Chairperson, the Campaign Manager, the Campaign Secretary, and the Political Campaign Consultant.

The Research Committee assists the Candidate in researching the issues, the incumbent's voting record, the polling data, and current activity in the political and economic world as it pertains to the particular office for which the Candidate is running.

Definition
The Research Committee assists the Candidate in researching the issues, the incumbent's voting record, the polling data, and current activity in the political and economic world.

Some campaigns establish additional committees, but in my experience, to establish more than three committees usually proves to be time consuming and simply complicates the process. It is my opinion that dividing all responsibilities among these three committees is both sensible and efficient. Some campaigns have so many committees, forms, and procedures that they become in themselves, unwieldy bureaucracies.

The campaign staff should consist of the Campaign Manager or Administrator, the Campaign Secretary, Finance Director, Media Secretary, Field Operations Director, Phone Bank Director, Driver/Aide, and three secretaries, preferably with personal computer experience. Regrettably, most campaigns have to make do with less because of budget considerations. The Campaign Manager usually ends up being the Finance Director and Media Secretary combined, the Field Operations Director is also the Phone Bank Director, and there are only two secretaries instead of three. Key volunteers should be used to assist in these functions. The Campaign Secretary is also the scheduler. One secretary normally doubles as the bookkeeper and Finance Committee Secretary, while the other secretary becomes the computer operator.

These six people are critical to the successful implementation of the Political Game Plan. They are usually paid very poorly and many respond out of personal regard for the candidate. Often younger and single people are recruited for these positions because of the demands on time. If a person is married, you must be certain that the volunteer and their entire family understand their job and its time requirements. The hours are not only outrageously long, but both stressful and demanding.

There are two other positions on the campaign staff that are usually filled by volunteers. Here again however, if the budget permits, they should be full-time paid positions, i.e., the Director of Volunteers and the Director of Research. If volunteers cannot be found, the Campaign Secretary assumes the Director of Volunteers position and the Campaign Manager or Media Secretary combines their regular responsibilities with that of the Director of Research position.

For discussion purposes within *The Campaign Manual,* I have used the average and presumed a six-person staff. Actually, with a Political Campaign Consultant who is management oriented and a modern computer system with a capable campaign management software like GOTV *Campaign Optimizer*, a core of active headquarter volunteers can work very well. The key is for the group to be well organized, well trained, and well disciplined and all rowing the boat in the same direction. If the Candidate and staff expend the time and energy to prepare for the campaign using the guidelines in *The Campaign Manual*, he or she can build a tight organization that will function smoothly throughout the campaign. This is especially important during the latter stages when the pressure becomes intense and an inevitable crisis develops.

The Campaign Manual is sold in an economical work book edition to be circulated among key staff and volunteers alike, keeping everyone trained by the same teacher and focused on the same set of objectives.

In my attempt to make *The Campaign Manual* as functional as possible, I have minimized lengthy discussions of the many variables that can exist in a campaign. Primarily, I focus the candidate on the essentials, i.e., the constants that exist in all campaigns. Unless you build a solid foundation, you cannot build a solid house. The best strategy devised is useless unless the structure to implement it is as precise as possible. This is the unglamorous part of a campaign. The part that the media and public do not see, which results in the part that the media and public do see. It is for this reason that they are essential to a successful outcome. Consequently, the candidate must realize that the solutions for the variables are a result of sound implementation of the constants and common sense.

After the foundation is built and the Political Game Plan developed, the campaign should follow it to the end. Unless a major event occurs that clearly threatens the outcome of the campaign, the Candidate should not give in to the overly abundant "well intentioned" advice that he or she will be inundated with during the later stages of the campaign. If the plan is sound when everyone is relatively cool, calm, and collected, it will still be sound when the pressure develops. A good Political Game Plan has a built-in tolerance for adjustment that will be more than sufficient for the normal campaign. However, you should always be aware that a normal campaign usually consists of some confusion, countermoves by the opponent, aggravating press coverage, volunteers failing to perform as promised, and interruptions in the cash flow. Do not panic; rather stick to the plan. In the final analysis, the percentages will be in the favor of a campaign's well thought out Political Game Plan.

Preparation - The Campaign Task List

There are fundamental Campaign Tasks that must be completed before the official start of the campaign, i.e., before the public announcement of your candidacy.

For a reasonable expectancy of success, whether a Candidate is an incumbent or a challenger for the first or second time, there are fundamental procedures that must be followed before the official start of the campaign, that is before the public announcement of your candidacy. I will list and discuss each here, in no order of importance as they all have a relative importance to the whole of the campaign strategy and Political Game Plan.

Do not read The Campaign Manual, study The Campaign Manual.

Study The Campaign Manual

By definition, to read is to apprehend or grasp the meaning of the relation of groups of printed characters. By definition, to study, is to apply the mind in acquiring knowledge; to examine; to scrutinize; to endeavor to memorize; to give attention to as something to be done; and finally to follow a regular course of instructions. In other words, do not read *The Campaign Manual*, study *The Campaign Manual*.

The Feasibility Survey helps to determine the degree of an opponent's vulnerability, the focus of any vulnerability, the Favorability rating, both name ID ratings, and the major issues in the district.

The Feasibility Survey

A number of political manuals and advisers will suggest potential candidates arrange for a feasibility study, a survey done by a professional polling firm, usually costing from $12,000 to $15,000, before making this commitment. This study helps to determine the degree of an opponent's vulnerability, the focus of any vulnerability, the Favorability rating, both name ID ratings, and the major issues in the district. The survey is usually done in September of the year before the election.

I believe that a feasibility survey is money well spent and strongly urge candidates, especially challengers, to commission one. However, the vast majority of candidates, eager to conserve precious dollars do not. Most will form focus groups as we discussed in the earlier chapters and analyze previous election results to make their determination without spending the money on a professional feasibility study. This decision, in my opinion, should be based on fiscal responsibility and therefore a function of the total amount of contributions to be spent on the campaign. If you plan to raise $100,000, which is certainly a low figure based on today's average campaign cost, the feasibility study would represent an expense of $15,000 or 15%. This expense will insure that a responsible decision is made on behalf of those that contribute to your campaign. Naturally, as the total of the contributions rises, the percent spent on the feasibility study falls and in that way, it behooves the responsible Candidate to seek a professional analysis over the biased view of a handful of supporters in a self formed focus group. In any event, contributions, for the most part, pay the cost of the analysis to insure the fiscal responsibility that is deemed necessary.

For a Candidate in a lower budget campaign, then I suggest he or she attempt to obtain a copy of a previous survey done in the district involving the opponent. Usually the Party or a former Candidate has commissioned one and even a 1 or 2 year old survey can be helpful in the decision making process of whether to run or not. If unfamiliar with surveys, ask a Party representative, a former Candidate, or a consultant to help with the correct interpretation and analysis.

From this point on, we will presume that the Candidate has decided in favor of, and is firmly committed to running. With that decision made, we can turn our attention to the balance of basic requirements that a Candidate needs to complete *before* making a formal announcement regarding candidacy. Since, I estimate at least 200 hours of work to complete this list, the sooner you start the better. I would suggest that this work be completed nine (9) calendar months before Election Day.

Hiring a Political Campaign Consultant

The Candidate should decide on the need for a professional Political Campaign Consultant.

As soon as possible after making the decision to run, a Candidate should decide on the need for a professional Political Campaign Consultant. This decision should be based on the same logical concept discussed regarding the feasibility study.

If the decision is yes, contract a Political Campaign Consultant to help with the campaign strategy, plan, and management. There are only about 400 full-time Political Campaign Consultants in the country and many of them are completely scheduled by October of the year before the election. Most of them have their own style of operation and a Candidate may need to redo their initial plan if it and they do not fit with the consultant's method of operation. Most Political Campaign Consultants, if they decide to take a campaign account, will usually work out budget payments for the campaign. They fully understand the need to be thrifty, especially in the early stages of the campaign.

The Candidate should be aware that although some standardization has evolved in recent years, there is no universal consensus or definition for a Political Consultant or his or her job definition. To a large degree, it is defined by the campaign need. Later and in more detail, I will discuss the many functions that are performed by the Political Campaign Consultant, depending on the definition of his or her services. For now, defined in the broadest terms, the

Political Campaign Consultant is the person who by virtue of education, training, and experience is able to advise a Candidate on how to design, plan, and manage a well organized campaign that will result in the strongest likelihood of an election victory.

The Political Campaign Consultant could be responsible for some or all of the responsibility to develop the Political Game Plan, the over all strategy, the Time Line, the organizational structure, and will provide guidance on developing issues.

Since no two campaigns are alike, the job description of the Political Campaign Consultant may never be alike as well. By definition, he or she could be responsible for some or all of the responsibility to develop the Political Game Plan, the over all strategy, the Time Line, the organizational structure, and will provide guidance on developing issues. The consultant may also be responsible for directing the various elements within the campaign, that is, the Candidate, the staff, the major volunteer groups, the polling firm, as well as the media and fund-raising consultants if he or she is not providing those particular services. The needs and the consulting fee will be agreed upon, on a campaign by campaign basis.

Definition
Seed money refers to the money necessary to fund the beginning of the campaign. It must be raised before the campaign begins.

Seed Money

The question always arises as to how much seed money is necessary before beginning the campaign. This is dependent on the type of campaign being run. For a Congressional candidate, I recommend a minimum of $75,000, or approximately 10% of the anticipated campaign's budget. This percentage can be used as a rule of thumb for most other types of campaigns.

This money should be in the bank before starting anything beyond filing the statements of candidacy and organization with the Federal Election Commission (FEC), or its equivalent, in the state capitol. By federal law, at this writing, these forms must be filed, when a person raises or spends $5,000.00, or by definition has ceased "testing the waters" and begins to campaign, by definition, as a candidate would. Write to FEC, 999 E Street, NW, Washington, DC 20463 or visit their web site at www.fec.gov for the FEC Campaign Guide and to review the necessary forms. As of February 2001, it became mandatory to file these forms electronically, which is another pressing reason to invest in a software application like GOTV *Campaign Optimizer*, which will file these forms electronically. For State and local campaigns, the filing requirements can be found on your state web site or at the State Board of Elections office in your district. The FEC and SBE rules and regulations regarding election filing and fund-raising will change on a legislated basis and will require you, by law, to make yourself aware of these changes and comply, subject to penalties, i.e. jail terms or fine or both. More on this subject later.

As for the seed money, it can come from a Candidate's own funds or from an initial group of campaign contributors who are actively supporting the candidacy. Without this required seed money, the viability of any campaign will usually be in doubt from the onset. Many Political Campaign Consultants will not accept a new candidate unless a person has at least this level of proven fund-raising ability.

The old adage "it takes money to make money" is especially true in politics. No matter how skilled the Political Campaign Consultant or fund-raiser, money is needed for the initial brochures, stationery, envelopes, and postage necessary for the initial fund-raising programs. In addition, unless a candidate can raise an appropriate amount of seed money, neither the Parties nor the Political Action Committees will be likely to take the campaign seriously and consider support.

The Candidate's Biography

The Candidate should prepare a complete and detailed biography in two formats; one should be produced in resume format, the other in a narrative style.

The Candidate should prepare a complete and detailed biography in two formats; one should be produced in resume format, the other in a narrative style. In addition, a frank and honest statement of personal strengths and weaknesses as described in the previous chapter on Characteristics should be completed as well. Be thorough. Start literally at "day one" and continue to the present. Include church and organization affiliations, military service, grade point averages, and everything else inclusively. This is not the time to be humble or brief. If need be, it can be condensed and the most pertinent facts highlighted in other forms later. For now, however, produce a complete description of your life and life's accomplishments. It is preferable to do this in an electronic format. In this way, whenever the need arises, for whatever purpose, a computer operator can cut and paste to emphasize any given details for any given situation.

It is essential that the Candidate be honest about every detail in his or her biography. Especially anything conceived to be a negative. There is nothing worse than having some skeleton surface during the later stages of the campaign. You can bet your last dollar that it will surface sooner, or later. It is far better to personally expose the "negative," defined in your terms, rather than being forced to defend yourself against the "negative," defined in their terms. Be honest, get any negatives out in the open, up front, where anything can be dealt with, the earlier in the campaign, the better.

The Family Biography

A brief biography should be prepared on the Candidate's spouse, children, and parents.

Prepare a brief biography on your spouse, children, and parents. If the Candidate has a noteworthy sibling, relative, or ancestor, make mention of that separately. As you did with the Candidate, since some like to presume guilt by association, make note of any serious negatives involving close members of the family.

Statement of Why You Are Running

The Candidate should prepare a statement covering why he or she is running for the office vied for.

The Candidate should prepare a statement of at least 1,000 words covering why he or she is running for the office vied for. If one could generalize in regard to the most likely question that a reporter will ask a candidate, it would be, why are you running for this office or why are you running for re-election to an office? It would amaze you to know how many candidates are unable to give a clear, convincing answer. This statement will also become part of the initial press and PAC kits and a useful fund-raising tool. Parts of the statement will also be used in most candidate addresses, and in campaign literature.

Speak to your feelings as well as the intellectual reasons for running. People tend to develop a "sense" of a person more by the impressions they receive rather than the rational arguments a Candidate might present for or against a particular issue. Voters want to feel they can relate to the Candidate and probably more importantly, want to know if the Candidate can relate to them. The average voter does not understand the complexities of the trade deficit or the ramifications of import/export quotas, but they do understand being out of work and the fear of not being able to afford medical coverage for their family.

It is worth emphasizing that I am not in any way saying that a Candidate should not do his or her homework and be very aware of the various arguments for and against the important issues over which he or she will have influence, if elected. In reality, the most preferred candidate will blend intellectual prowess on the issues with sensitivity toward the average voter's concern, and know which to emphasize when. We will discuss this in more detail later.

Appraisal of Voting Record

A complete analysis and appraisal of the opponent must be completed. Much of this information is available on the Internet at different sites depending on the elected office.

Do an appraisal of the opponent on his or her voting record or position statements, constituent service if an incumbent, community service record if a non-incumbent, sources of financial and political support, personal strengths and weaknesses. An incumbent's list of contributors and expenditures and the FEC report for Federal candidates, can be obtained from either the FEC in Washington, DC or the Secretary of State's office in the State Capitol. There are usually six reports filed by candidates during a campaign year and two or three in the off year. Be sure to obtain all of them for at least the two previous election cycles. The rest of the information can be obtained by talking with community leaders, local Party politicians, the local daily newspaper's political reporter, the Party's national research division, or by checking the files in the daily newspaper's morgue.

Be as thorough and complete regarding your opponent as you can expect your opponent to be regarding you. A Candidate should attempt to know the opponent as well as himself, or herself. A thorough investigation can even uncover the opponent's "hot buttons." Most of us have certain issues that can trigger an overly emotional response. When this happens, mistakes are made, sometimes making a significant difference in how one is perceived, affecting the outcome of the campaign.

Registered Voters List

Obtain a recent copy of an electronic file containing all registered voters in the district to be imported into your database. If this is not available or your campaign is not computerized, obtain a printed copy.

Obtain a recent copy of an electronic file containing all registered voters in the district, by Party and by precinct. If your district does not have the voter list available in electronic format, obtain a printed list. The list is usually available from the local Party headquarters, the County Registrar of Voters, The Board of Elections, or the Secretary of State's office. Ask when the next scheduled update will take place and time your acquisition accordingly, provided the acquisition will not be too late into the campaign year (or no later than February). Most locales update their lists 30 to 60 days following a major election. If this is the case in your district, wait until then and take advantage of the update. Since telephone numbers are optional information on voter registration forms, you will have to allow for time to research the missing telephone numbers that will be needed for your phone bank campaign.

A quality campaign management program like GOTV *Campaign Optimizer* can import and convert this electronic file of voter information, including voting history into its database system for analysis and targeting communication.

Zip Code Map of the District

Obtain a zip code map of the district to assist with the division of your regions and areas and direct mail campaign.

At the local Post Office, you can obtain a zip code map of the district. If this is a rural district, write to all major Post Offices requesting one for their area. Zip codes are the only geographic common denominator in every district throughout the country and all direct mailing firms are keyed to them. If possible, it is cost effective and efficient to structure your internal campaign boundaries, defined by your 5 on 5 Organizational Plan, along these established zip code lines.

Electoral District Map

Obtain a map showing the electoral district boundaries, the precinct designations, and a state legislative map showing Assembly or Senate district lines.

Obtain a map showing the electoral district boundaries and the precinct designations. In addition, obtain a state legislative map showing Assembly or Senate district lines. Ideally, an overlay should be made of these two maps on top of the zip code map before defining the Region and Area boundaries (5 on 5 Plan). If this is not possible, using the zip code map as a base, draw in the electoral district lines and then, with a dotted line, draw in the legislative, or other electoral district boundaries, using the resulting visual to assist in defining your Regions and Areas.

Analysis of The District

Prepare a written analysis of the district.

Prepare a written analysis of the district describing geographic, demographic and political boundaries, and geopolitical makeup. Demographics include race, sex, number, density, economic levels, or Party registration. This information is available from regular and political almanacs and the U.S. Census Tract data, available on the Internet at www.census.gov.

List of Other Elected and Party Officials

Prepare a list of all elected officials from either Party within the electoral district.

A complete campaign management program will have a memo pad related to each record to make memos and notations.

Prepare a list of names, addresses, telephone numbers, and offices held by all elected officials from either Party within the electoral district. Note the Region and Area where they reside. A program like GOTV *Campaign Optimizer* will enable the user to easily make this designation on the voter record. Make notes following each name regarding their political strength, base of support within their political areas, and whether they might be willing to assist you with your campaign. Do the same for all county, city, and district Party chairpersons. Be sure to include any auxiliary groups, such as women's federations or youth groups, especially those on college campuses.

This accumulated data could result in some sensitive political and personal information and should, therefore, be treated confidentially. The information should be entered directly into the campaign's database and password protected for security.

Previous Election Results

Obtain the results from at least the last two election cycles in the district.

While arranging the registered voter information, you can obtain the results from the last two election cycles in the district. When you develop the voter objectives for each precinct, the campaign will need these figures to examine a low, a high, and median vote level for each precinct (PIPS analysis - Precinct Index Prioritization Schedule).

The PIPS analysis is not only used to establish voter objectives, such as the number of votes a Candidate must achieve in each precinct in order to win. It is also used to target Candidate scheduling, direct mail, phone bank activity, and the Get Out The Vote (GOTV) program.

Be sure to include at least one previous race from within this electoral district. If the state does not compile this data in a ready format, select specific races such as a Presidential election, a gubernatorial race, a race for Secretary of State or State Treasurer, or a Congressional race, rather than wasting your time going through reams of unsorted voting results.

Committee Membership Lists

Create lists, organizing the information regarding all campaign committee members.

From your list of supporters, organize the name, address, office and home telephone number, occupation, and employer of all members of the Advisory or Steering, Field Operations, and Finance Committees. This is the first of many lists, other than the registered voters' list, that the campaign will need to develop. When completed, the total number of names and addresses, plus relevant data, will result in many thousands of records for the average campaign. To attempt to manage a data base of this size manually is extremely difficult and inefficient. I strongly recommend that the Candidate obtain a computer system with software designed like GOTV *Campaign Optimizer*, specifically for campaign management. The savings in time and strategic capability will greatly outweigh the cost of the software many times over.

It is also recommended that the Finance Committee should have a list of the leading representatives from the major occupational and professional groups that you plan to solicit, in addition to, a list of the "heavy hitter" types. Include all essential groups such as doctors, dentists, realtors, life insurance agents, builders and contractors, business executives, lawyers, manufacturers, major retail outlets, and producers and distributors from the petroleum industry.

Prospective Major Contributor List

Develop a list of supporters who will contribute $1,000 each to both the primary campaign and the general campaign.

The Candidate should develop a list of supporters who will contribute $1,000 to both the primary campaign and the general campaign. In addition, a list should be developed of prospects that are able to contribute $1,000 to both primary and general campaigns. Do the same for those that will, and those that are prospects to contribute between $500 and $1,000 in each of the same election periods. Be sure to research their names, addresses, telephone numbers, occupations, and employers.

After exhausting the candidate's personal list, tap the personal lists of members of the Finance or Advisory Committee, friends, relatives, acquaintances, and then move on to prospects for major contributions that are not known to anyone, but may be convinced to support your campaign.

Prospective Minor Contributor List

Develop a list of all potential contributors.

Develop a list of all potential contributors.

Campaign Photos

The Candidate should have a series of 5x7 black-and-white glossy photos taken in various poses, standing, sitting behind a desk, head and shoulders or 3/4 turn, in dark suit, white shirt, and conservative tie for a man or a business

The Candidate should have a series of black-and-white glossy photos taken in various poses.

ensemble for a woman. Have a series of family portraits taken in both formal and informal poses. Some should be formally dressed indoors and others in casual clothes outdoors. I strongly recommend having a professional photographer take these photographs.

In addition, research the family photo albums and pull out good pictures with others such as parents, family, children, senior citizens, or those illustrating community activities.

Filing with Federal (State) Election Commission

Schedule and file Federal or State election filing forms.

Record the pertinent information regarding the Candidate, Campaign Committee, its officers, the Chairperson, Treasurer, Assistant Treasurer, the location where the campaign's books, and records will be kept and relevant campaign banking information. It will be necessary to file this information according to the election regulations regarding the office that is vied for. I recommend calling the committee by the Candidate's Name and the Office you are running for Committee, e.g., Guzzetta for Congress Committee.

Arrange a large delivery box at the Post Office closest to the future site of the campaign headquarters. While there, obtain a Bulk Mailing Permit for the election year, which will cost about $125 for the application fee and $125 for the permit.

Although it may be too soon to install a headquarters telephone line, arrange to reserve a number for the campaign in an exchange area where the campaign headquarters will be located. Be sure to discuss any additional lines and service features that will be required for the phone bank installation.

Position Papers

Develop position papers on relevant issues.

If a Federal candidate, complete an opinion paper on the state of the economy, unemployment, defense, a balanced budget, taxes, abortion, school subsidies, crime, drug related issues, foreign trade, farming, business, welfare reform, gun control, senior citizen issues, social security, health insurance, communications with constituents, and any other subject of particular concern to this campaign or your district. If running for a non-Federal office, pick subjects from the list that are applicable to the particular office for which you are running. The Candidate should state the highlights of the problem as he or she sees it, tell what the opponent has or has not done or proposes to do and then develop, in general terms, what he or she would like to see done and specifically how he or she would accomplish the improved circumstance. Use all of the hard data and statistical information available, *but in all cases be certain of the accuracy of the facts.*

The national and state parties will prove to be gold mines for research data on many of these issues. Contact the appropriate ideological and association PAC's for their assistance. These organizations are usually very eager to share their research. The local library should have a copy of the national directory of associations and their addresses. The Internet is an excellent source for this research.

Wherever possible, position papers are best kept to 1,000 words or less. When the Candidate is satisfied with the results and has the position papers in final form, he or she might want to consider having them bound. I have had clients do this in some campaigns and it makes a very professional looking package, facilitating their use. The binding does not have to be expensive.

Web Site and Design

Many of today's voters and *all of tomorrow's* are not only connected, but also likely to be Internet dependent.

As stated earlier, the Internet is the fastest growing form of media communication in the world today. If you are not familiar with it, and its use, arrange formal training to bring your understanding and skill "up to speed." Be cognitive of the fact that television is to the baby boomer, as the Internet is to the generations that followed.

Owning and operating a web site is not as difficult or as mysterious as it may seem at first. It is simply an electronic address in cyberspace, where the public can come to visit at their leisure, stay as long as it holds their interest, and return as often as they want. Most importantly, the visit, stay, and gained insight cost the visitor virtually nothing more than the time that they invested.

Your first step will be to reserve a domain name and associated address (analogous to a postal box, only electronic). Many Internet Providers will do this on your behalf. There will be a charge associated with the name search (the name must be unique) and setup. A monthly charge will apply for the "rental" of the "cyberspace" domain address and space usage. There are as many pricing "plans" as there are providers. You should attempt to register a name associated closely to the Campaign Committee name. Your Internet Provider will assist you with the name search. Your Internet address will appear in the format www.websitename.com. Once registered and setup, anyone who has access to the Internet across the street or around the world, will be able to visit your site or contact you through your web e-mail (electronic mail) address. The e-mail address will also be unique to you. Most plans will allow a number of e-mail accounts, which can be personalized for the essential personnel within the campaign structure. A general e-mail address, such as info@websitename.com can be used for general inquiries.

Anyone who has access to the Internet across the street or around the world, will be able to visit your site or contact you through your web e-mail (electronic mail) address.

After the web site is arranged, a firm or individual must be contracted to manage your web site as the campaign progresses. The web master will be responsible for designing the web site, building the web pages, and keeping the information fresh, interesting, and updated. You must find someone with whom you feel compatible, who will give you sound advice, and valuable results regarding the development of a successful web site. The number of visitors that are attracted to the site measures success; more important may be, how long they stay. These statistics will be available through your Internet web site provider.

District Media Outlets

Prepare a list of all media outlets (radio, TV, magazines, and newspapers) that have any impact on your electoral district.

Create a Media list containing the names of the editor, manager, political reporters, publisher, or owner of each. Find out what their history has been regarding the type and amount of coverage for the opponent and past candidates. Find out if they endorse candidates and what local politicians think about the importance and impact of that endorsement. Measure this impact further through your polling company or initial focus groups. Obtain the necessary names by simply calling them. Make a list or key this information into your database. Your campaign software program should have a special record section for this data.

Press Kits should be prepared in advance, containing all the information that will be required by the media outlets. The kits should be first distributed at the candidacy announcement.

After the list of media outlets is organized, the Press Kits can be prepared and personalized to distribute to media contacts attending the announcement and to the balance of media contacts later. The kit should contain the following:

a) the candidates biography,
b) a 3 x 5 glossy photo,
c) the position booklet or six of the major issue papers,
d) a copy of the campaign brochure,
e) a copy of the announcement speech, and
f) a cover letter volunteering to provide any additional information, if needed, and a solicitation of their endorsement.

Potential Volunteers

Develop a list of people who might volunteer to work for the campaign.

Develop a list of volunteers, including their address, occupation, place of employment, and telephone number. This group is in addition to the people already asked to chair the various committees.

Naturally, entering names directly into a database will save considerable management time later. If the campaign does not have a computer with a campaign software program, like GOTV *Campaign Optimizer*, create 3 x 5 volunteer cards to be sorted and filed by zip code. The cards will be distributed later to the appropriate members of the Field Operations Committee for use in recruitment and task assignments.

District Telephone Directories

Obtain copies of all yellow page directories covering the district.

Obtain several copies of the yellow page directories and the crisscross directory. These directories are much easier to use when looking up telephone numbers at the phone bank. Since they are usually available only by subscription, the campaign may have to borrow some from a local real estate or insurance office. Looking up telephone numbers, even with a crisscross directory, is a very tedious and time-consuming project. If the electoral district has more than 10,000 homes with registered voters, I strongly recommend that the campaign have the numbers tele-matched to the electronic registered voter files by a local computer service bureau.

Possible Staff Personnel

Develop a list of people who might serve as staff personnel.

Develop a list of people who might be available in-district, preferably with campaign experience, to serve as the Campaign Manager, the Field Operations Director, the Campaign Secretary, the Bookkeeper/Secretary, the Media Secretary, and as Driver/Aide. These people will certainly not be paid well, in fact, in many cases they will be volunteers. Nonetheless, they are critically important to the campaign's success. They must be bright, talented, reasonably well educated, of good character, personable, able to manage others, and must have a strong sense of dedication and purpose.

Discuss each person with the Political Campaign Consultant before making any offers or commitments. Incidentally, Federal law, as well as the law in most states, prohibits any Candidate for public office from promising a government position to anyone in exchange for their support. It is not a stretch to believe that a promise of any job, of any kind after the election, since they worked on the campaign, would also breach this law. Be safe and make no promises.

If the campaign is having difficulty recruiting the right people from within the district, you might check for referrals with the state and national party, or with one of the many campaign institutes around the country. Frequently, they will have the names of talented and well-trained people who are seeking campaign positions throughout the state or country.

Centers of Influence List

Prepare a list of all Centers of Influence within the district.

A list of Centers of Influence will include community leaders such as religious leaders, civic leaders, presidents of civic clubs, homeowners' associations, PTA's, community leaders at local country clubs, editors, media station managers, key reporters, directors of service, or senior citizen clubs to name a few categories. Enter this data into your database or on 3 x 5 cards. On each card, put their address, telephone number, and Region / Area number as well. Much of this information is available at the City Hall, the Chamber of Commerce, or from the county Party.

Local Party Volunteers and Contributors

Obtain lists of contributors and volunteers from state, county, and city party headquarters.

Contact either the Chairperson or Executive Director at the state, city, and county party headquarters. Ask if they will share their lists of party volunteers and financial contributors in the district and state. Many will be cooperative. Alternatively, a good list of potential contributors can be obtained at the Secretary of State's office from all state candidates' contributor lists filed in the last 4 years. Enter these names into the database or on 3 x 5 cards. Separate the names by in-district and out-of-district (OD).

Federal law prohibits anyone from soliciting contributions from people whose names are taken from an FEC report.

Many states do not prohibit soliciting contributions from people whose names are taken from state financial reports. Usually, someone who has contributed to a state Candidate, regardless of the office, is a good prospect for contributing.

The Campaign Colors

Part of the campaign logo is the color or combination of colors used in campaign graphics. After a while, the viewer identifies the logo with the Candidate and the campaign without necessarily being conscious of the actual message.

Select the campaign color scheme.

Red, white, and blue are overused. Get professional assistance from your graphic designer. There is no regulation that states that the Candidate should not be happy with his or her own campaign colors, as long as they send an appropriate message. Check out the possibilities with a professional. Enjoy the break, for a change, this task can be enjoyable.

Personal Campaign Activity Preferences

The Candidate should consider the preferred types of campaign activity.

Before the Political Game Plan is developed, a Candidate should give some thought to the types of campaign activities that are preferred and to any kind of campaign activities that the Candidate has an aversion to. If possible, the Political Game Plan can be developed avoiding the aversions of the Candidate as much as possible. Rarely is any particular campaign style essential to the outcome of the election.

The Family Role

Consider the family's role.

Consider how active a role the Candidate's spouse, children, and family in general will play in the campaign. Is there any type of normal campaign activity that they cannot, or will not do?

Fairs, Festivals, and Parades

Prepare a master calendar of public events.

Prepare a Master Calendar illustrating the dates and times of local fairs, parades, festivals, and major public events. This information is usually available at the Parks and Recreation Department or City Clerk's Office. Strong political campaign software will incorporate a scheduler, day timer, and calendar within the program. Activities should be cross-referenced against the Region and Areas, which will host the activity.

Restrictions on Contributions

Assess any need to place restrictions on the source or amount of campaign contributions.

For any reason, does the campaign or Candidate need to place any restrictions on the source or amount of campaign contributions? Discuss this with any advisors and essential members of the Advisory Committee and Financial Committee. Remember that you do not want this to become a campaign issue. In some districts, the opponent could develop accepting money from a tobacco or oil company into a serious campaign issue, while in other districts, it might not mean anything. Regardless of what is decided, think these issues through very carefully. The aggravation and loss of votes may not be worth the dollars received. In addition, a Candidate needs to be very careful about public announcements, since it is hard to change your position after the fact.

Campaigning Time Available

Consider the actual time available for campaigning.

On the Master Calendar, aside from scheduling fairs, parades, etc., calculate on a day by day basis, how much time the Candidate will be able to spend actively campaigning or raising funds. The time spent actively campaigning is one of the advantages that a challenger has over an incumbent. Use it wisely.

Presuming an uncontested Primary, most candidates will try to arrange their schedules so they are able to spend about 20 hours a week on the campaign through May, and full time from then until the election. Make whatever arrangements are necessary, both at work and with the family, to accomplish this.

The Candidate Campaign Wardrobe

Candidates should assess both themselves and their wardrobe.

Candidates should assess both themselves and their wardrobe. If their wardrobe is not adequate or does not present the image that people expect of an elected official, find a quality local clothing store and ask the manager to assist in selecting an appropriate wardrobe. Stay with darker colors and conservative styles. Unfair as this may be, all visual characteristics should be considered carefully. On a male candidate, long hair and/or facial hair are known to be examples of visual characteristics that will change a finite percentage of prospect supporters into firm votes for the opponent. All similar characteristics within ones control should be considered in light of the votes that may be lost because of a choice regarding personal style.

Chapter 4 - Development of the Game Plan

Internal Preparation

A Candidate should spend time preparing mentally for the grueling campaign that lies ahead.

The next 12 months will likely be the most demanding on not only his or her personal life, but the lives of everyone in the family as well. He or she will spend 12 to 16 hours a day, 6 days a week, sometimes 7, focusing every moment on campaigning.

The Candidate's life is going to emulate a fishbowl where total strangers will constantly challenge, probe, ridicule, and question every aspect therein. No matter how nice a candidate is in reality, there will be those who will tear him or her down, more than likely because he or she is simply daring to challenge their personal choice for the same office. Cynics are going to hold suspect almost everything that is said. Doors will be slammed in your face and you will be constantly subjected to defending yourself against misstated quotes in the local newspaper. The Candidate must to learn to enjoy both "rubber chicken" dinners and panhandling for campaign donations. In addition, you can count on your opponents direct or indirect attack on you for your views and/or lack of experience each day.

The opponent is going to do everything possible to shake your resolve and to push your "hot buttons" in the hope that you will make a mistake.

If I have not scared a potential Candidate out of the race by now and he or she is still determined to run this gauntlet that we call the campaign process, then take this advice to heart. While you still have the chance, escape for a few days to think about yourself, your beliefs, and why you are doing this. Just as an athlete conditions the mind, body, and emotions for the event ahead, you too must prepare yourself. The opponent is going to do everything possible to shake your resolve and to push your "hot buttons" in the hope that you will make a mistake.

Few Political Campaign Consultants could not relate a story or two about a Candidate who collapsed either physically or emotionally in the latter stages of a campaign. All too often, it happens. Strengthen yourself before your campaign begins and schedule re-energizing time for yourself and with your family throughout the campaign. Set your schedule to avoid any possibility of "burning out" before reaching the finish line.

The Campaign Headquarters

Plan your campaign headquarters.

As the formal announcement date approaches, plan your campaign headquarters. The headquarters should have at least four private offices in addition to the common or reception area, totaling about 2,000 sq. ft. Make installation arrangements with the telephone company for the previously reserved lines and telephone system features. Do not forget to consider your line needs regarding modem access to the Internet (telephone or cable).

In another location, preferably a storefront facility, the campaign should arrange to set up the phone bank, if it is going to use one. This facility becomes the volunteers' headquarters. It should be at least 1,500 sq. ft. and have at least one private office. The central area should be arranged to accommodate the telephone lines and a work area for processing mail. Normally, a phone bank for a Congressional level campaign would have at least 10 telephone lines for calling voters and 2 lines for routine calling in and out.

If AT&T, MCI, Sprint or a similar long-distance service company is available in the district, arrange for it on the main telephone number. The savings on long distance calls to PAC's, Washington, or the state capitol can be substantial. I also recommend that the campaign look into the possibility of purchasing, or leasing, the actual telephone units from one of the many telephone stores around today. A campaign can usually save a considerable amount by doing this instead of leasing the units from the telephone company. Be sure to choose a location where exchanges are available to reach all parts of the district without long distance charges. Investigate and eliminate pro rated charges, such as a charge per number of calls made.

Scrounge, wherever possible, for office furniture. Churches, old office buildings, or law firms are often good sources for donations. Be careful and specific with the terms regarding donated items. Check out what you plan to do with the FEC or Secretary of State to be sure it is not a violation and is considered a contribution-in-kind. If a non-Federal Candidate, check with the Secretary of State's office or the appropriate election law official in your state.

Basic Campaign Headquarters Equipment

Here is a checklist of the basic equipment that the campaign office will require:

1 Memory Typewriter
6 Desks, chairs, tables, and file cabinets
1 Medium-sized Copier with 10 bin sorter and collator
1 Tape Cassette Recorder with a Telephone Coupler
1 Stamp Machine with Automatic Sealer
1 Refrigerator
1 Automatic Coffee maker
1 Pentium based computer system with campaign software like GOTV *Campaign Optimizer* and two laser printers. Larger campaigns will require more than one computer and the likelihood of networking several machines together. The disk space in any event should exceed 20 gigabytes and memory not less than 64 MB. Other accessories to consider would be a zip drive and or CD-RW disc drive.
4 Cell Phones (or whatever number is required to connect all key personnel with the candidate at all times)

Every Candidate for political office, regardless of the size of the electoral district, should obtain a personal computer with the appropriate software as the first campaign acquisition.

I strongly recommend that any Candidate for political office, regardless of the size of the electoral district or type of office, obtain a personal computer with the appropriate software as the first campaign acquisition. You should have already noted while reading this manual, the degree to which the preparatory work requires that you enter research into a database for future access. Based on the workload that a computer can manage and the time that it can save, a computer is a very inexpensive commodity. Give consideration to used equipment. Since technology is moving at such an incredible rate, there is always used equipment available that will be offered at substantial savings. Your computer system does not need to be leading edge technology, but should support a Windows 95 or later operating system.

Somewhat more important than the specifications of the computer, is the software on the computer. Software developed specifically for campaign management is available from several companies. Some companies, lease a "permission for temporary use" license over their product at a monthly or yearly stipend, while others sell a "user license" outright. The logistics regarding this option are similar to those associated with the lease or purchase of any capital equipment.

A candidate should not be surprised if a company will not lease to his or her political campaign, as most will not. One solution is to sublease items from a commercial firm friendly to his or her candidacy; another would be to sign the lease personally.

Newspaper Clipping Service and Files

Research the daily newspaper's morgue

Research the daily newspaper's morgue and make copies of all newspaper articles related to the Candidate and the opponent during the last 4 years. Then, either retain a local newspaper clipping service (about $80 a month) or have a volunteer begin clipping all articles on the Candidate and his or her opponent and maintain a file for future reference.

Preparation Summary

The preceding line items constitute the preparatory activity. Everything outlined in this chapter is necessary and useful in some facet of the campaign. I have tried to avoid those activities or items based on theory or the unlimited number of variables in a campaign. Much of it must be done by December 15th, in the year before the election. It should be apparent by now, with the level of work required to prepare for the campaign, that the sooner a Candidate starts, the better will be his or her chances for victory.

I would point out that a Candidate can usually arrange for his or her Political Campaign Consultant to accumulate much of this data, but like anything else, it will cost the campaign in extra fees. As it is, the analysis of all this material will require at least 80 hours of the consultant's time. It must be accomplished before a Political Game Plan can be developed and is usually one of the reasons a consultant's base fee is so high.

A campaign plan is only as good as the research upon which it is based. Be thorough, complete, and accurate. The time, energy, and money will be well spent.

There is a saying in the computer industry that "you only get out what you put in," or put another way, "garbage in, garbage out." This cliche is also very appropriate in the campaign industry. *A campaign plan is only as good as the research upon which it is based. Be thorough, complete, and accurate. The time, energy, and money will be well spent.*

Most of these suggestions are constants in a good campaign and in many cases will help determine the strategy, Political Game Plan, implementation, actions, and therefore, the outcome of the election.

Candidate Checklist

I developed a checklist for candidates outlining items that the candidate needs to arrange for and send to the Political Campaign Consultant or Advisor.

1) Prepare a detailed biography and self-evaluation of personal strengths and weaknesses.
2) Prepare biographies of wife, children, and parents.
3) Prepare a statement of at least 1,000 words on why you are running for this office.

4) Prepare an appraisal of your opponent, his or her voting record; if an incumbent send constituent services, sources of financial and political support, personal and political strengths and weaknesses.
5) If available from your Registrar of Voters, obtain and send a list of all registered voters in the District, by Party and Precinct. If not available in electronic file format, send a hard copy of the data.
6) Send a ZIP code map of the District.
7) Send a Congressional and Legislative Precinct map of the District.
8) Develop and send a list, identified by Party, showing name, address, and telephone number of elected officials within the District.
9) Send the names of your County and District Party Chairpersons with comments regarding strength and potential support.
10) Send previous results of the last two election cycles, by Precinct, for Presidential, U.S. Senate, U.S. Representative, Governor, and Secretary of State, plus the office for which you are running.
11) Prepare a written analysis of the District, describing geographic, demographic, and political boundaries and characteristics. Demographics include race, ethnic origin, economic levels, and population density.
12) Send name, address, telephone number, occupation, and employer of all members of finance and advisory committees.
13) Send 3" x 5" black and white glossy photos, formal and informal, of self and with family.
14) Send the name of your campaign committee, its officers, and P. O. Box number. Ask the telephone company to reserve a number in the area where headquarters will be located. Obtain bulk permit mailing number from Post Office for current year and send the number. If you have not already done so, file your Committee with the Clerk of the House, Washington, DC and the appropriate State office. They will also need to know the name of your Committee's bank and its account number. I suggest opening two accounts when necessary; one designated Primary Account and the other General Account. Register a domain name for the Candidate web site and contract the services of a web master.
15) Develop position papers on the subjects of inflation, unemployment, defense, taxes, abortion, school subsidies, crime, drugs, foreign trade, farm problems, business, welfare, arms reduction, balanced budget, and any other subjects of particular interest to you or your District. Send them to your Political Consultant or Advisor by January 1st.
16) Develop a list of at least thirty (30) people whom you are certain will contribute at least $1,000 to your campaign before and after the Primary election. Do the same for those who will give between $500 and $1,000. Send a copy of the list to your Political Consultant or Advisor and begin soliciting them during November and December. Include the telephone number, occupation, and place of employment.
17) Develop a list of all potential contributors including friends, relatives, and any acquaintance who might give any amount. Be sure to give complete addresses, telephone numbers, occupation, and place of employment. Enter this list and the names of those above, into a database and send a copy to your Political Consultant or Advisor by January 10th.
18) Send a list of major media outlets, radio, TV, and newspapers, daily or weekly, in the District. Indicate what their past history has been regarding types of coverage for an incumbent or challenger. Do they endorse, and if so, what is your opinion of the impact the endorsement has on the District?

19) Develop and send a list of *all* people who will volunteer to work for you on this campaign. Rate them from 1 to 10 (10 being those who will "slave" for you and 1 being those who will put up a yard sign). Be sure to include addresses, occupations, and telephone number of these people.
20) Send a copy of all telephone books, Yellow and White pages, covering your District.
21) Call *Congressional Quarterly* or *LEGI-SLATE* in Washington, DC and order a copy of the *Opposition Research* book on your opponent and have it sent to your Political Consultant or Advisor. They will copy pertinent pages and forward them to you along with comments.
22) Advise if you have anyone in mind, preferably with campaign experience, to be your Campaign Manager, Field Coordinator, and Campaign Secretary. If you do, ask them to send a biography on themselves to your Political Consultant or Advisor before January 15th. If not, let them know by January 1st so they can begin a search at their end.
23) Contact State and County Party headquarters and see if they will share lists of financial contributors with you. If not, visit the Secretary of State's office in the State Capitol and make copies of all major State candidates' contributors' lists in the last 4 years and send them to your Political Consultant or Advisor, unless that is specifically prohibited by State law.
24) Prepare a list in the database of *all* Centers of Influence within your District, such as, religious leaders, civic leaders, presidents of civic clubs, editors, station managers, key reporters of print and electronic media, directors of service and senior citizen clubs, and nursing homes by January 15th. Most of this information is available at City Hall or the Chamber of Commerce.
25) Make them aware of any campaign color preferences you have.
26) Make them aware of any campaign activity that you have an aversion to.
27) Make them aware of the role that your spouse, children, or parents will play in the campaign.
28) When are your local fairs, parades, or festivals? Let them know by January 15th.
29) Let them know if you feel that you need to place any restrictions on the source or amount of your campaign contributions.
30) Make them aware of how much time you will be able to devote to campaigning. Break it down by month, starting in January.
31) Arrange a central headquarters and a "storefront" by January 15th, to be opened by February 15th. Central headquarters should have at least 4 private offices plus a common area of about 2,000 sq. ft. and the storefront should have at least 1 office and 1,500 sq. ft. of common area.
32) Report on arrangements with the telephone company for 4 rotating lines, plus hold on 5 units, one in each office plus 1 for the receptionist, 1 dedicated line for the computer, and 10 single lines for the phone bank in the storefront, plus 2 lines for incoming and outgoing calls. Installation should be by February 15th.
33) Report on the arrangements for headquarters furniture.
34) Report on the arrangements for 4 computers with printers, Pentium with 20GB Hard Disk, 1 Memory typewriter, 1 medium-sized copy machine with sorter and 10 bin collator, 1 good tape recorder with telephone coupler, 1 used refrigerator, 1 coffee maker, and 1 mailing machine with automatic sealer. All should be delivered by February 15th, except for one computer, which must be on hand at the start of campaign planning.

All of the above must be completed by December 15th unless otherwise indicated. The formal announcement that you are a candidate will be made during the 1st or 2nd week of March.

35) Research the main newspaper morgue and copy all newspaper articles on you and your opponent during the last 4 years. Begin clipping all articles on you and your opponent and maintain a file to be sent when required.

Chapter 4 - Word Index

Chapter 5
Implementing the Campaign

A Time for Action

Defining the Problem / Finding the Solution

Why is it difficult to define campaign strategy? Because every variable creates its own nuances and subsequent need for a different set of responses.

As we are learning, there are many variables determining campaign strategy. In fact, the variations make it virtually impossible to write a Manual that can define a specific strategy to be employed in all campaigns. Every combination of factors, every variable creates its own nuances and subsequent need for a different set of responses.

Variables include the demographic and geographic composition of a district, the length of time an incumbent has been in office, the number of times a challenger has run, the name ID rating of the incumbent and challenger, the Favorability ratings for both, the availability, dedication, and skill of volunteers, the political, sociological, and economic conditions prevalent at the time, the political philosophies of the incumbent and challenger, the availability and cost factors of media outlets in the district, whether this is an incumbent or open seat campaign, the base of financial support available to the incumbent and challenger, the physical appearances and endurance levels of the candidates, the public speaking skills of both individuals, whether it is a Presidential election year or an off year, whether it is a special election or a regularly scheduled one, and I can go on and on and on and on, ad infinitum.

Sorting through these situational combinations and permutations, with experience, is the most valuable contribution that a professional Political Campaign Consultant makes to the campaign.

The factors and situational combinations are seemingly endless. It is in this area, probably more so than any other, that a professional Political Campaign Consultant is most valuable to the Candidate and his or her campaign. For a novice or relatively inexperienced individual to attempt to develop a sound strategy and Political Game Plan amongst all these variables, is not only difficult, but because of the financial cost of a campaign, it is also very risky. Between cash outlays, time, energy, and effort, the average Congressional campaign is currently valued at $1.2 million. This is an awful lot to risk on hunches and uneducated guesses. In addition, a political campaign, unlike a business, can not make a mistake and subsequently correct it without disastrous results. The campaign has only one chance to win the election. A prudent person will do everything possible to make that chance their best chance.

Two Basic Groups of Voters - Two Methodologies

Voters can be divided into two groups, the “above average” voters and “average” voters.

Extensive studies done by the University of Michigan, following every major election since the mid-1940’s, indicate there are two groups of voters. They are sometimes referred to as the “intelligent” and “non-intelligent” voters, or the “educated” and “uneducated” voters. I find these labels insensitive and therefore refer to the two groups as the “above average” and “average” voters.

In these studies, the average voter is usually described as the one who votes for a Candidate based on the following characteristics, in the following order of priority,

Studies indicate that approximately 86% of voters are "average" voters, leaving only 14% in the "above average" group.

1) name ID;
2) Party;
3) the assumed religion, nationality, race, or sense of familiarity with the name of the Candidate by virtue of previous experiences, i.e., they knew someone in their past with that name;
4) indiscriminate patterns, and
5) an automatic vote for or against all incumbents.

The above average voter is a person who knows one or more things about the Candidate over and above the preceding characteristics. These same studies also indicate that approximately 86% of voters are "average" voters, leaving only 14% in the "above average" group.

The results of these studies deserve serious consideration. Assuming these figures are accurate, and frankly I believe the above average group to be slightly smaller, especially as you go below the Congressional level, *86% of the voters know virtually nothing of substance about the person for whom they are voting.* They will usually have a positive, negative, or neutral feeling about the individual but relatively speaking, will know nothing about where the Candidate stands on the issues. Incidentally, the percentage of above average voters was only 6% in the 1940's. The 14% estimate indicates a slow improvement. The improvement is likely a result of the major increase in media coverage.

Fundamentally, two groups necessitate two strategies. One strategy must be directed to all voters and the other must be directed at voters in the above average category.

The strategic elements to be incorporated because of these findings must be recognized in order to develop a successful Political Game Plan. In a "landslide" election, elements are obviously in play that stimulate both average and above average voters to vote for the same candidate. On the other hand, in a close election, we can assume that winning the majority of the above average voters will determine the outcome. *Consequently, two strategies must be developed and implemented, one in conjunction with the other. One strategy must be directed to all voters and the other must be directed to voters in the above average category.*

A Prototype Plan

The Parameters

Ultimately, the strategies developed are dependent on the factors previously discussed. To demonstrate the process used in determining the strategy and Political Game Plan, I will develop a prototype campaign plan based on a Congressional Candidate, under the following conditions:

1) running with no previous experience, no seriously contested primary;
2) a statistically insignificant name ID rating. In any given poll, a statistically insignificant rating is +12% rating. Almost universally, any name will elicit this positive (+12%) response since a finite percentage of people do not want to appear ignorant to the pollster. This factor is considered insignificant because *any name* would receive around 12%.

3) in an urban/suburban district. For political offices below the statewide level, there are essentially four types of electoral districts: urban, urban/suburban, suburban, and rural.
4) a relatively self-contained media market;
5) a relatively good base of potential volunteer and financial support to build on;
6) an average district, slightly skewed toward the industrial side.

In addition, the Congressional Candidate is a political moderate and fiscal conservative. He or she is well educated, successful in business or profession, a good family person with no skeletons in the closet, average personality, excellent character, average looking, and not overly dynamic. For our study, the opponent's Favorability rating is a "soft" 50%, (meaning he or she does not elicit a strong emotional response from the voters in the district) and a "hard" name ID rating of 90% (meaning 90% in the district can name this person without any prompting by a pollster).

Building Name ID

You can be certain that a Candidate, who does not achieve equality with the opponent in name ID by the election, will lose.

As I have stated, the name ID rating measures the percentage of polled voters that recognize the name of a particular candidate at any given moment. Unless affected by extenuating circumstances, such as a scandal that would increase the name ID dramatically, but decrease the Favorability rating equally, you can be certain that a Candidate who does not achieve equality with the opponent in name ID by the election, will lose.

Name ID can be built in a variety of ways that place a name and the office vied for in the public's view over an extended period. Radio, TV, billboard and newspaper ads, bus signs, magnetic vehicle signs, lawn signs, window signs, bumper stickers, press releases, news conferences, personal campaigning, brochures, printed tabloids, direct mail, and Internet Web Sites are the most common vehicles.

Both FEC law and most state laws require a disclaimer on most public advertising stating who authorized and paid for the advertisement.

A gradual escalation of coverage by a combination of advertising methods proves to be very effective and cost efficient for most candidates. In the 2nd and 3rd Stages of the campaign, use a combination of billboards, lawn signs, window signs, bus signs, magnetic vehicle signs, bumper stickers, brochures, personal campaigning, the candidate's web site, direct mail, press releases, and news conferences. During the 4th and 5th Stages, add more direct mail pieces in conjunction with tabloids, newspaper ads, Radio, and TV commercials (if utilized). In the late stages, continue with direct mail, especially directed toward the above average voter and phone bank execution should assure the Candidate of a 90 percent name ID rating by the week before the election.

Since one of the primary objectives is to build name ID, as opposed to raising issues, billboards and signs should contain the name of the Candidate, the office being sought, and the web address if one exists. A graphic symbol and/or campaign slogan is optional. Normally, a motorist has only 4 seconds to read a sign making more than a few words (six to eight) a waste, or even counterproductive. Avoid the use of photos in the first advertising series and change the poster paper and locations every 3 months (this schedule assumes

Definition
The "rotation" refers to the advertising rotation, i.e., the three month schedule regarding message, poster paper renewal, and location.

a 9-month "showing" from Feb. 4 through Nov. 4), keeping the campaign fresh. It is also wise to make several editions of the same message and "rotate" each throughout the district. In advertising, the three month schedule regarding message, poster paper renewal, and location is actually referred to as the "rotation."

In the second series, the Candidate should introduce his or her portrait. The photo must be a quality, black and white portrait, professionally done so that the resolution will be at an acceptable level for the application. The third and final series should be similar to the first and consistent with the graphic look used on all other stationery and signs being distributed in the final 3 months. It is strongly recommended that the poster artwork be shown to the billboard company before having it printed. The billboard companies are usually more than willing to help with the decision making process and can save you from making any costly errors. Some companies have their own art departments and can do the art layout on behalf of the campaign.

Always, ask for the GRP rating of any display. Advertising companies periodically test the traffic flow for each billboard site and will be able to tell you accurately what the total showing should produce.

Normally, ten billboards strategically placed around the district will produce a 50 percent GRP rating (Gross Rating Points) in a district of this type. A 50 percent GRP means that about 50 percent of the district's motorists on the roads in any given day will see at least one of the billboards. If locations can be found and local sign ordinances permit their erection, the campaign should supplement the billboards with miniature duplicates of the billboards produced by a local silk-screen company on 4 x 8 sheets of plywood or corrugated boards. By placing them in carefully targeted areas, billboards and 4 x 8 corrugated signs will enable you to pinpoint the voters that you are trying to reach. Twenty or thirty of these signs throughout the district are very effective. If you erect the signs with metal poles, they will last longer and will resist the damage of vandalism.

To successfully increase the name ID rating, a Candidate must achieve a high saturation on a continuous basis.

The campaign is not only in competition with hundreds of commercial products, other candidates are being advertised daily as well. It takes maximum saturation to penetrate the consciousness of the average voter against this massive bombardment. It is for this reason that I am not in favor of radio and TV during the early stages of the campaign. It is very expensive in comparison to sign coverage, making it difficult to attain any similar saturation point.

The Candidate's personal campaigning activities (speaking before groups or press conferences) will act as a supplement to the campaign sign coverage. The most important of these personal activities are appearances in the newspapers and on radio and TV news programs. In addition, the newsworthy appearances are of greater impact, especially with the above average voters.

Never apologize for your name or the sound of your name.

Since there is nothing that a person should have to do about the sound of his or her name, nothing should be done. Never apologize for your name or the sound of your name. I have seen candidates try to make self-deprecating remarks about their particularly ethnic sounding name only to have it boomerang on them. There is also not much a Candidate can do about his or her Party label in a partisan race. It must appear on the ballot or voting machine. However, if it would be a liability in the district because of overwhelming registration by the opposite Party, it can be lightly diffused by not calling attention to it on the graphic and electronic advertising. In this Prototype Plan, the voter registration by Party is 2 to 1 against the Candidate. Therefore, we will not be calling attention to his or her Party affiliation. Incidentally, the FEC law, which supersedes state laws on this subject, does not require the naming of the Candidate's Party on public advertising. Speaking frankly, with 30 - 40 percent of voters today claiming to be independent, either Party label can be a liability. When the campaign does its 1st Stage direct mail and the GOTV program, the Candidate will be making an appeal to his or her own party members for support and that should be sufficient.

Both FEC law and most state laws require a disclaimer on most public advertising stating who authorized and paid for the advertisement.

Creating a Favorable Impression

It is almost equally important for a Candidate to create a favorable impression in conjunction with a positive name ID rating.

In order to increase the Favorability rating, the Candidate is dependent on direct mail, the volunteer program, free media coverage, personal campaigning in the early and middle stages, and the TV and radio commercials in the final month of the campaign. During the 2nd and 3rd Stages, the Candidate should endeavor to take part in many public activities and enjoy the growth in the voter recognition factor. The candidate must be sure to avoid any activity that might result in creating a negative feeling. Always stay on the middle ground if possible and do not let the opponent or the media label him or her as an ultra this or that, or as a negative candidate.

With all this done, the Candidate in our Prototype Campaign will have effectively neutralized the opponent's advantageous high name ID rating and the average voter group as expected will split evenly on Election Day. The outcome will be decided by the 14 percent of above average voters, that is, the voters who will vote for a Candidate because of his or her respective positions on an issue or issues of concern to them.

Communications with the Above Average Voters

Having equalized the name ID rating and Favorability rating, the average voter group can be expected to split evenly and the outcome will be decided by the (14%) above average voters.

Communication with the above average voter regarding the Candidate's position on the issues and the opponent's voting record is the second basic strategy. There are two approaches to successfully handle this strategic discipline: the "catch all" method (sometimes referred to as the shotgun method) and the "targeted" method (sometimes referred to as the "rifle" method).

Every effort must be made to identify the above average voters in your district. How well the campaign accomplishes its objectives among this group usually determines the outcome. This is why so many serious campaign elections are determined by 5 percent or less of the final vote and frankly, it is why so few incumbents are really that secure. It is not so much that incumbents beat challengers, but more often than not, the challengers beat themselves by failing to give the appropriate attention in terms of money, energy, and effort to both basic groups of voters. Invariably, they will focus on one and exclude or minimally address the other.

How successfully the campaign identifies and targets the above average voters usually determines the outcome.

Unfortunately, since it is only possible to identify a part of this group, a considerable amount of time, effort, and money must be spent directing a detailed message about the relative positions and differences between the candidates to a larger segment of the voting public. The most cost effective vehicle for this communication is direct mail. In a letter containing a flyer or brochure, or in a tabloid format, a Candidate has the space necessary to cover several pertinent points about the issues. These are the details that the above average voters want and need before making their decision. A 30 or 60 second TV or radio commercial essentially projects an impression, but a printed message projects substance.

Since many of the above average voters are in the middle to higher socio-economic levels, the campaign can save money by using zip codes to target its mail more effectively. Watch carefully for communities that are going through a redevelopment program, as they will usually have a significant mix of all socio-economic groups. This is where some of the preliminary research outlined will pay off. This method is similar to the "Claritis System" developed by the late Matt Reese who was a founder and godfather of the professional political consulting business. During a career that spanned more than three decades, he worked in more than 450 political campaigns in the United States and abroad. Among his candidates were Senators Edward M. Kennedy (D-Mass.), Robert F. Kennedy (D-N.Y.), Russell Long (D-La.), Charles S. Robb (D-Va.) and John Glenn (D-Ohio); House Speaker Thomas P. "Tip" O'Neill Jr. (D-Mass.); and several governors and local officials.

If possible, Radio and TV talk show programs, videos, public debates with the opponent, and interviews with people who are Centers of Influence should be arranged, in addition to, printed communication.

Most incumbents do not invest their resources on the above average voter since incumbents have campaigned previously, sent franking mail through their elected office, and have a stronger name ID rating in the first place. When presented, a Candidate should not miss the opportunity to capitalize on an incumbent's failure to focus on the above average voters. **An incumbent, who concentrates his resources on the average voters, while excluding the above average group during the campaign, will in all likelihood lose to a challenger who builds his or her name ID rating to equal that of the incumbent and communicates a message relevant to the above average voters. In fact, the incumbent will likely lose badly.**

This list will help summarize the primary methods of communication for each group:

Average and Above Average Groups

Direct Mail (Stages 2, 4, 5)
Precinct Operations (Stages 2, 5)
Tabloids (Pictorial)
Campaigning (Catch All)
Billboards, 4 x 8 Signs, Window and Lawn Signs
Magnetic Vehicle Signs and Bumper Stickers
Bus and/or Mobile Signs
Brochures
Radio and TV Commercials

Above Average Voter Group

Direct Mail (Stages 3, 4)
Precinct Operations (Stages 3, 4)
Tabloids (Issues)
Web Site
Campaigning (Targeted)
Position Papers
"Comparative" Flyers
Newspaper Ads
Debates
Radio and TV shows
Free Media Coverage
Videos

The Candidate must establish name ID for the targeted messages to the above average group to be considered.

Until the Candidate establishes name ID, the targeted messages to the above average group, for the most part, are unlikely to be considered. Usually, public image and recognition demonstrate credibility in a viable Candidate. It is at the point of established credibility that the above average voter will invest their attention in the messages being directed to them.

In the 2nd Stage of the campaign, the Candidate should concentrate on a targeted or selective method of campaigning rather than a "catch all" or "shotgun" method. A Candidate would be wasting much of his or her time walking precincts or working plant gates and shopping centers, before the general public begins to develop an awareness as to who he or she is as a Candidate. A Candidate's time would be better spent concentrating on visits with Centers of Influence, recruiting volunteers, solidifying his or her base of support, and assisting the Finance Committee with fund-raising from major contributors. Of course, an exception would exist if a candidate is walking precincts as a method of volunteer recruitment or working a plant gate as a staged media event.

In addition, the maximum exploitation of free media through press releases and conferences should give a Candidate more than adequate supplemental coverage and exposure during this Stage. Heavier emphasis on "catch all" methods should be incorporated into the 3rd and 4th Stages after the name ID has been built and the Candidate's credibility established.

What Should Be Communicated

Careful consideration must be given to the content of the message being sent. The challenger must give the voters in both groups a reason to vote against the incumbent, while projecting a positive feeling to the voters.

Consider the message that is being sent. Is the intention to develop a "positive" campaign based on the Candidate and his or her position on the issues while virtually ignoring the incumbent or is the intention to develop a "negative" campaign attacking the opponent or the opponent's stand regarding the issues? These intentions are described as taking the "high road" or the "low road." If you are an incumbent or in an "open" race, you would automatically take the high road. Many Political Campaign Consultants and strategists will advise the challenger to attack the incumbent, while advising the incumbent to downplay the challenger. They point out that generally voters are more inclined to vote "against" someone than they are to vote "for" someone. I agree with this theory to a certain extent. All other factors being equal, people will not usually vote against an incumbent that they are satisfied with. The most notable exception that comes to mind is Robert F. Kennedy's defeat of the incumbent Ken Keating for the U.S. Senate in New York State. In this campaign, both incumbent and challenger were very popular. Unless an incumbent has a high negative rating, usually as a result of neglect of the district, moral impropriety, or a notoriously poor voting record, the challenger must give the voters in both groups a reason to vote against the incumbent, while projecting a positive or at least neutral feeling about himself or herself to the voters.

Even more important than whether a candidate opts for the "high road" or the "low road," may be the timing and the degree of intensity of both.

As stated earlier, timing is everything. If a Candidate begins attacking too early and too aggressively, the media and the opponent will immediately tag the Candidate and the campaign as being negative and the subsequent loss of credibility will be very damaging. To avoid this possibility, I usually recommend a gradual escalation of the public "attack" during the various stages of the campaign. An axiom for this strategy is never to attack without offering a positive proposal to rectify the problem. Accompanying the attack with a positive proposal of your own is especially important when dealing with the media, either in person or through press releases.

A Candidate should show compassion, while offering hope for a better life by following his or her leadership.

A Candidate should concentrate, especially during the 1st and 2nd Stages, on building not only a positive personal image, but also a positive image of the campaign. A positive image is built by stressing a candidate's qualifications, record of community service, family background, local roots, and positions on the major issues. A campaign's positive image is built by appearing to be well organized and efficient. After the Candidate has solidified the base and established credibility, begin the attack in calculated, gradual steps designed to keep the opponent off-balance and constantly on the defensive. Since a Candidate is to be a leader of the people of a district, he or she must act like one. A Candidate should show compassion with the electorate, indignation, outrage, and concern over the problems affecting them, while offering hope for a better life by following his or her leadership.

A smart Candidate gives the voters confidence about the future. The Prophets of doom and gloom or those that baffle the voters with detail, rarely find themselves in the winner's circle.

Some candidates think that they must act like prophets of doom and gloom in order to win an election, while others believe that their alternative plans must be so specific and detailed that it would take a graduate engineer's degree to begin to understand them. In the final analysis, the Prophets of doom and gloom or those that baffle the voters with detail, rarely find themselves in the winner's circle on Election Day. It is sufficient for most people that a Candidate has a dream for the future and a plan for realizing it. A smart Candidate gives the voters confidence about the future and avoids any increase of the "doom and gloom" attitude that voters may already have. The Candidate should always leave the voters feeling good about themselves, the candidate, and the candidate's plan for their future.

How to Establish and Reach Voter Objectives

The campaign must structure objectives regarding the number of households in which he or she must establish support.

The campaign must establish objectives. Currently, each Congressional District has about 500,000 people living in it. Of those, approximately 370,000 (74%) are eligible voters. Of the eligible voters, 296,000 (80%) will be registered to vote. Of those registered to vote, usually no more than 228,000 (77%) will actually vote on Election Day. In this case, a Candidate for this office would need 114,001 votes in order to win, or one half plus one of the votes cast. We can assume that the 114,001 voters are statistically normal and live 1.7 votes per household. A Candidate, therefore, must solidify the support of approximately 67,000 households that will get out and vote for him or her on Election Day.

Victory can be insured if the Candidate, the consultant, the staff, and the volunteers resign themselves to a lot of hard work, and the campaign has access to enough money to insure that victory.

A Candidate might expect that all of the campaign and media activities would influence the 67,000 households in a positive manner, resulting in 67,000 household votes for him or her on Election Day. In truth, there is a two pronged plan to persuade the 67,000 households to get out and vote for the Candidate. As a bonus to this plan, the campaign manager can measure the progress of the campaign while it progresses, rather than waiting for the results on Election Day. Consequently, victory can be insured if the Candidate, the consultant, the staff, and the volunteers resign themselves to a lot of hard work, and the campaign has access to enough money to insure victory. Despite its ability to guarantee victory, this two-pronged attack plan is rarely fully implemented by challengers because of their underestimation of the commitment to hard work and/or insufficient financial backing.

I will discuss more of the specific details later, but the plan involves a combined volunteer program of precinct canvassing, in person and by phone. In the 1st Stage the objective is simply to identify how the registered voters currently see themselves voting on Election Day. Are they definitely for the opponent, definitely for the Candidate, or undecided? In the following stages, the undecideds are again contacted in person, by phone, and by mail in an attempt to persuade them to support the candidate. In the final stage, the GOTV Stage, those who are definitely for the Candidate are contacted first to remind them to get out and vote for him or her. The second contact is to sway the undeclared or undecided members of his or her Party and the final contact is a last minute "pitch" to the independents to vote for him or her.

The advantages should be obvious. The Candidate eliminates from the direct mail program, those voters who are definitely supporting the opponent and those voters who are supporting the Candidate. The campaign is then able to target its resources, the "rifle" method, on those voters with whom it will do the most good. As follow up surveys indicate that voters have decided one way or the other, voters are taken from the undecided column and added to the support total of the Candidate or to the support total of the opponent. The Candidate is then able to measure the progress toward the goal of capturing the support of the 67,000+ households. In the vernacular of the business, "it makes no sense to preach to those already saved or those already damned." Wherever possible, I have used this method during my career and have never failed to call the outcome of the election accurately at least one week before Election Day.

The disadvantages are just as obvious. There is a tremendous amount of hard work and extra expense involved. However, this is somewhat offset by the savings in the direct mail program. It requires a small army of volunteers, anywhere from 1,000 to 2,000, depending on the amount of turnover the campaign experiences. As I will discuss in detail, using the electronic telemarketing system to which I previously referred can substantially reduce the number of volunteers. Most campaigns will experience anywhere from 20 to 50 percent volunteer turnovers during the campaign. High turnover can be avoided if the Candidate and key staff members have a strong ability to keep the volunteers motivated. I was involved in several campaigns where the volunteers were so dedicated to the Candidate that the campaign lost only 5 percent of the original volunteers over the 9-month period.

Each Candidate has to decide for him or herself whether to use this method. In the Prototype Campaign being developed here, I have used it. The last Chapter and the Appendix contain manuals and forms that further detail how to implement this program.

Paid Media Strategy

With paid media coverage, the campaign is in control of the decisions regarding the developmental aspects.

The final major area of strategy development concerns the content, cost, level, and timing of the paid media used within the campaign. Media is a general term used meaning things such as outdoor advertising, direct mail, newspapers, radio, and television. Since here we are concerned with paid media coverage as opposed to free media coverage, the campaign is in control of the decisions regarding the developmental aspects.

We have discussed the use of outdoor advertising extensively. The strategy of the Prototype Political Game Plan calls for outdoor advertising starting in early February and continuing through to the election.

The basic functions of direct mail are communication and fund-raising. During the 2nd Stage, direct mail will be devoted to fund-raising, except for one political communication piece making an appeal for volunteer support from registered members of the Candidate's Party. The Candidate must target his or her Party in order to solidify base support among the "natural" constituents. During the 3rd Stage, direct mail will target the undecideds and the independents. This strategy will capitalize on the campaign activity that has transpired to this point (the Candidate's activities, the free and paid media activity, and the combination of the precinct and phone bank workers' efforts). In the 4th Stage, an "attack" direct mail piece should target the undecided members of both major Parties and the remaining independents. It should be remembered, that every vote taken from the opponent is, in effect, two for the candidate. In the 5th Stage, the direct mail program must target two groups. Direct mail pieces must continue to solicit the still undecided members of both Parties and the independents, while those who are definitely committed to the Candidate must be sent an appeal to get out and vote. The total volume of direct mail for both fund-raising and political purposes will be around 300,000 pieces.

Newspaper ads can take several approaches such as endorsement ads, issue-oriented ads, ads for name ID purposes only, attack ads, or GOTV ads. I have difficulty justifying the use of newspaper ads on a cost and vote effective basis in a congressional race of the type used in the Prototype. These ads are primarily aimed at the 14% above average group and are competing with or at least duplicating, the direct mail campaign. Frankly, whenever the ads are used it is often a means to encourage favorable news coverage from the editor or owner of the newspaper. Even then, I would recommend using them sparingly in the last 15 days of the campaign. As to content, that will depend on the circumstances at the time. The final poll will focus the decision on the targeting required at that point. Targeting in the final stages of the campaign is a decision that is usually best left in the hands of the Political Media Consultant, adviser, strategist, or ad agency.

Generally, depending on the cost factor in the district, I recommend investing 20% of the campaign budget in electronic media.

There are several theories on the timing and the best purchase methods regarding radio and TV time. For challengers, I recommend investing 20% of the campaign budget in electronic media. I favor allocating the funds using the 10, 20, 30, 40 plan. This strategy invests 10 percent of the electronic media budget in the fourth week before the election, 20 percent in the third, 30 percent in the second and 40 percent of the media budget in the final week prior to Election Day. This spread, in combination with the other media and campaign activities, works most effectively in continuing positive name ID and builds a steady momentum to Election Day. A real problem in campaigns is that of peaking too soon. This spread acts as a natural deterrent to this happening.

The content and timing of an average campaign would be scheduled as follows:

Time	Run / Content
First Week (4 weeks prior to Election Day)	a 60-second biographic spot
Second Week (3 weeks prior to Election Day)	two 30-second man on the street
Third Week (2 weeks prior to Election Day)	two 30-second issue-oriented spots, one positive, one attack
Fourth Week (last week prior to Election Day)	one 30-second appeal for votes by the Candidate, plus some interspersing of the positive and attack spots

Radio spots are usually taken from the sound track on the TV spots and follow the same spread pattern. In order to qualify for the lowest rates available on both TV and radio, the law states that either the candidate's voice must be used somewhere in the spot or that he or she must appear in the spot. For those spots where neither of these conditions prevail, the normal procedure is to have the candidate state the disclaimer which is tagged at the end of the spot, i.e., "Authorized and paid for the (Your Name) for (Office) Committee."

Regarding the exact location of the media buys, a Candidate should not make these purchase arrangements on his or her own. The Radio and TV stations pay media placement agencies a commission for arranging the placement of media spots. The placement arrangement is similar to the commissions paid to a travel agent by an airline company. It is only available to the travel agent. You receive no discount when buying direct; the airline simply pays no commission. If the Candidate does not have a Political Media Consultant or a consultant able to do ad work or media placement, the Candidate should contract a media placement agency or other local firm. Since placement agencies are paid a commission by the stations, this service should not be expensive. However, this statement is only true if the total amount of the buy is large enough for the agency to make a profit on the commission. Many agencies will surcharge this commission if the total size of the buy is not large enough.

A considerable amount of research from polls and studies of the official ratings for each show is referred to as the Arbitron ratings. The Arbitron ratings must be considered in order to obtain maximum voter impact effectiveness for each commercial. This attention to detail will not apply to bulk purchases on a local cable network as no choice of spot is guaranteed. Local purchases from these sources are usually made on a ROS (Run of the Station) basis. In this case, purchasers are sold spots at a set price and the cable network distributes the spots over an equal number of program times and types.

By law, Candidates are to receive the same discounted rate that a major advertiser like GM would receive.

Many candidates know that if the above conditions are met they are entitled to the lowest commercial rate a station is currently charging any active client no matter the size of their account. What they usually do not know is that some stations have three additional methods of buying time within that rate structure. Since stations are profit making operations and ad or media buying agencies are paid a commission on the total number of dollars spent, there are some that do not volunteer this additional information quickly, if at all. Legally, they are not required to do so.

Anytime a spot is bumped for any reason, the station, according to the law, must offer a replacement time of equal value. Normally, the station will discuss your options and choices because of strict audit procedures. For this reason, a Candidate can usually depend on a fair adjustment being made every time.

The three additional methods, or rate structures, are usually referred to as pre-emptible time, semi-fixed time, and fixed or guaranteed time. The terms are self-explanatory. If a Candidate buys time at the pre-emptible rate and another advertiser comes along who wants that time slot and is willing to pay the next higher rate, the Candidate will be "bumped." There is less risk with semi-fixed time and no risk with fixed time.

If the specific locations of the spots are so important one could ask, why would a Candidate want to risk losing them? Pre-emptible time costs about 30 percent less than fixed time. In my experience, I have always been able to reach an agreement with the station salesperson or manager so that if anyone threatens to bump a spot, I would be given a call and be offered the opportunity to cover it with the higher rate before it is bumped. I have rarely lost a spot and, even after paying the fixed rate for the few spots that are invariably challenged, my clients have saved thousands of dollars over the same number of spots at the fixed rate. In fact, for the average congressional campaign the difference is usually around $25,000.

Again, as to the specific content of the commercials, this should be reviewed with the campaign consultant, adviser, or ad agency. Generally, the commercials are not produced until at least one survey has been done so that they can be developed for the necessary demographic target groups. My only word of caution here is to avoid the "bells and whistles." Most candidates would like to have their commercials look as slick as commercial product advertising. Unfortunately, they do not realize that those commercials can cost hundreds of thousands of dollars to produce. Aerial photographs, the use of pop music, and graphics are very expensive. I can not deny that this gimmickry does help penetrate the consciousness of the viewer. However, for any campaign with a budget of less than one million dollars, it is usually a poor trade off. The extra money spent for this production gimmickry would be better spent on more airtime. As a rule of thumb, I rarely budget more than 10 percent of the media budget for the actual cost of production.

All other factors being equal, the strategy usually follows the same thrust as in the earlier stages of the Political Game Plan. The first commercials should focus on who the Candidate is, the biographical spot, and the MOS (man-on-the-street) interviews reinforcing the candidate's qualities and capabilities. The next three commercials should uncover any of the opponent's negative characteristics and strengthen the Candidate's Favorability rating. An attack spot for example, might emphasize an opponent "out of step" with voters in the district, the positive spot would focus on the Candidate with positive solutions for district problems, and the appeal spot would portray the Candidate as the better choice to lead the district into the future.

Strategy Review

Although the development of strategy is dependent on a number of variables, there are some constants to guide a Candidate's planning. There are two basic campaign methodologies. One directed toward all voters, the other toward the 14 percent above average voter group. To implement this dual strategy, a Candidate has two methods at his or her disposal, the "catch all" method and the "targeted" method.

A Candidate's first objective should be to "castle the King," solidify his or her base, raise funds, organize, and train the volunteers. Only then can a Candidate begin to attack from a position of strength. A Candidate should always offer a positive alternative program in conjunction with any negative attack.

The "catch all" campaigning method should be limited to the 3rd, 4th, and 5th Stages. During the 1st and 2nd Stages, the primary concentration should be on Centers of Influence, raising funds, and utilization of free media. The range of campaign activities should be expanded during the 3rd, 4th, and 5th Stages, playing to the Candidate's natural strengths.

The opponent is fair game on the issues, sources of financial support, voting record and campaign tactics. On the other hand, **"If you can't prove it, you can't use it."**

Once the attack has begun, it should be kept up on a hit and run basis, in order to keep the opponent off guard and on the defensive. Find his or her "hot buttons" and push them. Personal attacks usually backfire, but the opponent is fair game on the issues, sources of financial support, voting record, and campaign tactics. Certainty of the facts regarding an opponent's position is imperative. If it can not be proven, do not use it. Do not "beat" on an issue too long, unless it appears to be having a major impact. A sustained attack on a single issue might give the opponent a chance to recover and gain the offensive. The average voter group is only concerned about impressions such as, the candidate is stronger, the opponent is weaker, the opponent is part of the problem, or the candidate is the solution. Keep it simple.

A Candidate should find a respected third party to lead the attack. It is preferably that the third party is not directly connected with the campaign, giving the attack more credibility. It is imperative that the Candidate be sure of the facts about the issue and/or position taken by the opponent regarding any attack. The Candidate should never resort to half-truths or misleading statements.

Develop voter objectives based on the actual statistics within the district. Then develop a Political Game Plan to accomplish those objectives, using a combination of precinct captains, phone bank volunteers, and direct mail.

Start outdoor media in the 2nd Stage and continue throughout the campaign. Intensify with additional mobile outdoor signs and yard signs in the 4th Stage.

Develop and target the electronic media with great care and the help of professionals. Plan to use about 20 percent of the campaign budget for electronic media. Use the 10, 20, 30, 40 plan for maximum effectiveness. Do not over buy. Over saturation is almost as bad as not enough. Decide which subgroups the campaign has to reach, based on an analysis of the cross-tabs in the survey and buy a sufficient number of spots to reach those groups. Do not buy spots going primarily to non-targeted groups. Analyze the Arbitron ratings.

Use newspaper ads sparingly. Scheduled and targeted properly, a direct mail program is more effective than random newspaper ads.

The campaign should be timed to reach its peak momentum about 10 days before Election Day. Any sooner and it will be unable to sustain that peak.

Remember the campaign's appeal should be as broad-based as possible. If possible, stay on the "middle ground" from beginning to end. A Candidate should strongly resist any attempts by the opponent or the media to hang a label on him or her that might automatically alienate a large segment of the voters.

A Candidate should be careful about which PACs are allowed to contribute money. Some are so ideologically pure that some will assume that if one takes money from them, then he or she must be like them or pure enough to have passed their "litmus tests." The best solution in order to diffuse this issue is to develop the broadest possible base for financial support in terms of numbers, occupations, and ages.

Start gradually and control the buildup of momentum in the campaign. It is critical that a campaign reaches its peak momentum about 10 days before Election Day. If the campaign peaks earlier then it is too difficult to sustain the peak. In addition, to peak sooner, much of the campaign's energy will be directed on a segment of the electorate that is not yet ready to receive your message and make a decision that will favor you.

No matter how busy the Candidate or Campaign Manager is, they should monitor the campaign's progress by using the voter status ID program (vote for, undecided, or against) carefully and regularly. Post a "thermometer" in the campaign headquarters during the 3rd and 4th Stages as a visual reminder to staff and volunteers of where the campaign is and what is still needed to reach its goals.

The methodology profiled contains "safety nets" staggered, one on top of the other, ensuring that if one method of communication does not reach a particular voter, the second or third will. The anticipated result by Election Day is to

Once the campaign strategy and Political Game Plan has been adopted, DO NOT CHANGE IT unless something unexpected, even drastic happens. Feelings, hunches, and sure-fire advice from friends do not count as an unexpected or drastic occurrence.

afford the above average voters an opportunity to learn about the Candidate and the opponent well beyond superficial characteristics. As the campaign peaks, the average voter group will be equally familiar with the Candidate and the opponent. If the campaign has successfully accomplished these objectives, the electorate has been offered a real choice, creating at least a 50/50 chance of a Candidate victory over the incumbent opponent.

Misfortune in the form of negative outside factors might play a part, but the campaign's efforts will have gone a long way toward minimizing its potential impact. Even after the Watergate scandal, some Republican campaigns survived.

Chapter 5 - Word Index

Chapter 6
The Game Plan, Budget, and Cash Flow

"The Blueprint of Happiness"

The Game Plan

As tools, the Political Game Plan and Budget serves a twofold function - to measure the campaign's progress against any moment in time and to illustrate to prospective supporters that the Candidate has a sound and practical method to achieve success.

The development of the Political Game Plan and Budget is directly relative to the overall strategy of the campaign. Its function is twofold. First, design and write a plan to implement the strategy outlining how the Candidate will accomplish the goal. The plan will measure progress at any given point in the campaign, alternate plans, strategic methods, and the cost of the plan overall. Second, the Political Game Plan and Budget is a tool to be used in convincing potential volunteers and financial supporters that the Candidate knows what needs to be done and has a sound and practical method for reaching the planned objective.

It never ceases to amaze me as to how so many people expect others to invest in their campaigns without preparing a detailed "prospectus" on the campaign's chances for success. Many of these same people are astute business persons who would not dream of investing in a business or attempting to secure a loan without a detailed analysis of the operation, including a budget, growth projections, market analysis, and plans for implementation.

A Candidate can not expect contributors to invest sizeable sums of money without reviewing a detailed "prospectus" on the campaign's chances for success.

A campaign is serious business, like any other business. All the emotions and "righteousness" of the Candidate, his or her background and accomplishments, and the dedication and enthusiasm of grass-roots volunteers will not convince individuals and organizations to contribute relatively large sums of money to a campaign. *The Candidate can only convince them if he or she has a viable plan to win the election*. This truism can be applied to the essential volunteers needed on the advisory and fund-raising committees, the media, and the Centers of Influence in the district that will be a required aspect of the campaign. Simply put, without money and the support of key individuals, a Candidate cannot win. The Candidate must, therefore, develop a well-written and realistic Political Game Plan before beginning the campaign.

The heart of the Political Game Plan is the *Timeline*.

The Campaign Timeline is a day by day, even hour by hour calendar projecting the political activities for the three operating levels of the campaign, broken down by stages. The Campaign's cash flow schedule tracks the collection of contributions against the cost of each activity and runs concurrently with the Timeline.

The preface should demonstrate to the reader that the campaign is winnable. The Candidate can then proceed to demonstrate how he or she is going to win.

The Preface

The preface should set the stage for the reader by providing:

a) a brief, but detailed description of the district, including demographics, geographic, and economic characteristics;
b) a listing of the major interest groups that have an impact on the district, such as, manufacturing plants, retail businesses, unions, and farmers;

c) if the opponent is an incumbent, highlight his or her voting record and provide an analysis of his or her strengths and weaknesses;
d) provide details on previous voting results in other races within the district, as well as the one being sought;
e) include the latest polling data available along with the latest published ratings by organizations like the ACU (American Conservative Union) and COPE (Committee On Political Education, a part of the AFL-CIO);
f) a biography of the Candidate, including an analysis of his or her strengths, base of support, and stand on the major issues is essential.

Some Political Campaign Consultants recommend that the Political Game Plan and Budget be kept a closely guarded secret. By doing so, the plan's use as a fund-raising and recruiting tool is mitigated. I agree with this recommendation under the following circumstances:

The risk implied by publishing and selectively distributing their Political Game Plan and Budget is not as great as it might seem.

1) the Candidate is an incumbent,
2) the Candidate is an individual able to fund the bulk of the campaign personally, and / or
3) the Candidate had such a strong record of accomplishment because of a different elective office or other position held that he or she could garner the needed support on the strength of this candidacy alone.

Candidates who do not fall into one of the three categories must take the risk implied by publishing and selectively distributing their Political Game Plan and Budget. It is my belief that the risk is not as great as it might seem. So long as the actual contents of the media messages and the actual dialogue of letters or commercials is not revealed prematurely, there is little an opponent can do regarding the plan. I have also found that opponents tend to consider an open and honest Political Game Plan and Budget a "smoke screen," that is a fictitious plan designed to throw them off guard. It seems some people will only believe "inside" information if it is gained surreptitiously.

Finally, many opponents, especially those with a political campaign consultant, know that a challenger must implement a valid plan in order to win. Eventually, because of their political knowledge and experience, a Political Campaign Consultant will recognize a challenger's strategy. In the case of incumbents, not only are they not fools, they were once in need of defeating an incumbent themselves. As far as I am concerned, the advantages of full disclosure for most candidates outweigh the risks. In fact, I recommend using the Political Game Plan and Budget vigorously. I do not recommend calling a press conference to announce its details, but I do recommend that it be a part of the press kit distributed to the media.

The Political Game Plan and Budget should also be distributed to the major PACs in a PAC kit. See pages 258-259

Summarize the Strategy

After completing the preface, summarize the general strategy. Avoid being too specific regarding the actual details of attack and media messages. Follow the Prototype Plan outline established in Chapter 5 regarding the two basic voter groups, the parameters, building name ID, Favorability, communications, the message, voter objectives, and paid media strategy.

Developing the Timeline

Before developing the Timeline, a "shell" must be prepared to contain it. I have previously referred to campaign "stages." During each of the "stages," the workload and general activity for each level in the campaign should be the same. As an example, I have developed an overview of these stages within a specific timeframe.

1st Stage - Primary Objective - *to lay the groundwork for the campaign.*

1st Stage - (10/1/— to 3/1/—) - Pre-Announcement

During the Pre-Announcement Stage, the research, organization, and detail work is completed. Recruit, select, and train essential volunteers, staff, and committees, along with Regional and Area Chairpersons. Begin to recruit and train Precinct Captains and Phone Bank volunteers. Contract by November 1st with a Political Campaign Consultant and other professional support as needed. Make contact with important Party persons, local, state, and national, to discuss intentions and to review possible support. Make all arrangements to establish headquarters and provide equipment. Prepare for formal announcement and the first direct mailer. Let rumors leak to the media regarding candidacy, but neither confirm nor deny. Arrange a press conference for March 1st in order to make a formal announcement of candidacy. Purchase and familiarize essential individuals regarding a capable campaign management software application.

2nd Stage - Primary Objective - *to identify and classify registered voters.*

2nd Stage - (3/2/— to 6/1/—) - Voter ID Stage

During the Voter ID Stage, continue recruiting and training activities. This is an on-going process in most campaigns. Solidify the base of support. Attend all Party functions and meetings, if possible. The Candidate should meet personally with as many Party precinct workers as possible in an effort to recruit and motivate them to work on the campaign. Contact key groups of "natural support." Put heavy emphasis on fund-raising. Precinct Captains and Phone Bank volunteers should then begin identifying where the electorate currently stands on the Candidate and opponent. Input results into a computer database monthly. Begin to develop a more extensive Support File, using GOTV *Campaign Optimizer*. Send direct mail piece to all registered members of Candidate's Party, requesting volunteer and financial support. Post billboards, 4 x 8 corrugated signs, lawn signs in protected locations, and window signs. Hold a press conference to open headquarters and to formally announce your candidacy. Begin systematic program of press releases. Be sensitive to media events Candidate can tap into. Visit and obtain endorsements from as many Centers of Influence as possible.

Normally, it is very difficult to obtain a high turnout and vote in an uncontested Primary. However, every effort should be made to maximize this vote as some potential contributors and media people will attempt to predict the General Election results from the current and previous Primary results, and as an indication of numeric strength. Consequently, even if uncontested in the Primary Election, have volunteers go through a simulated GOTV program on Primary Election Day to test the program and increase the vote overall.

3rd Stage - Primary Objective - *to build a positive image.*

3rd Stage - (6/8/— to 9/6/—) - Positive Advocacy Stage

Schedule a break in major campaign activity for a few days after Primary. Begin to campaign full-time during the Positive Advocacy Stage, if not already doing so. Increase public exposure by walking selected precincts, campaigning when shifts change at local plants, attending fairs, festivals, parades, and other public events. Increase speaking engagements before groups, visit nursing homes, senior citizen centers, begin regularly scheduled visits with reporters for in-depth interviews, continue regular drop-in schedule with radio stations to do on air or taped interviews, likewise with the weekly newspapers, and walk local business districts. Continue putting out substantive press releases regarding position on the issues.

Hold press conferences at least once a month on location, for example, if talking about the price of gas, hold the conference at a gas station. During July do a "benchmark" survey. In August, begin production on commercials. Volunteers begin callback on undecideds, encouraging their vote for Candidate. Send the direct mail piece to all undecided and independents, containing a computer letter, position piece, brochure, and BRE (business return envelope). The latter might pick up enough contributions to pay for the mailer and recruit some additional volunteers. Rotate and continue sign program with heavy emphasis on bumper stickers.

4th Stage - Primary Objective - *to weaken your opponent's Favorability rating by an attack on his or her position on the issues.*

4th Stage - (9/6/— to 10/18/—) - Negative Advocacy Stage

During September canvass again, those voters not contacted during 2nd Stage, especially in high priority Precincts. Contact, once more, undecided voters during October. Begin debates with opponent and try to schedule as many talk-show appearances as possible. Increase speaking engagements before groups such as Optimists, Lions, Kiwanis, Chamber of Commerce, civic or political science classes, or homeowners' associations. Escalate the attack on the opponent's voting record or position on issues, sources of support, and campaign tactics. Be sure to discuss alternative programs with equal emphasis.

Implement absentee ballot program. Distribute tabloids and comparison sheets. Send direct mail piece to remaining undecideds, independents, and unidentified members of the opposite Party with letter, comparison sheet, brochure, and BRE. Rotate billboards for the last time. Begin radio and TV commercials and put up additional lawn signs in October. Change tone of press releases and conferences to reflect "attack and alternative" approach with graduated increase in frequency.

In mid-September complete a final update of computer data on registered voters and obtain new printouts deleting identified opponent supporters. Continue updating manually. During the third week of September, mail fund-raising appeal to registered members of Candidate's Party, emphasizing need for funds to run commercials. Early in September do the first follow up survey. By the end of the first week in October, complete second follow up survey. Coordinate field activities with other campaigns and Party activities within the district.

5th Stage - Primary Objective - *to motivate supporters to get out and vote.*

5th Stage - (10/19/— to 11/1/—) - GOTV Stage

Contact all Centers of Influence. Stress the need for them to contact their members, or people influenced by them, to vote for the Candidate on Election Day. This is especially important for senior citizen centers, nursing home directors, and religious leaders. Increase public visibility. If a Candidate believes positive benefit would result, he or she should make joint appearances with other candidates of the Party. Drop postcard mailers from volunteers to their friends and relatives urging them to vote for the Candidate. Organize groups of volunteers to make literature drops on October 29th and 30th in precincts that, for all intent and purpose, have been neglected during the campaign, but have a high priority. Phone Bank volunteers and Precinct Captains should begin calling identified supporters and Party members, reminding them that the Election Day is approaching quickly and ask them to be sure to vote and to ask at least three of their friends and relatives to join them in voting for the Candidate.

If time permits, contact known undecideds for one last effort to persuade them to vote for the Candidate. Review the Election Day program for poll watchers, drivers, ballot security, voter contacts, and "host" homes. Send final direct mail piece listing location of polling place and other pertinent Election Day information to identified supporters, unidentified members of the Candidate's Party, and known undecideds. This mailing should be timed for arrival by October 31st. Newspaper ads, if used, run during this stage.

On Election Day, after the Candidate goes through the traditional ritual of voting with media present, he or she should make the rounds of major phone banks, visit briefly with volunteers, provide encouragement, and then stay out of everyone's way for the rest of the day. It has been said that the two most useless people on Election Day are the Candidate and the consultant.

Regardless of the outcome, you must "clean up" afterwards. Salvageable election yard and 4 x 8 corrugated signs must be removed and stored. It is very important to collect all of the data material as soon as possible from the phone bank, the host homes, and the Precinct Captains. Otherwise, it has a way of quickly disappearing. Win or lose, the data base is valuable for the next election. After you assemble all of your information, update your computer files or send it to the data processing computer firm for updating. In addition, thank you letters need to be mailed to all volunteers, endorsers, and contributors, sharing the Candidate's feelings about the result and reminding them that the next campaign began as soon as this one ended.

These dates are examples only. By no means is this Timeline considered complete. It is shown for illustrative purposes only.

In reviewing this "shell," keep in mind that the dates are examples only. By no means is it considered complete and is shown for illustrative purposes only. When a Candidate develops his or hers, it should be more specific and detailed. It should show fund-raising activity as well as political activity. Conceptualize the whole campaign in stages, week by week and day by day with the actual dates involved.

Political Timeline

10/01/—	**Begin 1st Stage: Pre-Announcement Stage** Begin meeting with prospective members of Finance and Advisory Committees and interviewing Political Campaign Consultants. Obtain computer and software application such as, GOTV *Campaign Optimizer*. Open P.O. Box.
10/15/—	Appoint Finance and Advisory Committee members, Campaign Chairperson(s) and Treasurer. Open campaign bank accounts. Begin developing Support and Prospect Files.
11/01/—	Contract with Political Campaign Consultant and other suppliers. File as a Candidate with the appropriate agencies. If a Congressional candidate, file with the Clerk of the House and the FEC.
11/15/—	Travel to Washington, DC, or state capitol. Visit with key national or state Party staff people, elected Party officials, and key PAC directors, to discuss candidacy and develop support / 2-3 days.
12/01/—	Select location for headquarters. Obtain assigned telephone numbers. Meet with Finance Committee. Order campaign graphics, logo, and brochure.
12/15/—	Order brochures, press release masthead paper, stationery, envelopes, bumper stickers, and billboard paper. Obtain lists or electronic file of registered voters. Meet with Advisory Committee.
12/20/—	Meet with Finance Committee. Establish Regional and Area boundaries.
01/03/—	Arrange for direct mail piece to all Party households. Drop date 2/15/—. Order billboards, lawn signs, and corrugated four x eight signs and select initial placement locations. Posting time 3/1/—.
01/15/—	Begin contacting Centers of Influence on regularly scheduled basis.
02/01/—	Make deposit on headquarters, telephones, equipment. Formal opening is scheduled for 3/1/—. Arrange location of first press conference for announcement of candidacy on 2/15/—. Assemble press kits. Begin interviewing staff members.
02/07/—	Send press release announcing a press conference for 2/15/—. Check progress of Party direct mail. Meet with Finance Committee. Hire key staff.

02/08/— Invite attendees, essential community leaders, chairpersons, treasurer, and volunteers to press conference 2/15/—. Develop announcement speech. Meet with Advisory Committee.

02/12/— Confirm media attendees for 2/15/— press conference. Mail kits to media outlets unable to attend.

02/15/— Press conference to announce candidacy. Refreshments afterwards. Drop Party direct mail. Order signs for headquarters.

02/16/— Complete hiring of staff. Arrange installation of phones and delivery of equipment. Begin assembly of Precinct kits and Phone Bank manuals. Arrange for tele-matching of telephone numbers on voter registration lists.

02/18/— Headquarters opens informally. Equip and make headquarters operational. Establish procedures.

02/25/— Send press release announcing grand opening of headquarters 3/1/—. Invite all volunteers to grand opening. Plan for light party.

02/26/— Training sessions for Precinct Captains and Phone Bank volunteers. Meet with Finance Committee.

03/01/— Formal grand opening of headquarters, 7:30 P.M. Party for volunteers, staff, and media. Post billboards, lawn signs, and corrugated 4 x 8 signs.

03/02/— Begin 2nd Stage: Voter ID Stage
Prepare copy for first mailing to support file on 3/15/—. Precinct and Phone Bank operations begin.

03/03/— Assemble PAC kits and order material for first PAC mailing. Meet with Advisory Committee. Meet with Field Operations Committee.

03/04/— Meet with Finance Committee.

03/10/— Drop first PAC mailing. Order out-of-district (OD) mail materials. Drop date 4/10/—.

03/15/— Drop first Support File mailing. Send invitations to prospective speakers for 5/14/— fund-raising dinner.

03/26/— Meet with Precinct Captains and Phone Bank volunteers. Define objectives and priority Precincts. Begin PAC mailing follow up to key PACs.

04/01/—	Meet with Advisory Committee. Meet with the Finance Committee. Confirm guest speaker for 5/15/— dinner. Order tickets. Arrange for promotional mailing on 4/15/—.
04/10/—	Drop out-of-district mailing.
04/15/—	Drop dinner mailing.
04/20/—	Meet with Finance Committee. Distribute prospect cards for sale of dinner tickets.
04/28/—	Meet with Advisory Committee.
04/29/—	Begin telephone follow up to persons who received dinner tickets in mail, but did not respond.
05/02/—	Order new poster paper for billboards.
05/05/—	Meet with Finance Committee at dinner. Send press release on 5/15/— dinner. Announce time of press conference to be held on 5/15/—.
05/15/—	5:00 p.m. Press Conference with guest of honor. 6:00 p.m. Private Social Hour. 7:00 p.m. Public Social Hour. 8:00 p.m. Dinner.
05/22/—	Meet with Field Operations Committee. Discuss and arrange for modified GOTV on Primary. Order direct mail piece for undecideds. Drop on 7/7/—.
05/31/—	Begin modified GOTV Stage.
06/07/—	Primary Election Day GOTV action.
06/08/—	**Begin 3rd Stage: Positive Advocacy** Hold press conference setting stage for General Election period. Order direct mail for 2nd PAC and OD (out-of-district) mailing. Drop 06/22/—. Rotate billboards. Order tabloids for general distribution and do Phone Bank follow up. Send ID data to computer firm for update.
06/09/—	Meet with Finance and Advisory Committee.
06/11/—	Training seminar for all volunteers on 3rd Stage.
06/22/—	Drop 2nd PAC and OD (out-of-district) mailing. Order direct mail for 2nd Support File mailing. Drop date 7/18/— and tie in to mini event, if possible.
07/04/—	Ride in annual parade and attend major picnics.

07/07/— Drop direct mail piece to undecideds.

07/10/— Begin telephone follow up to 2nd PAC mailing. Secure items for auction on 8/7/—.

07/13/— Do benchmark survey.

07/18/— Drop 2nd Support File mailing. Send notice of picnic/auction to volunteers and contributors.

07/25/— Meet with Finance Committee. Review prospect cards.

08/03/— Meet with Advisory Committee. Review survey and do major campaign analysis. Complete arrangements for speaker and dinner on 9/10/—. Order new poster paper for billboards.

08/05/— Make final arrangements for 2nd major dinner on 9/10/—. Order tickets and direct mail. Drop on 8/15/—.

08/07/— Picnic and auction for volunteers, staff, and contributors.

08/08/— Begin production on commercials.

08/15/— Drop 2nd major dinner mail. Order direct mail for 3rd PAC and OD (out- of-district) mailing. Drop date 9/6/—. Order direct mail on 9/7/00 for 3rd Support File mailing, if not incorporated in dinner mailing. Order direct mail for 9/14/— mailing to undecideds, independents, and unidentified members of the opposite Party. Meet with Advisory and Finance Committee.

09/01/— Send out press release for 9/10/— dinner. Meet with Finance Committee. Order additional yard signs.

09/06/— Begin 4th Stage: Negative Advocacy
Drop 3rd PAC and OD (out-of-district) mailings. Rotate billboards. Review and analyze results of 3rd Stage program. Meet with Advisory Committee.

09/07/— Drop Support File mailing. Contact media regarding Press conference 9/10/—.

09/10/— 4:00 p.m. Press conference or rally.
6:00 p.m. Private Social Hour.
7:00 p.m. Public Social Hour.
8:00 p.m. Dinner.

09/12/— 1st Follow up survey. Reserve hotel for victory party 11/5/—.

09/14/— Drop political mailing to undecideds, independents, and unidentifieds. Order final fund-raising mailing for key PACs, OD (out-of-district), previous contributors, and members of Party. Drop date 10/4/—. Begin PAC Telephone follow up and third mailing.

09/16/—	Send accumulated results of Phone Bank and Precinct operations to computer firm for final update and preparation of GOTV printouts.
09/17/—	Training seminar for 4th Stage. Meet with Field Operations Committee. Prepare mail program from elected and party officials to their supporters, plus postcard mailer from volunteers, endorsers, and contributors to their friends and relatives. Drop 10/23/—.
09/19/—	Meet with Finance and Advisory Committee. Begin absentee ballot program. Begin developing Election Day program.
09/30/—	Organize ad hoc GOTV committee.
10/04/—	Drop final fund-raising mailing to key PACs, OD (out-of-district), previous contributors, and members of Party. Begin TV and radio commercials. Order final direct mail to ID'd supporters, members of Party, and remaining undecideds. Drop date 10/25/—. Meet with Finance Committee.
10/10/—	2nd Follow up survey. Prepare GOTV kits. Put up lawn signs. Secure host homes to supplement Phone Banks on 11/5/—.
10/14/—	Meet with Advisory Committee. Last possible turnaround day or chance to make changes in final media program. Begin final PAC telephone follow up.
10/19/—	**Begin 5th Stage: GOTV**
10/21/—	GOTV training seminar for everyone.
10/22/—	Precinct blitz. Political rally.
10/23/—	Drop mail from party and elected officials and supporters.
10/25/—	Drop final GOTV mailing and use special political mail tags to insure timely delivery. Begin newspaper ads, if being used.
10/29/—	Precinct blitz. Call all ID'd supporters.
10/30/—	Precinct blitz. Call all ID'd supporters, undecideds, and members of Party.
10/31/—	Check final preparations for Election Day program. Confirm host homes, poll watchers, and ballot security program. Final press conference.
11/05/—	Election Day program. **Victory Party!**

The campaign can enter every key or special event on its Timeline, as developed, or as strategy dictates. Note that the lead-time for most production work is assumed 30 days. Anything less will strain a supplier's ability to deliver on time, resulting in added or unnecessary costs and missed deadlines. Know exactly what the campaign's needs are and order in advance to keep the costs down.

GOTV *Campaign Optimizer* has a built-in Timeline module designed to work very effectively for this purpose. The pace of the campaign becomes so hectic, at times, that it becomes easy to forget or overlook even important events. The Timeline should not be used as the Candidate's Campaign Calendar. The Candidates daily calendar is separate and should be maintained by the Campaign Secretary. A capable campaign management software should afford the opportunity to track the Campaign Timeline and the Candidate's Daily Schedule as complete and separate entities.

Develop the strategy and Political Game Plan first, the budget second, and the cash flow projections last.

The Political Game Plan that maximizes a Candidate's opportunity to win should be developed, and then, every effort should be made to raise the necessary capital to support that plan.

The next part of the Political Game Plan is the budget and cash flow schedule. Develop the strategy and Political Game Plan first, the budget second, and the cash flow projections last. Unlike some consultants, I do not subscribe to the theory that a campaign should develop a high and a low Budget. I believe a Political Game Plan should be developed that maximizes a Candidate's opportunity to win, and then every effort should be made to raise the necessary capital to support that plan. This schedule of activity also eliminates the likelihood of excluding a campaign activity because of financial constraints. Inevitably, I am asked during the course of a campaign what effect will the elimination of a particular planned activity have on the outcome of the campaign. My answer is always the same. If the activity were not considered important, it would not have been part of the plan in the first place.

The Campaign Budget

Congressional Campaign Budget

Expense	Budget
Computers, Printers, Software, and Supplies	10,000
Staff salaries, including tax and insurance	95,000
Headquarters rental, including utilities	15,800
Phones, including deposits	23,000
Office postage	2,700
Office equipment and supplies	18,000
Telemarketing	25,000
Web Site Design and Site Service	5,000
Miscellaneous printing	16,000
Polling - 1 Benchmark, 2 Follow ups	35,000
Political Campaign Consultant's fee	50,000
Political Campaign Consultant's expenses	12,000
Candidate's campaign expenses	12,000
Graphics and typesetting	4,000
Brochures - 200,000	15,000

...continued

Expense	Budget
Campaign and PR stationery	6,000
Billboard production	7,000
Billboard rental	32,000
Yard, Window, and 4 x 8 signs	14,400
Bumper Stickers - 10,000	4,000
Computer Services, data entry, and printouts	15,000
Tabloids - 80,000	6,800
Political and Fund-raising direct mail pieces - 320,000	86,000
Direct Mail and Tabloid postage and permits	73,500
Radio and TV commercial spots	150,000
Production, 6 commercials	25,000
Promotional Items	3,400
Major Event expenses	20,000
Miscellaneous expenses	4,400
Total Estimated Expenses, including fund-raising	**786,000**

Sources of Funds (Contributions)

Contribution Source	Total
Candidate	100,000
30 Major Contributors, Primary and General	100,000
Individual solicitations, Minor Contributors	100,000
Direct Mail	100,000
PACs, $150,000 and OD (Out-of-District), $50,000	200,000
2 Major Events, total 600 @ $150 + social	90,000
Party contributions (national, state, local)	96,000
Total Income - $490,000 in-district	**786,000**

Fund-raising Schedule (Cash Flow)

Date	Contribution Source	Total
11/1/--	$50,000 Candidate, $20,000 Major Contributors, $5,000 Individual Solicitations	75,000
12/1/--	$50,000 Candidate, $30,000 Major Contributors	80,000
1/15/--	Individual Solicitations	25,000
2/15/--	$40,000 Direct Mail, $40,000 Individual Solicitations	80,000
4/1/--	PACs	35,000
4/30/--	OD (Out-of-District) contributions	20,000

...continued

Date	Contribution Source	Total
5/15/--	1st Major Event, dinner and social.	45,000
5/19/--	Party contribution	30,000
6/15/--	$50,000 Major Contributors, $30,000 Individual Solicitations	80,000
7/15/--	PACs and OD contributions	60,000
8/15/--	$25,000 PACs, $30,000 Direct Mail	55,000
9/10/--	2nd Major Event, dinner and social	45,000
9/15/--	$46,000 Party contribution, $30,000 Direct Mail, $30,000 PACs & OD contributions	106,000
10/7/--	$20,000 Party, $30,000 PACs & OD contributions	50,000
	Total Income	**786,000**

Budget Analysis

When creating the budget, do not overlook the cost of fund-raising. It should represent at least 20% of the campaign budget.

One note of interest in analyzing these figures is that approximately $150,000, or 20 percent of the Budget, is spent on fund-raising activities. This is a cost factor so often overlooked by candidates. However, most of the contributions would not be raised without it. The percentage, 20%, is very conservative and when fund-raising, one might remember the cliché, “the more you spend, the more you get.”

Of the $630,000 spent for political purposes, the largest percentage is spent on communications. This total amount, $630,000, translates to an average of $1.50 per adult person in the district and will be spent over a period of 12 months (13 cents per person, per month). The average cost per adult would increase slightly for smaller, state legislative races and decrease for larger or statewide races. A Candidate should use these cost comparisons when and if the opponent or the media attempt to make an issue of the campaign budget. Surely, no one would deny the right of the electorate to be afforded the opportunity to learn about you and the issues.

The cash flow schedule and the dates shown on the political and fund-raising Timelines should not appear in the Political Game Plan developed for public dissemination.

The cash flow schedule and the dates shown on the political and fund-raising Timelines should not appear in the Political Game Plan developed for public dissemination. This information is too sensitive for the opponent to see and does not enhance the use of the Political Game Plan as a fund-raising tool.

Keep in mind that a few Congressional Candidates, or any others for that matter, will win in any given year in spite of themselves or their campaigns. Those who do win by design, i.e., challengers at the congressional level, will invariably spend between $600,000 and $800,000 for the political portion of the campaign. In fact, during the last 18 years this has been one of the few common denominators among winning Congressional challengers.

Incidentally, some of the cost factors used in this budget are lower than most candidates can expect to pay. Most Political Campaign Consultants invariably save their clients more than their fees by obtaining other campaign items and services at costs lower than they could realize on their own. I would point out that I have used the term "Political Consultant" very loosely throughout this Manual. Unfortunately, there are few precise definitions in this business and almost anyone can call themselves a Political Consultant. For my purpose here, a Political Campaign Consultant is a specialist in organizing and managing a political campaign, possessing both the knowledge and experience in all political campaign components.

Definition
A generalist or Political Campaign Consultant, for my purposes here is one who develops strategy, the game plan, the fund-raising plan, the media plan, and supervises the campaign on a regular basis.

Many Political Consultants, even those who are not generalists have arrangements with some suppliers to provide their goods or services to the consultant's clients at reduced prices. This is possible because the Political Campaign Consultant is able to negotiate a lower price, based on volume, than can the individual Candidate. For example, the current, average rate for polling is around $35 per interview. Some consultants have associate arrangements with reputable polling firms that will provide the same service for their clients at $30 per interview. An associate printer might provide a two color, three-fold brochure on glossy stock for 12 cents each. In other cases, candidates might pay between 14 and 18 cents for exactly the same brochure. In direct mail, many consultants have associates who will provide a client with an individualized computer letter, #10 window envelope, #6 1/2 business return envelope (BRE), and a brochure or insert piece for a total of 44 or 47 cents. This includes materials, printing, folding, inserting, sorting, and preparing for a direct drop at the Post Office. The Candidate buying directly could expect to pay between 52 and 55 cents per unit for the same piece of mail and service.

There are also differences in the fees charged for support services when combined in one agency. For example, Political Campaign Consultants' fees for a campaign of this size will average $50,000 plus expenses. Average media creative fees are $35,000 for six commercials plus the crew and expenses. Political fund-raisers' fees average $20,000; in addition, a 5 percent commission on the amount raised, plus expenses. Separately, the fees would usually average $105,000 plus $35,000 in fund-raising commissions. By using a Political Campaign Consultant, a campaign could save around $45,000. Normally, however, a Political Campaign Consultant will only give this preferred rate if he or she is also responsible for all the media production and placement in the campaign.

Considering these differentials, the budget used in the Prototype Plan is very realistic for the campaign we are developing in *The Campaign Manual*. Variations will occur, of course, depending on the many variables discussed.

Political Game Plan Summary

The cash flow schedule and the dates shown on the political and fund-raising Timelines should not appear in the Political Game Plan developed for public dissemination.

In summary, the Political Game Plan should include the following:

a) A Preface, giving the reader reasons why the race is winnable.

b) A summary of the strategy that the campaign will implement.

c) The Political Game Plan it will follow to implement the strategy and an overview of the stages, campaign organization flow chart, and a detailed Campaign Timeline.

d) The Campaign Budget needed to implement the Political Game Plan, including the anticipated sources of income and a fund-raising schedule with dated detail for internal use only.

e) The Cash Flow Schedule, for internal use only.

When completed it should be neatly typed and bound in a plastic cover. Excluding the Cash Flow Schedule, 150 copies should be prepared for distribution to major contributor prospects.

"The Best Laid Plans of Mice and Men"

There is a direct relationship between the size of the population in your geopolitical district and the amount of money spent in the campaign.

How to Estimate the Budget

Defining Objectives

The budget is a by-product of your campaign plan, which is a by-product of your strategy. However, there are general rules of thumb that are valid in most campaigns. There is a direct relationship between the size of the population in your geopolitical district and the amount of money spent in the campaign. Interestingly, it is usually an inverse ratio. That is, the larger the population, the less spent per capita.

The average congressional district has a population of 500,000 people. The average amount spent on a congressional campaign today will be $750,000 or $1.50 per person. A state senatorial district in a large state will have an average population of 120,000 people. The average amount being spent for these races will be $156,000, or $1.30 per person. State representative districts in larger states will have an average population of 60,000 and the average amount being spent will be $102,000 or $1.70 per person. The smaller the population, the more the per capita cost increases. There are, of course, exceptions, but these averages tend to remain constant in seriously contested races.

Specific Costs Involved

One of the reasons the above inverse ratio exists is because there is an inverse ratio in the purchase of goods and services used in a campaign. As with so many products, a discount is offered for volume buying. For example, in the area of printing costs for brochures, a two-color, three fold brochure, with 4 pictures, half-tones, 8.5 X 14", on 70 lb. glossy stock will average $.15 a piece in quantities of 10,000. That same brochure in quantities of 100,000 might drop to $.08 a piece or less. Envelopes which cost $.055 a piece in quantities of 100,000, might increase to $.095 a piece for quantities of 10,000. These prices will not be proportionate as you increase in volume from 10,000 to 100,000. Printers, and many other distributors of products or services, have price breaks at fixed levels. Until you reach that specific level, the unit price remains the same. The concept is true of advertising outlets. Practically all of them, television, radio, newspapers, and billboards have substantial discounts for volume purchasing.

Even postal rates have discounts. First class mail, at present, is $.34 for the 1st ounce. If you purchase a bulk rate postal permit and are sending 200 or more pieces, properly separated, you can mail them at bulk rates, which would be less than $.20 per piece. The cost of such a permit is about $120.00. If you are doing a concentrated mailing in one precinct, you might qualify for a further discount for a carrier-route rate, reducing your cost to about $.15 per unit piece.

Two rules of thumb to guide you: the more you buy, the less the unit cost; neither the cheapest, nor the most expensive, are necessarily the best.

Television and radio stations are required by law to sell a political candidate airtime at the lowest rate available, regardless of volume. Newspapers and billboards are not bound by this requirement.

After you have developed your strategy and game plan, itemize the goods and services your campaign will require. Then obtain bids from the various suppliers in your area, or wherever available. Check with the media outlets to determine their prices, based on the time and amount. Once quotations from various suppliers of the goods and services are in hand, you can make a wise choice regarding which suppliers are offering the best purchase opportunity for your campaign needs. Do not forget to factor in "delivery and timeliness." Remember that neither the cheapest, nor the most expensive, are necessarily the best.

Calculating the Budget

Almost all suppliers will demand payment in advance.

Costs will be based on the quantity, quality, and (lead-time) delivery of the items purchased. Regardless of what is purchased, keep in mind that political campaigns and candidates are one of the worst credit risks in the marketplace. Almost all suppliers will demand payment in advance.

Before calculating your budget, analyze your campaign's Timeline. The budget should indicate the date that payments for your goods or services are due. Usually, there is a lead-time of 2-4 weeks. If you need faster service, you will pay a rush charge. Keep in mind that most suppliers usually have a regular customer base whose needs will always take priority over a campaign. Be sure to obtain firm delivery dates for everything you order.

In order to estimate your budget requirements, work backwards from the date of the election.

Working from the date of the election backward, post each item. Indicate the date needed and the order date. On the order date, post the amount of money that will be needed with the order. As a precaution develop an alternative, or low budget, if for some reason your campaign is unable to raise the full amount required for your regular budget. Although every effort should be made to raise the amount called for in your game plan, the fact remains that things will happen beyond the campaign's control and alternative plans are a sound idea. As a practical matter, the alternative budget information should not be distributed. People have a tendency to work only as hard as they think they have to work to accomplish an objective. The pressure should always remain to raise the total amount needed for the Political Game Plan.

Once you have a preliminary estimate of your budget, through quotations, obtain the best possible unit price for the goods and services that you require. Substantial competition exists between the suppliers that you will be soliciting; use it to your advantage when negotiating prices.

The most efficient way to do a cost analysis is to prepare a specification sheet that details exactly what you need. Your specification sheet should include all of the cost factors involved in the production and purchase of the item. As an example, examine the brochure more closely:

1. The paperweight is 70 lb.
2. It is a coated or glossy stock.
3. It will be printed in 2 colors, both standard.
4. Including 4 pictures or half tones.
5. The size before folding is 8.5" X 14".
6. It requires two folds, no binding.
7. The quantity is 10,000.
8. The finished size is 8.5" X 4.66"
9. You will provide camera-ready artwork.
10. Lead-time / Delivery

Deal with the supplier offering the lowest *qualified* quote.

With these specifications listed as discussed, you could ask any number of printers to quote this job. Since everyone would have the same information, you would be certain of a fair price comparison. You will be surprised by the differences in the quotes that you receive. Be aware that it is easy for shrewd suppliers to take advantage of unprepared campaign purchasers, since in general, they are not familiar with the purchase of these products. Arranging the best value is a result of taking the time and investing the energy in a price comparison analysis. Remember that when you look at a bid that the lowest quote is not always the best quote. You want to deal with the supplier offering the lowest *qualified* quote.

You can not assume that the most competitive supplier on one specific purchase will automatically offer the lowest quote on another. Each time you place a major order, you should repeat this process. When a supplier can not be

Political Resource Directory is available from Carol Hess at Political Resources, Inc., P.O. Box 3365, Burlington, VT 05406 800.423.2677 or www.politicalresources.com

found locally, you will likely find a listing in a political publication like the Political Resource Directory. This reference book lists every campaign supplier in the United States, state by state, and is indexed by goods and services. If you don't feel the cost is justified just for your campaign, you might want to ask your county party chairperson to purchase it as a reference for all of the Party candidates running in that area.

My point is that prudent shopping can save the campaign anywhere from 5% to 15%. It is a comparatively easy way to do your fund-raising in reverse, since a penny saved is a penny earned. Your campaign should operate like an efficient business and successful business managers are prudent people. It is not a case of being afraid to spend money; it is a case of attaining the most value for every dollar spent.

An argument can also be made that a candidate, a PAC, and/or a party committee has a fiduciary responsibility to spend their contributors' funds in the most prudent manner possible, for the purposes for which it was intended.

Chapter 6 - Word Index

Chapter 7
Organizational Flow Chart

Who, What, When, Where, Why, How

Introduction

In this chapter, we will discuss the implementation of the campaign's Political Game Plan and identify the basic responsibilities of each individual in the campaign organization. We will be looking at who does what, when, where, why, and how.

Throughout the Manual, we attempt to emphasize the constants. That is, those activities and responsibilities that should be basic to any well-run campaign. The variables will depend on the individuals involved, their personalities, skills, experience, available time, dedication, the actual strategy, and the Political Game Plan.

Although the Prototype Plan calls for the Campaign Manager to perform the duties of Finance Director, I will outline each position as though a single individual was hired to do each of them. Keep in mind that all of these functions are necessary in all campaigns and must be performed by someone, either a paid staff member or a volunteer.

The Campaign Organization

The Candidate should complete an organizational flow chart during the 1st Stage of the campaign. The hierarchy should be strictly enforced in order to avoid confusion.

It is necessary to develop an organizational flow chart for the campaign. This project should be completed during the 1st Stage by the Candidate and be based solely on his or her own situation. All members of the committees and staff should be given a copy and it should be made a part of the Political Game Plan. The campaign organizational flow chart helps to illustrate and clearly define the lines of authority, responsibility, and communication within the campaign. Once established, the hierarchy should be strictly enforced in order to avoid confusion during the campaign.

The Candidate

Role The Candidate is the ultimate decision-maker responsible for every detail.

The Candidate is the ultimate decision-maker within the campaign. As stated in the old adage, "The buck stops here." It is the Candidate that receives all the praise when things go right; it is that same Candidate that takes the "heat" for things that are deemed wrong.

The Candidate must be informed and wise regarding all FEC and State regulations that apply to the elected office that he or she has aspired to.

Based on both FEC and State regulations, the Candidate is responsible to see that all laws and regulations are followed by his or her campaign. It is imperative that the Candidate is informed and wise regarding all of the regulations that apply to the elected office that he or she has aspired to. The Candidate must be able to identify and correct any regulation irregularity within the campaign well before any irregularity has any opportunity to become public or even worse, result in criminal liability. Since these regulations are not fixed, ever changing as legislation is passed, this is an on-going responsibility that must be regarded as most serious, both before and after the election, win or lose.

Nothing should ever be made public in either the Candidate's name or the campaign committee's name, without the Candidate's consent or approval.

He or she has the final say on all strategy, implementation, procedures, budget, contracts, graphics, copyrighting, commercials, and issue statements. Nothing should ever be made public in either the Candidate's name or the campaign committee's name, without the Candidate's consent or approval. Candidates, out of necessity, will usually delegate much of this responsibility to the Political Campaign Consultant and senior members of the staff. However, the parameters of this delegated authority should be clearly defined and enforced.

To analogize, the Candidate activities, coupled with the media program are designed to cultivate, to plant, and nurture the seeds.

Since the Candidate is responsible to the thousands of people investing in the campaign, both in terms of money and effort, certain behavioral patterns should be established and followed that will help insure the safety as well as the physical, emotional, and intellectual fitness of the Candidate during the campaign.

Candidate "Do's & Don't's"

a) The Candidate should always travel by commercial airlines or, if not available, a twin-engine, dual piloted aircraft. Travel safely regardless of how far behind schedule the Candidate may be. During the campaign, all recreational activity that involves a high degree of risk should be avoided.

Consider the threat of burn out seriously. First time Candidates have no real idea of how utterly exhausting the campaign process is and they invariably overestimate their strength and endurance.

b) Establish a reasonable schedule of activity, within a sound timetable and adhere to it. A Candidate runs a high risk of a physical and/or emotional collapse that could jeopardize the outcome of the campaign. An exhausted Candidate might result in a damaging slip of the tongue at the wrong time or place. Respect the tremendous demands on the Candidate. He or she will constantly be subjected to requests for attendance at numerous functions, often within the same time frame. Many well-intentioned friends and volunteers will forever suggest a meeting or activity that is a "must" if the campaign is to be won. In the later stages, a Candidate is vulnerable because of self-imposed pressure on themselves to see just one more person or shake just one more hand.

c) A Candidate must plan rest and relaxation, especially during the first three Stages, if he or she is going to make it to the end of the race alert and energetic enough to make it through the home stretch. Like a marathon runner, the Candidate must pace the race or run the risk of collapsing before reaching the finish line. R&R time means just that. It means rest and relaxation with no phones, meetings, writing, research, visits, or campaign related visitors. During this time, the Candidate should try to keep his or her mind off the campaign.

The Candidate must accept the fact that it is physically impossible to be at all events all of the time.

d) During the first three stages, the Candidate must schedule 1 full day off per week, regardless of what is going on in the campaign. It is physically impossible to be at all events all of the time. He or she must accept the fact that some events are going to be missed. Try to prioritize the impact of the event and go with the highest priority. Have a surrogate cover other events.

e) While a Candidate is still employed full time, he or she should limit campaign activity to 4 hours a day during the week and 10 hours on Saturday. When the Candidate begins campaigning full time, he or she should never put in more than a 14-hour day. Twelve hours on a regular basis is also considered excessive.

f) At least twice during the campaign, the Candidate should take a 3 day holiday away from the district, especially, just prior to the 4th Stage. The 4th and 5th Stages are the exception. The Candidate will find there will not be a chance to take many days off and the pressure will really begin to build. Therefore, when possible the Candidate should take a break occasionally and regenerate his or her physical and mental resources. The improved *quality* of the campaigning will more than make up for the loss of *quantity*.

g) A Candidate should make sure his or her wardrobe is in good shape before the start of campaigning. Stay with the basic outfits and avoid anything too flashy or ostentatious. Keep a complete change of clothes sealed in a plastic bag, plus an overnight kit in the trunk of the campaign car for emergencies. An American (made) vehicle is preferable.

A few additional considerations the Candidate should keep in mind while campaigning:

1) Avoid drinking alcoholic beverages. The Candidate could begin to slur speech, become overly tired, and make a serious mistake;

2) Avoid holding a cold glass in the right hand. No one likes a cold, wet handshake;

3) If possible, never be photographed with a glass in hand. Even water looks like an alcoholic drink in a photo. The Driver/Aide should be trained to be on the alert for a possible photo and automatically take the glass from the Candidate's hand before it happens. After awhile this becomes routine. The Candidate becomes sensitized to releasing the glass when it is being lifted. Soon this signals that a picture is about to be taken and stimulates a pose;

4) Do not wear a ring on the right hand. After a day of shaking hands, it could cut into your finger;

5) When shaking hands, thrust your hand firmly forward. Lock the hand in between the thumb and the first finger avoiding a limp handshake and protecting the fingers, preventing a swollen hand by the end of the day;

6) When "working" a crowd, the Candidate should let the Aide move him or her along. The standard signal is a light touch on the inside of the Candidate's left elbow. It is the signal that he or she is spending too much time with that person, as others are waiting to speak with him or her. The Aide should be trained so that when the signal is ignored for a second time, it means the Candidate feels the present conversation is too important to interrupt. At that point, to avoid anyone feeling slighted, the Aide turns to the people waiting and assures them the Candidate will be with them shortly;

7) If offered, the Candidate should let the Aide take notes, cards, or contributions from any individual with whom he or she is speaking;

8) When the Candidate is a guest speaker at a scheduled event that the campaign has not set up, he or she should keep the prepared speech to 15 minutes, covering no more than two or three major points and then open the event for questions and answers;

9) The Candidate should avoid detailed or complicated explanations. Most people only want to know where the Candidate stands, generally, on the issue(s);

10) If comfortable doing it, the Candidate should ease tensions with a humorous anecdote or two, but should not overdo it;

11) Avoid personal attacks on the opponent and, if present, show the proper respect and courtesy for the Office held, or position sought;

12) Be extremely courteous, gracious, and pleasant at all times;

13) Watch overeating. For some reason, it seems everyone wants to feed the Candidate and it is not at all unusual to add 10 to 20 pounds during the campaign;

14) If the Candidate is a male, he should keep a re-chargeable electric razor in the car;

15) The Candidate should make sure the Aide always has a camera on hand, loaded with black and white film, and knows how to use it. Photos should be taken of the Candidate with dignitaries and other people present. These photos will be valuable at press conferences and in future tabloids. In addition, it is great PR to send copies to the people in the pictures with the Candidate.

16) The Candidate should always avoid arguing in public with anyone who disagrees with him or her. Offer to discuss the issue later or suggest that the campaign will be pleased to send them a copy of the specific position paper on the issue of concern to them;

17) The Candidate should be sure the Aide always has an adequate supply of campaign material with him or her. The campaign vehicle should be outfitted like a mobile office;

18) If the Candidate's spouse or children are present, he or she should not forget to introduce them. Likewise introduce the staff, committee members, or other candidates and elected officials;

19) The Candidate should expect foul-ups. They always happen, no matter how well things are planned. Never criticize the Aide or staff in public;

20) The Candidate should be patient and keep a sense of humor at all times. Rarely is any one thing that critical or insurmountable.

Types of Campaign Activity

Canvassing Precincts

This is one of the most difficult types of campaign activity for most candidates, but it can be very effective for gaining support and recruiting volunteers. For candidates below the congressional level, with relatively small districts, it is usually essential. Before beginning the canvass activity, the Candidate should have a supply of campaign brochures, 3 x 5 cards or door hangers (signed by the Candidate, expressing, "Sorry, I missed you") that can be left on the door with a brochure when no one is at home, a copy of the voter registration list for that Precinct and a supply of any promotional items the campaign may be using.

When the person opens the door, the Candidate should introduce himself or herself, mention the office for which they are running, tell the person he or she would appreciate their support, and hand them a brochure. Unless the person wants to talk further, the whole visit should last no more than 30 seconds. If they do want to talk, try not to let it last more than 2 minutes. Whether they indicate support or opposition, mark the voter registration sheet accordingly. If they are supporters, ask them if they would like to volunteer to help on the campaign or put up a yard sign. If they say yes to either, mark the sheet and tell them the volunteer coordinator will be in touch with them soon. Be sure to give this data to the appropriate staff person for follow up on a regular basis.

Plant Gate Campaigning

The preparation for this type of campaign activity is basically the same as for precinct canvassing except that the materials on hand should include all voter registration lists. In most cases, the campaign will have to obtain prior permission from the plant supervisor for the Candidate to campaign there.

This type of campaign activity usually involves being at a main plant gate when the shifts change. This provides the Candidate with an opportunity to introduce him or her, hand out literature, and shake hands with the workers as they enter or leave. It helps to have a few volunteers with the Candidate holding signs on poles to draw attention to the Candidate and maximize the impact. The media should be alerted when this type of activity is planned since they will occasionally "cover it" for background footage on the campaign.

Coffee "Klatsches"

Definition
Coffee "Klatsches" are informal meetings held in the home of a supporter with some of their neighbors and friends.

Preparation for coffee "Klatsches" is essentially the same as for precinct canvassing and plant gate visits, with the addition of position papers, bumper stickers, and BREs for the materials on hand.

"Klatsches" are informal meetings held in the home of a supporter with some of their neighbors and friends. Usually, a Candidate can do three of these a night by staying at each one for only 30 to 45 minutes. Standard procedure is a basic 5 to 10-minute talk, followed by Q&A, and an appeal for volunteer and financial support. This is an excellent way for a Candidate to help the Area Chairperson recruit volunteers during the 2nd and 3rd Stages. I normally suggest that the host invite two to three times as many people as they expect to attend. The no shows for these events are very high.

The host should be responsible for making sure everyone who attends receives campaign literature and a BRE. They can leave a contribution, mail it in to the campaign, or volunteer for some activity. Encourage one or more of the attendees to host a coffee "Klatsch" in their home for their friends and relatives.

Public Speaking / Civic and Business Groups

The Campaign Scheduler should try to promote as many of these as possible by sending letters early in the campaign to appropriate groups advising them that the Candidate would like the opportunity to meet with them at a scheduled meeting. The invitations will usually be slow in the early stages but will pick up after Labor Day. If appropriate, the Aide should bring brochures, position papers, bumper stickers, and BREs to the event. Appropriateness should be confirmed with the Program Chairperson.

Some groups have prohibitions against candidates making a political speech at their meetings but they will allow a speech to be given on a topic of interest such as the economy. If this is the case, no campaigning, as such, is allowed. If this is not the situation, then follow the procedure for a coffee "Klatsch." The candidate should give a 15-minute basic speech, followed by Q&A, and an appeal for votes and assistance.

Debates with the Opponent

Never debate with a *substitute* opponent.

Usually a challenger Candidate will issue an invitation to the opponent to debate the issues during the Primary Election's "victory speech." Press hard if the opponent does not acknowledge, respond, or agree. Usually these would be scheduled wherever and whenever possible. Be sure the rules are fair, agreed to in advance, and followed. The Campaign Manager should meet with the opponent's Manager to work out the details. Remember this one rule of thumb, whoever starts finishes. Formats can vary considerably but usually involve opening statements for 5 minutes, rebuttals for 3 minutes, and closing statements for 3 minutes. Sometimes Q&A from the audience or a panel, precedes closing statements and occasionally several rebuttal exchanges of 1 or 2 minutes are agreed upon.

Usually debates are news events and therefore, generate free media coverage that is especially beneficial to a challenger. This is why some incumbents avoid them, or try to minimize the number, especially in the early stages of the campaign.

Never send a substitute to a debate.

When preparing for a debate, it is usually a good idea for the Candidate to go through mock debates with a sharp staff person or volunteer. Try to anticipate every question that might be asked and how to frame the response within the allotted time frame. If the debate is being televised, be sure to look straight into the camera when answering. Never look at the opponent, the moderator, or the panel. If no television camera is present, look at the audience when answering.

Dress conservatively; use only light powder make up if being televised, to avoid reflection from the TV lights. Speak distinctly, avoid excessive hand gestures, be personable, and not combative. Be sure to thank the opponent, host organization, panel members, and the moderator for providing this opportunity to debate the issues.

Fairs, Festivals, Parades

Almost every district in the country has fairs, festivals, and parades. A Candidate should make every effort to be personally active in as many as possible and have volunteers cover those he or she cannot attend. These activities are "meet and greet" types, giving the public a chance to see the Candidate in person.

At the fairs, the campaign should try to have a booth with volunteers to pass out literature and draw attention to the Candidate. All kinds of gimmicks have been used to draw people to the booth and to give them an awareness of the Candidate and the campaign. These range from passing out balloons to giving free pony rides to the children. One of the least expensive, and most effective techniques is to have a 25 or 50 gallon metal container filled with ice water and offer free drinks to the public. Normally, these events are held during the hot summer, and it is amazing how many people will appreciate and remember this simple gesture. Another popular and inexpensive idea is to have a portable audio-visual display running continuously. Alternatively, show a video of the Candidate campaigning, including a biographical spot, why he or she is running, and his or her stand on the issues. Almost every fair has a local radio station broadcasting live from a portable set-up. The Candidate should try to have a live interview with the DJ at least once a day.

At festivals, the Candidate would normally circulate through the crowd, if permitted, making introductions and shaking hands while volunteers pass out campaign literature. Some festival committees will allow candidates to set up booths. If that is the case, the routine should be the same as for the fairs.

More and more parade committees are discouraging candidates from riding in the traditional convertible with the signs on the side. If a Candidate can get in a parade, do so. Have volunteers walking the sides of the parade route, just ahead of the car, passing out brochures. If unable to get into the parade, just have the volunteers walk along the sides of the parade route passing out literature.

Community Centers of Activity

Some candidates find it helpful to work the crowds at the parks and beaches on Sundays and holidays during the summer months. If this type of activity is traditional in the Candidate's district and he or she does not mind doing it, that's fine, as long as it does not take away from his or her R&R time. Normally,

A Candidate should make every effort to campaign at all the Senior Citizen clubs and homes in the district. As a group, senior citizens have one of the highest voter turnout rates and they often make a critical difference in the election outcome.

Unless a Candidate is well organized and disciplined enough to keep to a schedule, the opportunity to maximize his or her personal impact on the campaign will be proportionately limited.

I would discourage it on the basis that this is semi-private family time for most individuals and the risk of turning people off by invading it may be greater than the political gain that might be realized.

A safer form of this activity is to campaign, periodically, at the local shopping centers and farmers' markets using the same procedure as at the festivals. The campaign should obtain permission from the directors of Senior Citizen clubs and homes in order to visit with these reliable voters. Follow the guidelines for a coffee "Klatsch." Give a short talk, Q&A, and distribute literature.

If a Candidate is so inclined, churches can be an excellent place to campaign. Many churches will give a Candidate an opportunity to participate in some manner during their Sunday services, perhaps reading prayers, giving a short sermon, or singing. Investigate this opportunity and make arrangements when making Center of Influence visits with the religious leaders.

Additional activities include visits with Centers of Influence, fund-raising, and meetings with individuals and committees. Signing letters, research, study, reviewing campaign material, making progress reports, and preparing budgets are all required activities of the Candidate.

In the section on the Media Secretary's role, I will discuss the type of activity recommended to promote free media coverage, as it relates to the Candidate's role.

Role The role of the Candidate's spouse and family is entirely dependent on the individual.

The Candidate's spouse is generally the only acceptable substitute for the Candidate and is speaking for the Candidate, not for himself or herself.

The Candidate's Spouse and Family

The role that the Candidate's spouse plays in the campaign is entirely dependent on the individual. There is no constant.

Some spouses prefer, even insist, on staying in the background. At best, they will occasionally provide some assistance at headquarters or attend essential events with the Candidate. Others are able and willing to take a much more active role. This provides an extra dimension to the Candidate's campaigning that is not possible from any other source. In the public mind, the Candidate's spouse is generally the only acceptable substitute for the Candidate. An active spouse, therefore, can almost double the impact of the Candidate's activities on the campaign.

If the spouse does take an active role, he or she can do all of the activities similar to the Candidate and in some cases do them even more effectively. The spouse should be thoroughly briefed on the issues and the Political Game Plan. The spouse must remember at all times, he or she is speaking for the Candidate, not for himself or herself. The same rules regarding behavior, safety, and dress that apply to the Candidate apply to the spouse. The spouse should always travel with a volunteer aide when campaigning.

If the spouse is playing an active role, he or she should be a member of all committees and be encouraged to attend and participate in meetings. The spouse should be especially cognizant of his or her role as a morale builder with the staff and volunteers. Many who would hesitate to communicate with the Candidate when there is a problem will usually be more comfortable speaking to the spouse, if they feel encouraged to do so.

Role The children's role depends on age and willingness. The children should always remember they are part of the Candidate's image and conduct themselves accordingly.

The role of any children in the family depends on their ages and willingness or ability to become involved. If they are older, they should be encouraged to work with the volunteers in the Phone Bank. It is good for volunteer morale to see the Candidate's children working side by side with them.

If they are post teens, they could be used as the Driver/Aide or to do messenger work, the traditional "gofer" job. If they are adults, they can be utilized as surrogate speakers. The children should always remember they are part of the Candidate's image and conduct themselves accordingly.

Role One Campaign Chairperson oversees the activities of the Field Operations Committee; the other oversees the administrative and financial parts of the campaign. Together they oversee the entire campaign.

The Campaign Chairperson(s)

Ideally, there should be two Chairpersons, a man and a woman. Both individuals should be close associates of the Candidate and must be trusted implicitly. As can be seen from the Candidate's activities, a Candidate rarely has time to oversee the campaign closely and should not have to take the time to do so. The Campaign Chairpersons have this primary function. To that extent they should be capable, qualified individuals.

In addition, it is their responsibility to make sure the Candidate's and staff morale stay high. At the first sign of a problem, in this regard, they should step in and take corrective action. Most of the time, just "lending an ear," giving someone a chance to speak or even a chance to let off steam is all that is needed. They should be especially sensitive to the Candidate and the Campaign Manager. Since these two positions are "dumped on" most often, they are subject to the most internal pressure since neither one can afford to show anger or emotional upset.

From time to time a little staff party is helpful. Some outward sign of appreciation at just the right time can make a significant difference in attitude and productivity. The Chairpersons should be certain that the staff take regular R&R so that they too are in the best mental and physical condition for the final stages.

Chairpersons are also called on, from time to time, to speak to the media on behalf of the campaign and to fill in for the Candidate as surrogate speakers, when both the Candidate and spouse are unavailable. Most organizational press releases are issued in their names. In a sense, they are the visible head of the volunteer campaign and represent all volunteers with the Candidate and the public. They chair the Advisory Committee meetings and are members of all other committees. As such, they should alternate in chairing the Advisory Committee meetings and establishing the agenda for them. If present at formal functions, they usually make the necessary introductions.

The Campaign Treasurer

Role The Treasurer is responsible for the campaign accounting and reporting procedures.

The Treasurer is responsible for the campaign accounting and reporting procedures in accordance with the Federal Election Commission or regulatory state agency rules and regulations. It is a very detailed and difficult responsibility. Ideally, the Treasurer is an accountant or tax attorney familiar with campaign accounting procedures. The Treasurer is responsible for the deposit of all campaign receipts and expenditures.

No monetary transaction may take place while there is a vacancy in the Treasurer's position.

When the Candidate files the campaign committee form with the Clerk of the House and the FEC in Washington, DC, or the appropriate state agency if a non-Federal Candidate, it must show the name and address of the Treasurer and the bank where all deposits will be made. Once filed, the Treasurer is legally responsible for the reporting of all transactions, including the filing of the required periodic reports, until a formal change of Treasurer is made. Technically, no monetary transaction may take place while there is a vacancy in the Treasurer's position.

Since it is now mandatory to file FEC reports electronically, and since state agencies are moving in this direction, we have another reason to convince the campaign to computerize.

The FEC and most state agencies are not concerned about which accounting method is used as long as it is detailed and accurate. Normally, the use of the contributor's card (a sample can be found in Appendix M) is sufficient for recording receipts. The campaign checkbook stubs together with the canceled checks are adequate proof of disbursements. Long term contracts and loans can be recorded in a simple ledger book. Computer software available for campaigns, including GOTV *Campaign Optimizer*, include a section to record the data necessary for the completion of these requirements in an acceptable format. It is now mandatory to file all FEC reports electronically and most states are moving in this direction. You should check to see if this arrangement is possible in your state.

The Campaign Treasurer is responsible (on behalf of the campaign committee) for compliance with all FEC and State laws and regulations regarding the elected office that is being sought. Although, the Candidate will be legally liable for breaches of campaign finance regulations, the Treasurer will be responsible for the day to day compliance and shares this burden on an ethical, if not legal level. Financial transactions involving contributions, disbursements, debts and obligations, and campaign loans all fall under the auspices of the Treasurer's responsibility and are all subject to FEC and State regulatory agencies. The Treasurer will certify that all receipts and expenditures are legal. As these laws and regulations change with legislation, the Treasurer must remain informed and wise regarding all campaign finance laws and regulations before, during, and after the campaign and election. A campaign finance guideline is automatically sent to the Treasurer of Federal campaigns, along with a basic supply of forms, when the committee is filed. State Agencies model a similar procedure.

Since few Treasurers can work full time on the campaign, it is usual for them to delegate many of these responsibilities to the staff, especially the secretary/ bookkeeper and the Finance Director, if there is one, or to the Campaign Manager. Normally the records are kept under lock and key in the headquarters. Records of receipts and bank deposits are filed by the bookkeeper. Disbursement checks prepared by the Campaign Manager, or the bookkeeper, are for the Treasurer's signature. The Treasurer verifies all transactions at the time of filing the FEC or state reports. The Treasurer, along with the Campaign Manager, is also responsible for keeping the Candidate informed if the campaign is staying within the Budget and the Cash Flow. The Treasurer is automatically a member of the Advisory and Finance Committees.

The Treasurer, the Campaign Manager, and the Candidate are usually the only three individuals with check signing authority. Normally any one of them can sign checks up to a predetermined amount, usually $1,000, with two of the three signatories being required for larger disbursements. It is inadvisable to require two signatories for checks below $1,000 as this can present numerous problems during the final stages of the campaign.

As previously stated, the Treasurer should establish two checking accounts at the bank, one account designated for the primary election period and the other account for the general election period. In general, funds may be deposited to either account. In addition (at this writing), the campaign can deposit contributions into the "primary" account, even after the primary election. This is allowed if a debt has been "carried forward" from a previous period, and a donor, who has not contributed their maximum amount for the previous period, designates a contribution for that specific election period. Again, always verify these regulations with the FEC or state agency.

Presently, accounting and law firms are the only exceptions to the FEC law regarding the prohibition of corporate contributions to federal candidates, as the campaign is allowed to accept their services as a contribution-in-kind.

If the campaign has a Political Campaign Consultant, he or she will usually be able to provide any needed assistance to the Treasurer in setting up the basic procedures. An accounting firm even if a corporation may donate its services to the campaign for the purposes of performing this function, but someone must still sign and be responsible as Treasurer.

The Assistant Treasurer

Role The assistant treasurer acts as, and is fully accountable for all Treasurer responsibilities in the event that the Treasurer is unable to perform that function.

In today's fast moving climate, it is wise to appoint both a Treasurer and Assistant Treasurer. Since no monetary transaction is allowed while there is a vacancy in the Treasurer's position, the appointment of an Assistant Treasurer circumvents this potentially disastrous possibility.

The Assistant Treasurer is responsible to the Treasurer and must be kept abreast of all of the campaign's financial activity. In effect, he or she must be ready, willing, and able to "come off the bench" and be "up to speed" at a moment's notice, should the Treasurer be unable to fulfill that role.

The Finance Committee Chairperson(s)

Role One Finance Committee Chairperson is responsible for the major contributors' program and major fund-raising events; the other should oversee the individual solicitation and fund-raising direct mail program.

Most of the duties for Finance Committee Chairperson(s) is/are described in the Fund-raising chapter. As with the Advisory Committee, it is desirable to have a man and a woman as co-chairpersons. One chairperson would be from the upper-level income group and be primarily responsible for overseeing the major contributors' program, and the major events. The other should be from the middle level income group and oversee the individual solicitation and fund-raising direct mail program. Both are responsible for overseeing the total fund-raising effort for the campaign.

Much of the success of the campaign is dependent on the efforts of the Finance Committee Chairperson(s). If they fail to be accomplished at their jobs, the campaign can suffer disastrous repercussions. Some candidates attempt to campaign without someone assigned to this responsibility, in almost every case, the campaign will fail.

The Finance Chairpersons must have the drive and ability to motivate the rest of the committee to realize the objectives.

Naturally, much of the success of the campaign is dependent on the efforts of these two individuals and the rest of the Finance Committee. If they fail to be accomplished at their jobs, not only in terms of dollars raised, but also regarding the financial timeline, the campaign can suffer disastrous repercussions. These individuals must be totally committed to the Candidate and the successful outcome of the campaign. Great care must be used in selecting people who have the ability and willingness to do this job. Unfortunately, it goes with the territory that most candidates learn that it is difficult to find anyone willing to take on this responsibility.

A solid Finance Committee, with good leadership, must be a top priority in the 1st Stage of the campaign. Frankly, unless they are willing and able to finance their own campaign, I normally recommend that candidates not attempt their campaign unless they first organize a capable Finance Committee. Although, a good fund-raising consultant, coupled with a strong Political Game Plan will help considerably, it is only with the success of a capable Finance Committee that the major portion of the plan will ever be implemented.

As the heads of this committee, they should alternate chairing the meetings. Both are automatically members of the Advisory Committee.

The Research Chairperson

Role The Research Chairperson analyzes and understands the basic issues and implications of the Candidate's positions.

Ideally, the Research Chairperson would also know how to read and interpret polling data, thus providing the Candidate and Campaign Manager with valuable assistance in this critical area of strategy development.

I recommend *The Almanac of American Politics* by Michael Barone and Grant Ujifusa, published by The National Journal, Inc., for federal or major statewide candidates. The National Journal can also be found at www.nationaljournal.com/about/almanac.

Normally the Research Chairperson is a volunteer recruited from the Political Science Department of a local college or a volunteer journalist. He or she helps the Candidate know and understand the basic issues and the implications of the positions taken. He or she provides supporting data, analyzes the record or position statements of the opponent, provides accurate comparisons of positions, and monitors the development of the issue-oriented segment of the campaign. The Research Chairperson also helps to prepare the Candidate for debates and provides assistance in the writing of basic speeches and press releases.

There are many resources available to the Research Chairperson to assist in the performance of these responsibilities. The "morgue" at the local daily newspaper is an excellent source for information on the opponent's previous campaigns if he or she has run before, including style, results, and promises made. If running against a Federal incumbent, the *Congressional Quarterly* or *LEGI-SLATE* will provide a complete record of the incumbent's votes, finances, and major speeches during the previous six years. Both national parties and many state parties have extensive research departments available on the Internet that will provide much of this information without charge. In addition, you will find the Party's position on most major issues, their reasons for these positions, and supporting data to justify them. Many of these resources are available through the Internet.

Some PACs will provide basic research as an in-kind contribution, especially on issues of primary concern to them. A current almanac is also an excellent source of data that is often overlooked. Alternatively, previous candidates for the office being sought have probably kept the research files developed during their campaigns and might be willing to share, if asked.

Almost every department in the government has reams of research data on issues within their purview and often a letter requesting assistance on a particular subject will produce an outpouring of data. In many cases, this data can be accessed on the Internet. If a Federal Candidate, write to the Superintendent of Documents, U.S. Government Printing Office, P.O. Box 371954, Pittsburgh, PA 15250 for a copy of their directory showing availability and price for all Federal government publications. You can also check their web site at www.bookstore.gpo.gov.

The Research Chairperson is responsible not only for the accumulation of all this data, but also for cataloging it in a manner that makes it available for quick and easy reference, when needed, and in many cases, recasting the data into concise position papers.

The Research Chairperson is automatically a member of the Advisory Committee.

The Regional Chairpersons

Role The Regional Chairperson is responsible for supervision and motivation at the region level.

In the geographic and organizational structuring of the campaign, we divide the district into five Regions and then subdivide each Region into five Areas. Two persons, preferably a man and a woman should chair each Region. Since their primary responsibilities are supervision and motivation, they should be people who are relatively aggressive and self-generating by nature, with experience in management and/or leadership roles.

The Regional Chairperson and the committees are conducting a grass-roots campaign within each Region. That is, a campaign within the campaign.

They are responsible for implementing their share of the two basic activities in the field operations program of the campaign, i.e., the Phone Bank and Precinct Operations. They must recruit, train, and supervise the Area Chairpersons and Regional Phone Bank Supervisors. Therefore, they must be thoroughly familiar with the Political Game Plan and help develop the Field Operations (a sample of this manual is in Chapter 14) Manual for the Precinct Captains and Phone Bank volunteers. During each stage, they should conduct training seminars for all volunteers on the procedures and objectives of the plan in that period.

Once the Regional and Area voter objectives are established, they must initiate a routine of receiving bi -monthly progress reports from the Area Chairperson and Phone Bank Supervisors in order to monitor their progress. There should be a special emphasis on whether the Region is on schedule.

If an Area is behind, they must determine why early enough to take the necessary corrective action, by either replacing the individual who is failing to do his or her assignment, by shifting personnel resources to assist temporarily, or by readjusting objectives.

In order to accomplish these responsibilities and objectives, they should maintain a card file or computer printout, listing the name, address, telephone number, and occupation of each volunteer in their Region plus that individual's personal objective, the number of registered voters by Party, the date assigned, and a place to record progress reports. In the absence of a computerized campaign, this information can also be maintained in a "control book."

The Regional Chairpersons should develop and maintain a procedural system for the constant recruitment of new volunteers, as well as for the retention of the old ones, for both functions. During the 4th Stage, they must also recruit and train volunteers who will serve as host homes in the 5th Stage.

Regional Chairpersons - Methods for Recruiting Volunteers

There are several methods generally used in recruiting volunteers:

1) The response to the information printed on the inside flap of the BRE envelope that the staff would forward to the appropriate Regional Chairperson as soon as they have finished processing them,

2) The recruitment activity built into the Phone Bank and Precinct programs during the 2nd and 3rd Stage,

3) Coffee "Klatsches,"

4) Personal appeals to friends, relatives, and members of organizations to which they might belong,

5) Appeals to Party precinct workers and members of their affiliated organizations,

6) Local religious leaders and church affiliated organizations,

7) The offers of assistance the Candidate receives while campaigning,

8) Local senior citizens clubs,

9) Local colleges and universities, especially from the Political Science Departments,

10) Seniors and juniors in high school civics classes,

11) Members of organizations or groups that are actively supporting the campaign, or

12) Asking existing volunteers to help recruit at least one other person.

The Regional Chairperson and the committees are conducting a grass-roots campaign within each Region.

Regional Chairpersons - Developing the Volunteer Kits

When developing the Precinct Captain and Phone Bank volunteers' kits, be sure to keep them consistent and relatively easy to understand. The kits should be self-explanatory, so that in the event a training seminar is not possible a volunteer will be able to understand what needs to be done and be able to get started on their own. Avoid complicated and highly structured "canned" messages. Provide the outline and let the volunteers use their own phraseology to fill it in (a sample kit can be found in Chapter 14).

The Field Operations Committee activities are designed to identify and inform the electorate during the 2nd through 4th Stages, so that they can be motivated in the 5th Stage to get out and vote for the Candidate.

The volunteer organization is one of the Candidate's critical advantages and must not fail the campaign.

Remember that every contributor, no matter how small the contribution, on the average will speak to seven other people and try to influence them to vote for the Candidate.

Objectives are to identify and inform the electorate during the 2nd through 4th Stages, so that they can be motivated in the 5th Stage to get out and vote (GOTV) for the Candidate. All of the Field Operations Committee activities are designed to accomplish these broad objectives.

To continue with our analogy, the Regional Chairpersons and their committee members will separate the chaff (those who are opposed to the candidate), from the wheat (those who are for the candidate), during the ID and Advocacy Stages. They will then bring in the harvest during the Get-Out-the-Vote (GOTV) Stage. Without the Field Operations Committee effort, the chances of a successful harvest are greatly reduced, if not entirely eliminated. Remember that one of the few advantages most challengers have over an incumbent is the ability to rally a committed volunteer organization. It is a critical advantage and must not fail.

Regional Chairpersons - Minor Events / Other Activities

At least once during the campaign, the Regional Chairperson should plan a minor fund-raising event in the Region with their counterpart on the Finance Committee. To the extent that the Regional Chairpersons can, they should help supplement the Finance Committee's fund-raising activities at the precinct level. Mini projects, like selling campaign buttons, car washes, garage sales, and passing the hat at coffee "Klatsches," are helpful, both financially and politically.

Previously, we discussed the use of 4 x 8 corrugated signs to supplement the billboard program. Normally, an ad hoc committee would be established to prepare the signs, and the Regional Chairperson would organize a separate group of volunteers to find suitable locations and to erect the signs during the 2nd Stage. In addition, another part of the program entails the distribution of bumper stickers early in the 2nd Stage and the precinct literature drops scheduled during the 4th Stage. The Regional Chairperson should keep a separate list of all people who have volunteered to put up yard signs in the Region during the final month of the campaign and organize the volunteers needed to implement this program.

The Regional Chairpersons should be sensitive to morale, especially the morale of the Area Chairpersons and the Phone Bank Supervisors. They have the hardest volunteer jobs in the campaign. The Regional Chairpersons should always make sure the efforts of the Area Chairpersons are recognized and appreciated. From time to time, they should have a luncheon or social gathering for them with the Candidate present. They should also keep the Area Chairpersons informed about what is going on in the rest of the campaign. It is especially aggravating when these people learn from the newspaper something that they should have been informed of in person.

As the heads of the Regional Committee, the Regional Chairpersons should alternate chairing the scheduled meetings and seminars. In dividing responsibilities, one Chairperson is usually responsible for the Phone Bank, events, and bumper sticker programs, and the other for Precinct sign and literature drop programs. Both should be thoroughly familiar with all the programs since they are responsible for overseeing all of the activities within their Region.

Regional Chairpersons - Candidate Regional Schedule

During the campaign, the Candidate will be scheduled on a prioritized basis for the specified number of days allotted to each Region. After the scheduler has worked out with the Regional Chairpersons their assigned days, they should be sure to maximize the Candidate's activities and impact for that day by carefully planning the program.

The Candidate is one of the best "tools" the Regional Chairpersons have to help them reach their objectives. For example, if they are having a problem with recruiting, they might want to arrange several coffee "Klatsches" for that evening in an effort to motivate prospective volunteers to get on board. If there is a high priority precinct remaining uncovered by a Precinct Captain or not generating the results expected, the Candidate could be scheduled to spend a few hours walking the precinct with the Regional or Area Chairperson in a concerted effort to recruit a Precinct Captain and/or improve the response there. If analyzing the Phone Bank results suggests that public awareness of the Candidate is low in a certain area, the Regional Chairperson might want to schedule a small rally at a local community shopping center.

In effect, the Regional Chairperson and the committees are conducting a grass-roots campaign within each Region. They assist in developing the strategy, the objectives, the Political Game Plan, and the program for its implementation. I often refer to it as the campaign within the campaign. As stated before, it is a critical part of the campaign and will play a major role in the determination of its outcome.

The Regional Chairpersons are automatically members of the Field Operations Committee and the Advisory Committee.

Role The Area Chairperson is responsible for implementation of Area Precinct operations, functioning not only in a supervisory capacity but in a supportive role as well.

The Area Chairpersons

The Area Chairpersons are responsible for implementing the precinct operations in their respective Areas. The exact number of precincts will vary relative to the size of the electoral district and the Political Game Plan. They share with the Regional Chairpersons the responsibility for recruiting, training, and supervising the Precinct Captains in their assigned precincts. They also help develop the objectives, monitor progress, submit monthly detailed reports to their Regional Chairperson and assist with the campaigning events and sign programs.

Like the Regional Chairperson, the Area Chairpersons should maintain a card file or control book listing the name, address, telephone number, and occupation of each of their Precinct Captains and of each volunteer in their Area plus that individual's personal objective, the number of registered voters by Party, the date assigned, and a place to record progress reports for, plus the names of backup volunteers in case their use becomes necessary. They should get to know their Precinct Captains through regularly scheduled meetings and keep them informed about the campaign's overall progress. If problems or local issues develop that the Candidate should be aware of, they should promptly share this information with their Regional Chairperson.

The Area Chairpersons should help plan the Candidate's schedule when campaigning in their Area and accompany him or her, if possible.

The Area Chairpersons are also responsible for maintaining and distributing the supplies and materials needed by the Precinct Captains. They should try to visit at least one Precinct Captain each day, to discuss progress, to help solve problems, and to bolster their morale. The Precinct Captains are in the front line of offense within the campaign and as such, they carry a heavy burden and responsibility. The Area Chairperson functions not only in a supervisory capacity but in a supportive role as well.

A regional newsletter is especially helpful in producing an element of competition, resulting in a deepening team spirit.

It helps to engender a team spirit. To encourage this, I suggest that the campaign develop an element of competition. Designate each Area committee with an unofficial, colorful, or descriptive name, and then compare internally the progress for all the Areas and the percentage of the objectives accomplished within a specific period by each team. When the Area Chairpersons really get into the swing of this method, prizes, such as having the other four Area Chairperson pick up the tab for a pizza party honoring the Area committee leading at the end of the 2nd and 3rd Stages, can be awarded and the results of the competition posted in a campaign newsletter. The formation of bowling or softball team competition can also be helpful in creating a team spirit.

Camaraderie is essential; a picnic or special night at a local professional baseball game are two other suggestions that might be considered to assist in creating the appropriate atmosphere.

The Area Chairpersons should organize other ideas that inject an element of fun and socializing into the campaign activities. Studies have shown, and my own experience has confirmed, many volunteers become involved in a campaign just for an opportunity to meet people and socialize. A sense of civic responsibility is usually second and the concern about issues and/or the Candidate is third. There is no rule that says working on a campaign should not be fun and self-rewarding.

Area Chairpersons are automatically members of the Field Operations Committee.

Role The Precinct Captain is the real "work-horse" who personally represents the Candidate on the front line.

The Precinct Captain

Often described as the real "work-horse" of the campaign, the Precinct Captain is the individual on whom the whole field operation's structure is built. On the front line, they are the ones who personally represent the Candidate and the campaign on a daily basis.

Before beginning, the Precinct Captain should be given a kit containing a biography of the Candidate, the public Political Game Plan, a synopsis of the Candidate's position on the issues, the comparative piece between the Candidate and the opponent, the Precinct Captain's manual, a map of the precinct, a "walk-sheet," and a supply of brochures and bumper stickers.

A dedicated Precinct Captain should canvass every home or apartment in the precinct, surveying each resident as to whether or not they are registered to vote, with which Party they are affiliated, and whether or not they plan to support the Candidate in the upcoming election. If yes, the Precinct Captain does everything possible to help them get to the polls on Election Day.

The Captains know the dynamics of their precincts. That is, who lives there, what their concerns are, and how they vote? After they have identified the voters in their precincts, they return to call on the undecideds, regardless of party preference, armed with position papers, the opponent's voting record, or positions on specific issues. They attempt to convince an undecided to vote for their Candidate, usually spending about a half-hour with the person and recording the results on the precinct walk-sheet. Every 2 weeks the Precinct Captains should meet with the Area Chairperson and update the results of their efforts. Precinct Captains are also expected to help with the sign program in their precincts and with minor events in the Region.

Since the average precinct usually has 200 families, the initial ID survey or canvass of the precinct will probably show around 40 for an incumbent and 25 for a challenger. This leaves around 135 undecided to be called on over the 3 months during the 3rd Stage. With each visit lasting about 15 minutes, the time required amounts to about 11.25 hours of work each month, plus the 7 hours per week needed for callbacks and meetings with the Area Chairperson.

The objective for the Precinct Captain, I might note, would probably be around 65 positive identified households for the Candidate presuming a 60 percent voter turnout. That figure includes a safety margin of 10 percent. With 25 households already predisposed to vote for the Candidate, if a challenger, the Precinct Captain needs to convert about 30 percent of the remaining 135 undecideds, or 41 households, in order to reach his or her precinct's objective.

The act of signing an endorsement sheet, like the act of giving a contribution, usually produces a multiplier effect.

One tool that can be used by the Precinct Captain to be more certain of a "committed" vote is to ask the person who says he or she is for the Candidate to sign an endorsement sheet. The act of signing, like the act of giving a contribution, usually produces a multiplier effect. Where a contributor will usually encourage seven others to join them in voting for the Candidate, an endorser will usually influence three others to join.

After the Precinct Captain has a completed endorsement sheet, a copy should be made and forwarded to the Field Director or Campaign Manager. There the names will be added to the support file for future contact with newsletters and fund-raising appeals. The names, addresses, and telephone numbers should, therefore, be legible. I normally recommend having the people print the information and then initial it.

Though they are operating independently of the Phone Bank, the Precinct Captains should, at the end of each Stage, compare their precinct walk-sheets with the duplicates being used at the Phone Bank to coordinate and update the results of both efforts. If the Phone Bank precinct sheet, usually referred to as computer printouts, does not have a telephone number for the registered voter, the Precinct Captain, if he or she has obtained it, should write it in, especially for the Candidate's supporters, Party members, independents, and undecideds. If it does not appear on the walk-sheet, the Precinct Captain should obtain these telephone numbers during their canvass of the precinct.

When the Candidate is campaigning in the precinct, the Precinct Captain should make every effort to accompany him or her while walking the precinct. They

The Precinct Captains are normally responsible for poll watching duties on Election Day.

should also assist the Area Chairperson in recruiting volunteers and the host homes needed for other campaign activities.

The Precinct Captain is a member of his or her Area Committee and should try to attend all meetings and seminars called by the Area Chairperson.

Role The Phone Bank and Supervisors provide back up for the precinct operation, follow up for the Finance Committee programs, and primary communication with the voters, especially in the GOTV Stage.

The Phone Bank Supervisors & Program

The Phone Bank, for a campaign the size of our prototype, would consist of ten calling units plus two regular units. It is located at the volunteer headquarters and has three basic functions in the campaign:

1) to provide a backup, or "safety net," program for the precinct operations,
2) to provide telephone follow up assistance for some of the Finance Committee's programs, and
3) to provide the primary communication with the voters in the GOTV Stage.

It is inadvisable to call on Sundays since many voters find this offensive.

There should be 12 Phone Bank Supervisors, of which two should be assigned to each Region and be under the supervision of that Region's Chairpersons, and two should be assigned to the campaign headquarters under the supervision of the Finance Director or Campaign Manager. Presuming a 6-day operation of the Phone Bank, two Supervisors would normally share the responsibility for each Region's day of operation at the Bank, plus 1 day for the Finance Committee. Since the Phone Bank normally operates from 10:00 a.m. to 9:00 p.m., the day is usually divided into two 5 1/2 hour shifts with one supervisor per shift. Calling before 10:00 a.m. would find many parents busy getting the children off to school; calling after 9:00 p.m. would find many people getting children ready for bed, or settled in with their favorite TV shows and in no mood to be disturbed. The Field Operations Director, who is the staff person responsible for providing logistical support to the Field Operations Committee, does this scheduling.

Each Phone Bank Supervisor, in addition to supervising the shift's activities and completing the appropriate tally sheets at the end of each day, should assist the Regional Chairperson in the recruitment and training of the Phone Bank volunteers. They should arrive 15 minutes before the shift begins to make sure the supplies, such as pencils and envelopes, are available and that the assigned printouts are ready for calling.

Normally, each Region would have the responsibility for the Phone Bank on the same regularly scheduled day of each week, e.g., Region I on Monday, Finance on Tuesday, Region II on Wednesday, etc. Although this arrangement is not required, it keeps things simple and, in this case, more effective. If mutually desired, a change of days between Regions could take place at the end of each Stage. In other words, each Region has the responsibility for recruiting an average of 20 volunteers, who will be needed to keep the telephones working at maximum capacity during both shifts each day.

Occasionally, there will be certain permanent Phone Bank volunteers willing to work several shifts each week. This helps recruiting efforts considerably.

However, the final responsibility always rests with the Region assigned for any particular day.

The Phone Bank - Procedures, Objectives, and Implementation

The Phone Bank surveys the registered voters in the district in an effort to determine how each voter is planning to vote.

During each stage, the Phone Bank serves essentially the same function as the precinct operation, surveying the registered voters in the district in an effort to determine how each voter is planning to vote in the upcoming election.

If the district does not have telephone numbers available on the voter tapes and the campaign is unable to have the numbers tele-matched by a computer service bureau, then volunteers need to be used to look up and post the numbers before the calls begin. Usually this activity is staggered so it stays about 2 weeks ahead of the telephoning. Crisscross directories are ideal for this activity as they list the names both alphabetically and by street address.

Phone Bank - Stage 2, Voter Identification

The 2nd Stage calls are not demanding. The volunteer simply identifies himself or herself and advising the voter that, "We are taking a survey and would appreciate a moment of your time regarding the upcoming election for (Office being sought). If the election were held today, would you be voting for (name of incumbent/opponent) (Alternate the names i.e., challenger/candidate), or are you still undecided?" If they say they are for the Candidate, then ask them if they would be willing to volunteer some time on the campaign. If they say no to being a volunteer, thank them for supporting the Candidate and encourage them to ask their friends and relatives to vote for the Candidate. If yes, advise them that, "Someone will be in contact with them soon and thank them for their assistance and say goodbye." After the call is completed, the volunteer would circle the "V" (indicating volunteer) on the printout sheet, transfer the personal information to a volunteer card, and give it to the Supervisor. Finally, the phone bank volunteer will record the answer on the print out or the tally sheet, by circling the appropriate symbol, usually "F" if for the Candidate, "A" if against the Candidate, and "U" for undecided. If the person being called is definitely for the opponent, a single pencil line is drawn through the individual's name. This will be the only time the opponent's supporters are personally contacted by the Candidate's campaign.

Notice that the volunteer does not indicate initially whom the survey is for since this might prejudice the response. Where a Political Campaign Consultant is involved in the campaign, they will usually authorize the campaign to say the survey is being taken on their behalf. The approach is as follows, "Hello, (his or her name), this is (volunteer's name); I am taking a survey today for Campaign Opinion Research of Washington, D.C."

At the end of each shift, the Phone Bank Supervisor collects the volunteer cards and tally sheets, summarizes them, makes sure they are dated, initials them, and turns them in to the Campaign Secretary. The printout sheets are marked in pencil only and no other markings, except as indicated, should be made. A number of people will be using the sheets over several months and if a computer company will be reentering the data into a database, the campaign will be charged extra if the sheets are not clean and clear.

An average congressional district will have about 141,000 households of registered voters with listed telephone numbers. The average phone volunteer can complete about 60 calls per hour in the 2nd Stage, allowing for 50 percent "no answers" or disconnected numbers, x 10 units = 300 completed calls per hour. If the Phone Bank operates efficiently, multiply 300 x 8 full hours per day of telephoning. Allowing 1 hour per shift downtime, it would take the Phone Bank about 12 weeks at that rate to complete the ID Stage of the program, 2,400 x 5 = 12,000 calls per week x 12 weeks = 144,0000. Starting in late February, this would complete the program by the end of the 2nd Stage, the last week of May. This formula can also be used to calculate the number of telephone units required for different sized districts. Divide 1,440 into the number of households and the result is the number of units needed over a 12-week period.

If the phone volunteer is able to determine that the person is deceased or moved form the district, the name can be eliminated from future printouts by circling the opponent's code "A" on the printout.

On average, it can be expected that about 25,000 households will not be contacted as a result of disconnected numbers and no answers. Of the 116,000 balance, the breakout would probably be around 29,000 for the opponent if an incumbent and 17,000 for the candidate/challenger, with the remaining 70,000 undecided or refusing to answer. Those who refuse to answer are treated as undecideds during the 3rd Stage and eliminated by marking the printout sheet with the opponent's designation "A" during the 4th Stage, if they still refuse to answer.

At the end of the 2nd Stage, the sheets should be compared with the Precinct Captain's results and be revised accordingly.

Phone Bank - Stage 3, Positive Advocacy

During the 3rd Stage, the undecideds are called again, then the independents, if time permits. This time the phone volunteers identify themselves as volunteers for the (Candidate's name) for (office) Committee and make a brief attempt to convince the voter to vote for the Candidate. If a positive response is given, the phone volunteer reinforces the positive response and asks them if they would like to volunteer, records the personal information on the volunteer card next to the phone, thanks them, and makes the appropriate designation on the printout sheet, erasing the previous one (thus the use of pencil only). The appropriate mark is then made on the tally sheet.

If still undecided, the phone volunteer advises that the Candidate will be sending some information that might assist them in making their decision. Closing with the hope that it is a favorable decision, the phone volunteer again circles the "U" designation on the printout sheet to avoid recalling the person during this Stage, then addresses a #10 envelope, with a special mailer or a tabloid and marks that result on the tally sheet. A supply of mailing materials should always be on hand next to the telephone.

If the voter indicates they have decided to vote for the opponent, thank them for their time, say goodbye, mark the sheet with the opponent's designation "A," draw a line through the name, and erase the previous "U" designation.

This interview from beginning to end will normally take 4 minutes. With time allowed for uncompleted calls, the average phone volunteer can complete 12 calls per hour x 10 units = 120 per hour x 8 hours, allowing 1 hour downtime per shift = 960 completed calls per day x 5 days = 4,800 calls per week. With approximately 14 weeks in the 3rd Stage, the total number of completed calls possible will be around 67,200. This is close to the 70,000 started with. Short of increasing the number of telephone units in the Phone Bank, the differential can be reduced by:

1) eliminating those who refused to answer by circling the opponent's designation,
2) ignoring the undecideds who are members of the opponent's Party and marking no different designation on the sheets for the time being,
3) concentration on the telephone calls in the higher priority precincts first, or
4) adding the data collected from the Precinct Captains to the Phone Bank results. The result of all these adjustments should reduce the original 70,000 total to the number of calls actually made.

Of the 67,200 completed calls, around 50 percent will probably still be undecided or refuse to answer. The balance should fall 60/40 percent to the candidate/challenger because of the personal contact. The process results in 20,000 additional positive households identified. That, added to the previous total obtained in the 2nd Stage, should bring the grand total by the end of the 3rd Stage to 37,000 households.

Phone Bank - Stage 4, Negative Advocacy

The phone volunteer's routine in the 4th Stage is similar to the 3rd Stage, except that the message in the letter mailed to the remaining undecideds should contain the negative attack. The first call backs should be made to the 50 percent who were still undecided in the 3rd Stage and to the 33,600 to whom literature was mailed. This time the phone volunteers should continue to identify themselves as volunteers for the (Candidate's name) for (office) Committee.

The time that is required to complete the calls should be similar to that of the 3rd Stage. As before, circle the "U" a third time if they are still undecided and address an envelope with the comparative flyer and a letter from the Candidate. Make the appropriate change on the printout sheets if they have decided for the Candidate or the opponent. This time the percentage of those who are still undecided should be substantially reduced and should probably number no more than 20 percent. The balance of 26,880 will probably split 60 percent for the Candidate and 40 percent for the opponent or approximately 16,000 to 10,000. This makes the Candidate's grand total 53,000 positive identified households. The balance needed should come from the precinct operation.

A sample procedure for handling absentee ballot distribution is in the Phone Bank Manual in Chapter 14.

During the 4th Stage, the phone volunteer would ask all persons answering affirmatively for the Candidate if they need an absentee ballot for the election. If yes, follow the procedure required by the Secretary of State, Board of Elections, or County Registrar of Voters Office.

The time required to the end of the 4th Stage is 7 weeks. It is reasonable to assume that the Precinct Captains will have added an additional 14,000 household to this total. For the 67,000 positive identified households, the respective sheets should again be checked and updated. Given a ratio of 1.7 adult voting members per household, the Candidate should have 114,000+ votes on Election Day, if they all get out and vote.

Phone Bank - Stage 5, GOTV

In the first 9 days of the 5th Stage, a brief telephone call should be made to all positive identified households to remind them that Election Day is fast approaching and to find out whether they will need assistance to get to the polls. If yes, the phone volunteer should note the name, address, and telephone number on the special transportation pads next to the telephone and submit the information to the Supervisor, who will forward it to the Campaign Secretary. The person being called should then be urged to bring a friend along to the polls.

In this stage the completion rate should be 40 calls per hour x 10 hours, no downtime x 10 units = 4,000 calls per day x 9 days = 36,000 completed calls. Obviously, using only 10 units makes it virtually impossible to complete the required 67,000 calls. In anticipation of this problem, additional units and volunteers need to be secured prior to the beginning of the GOTV Stage. As the project director for the GOTV program, the Campaign Manager will make both these special arrangements and those required for the Election Day program.

Definition
A "host home" is one that has agreed to let a phone volunteer come into their home and use the telephone for making calls during the day.

Possible sources that might be volunteered are offices with several units, such as, real estate, insurance, and law offices that can be used for calling after normal closing hours. Host homes are another source. A "host home" is one that has agreed to let a phone volunteer come into their home and use the telephone for making calls during the day. In addition, the Precinct Captains can be requested to make a number of calls from their homes.

If additional time becomes available during this 9-day period, callbacks should be made to members of the Candidate's Party who were still undecided.

Phone Bank - Election Day Procedures

During Election Day, it is critical that all positive identified households be called and recalled until verification is given that the person actually voted.

The final program takes place on Election Day. It is critical that all positive identified households be called and recalled until verification is given that the person actually voted. In some cases, as many as three calls to the same household may be required.

Calling usually begins around 9:30 a.m. and continues until around 7:00 p.m. or a total of 9.5 hours. With an average call taking 2 minutes, a phone volunteer can make 30 calls per hour x 9.5 hours = 285 calls. Given that 67,000 calls need to be made, plus callbacks, the campaign will probably need at least 235 units plus 470 phone volunteers.

The Phone Bank Supervisors, under the direct supervision of the Campaign Manager during these final 10 days, will probably be directed to supervise centralized, volunteered banks set up for this effort. Some will assist by "breaking out" those precincts that are being sent to host homes for calling, usually the lower priority precincts and then helping with the distribution within their Regions.

The Phone Bank Supervisors, the Regional and Area Chairpersons, the Staff, and the Campaign Manager will make it all happen by working together as a cohesive, management team.

As awesome as all this might sound, it is very possible in a well-organized, well-directed plan, with a lot of cooperation. Incidentally, the Precinct Captains are normally responsible for poll watching duties on Election Day. Therefore, they will be unavailable to serve as phone volunteers. However, a good campaign, especially one that appears to have a chance of winning, will always have a surge of volunteers working on Election Day.

The Phone Bank Supervisors are automatically members of their Regional Committee and the Field Operations Committee, except for the two only assigned to the Finance Committee.

The Phone Bank Volunteer

Role Although not in person, the Phone Bank Volunteers are an important part of the front lines. He or she represents the Candidate and the campaign.

Like the Precinct Captains, Phone Bank Volunteers are a part of the front lines. Though not seen in person, because of his or her personal contact with the electorate, he or she is a representative of the Candidate and the campaign through the telephone. As such, they must give a positive impression at all times by speaking clearly, talking courteously, and avoiding saying anything derogatory about the opponent.

Each Phone Bank Volunteer should be provided with a basic kit containing a biography of the Candidate, a synopsis of his or her position on the issues, the comparative piece between the opponent and the Candidate, any printed material being mailed to the public, a brief outline of the Political Game Plan, and the Phone Bank Manual. They must be aware, at all times, of what is being received and read, and be made familiar with where the campaign stands to date.

Before the phone volunteer begins telephoning, the material should be read and, if there are any questions, they should be discussed with the Phone Bank Supervisor. If a person being called asks about the Candidate's position on an issue, only information on the synopsis sheet should be relayed to the voter. If additional information is asked for, a note should be made on the pad next to the telephone as to the nature of the question, the name, address, and telephone number of the person. This request and information should be given to the Supervisor, who will forward it to the Campaign Manager. The phone volunteer should advise the person that the Candidate will respond to the question as soon as possible.

Telephone volunteers should be responsible, dependable people, who will honor their commitment to the phone bank schedule and who, during each stage, will follow instructions precisely. They should be made aware of the role they are performing in the campaign and how it interrelates with all of the other activities.

Unlike the Precinct Captain, who is out working alone most of the time, morale for the Phone Bank Volunteer is usually not a serious problem. The team spirit, working together in the volunteer headquarters, is relatively easy to achieve. However, it is intensive work and very difficult, to say the least. The staff and Phone Bank Supervisors should make every effort to make sure there is always plenty of coffee and cookies for refreshment during breaks. Because of this intense, internal pressure, I usually recommend a 10-minute break every hour as part of the downtime. Though the atmosphere should be friendly, care must be taken that it does not become too noisy or distracting.

Because this is such a critical element of the campaign, and because it is a difficult position to recruit for on a regular basis, a number of campaigns have resorted to hiring paid telemarketing as a supplement, or in some cases as a substitute, for the Phone Bank Volunteer. This method can be effective but it does have several inherent problems. There is a tendency of the volunteers of the campaign to become resentful toward the paid telemarketers and often leave the campaign. It is very expensive, averaging more than $3,000 per week or close to $120,000 for the whole campaign. The quality of the calls made tend to vary considerably, in spite of the claims of consistency made by the tele-communications firms that provide this service.

Technology is providing new devices today, which a campaign might wish to consider as an alternative. These devices, offered by several vendors, are called electronic telemarketing that enables the campaign to download the voter registration lists, with telephone numbers into a telephone dialing database. During the 2nd Stage the system can call and record the results of the ID survey. If the respondent is undecided, the system could generate a specific letter designed for that type of response. If a supporter of the Candidate, it would generate a different letter designed for that type of response.

This device can be programmed to ask any number of questions and to take responses by either pushing a number on the person's telephone unit, e.g., 1 for Yes, 3 for No, or 5 for Undecided. It can record a complete response to an "open-ended" question that asks for an answer that cannot be reduced to a Yes, No, or Undecided, e.g., "What are the most important issues facing you today?" The system is "logical" in that it can shift messages instantly based on a person's response. Since it is digitized, the computer's "voice" is actually the voice of whoever dictates the questions into the microphone. It could be the Candidate, the well-known voice of a local or national personality, or just a pleasant sounding person.

When I first saw this system, I was concerned about whether or not people would respond to a machine. Since having that concern, I have used it and found the results actually better than what would normally be achieved in a regular Phone Bank operation. Major advantages include the speed dialing advantage and the elimination of downtime resulting in a considerably higher number of completed calls, within the same time.

The system that I am most familiar with is a system called the ETS-1500 PRO by Kolker Systems, Inc., who can be reached at 760.431.9633 or at www.kolkersystems.com. The ETS-1500 PRO worked in tandem with your computer and was incredibly fast, despite a problem with doubling calls. It could handle two lines simultaneously and could be programmed to turn itself on and start calling at a certain time in the morning and shut itself off at a preset time in the evening. It could hold up to 100,000 names at a time, and will speed call these names over and over until a connection is made, or until the campaign tells it to quit and loads in another batch of names. Some systems are expandable to 10 lines, with an additional charge applying for each line over two.

These systems can also do double duty by doing follow up telephone calls for fund-raising events and serving as a very sophisticated telephone answering machine for call backs. Another utilization is its ability to serve as a 24 hour "hot-line" for people who want to know where the Candidate stands on the issues. By calling a set number, the computer would ask what issue the caller is concerned about. The caller would respond by pushing a specific number on their telephone and would immediately be routed to the appropriate response, given in the voice of the Candidate. By the time an ETS-1500 PRO system is programmed for a campaign's needs and integrated with the campaign software, the cost will rise to about $2,800. However, depending on the size of the campaign, I believe it is well worth the investment.

The latest model offered by Kolker Systems is called the Gemini 2000.

The Campaign Manager

Qualifications The one most responsible for the day to day implementation of the Political Game Plan. The Candidate needs his or her complete loyalty, absolute trust, and inherent ability to function as his or her alter ego.

The role of the Campaign Manager varies considerably from one campaign to another. Ideally, as the one most responsible for the day to day implementation, he or she is a highly-qualified, intelligent person, a first-rate administrator, politically astute, and able to manage and to motivate effectively the hundreds of players in the campaign.

In the Prototype Plan, the Campaign Manager functions as the chief administrative officer of the campaign and the Political Campaign Consultant is the chief executive officer. If a campaign does not have a Political Campaign Consultant, then all of the Political Campaign Consultant's functions and activities are done by the Campaign Manager, in addition to what is outlined in this and other sections of this Manual.

Campaign Manager - Duties / Responsibilities

Role The Campaign Manager functions as the eyes and ears of the Political Campaign Consultant, keeping in contact with the consultant on a continuing basis and reporting the results of each day's activities.

The Campaign Manager, as the chief administrative officer of the campaign must be thoroughly familiar with every aspect of it. The Campaign Manager is responsible for coordinating all of the separate activities, monitoring the Timelines and Cash Flow schedules, and making sure all materials and supplies are at the proper place at the proper time. Working with the Field Operations Director, the Campaign Manager helps to establish the voter objectives for the campaign and each entity within the field operations.

The Campaign Manager should meet with the Candidate, ideally every day. At each meeting, the Campaign Manager should bring the Candidate up to date on what is happening in all levels of the campaign. This also provides the

Candidate with an opportunity to share campaign results and to discuss ways and means to improve future activity.

In many campaigns, the Campaign Manager spends a considerable amount of time in communicating with the PACs, the Party at all levels, and other organizations and individuals outside the district with an interest in the campaign. He or she functions as a campaign spokesperson.

If there is no Finance Director and/or Media Secretary, the Campaign Manager performs these functions in addition to supervising the rest of the staff. In the event the campaign does not have a consultant, the Campaign Manager would also be responsible for implementing the direct mail program.

The Campaign Manager is a member of all committees.

Political Direct Mail Program

In implementing the political direct mail program, the Campaign Manager must work closely with the company doing the mail program and develop a thorough understanding of how their system and time frames relate. He or she must be aware of the lead time required, and who is responsible for providing the inserts (such as brochures, flyers, and BREs), for stuffing, sealing, stamping, sorting by zip code, bagging, and delivering material to the Post Office for mailing.

Normally, a computer company that specializes in direct mail will handle the whole process for the campaign, including the printing of inserts and mail processing. The campaign will need only to provide the "camera ready" artwork for the mailing pieces. The cost per unit piece, including the mail processing, can vary from 35 to 45 cents. The average is around 40 cents. As mentioned before, there is virtually no difference in quality, only in profit and overhead. Some companies will allow you to use unlimited variables in the body of the letter, while others will add an additional charge for additional variables over a set number, usually 12. Just to clarify, variables in a computer letter are paragraphs containing different copy. They are used to personalize the letter depending on the demographics of the recipient.

When writing the letter, be sure to format the message for the objectives of the stage that the campaign is in at the time and, of course, to the group receiving it. In most cases, individualized paragraphs can be written in the body of the letter, usually between the first and last paragraphs, and be targeted for males, females, party affiliation, independents, and presumed economic levels, based on zip codes or precincts. In some states, the date of birth for the recipient is available and provides another group.

Some computer service firms have developed targeting systems that enable them to merge variable paragraphs automatically with the appropriate groups as determined by the polling results. These systems are highly sophisticated and very accurate.

Develop a code with the computer firm for each grouping and then write a series of paragraphs with a personalized message for each possible group and/or combination of groups. For example:

Code 21 - Females, Democrat, Zip Codes 12345-12350 or Precinct Number
Code 22 - Females, Independent, Zip Codes 12345-12350 or Precinct Number
Code 23 - Females, Republican, Zip Codes 12345-12350 or Precinct Number
Code 24 - Females, Democrat, Zip Codes 12351-12361 or Precinct Number
Code 25 - Females, Independent, Zip Codes 12351-12361 or Precinct Number
Code 26 - Females, Republican, Zip Codes 12351-12361 or Precinct Number
And so on.

When a particular paragraph is appropriate for two or more codes, e.g., codes 22 and 25 indicate that on the order form to the computer company. This data is then fed into the computer and, when programmed to do so, the appropriate "personalized" letter is automatically generated.

The more personalized the letter, the greater its impact. As time consuming and difficult as this targeting is, it really pays off in helping to communicate the Candidate's message effectively. A preprinted form letter is easier and cheaper, but the results are not nearly as effective.

As to the specific message of each paragraph, initially the Candidate in conjunction with the Campaign Manager will have to identify the major concern for each grouping. After the first poll is taken, they will be more accurate after checking the cross-tabs, identifying the major concerns for each group, and then writing a specific paragraph addressing those issues. Many people with the same general characteristics will share the same concerns and aspirations. These common concerns become even more pronounced when you factor in age and marital status.

All letters except for the 5th Stage mailer should include an appeal for funds and volunteers either in the last paragraph or as a postscript.

The final mailer in the 5th Stage is usually a simulated mailgram or telegram written to convey a sense of urgency. With the election only a few days away, the letter must try to motivate them to get out and vote. If possible, about a month before this final mailer, a list of the polling places should be sent to the computer company with instructions to feed this information into the computer by precinct. Then the final mailer, as a voter service, can indicate where each individual's polling place is located and the times for voting.

Lead-time is extremely important with direct mail computer companies. Their primary business is established commercial accounts. Therefore, political business receives a low priority. Ask them to be frank about their timeframes and then see to it that the copy and artwork is sent to them on schedule.

A few additional tips on direct mail:

1) On the front of the envelopes used for the 3rd and 4th Stage direct mail, presuming the campaign is using window envelopes, have the words "Important Voter Information Enclosed" imprinted in block letters in the bottom right quadrant of the envelope. If it is not much more expensive, have this message printed in red.
2) Have the continuous feed or laser paper used for the letters imprinted with the same logo and colors as the stationery.
3) I recommend showing only the P. O. Box number, city, state and zip code for the return address on the mailing envelope printed in color and preferably on the back flap.
4) On the mailing envelope, have the computer/mail processing company use either a pre-canceled bulk rate stamp or a meter stamp with your bulk rate permit number, if possible. **Do not use printed postal indicia.**

5) Lead-time is extremely important with direct mail computer companies. Political business receives a low priority, so ask them to be frank about their time frames and see to it that the copy and artwork are sent based on their schedule.

In addition to the computer generated direct mail, form letters will have to be developed to send to the individuals who the Phone Bank identifies as still undecided in the 4th Stage and to those persons who will be voting by absentee ballot. Many campaigns simply address a tabloid to the undecided in both the 3rd and 4th Stages, and a computer generated letter in the 3rd Stage. Fund-raising direct mail is discussed later, as well as the mail program for the Prospect File.

The Campaign Secretary

Role The Campaign Secretary is the office manager, the scheduler, and personal secretary for the Candidate and Campaign Manager. He or she is the second most important administrative person in the campaign, performing the duties of the Campaign Manager when he or she is not available.

The Campaign Secretary is the second most important administrative person in the campaign, performing the duties of the Campaign Manager when he or she is not available. The Campaign Secretary is also the office manager, the scheduler for the Candidate and the spouse, if actively campaigning, Campaign Manager and surrogate speakers, the director of volunteers, and personal secretary for the Candidate and Campaign Manager.

Most of the responsibilities are normal and routine for a highly qualified executive secretary. However, as the "Number Two" administrative person, the Campaign Secretary must be thoroughly familiar with the Political Game Plan and aware of what is going on in the campaign at all times.

The Campaign Secretary - Scheduling

Definition
An "advance person" is someone who precedes the Candidate in order to make certain the activity is set up properly for maximum impact

The other unique responsibility, in addition to being Number Two, is that of scheduling. Since few campaigns below the million dollar budget category can afford to hire an "advance person," someone who precedes the Candidate in order to make certain the activity is set up properly for maximum impact, the scheduler must be able to make as many determinations as possible when scheduling the event.

If the campaign is not using an application with a scheduling calendar, there is, in the Appendix M, a form called Request for Appearance. It is imperative that it is used for all campaign activities or fund-raising events that the Candidate is requested to attend.

Once the request for appearance is completed and approved, the event and time are posted in the appropriate day on a large wall calendar, as well as in the computer. Absolutely no one except the Campaign Secretary, not even the Candidate or the Campaign Manager should be allowed to make changes on this calendar. I cannot stress enough the importance of strict adherence to this procedure. As the campaign progresses, the pressure for the Candidate's time and presence intensifies and results in many potential conflicts. This is the only system I know of that will help prevent chaos, confusion, missed events, disappointed or insulted hosts or hostesses, poor PR, and lost votes.

The calendar, manual or computerized, is the official schedule and only one person should be responsible and accountable for it. This is not to say the Candidate or the Campaign Manager may not authorize a change. However, only the scheduler can record it. If a change is made, the scheduler must notify all the individuals involved and attempt to reschedule the event or provide a surrogate.

From the scheduler's perspective, there are two types of events that require the completion of a Request for Appearance form. Those are requests for the Candidate's attendance or participation in some kind of activity by persons, groups, or organizations not directly connected with the campaign and those activities and/or events generated internally by the campaign.

All references to the Candidate in this section should be extended to the spouse, the Campaign Manager, and surrogates.

Administrative functions or activities, such as campaign committee meetings, seminars, office and telephone time, and personal activities of the Candidate do not require a Request for Appearance form but should be noted on the master calendar and the time should be blocked out. This should be done as far in advance as possible.

Definition
Scheduled outside requests for appearance emanate from outside the campaign without a promotional effort by anyone connected with the campaign. All such events require a Request for Appearance form. Administrative functions or activities and personal activities of the Candidate do not require a Request for Appearance form but should be noted on the master calendar.

Scheduling - Outside Requests for Appearance

Requests emanating from outside the campaign are either spontaneous, that is the requests are made either unsolicited or without a promotional effort by anyone connected with the campaign. In the early stages of the campaign, invitations will be slow in coming and it is up to the scheduler to develop a program that will actively solicit them. To do this a complete list of all business, homeowner, trade organizations, union organizations, civic, service and social clubs, and membership societies should be assembled. A form letter should then be sent advising their events or social chairpersons that the Candidate is anxious to meet with their group and would appreciate an opportunity to do so at their next regularly scheduled meeting or as early as possible. Letters directed to chairpersons or associations targeted for potential financial support, such as real estate and insurance associations, should be personalized. Similar mailings should also be made to high school junior and senior civic classes, colleges, and universities, particularly to Political Science Departments.

Together with the Candidate, the Campaign Manager and the Campaign Chairperson(s) should make a complete list of Centers of Influence in the district. Letters requesting personal visits with these individuals should be sent on a regularly scheduled basis. The chairpersons of outside community events, such as fairs and parades that the Candidate should participate in, should be contacted early in the 2nd Stage so that any requirements may be complied with, and where necessary, choice site locations may be selected.

About a week after the letters have been sent to event chairpersons, the scheduler should telephone the individual to firm up the details and if necessary, arrange a visit by the Candidate. A "Request for Appearance" form should be completed or all details entered, providing as much information as possible, into the scheduling module of your campaign management program. Care should be taken to make the event as successful as possible for the Candidate. The scheduler should detail what is expected of the Candidate. Will he or she be speaking? If so, for how long? Do they have a particular subject that they would like the Candidate to address? If so, what? Will there be time for a Q&A session? If so, how much? Is it a media event? Will the media be there, or may they be invited to attend? May literature be passed out? Is this a "meet and greet" opportunity alone, with no opportunity for the Candidate to speak? Will the Candidate be expected to have a meal with the group? May the Candidate's Driver/Aide join them? Will other candidates or dignitaries be there? If so, who? It is up to the scheduler to provide as much advance information as possible so that the Candidate can prepare properly for the appearance and avoid possible misunderstandings and/or embarrassments.

Careful attention must also be given to the timing, not only of the event, but also between events. The scheduler should be familiar with the district and be able to estimate accurately the travel time required for the Candidate to move safely from one place to another. They should always be sensitive to time of day issues such as rush hour traffic conditions and possible seasonal weather conditions when estimating travel time. In addition, remember that the Candidate is human and must be allowed some personal "break" time.

When the Request for Appearance form is completed, a copy should be forwarded to the Campaign Manager for final approval and then returned to the scheduler. At this point, make four copies, one each for the Candidate, the Driver/Aide, the Campaign Manager, and the Regional Chairperson covering that part of the district. It is then entered on the master calendar, a confirmation letter is sent to the appropriate contact, and the original Request for Appearance form is filed. If scheduling is computerized, these functions can be handled within the scheduling module.

The scheduler should maintain a logbook showing all letters sent soliciting invitations, to which individual they were sent, the date, when the follow up call was made, and the results. This is helpful when timing second or third mailings, avoiding potential criticism that the Candidate is avoiding certain groups or individuals.

Scheduling - Internal Requests for Appearance

Essentially, the same procedure is followed for events or activities generated internally by the campaign.

Prior to the beginning of the 3rd Stage, or earlier if the Candidate begins campaigning full time, the scheduler should determine the number of days the Campaign Manager will want the Candidate to spend in each Region during each Stage. Once the number of allotted days has been determined, the scheduler should call a meeting with the Regional Chairpersons and discuss the specific days that they will need. Once allotted, the Regional Chairpersons have the responsibility to plan that day's activities. If there were an event or activity already on the calendar for that day, they would fill in the time around it. Normally, they are expected to complete, in draft form, a Request for Appearance form for each event or activity that they plan with the Candidate. They then submit the form to the Campaign Secretary/Scheduler for completion and in turn, to the Campaign Manager for approval, distribution, and posting.

The type of events and activities the Regional Chairpersons should schedule will depend on their particular needs as the campaign progresses. However, the scheduler should offer suggestions and guidance as to the types of events or activity that are most productive. Fund-raising activity is usually the highest priority event and there should be some activity in each day's schedule that will generate funds, regardless of how much or how little will be raised. Next in priority are events where the media will be attending or can be encouraged to attend. This is followed by events or activities that will expose the Candidate to the largest number of people possible within a given timeframe. Selective precinct or business district walking and coffee "Klatsches" are low priorities and are used to fill in any gaps. The Regional chairpersons should also be cautioned about travel time considerations.

It will be difficult, but the scheduler should insist on having the Regional Chairperson turn in the Request for Appearance forms and the date itself, completely scheduled at least 1 (one) full week in advance. Ideally, the whole schedule would be known and completed 2 (two) weeks in advance.

When assigning dates 3 months in advance, the scheduler will find that invariably one Region will discover it needs a date already assigned to another Region. This may be for a special event that they were unaware of or an important meeting that can only be arranged on a certain date. When this happens, the Regional Chairperson who needs the different date should call the Regional Chairperson who has the date and arrange a swap, if possible. Once agreed upon, it is then the originating Regional Chairperson's responsibility to notify the scheduler of the change.

When a date's schedule is completed, the scheduler should complete a Daily Calendar (a sample of this form is in the Appendix M) and, using it as the cover sheet, staple it to the Request for Appearance forms for that date. Three complete sets should be prepared in this manner, one for the Candidate, one for the Driver/Aide, and one for the Regional Chairperson. Again, if computerized, the program will generate a "daytimer view" of the day's schedule and print the copies required.

A good Campaign Secretary will develop a sensitivity for the type of events important for the Candidate to attend, regularly scan the local newspapers for information about upcoming activities, call them to the attention of the appropriate Regional Chairperson and help them to work it into that date's schedule wherever possible.

Hard as it may be to believe, one serious problem in most campaigns is maintaining communications between the Candidate and the headquarters staff. With the Candidate literally on the run, a system usually needs to be established for transferring needed messages and material back and forth. One system involves the Campaign Secretary having two pouches, using different colors in order to avoid confusion in sending and returning materials. He or she should also arrange for the Driver/Aide to exchange them at the end or beginning of each day. In this way, the Campaign Secretary can return the previous day's Request for Appearance forms with notations regarding the outcome or results at the bottom, plus any directives or messages from the Candidate to the staff.

The returned Request for Appearance forms with notations should be given to the Campaign Manager for review and any action necessary. The Campaign Secretary should then send out the appropriate thank you letters to the essential organizers involved and enter follow up comments into the database.

When conflicts arise, and they always do, use a prioritization method to decide which event the Candidate should attend personally and to which event a surrogate should be assigned.

Scheduling - Event Prioritization

Every event to be scheduled should be rated as normal, important, or critical to have the Candidate present based on the following prioritization:

1) Fund-raising events
2) Media events
3) The size of the audience at a given time and type of activity. Debates, speaking engagements before organized groups, fairs, visits to senior citizen homes, visits with Centers of Influence
4) Canvassing small business districts

The balance of events should be rated as requiring the Candidate or Substitute, a Substitute only need be considered, or the event itself is optional, again based on the following prioritization:

5) Coffee "Klatsch"
6) Walking precincts
7) Plant gates and shopping centers

The Campaign Secretary - Director of Volunteers

Role The Campaign Secretary, acting as the Director of Volunteers is responsible for maintaining the volunteer activities.

Another unique responsibility of the Campaign Secretary is serving as the Director of Volunteers. In this role, the Campaign Secretary is responsible for maintaining the volunteer files on hard copy or in a database, allocating prospective volunteers to the appropriate Chairpersons, sending out thank you letters, maintaining a small pool of reserve volunteers for emergencies or special projects, and writing a campaign newsletter. The newsletter should be sent to all volunteers, contributors, and endorsers every month or every other month.

If the campaign has a Media Secretary, that person usually does campaign newsletters.

Sometimes, the Director of Volunteers can be delegated to a key volunteer that has the time to do it well.

The Field Operations Director and Voter Targeting

Role The Field Operations Director is responsible for success regarding activities controlled by the Field Operations Committee.

The Field Operations Director provides logistical support for the Field Operations Committee and is the staff person responsible for the successful accomplishment of its activities and objectives. This person attends all Field Operations Committee meetings and helps conduct the training seminars. He or she is also responsible for coordinating the activities of the Precinct and Phone Bank operations.

Working with the Campaign Manager, the Field Operations Director is responsible for developing the prioritization of the precincts, Regions and Areas, and the voter objectives for each. This individual then monitors the progress of the

Precinct and Phone Bank operations toward the realization of these objectives on a weekly basis and keeps the Campaign Manager informed of their current status by means of biweekly summary progress reports. If a problem develops, such as no significant progress in a certain precinct, and it continues for a period of two weeks, the Field Operations Director should immediately call it to the attention of the Region and Area Chairpersons involved and help them take the necessary corrective action. The Campaign Manager should be kept aware of these situations and be informed of what remedial action is planned.

The Field Operations Director is an ex-officio member of the Field Operations Committee.

Developing Precinct Objectives - PIPS Analysis

Precinct objectives are based on the theory that most precincts will follow previously established patterns of voting. When establishing objectives, the real key to accuracy is in the selection of the previous races that are used as points of reference.

The methods used to develop the voter objectives is relatively simple, but requires a considerable amount of tedious detail work to establish them. However, due to the natural limitations of time and resources that all campaigns experience, it must be done accurately and on a timely basis. The system is based on the theory that most precincts will follow previously established patterns of voting and that a careful analysis will help develop realistic objectives or goals in future elections, provided the campaign is conducted effectively.

The real key to accuracy is in the selection of the previous races that are used as points of reference. The first procedure is to determine the "base" vote that exists for the Candidate and the "high" potential vote available. This can be determined by identifying the highest number of votes received by a popular, winning member of the Candidate's Party in a different district race, but not restricted to it and a "median" vote, obtained by a person of the Candidate's Party who attempted a serious campaign, regardless of the outcome. This data should be obtained for the last two election cycles.

All of the vote totals needed are usually available from the Secretary of State, the Board of Elections, or the County Registrar of Voters.

If precinct boundaries have recently changed, the campaign will have to approximate from the previous precinct boundary totals.

The Field Operations Director should check with the national or state Party. Sometimes, they already have these figures and many times in an electronic file format. If so, the job becomes relatively easy. The Party may charge for the computer time required to accumulate the data and provide a printout, but the savings in time and energy, plus the assured accuracy, will be more than worth it. Since both Parties have done a considerable amount of research on precinct boundary lines for reapportionment purposes, they might even be able to help with the interpolation of the previous vote patterns in each precinct, or even provide the PIPS analysis for the campaign.

In any case, the "base" race for each cycle is usually the most recent race for State Controller or Treasurer. The candidates for these offices rarely conduct an active campaign and the vote they receive, therefore, is usually a strongly committed Party vote. If this is not the case in the Candidate's state, either choose another campaign that fits this description, or if the county's boundaries exceed the district's boundaries, then a lower level race, similar in type, is acceptable.

For the "high" race, look at a senatorial, gubernatorial, or other statewide candidate's race, for a member of the Candidate's Party who won. Personally, I do not like to use a presidential race, since too many factors can skew the results and the results might not be as meaningful for this analysis.

If there is a choice, try to pick a race that was won essentially on its own merits. Choose a hard fought, well run campaign, as opposed to an abnormal situation. The "median" race is usually the previous congressional campaign, unless the results for one reason or another were not significant. If the latter is the case, choose a campaign, one from the Candidate's Party and one that covered the district that was reasonably well run but the Candidate still lost.

Follow this procedure for each of the last two election cycles. Remember that a political cycle is normally every two years, though in some states that have odd numbered year elections, the cycle can be yearly. Once this data is compiled, total all six figures per precinct and divide by six. The result plus the added 10 percent as a safety margin, becomes a reasonable voter objective for the Candidate in that precinct.

For example, in order to analyze the objectives in Precinct #10, you would take note of the fact that Precinct #10 cast 200 votes in the last cycle 2 years ago. Of these votes, the Gubernatorial Candidate of the Candidate's Party received 120 votes or 60 percent. The Candidate for State Treasurer of the Candidate's Party received 60 votes or 30 percent. The Congressional Candidate of the Candidate's Party received 80 votes or 40 percent. Precinct #10 cast 240 votes in the cycle before the last one. Of those votes, the U.S. Senatorial Candidate of the Candidate's Party received 120 votes or 50 percent. The winning Candidate for County Clerk in a nonpartisan race received 111 votes or 45 percent. The Congressional Candidate of the Candidate's Party received 144 votes or 60 percent. (The arithmetic looks like 120 + 60 + 80 + 120 + 111 + 144 = 635 divided by 6 = 105.8 + 10.6 (10% safety margin) = 116 votes divided by 1.7 votes per household = 68 households). For Precinct #10, this Candidate needs 116 votes or 68 supporting households to carry the Precinct in this election.

Note: If the total of all the precinct vote objectives is not equal to the number of votes required to win, increase the individual precinct totals by the percentage necessary. For example, if the total adds up to 45% of the projected amount needed, based on projected voter turnout, increase all precinct objectives by approximately 11%.

The voters who make up the differential between the "base" and the "high" are usually referred to as ticket-splitters, i.e., those voters who are not knee jerk voters in either Party, regardless of how they register, and sometimes cast their ballot on the basis of factors other than Party affiliation.

In the simplified example above, there are approximately 50 to 60 ticket-splitters in Precinct #10. If the Candidate realizes his or her objective in this precinct, he or she will likely win it. However, this should not necessarily be the objective of this analysis. To set objectives based on a win in every single precinct is unrealistic and therefore, by definition, an unsound strategy. The campaign should strive for it, but not base its strategy and Political Game Plan on it. More appropriate, would be to use the analysis to identify supporting precincts, close precincts, and precincts in which your opponent is strong. I refer to this as prioritizing the precincts.

Prioritizing the Precincts

Expend only the resources necessary in the supporting precincts to retain the existing level of support, while expending the larger percentage of resources in the close precincts in order to win them. Your strategy must be realistic in its evaluation and realize that precincts, in which you are far behind, may not be salvageable.

The next calculation that the Field Operations Director and the Campaign Manager need to make is to establish the prioritization of the precincts and Regions. With limited time and resources, the campaign needs a system that will proportion these, when a choice has to be made, in the most effective manner possible. Resources must be directed where they will produce the greatest number of votes.

I normally recommend that the precincts be divided into six levels based on the ratio of vote objectives for the Candidate, determined by the formula given in the preceding section, to the average total vote previously cast in the district for that, or a similar race. The resulting percentage determines the level of the precinct. The levels have been arbitrarily established and could be changed to fit the campaign's particular needs.

Level 1	60%+
Level 2	55-59%
Level 3	50-54%
Level 4	45-49%
Level 5	40-44%
Level 6	-39%

Precinct Priority Equation
Projected Precinct Vote Objective divided by the average number of precinct votes cast in the previous elections analyzed equals the prioritization level (expressed as a percentage).

In the previous example, Precinct #10 would be a Level 3 precinct since the projected vote objective (116) divided by the average number of votes previously cast (220) equals 52.7 percent.

During the 2nd Stage, the strategy in the Prototype Plan calls for the Candidate to solidify his or her base, therefore, Levels 1, 2 and 3 should be the highest priority, in that order, followed by 4, 5 and 6. However, during the 3rd Stage, the Prototype strategy is to concentrate on the undecideds and ticket-splitters, most of who are in Levels 4, 5, and 3. These levels, therefore, become the highest priorities in the 3rd Stage, followed by Levels 2, 1, and 6. This prioritization continues for the most part in the 4th Stage, except for a direct mail piece that will be targeted on Level 6 precincts. Depending on the judgment of the Area Chairperson, some selective campaigning by the Candidate could be done in Level 6 precincts that might, with a little extra effort, be moved into Level 5. Usually, the Level 6 precincts chosen would be precincts that have been well canvassed by a Precinct Captain.

In the 5th Stage, the GOTV Stage, ideally all committed voters for the Candidate will have been identified and called, regardless of their precinct level. If for some reason the programs have failed (not enough telephone units and/or volunteers have been secured, for example) then, as a last resort, after contacting those households already known as being for the Candidate, the campaign would revert to calling the precincts in order of priority, starting with Level 1. This whole system of establishing vote objectives and prioritizing precincts acts as a back up to the Field Operation program. In those campaigns where volunteers are not available, this system can be used to maximize a Candidate's communication efforts by targeting the message where it has the greatest chance to be effective, primarily using direct mail.

Prioritizing the Candidate's Regional Activity

By extending the calculations used to determine the precinct's priority levels to the Regions and Areas, the prioritization levels for each can be developed. Depending on the stage of the campaign and the number of days available, the Candidate's campaign time should be apportioned accordingly.

In the 3rd Stage, it has been determined that the Candidate will have about 70 days to apportion to the Regions. This determination is based on approximately 95 days in Stage 3 minus 17 days for R&R, minus 8 days for meetings and other campaign activities = 70 days. For the sake of discussion, let's assume Region I is in Level 2, Region 2 is in Level 3, Region 3 is in Level 4, Region 4 is in Level 4, and Region 5 is in Level 6. The prioritization for the Stage 3 schedule based on the Prototype Plan's strategy, would be Levels 5, 4, 3, 2, 1, 6. On this basis, the breakout of days might be as follows:

Region 3 (Level 4) = 20 days
Region 4 (Level 4) = 20 days
Region 2 (Level 3) = 15 days
Region I (Level 2) = 10 days
Region 5 (Level 6) = 5 days

Where the Candidate campaigns in the Regions on those days should be decided on the individualized precinct prioritization levels.

All of these figures are examples only, designed to illustrate the procedures. They are not a point of comparison for any district.

Each campaign must make these calculations for their individual situation and weigh all calculations with all the other relevant factors. I have already referred to one important factor that must be considered and that is the expected turn out for the race. Estimating this is essentially a subjective judgment call, but obviously a significant one. Check with other persons to see if a valid consensus can be reached. Usually the County Registrar of Voters will have an educated guess as to the turn out, as will the political editor of the daily newspaper. The County Party Chairperson, especially if a seasoned veteran, will also have an opinion.

Some consultants and political publications refer to this method as "targeting." I find this can be too easily confused with the term targeting as it is used in reference to the strategic placement of media or direct mail. The term I prefer to use, and that I feel more accurately describes this activity, is "prioritizing."

If all else fails, then the decision should be based on the last comparable election year. If the year of this campaign is a presidential election year, use the actual turn out percentage in the district 4 years ago. Add 5 percent if the campaign wants to build in a reasonable safety margin. If the turn out was 55 percent of the registered voters, add a 5 percent safety margin and figure on a 58 percent turnout for this campaign. Then, if the results of the reference races used in the PIPS analysis were based on a 60 percent turn out, the campaign would decrease its final figures or objectives by 2 percent.

Care must be taken to differentiate between raw numbers and percentages. Factoring this into consideration when doing the evaluations, a Level 1 precinct might be expected to produce 60 percent of the voter turnout for the Candidate, but if the numerical turn out is considerably lower than in a Level 4 precinct, the actual number of votes for the Candidate could be virtually the same from both precincts, or even greater in the Level 4 precinct.

After the prioritizing process is completed, all concerned volunteers should be advised of the individual or group vote objectives in total and broken down weekly and by stages, 40 % - Stage 2, 35% - Stage 3, 25% - Stage 4. The Candidate, Political Campaign Consultant, Campaign Manager, Campaign Secretary, and the Campaign Chairperson(s) should be given a master copy, broken down within Regions by Stages, then summarized for the whole campaign.

The rate of accomplishment is dependent on the actual amount of time involved in conjunction with the number of volunteers. Nevertheless, in the Prototype Campaign it would be reasonable to expect 40 percent of the total to be achieved by the end of the 2nd Stage, 75 percent by the end of the 3rd Stage, and 100 percent by the end of the 4th Stage. As previously stated, the Field Operations Director is then responsible for monitoring the progress of the Field Operation's team, Precinct Captains, and Phone Bank volunteers in achieving those objectives. In this way, the campaign will know, with a degree of certainty, where the campaign's objectives are at any given time and the probable outcome, before the ballots are ever counted.

During the 5th Stage, the Field Operations Director works closely with the Campaign Manager in the management of the GOTV and Election Day programs. As this stage approaches, the Field Operations Director should be making a concerted effort to obtain host homes for Election Day. He should concentrate on training the volunteers who in cooperation with the Region and Area Chairpersons will be working the telephones. The Field Operations Director should also establish the poll watching procedures, depending on what the local laws will permit and in cooperation with the local Party programs, and make the necessary assignments of Precinct Captains in coordination with Area Chairpersons. He or she is also responsible for making sure polling place yard signs are in place early in the morning on Election Day.

The Field Operations Director is an ex-officio member of the Field Operations Committee.

Role The Finance Director should have extensive fund-raising experience in political campaigns or in community fund-raising campaigns.

The Finance Director

In our Prototype campaign, the Campaign Manager performs the duties of the Finance Director. However, I am showing them separately in the event that the campaign is able to hire an individual for this position.

The Finance Director is the staff person responsible for:

1) Providing the logistical support necessary for the Finance Committee,

2) Providing necessary guidance and training in procedures and methods,

3) Helping the Finance Committee Chairperson(s) establish individual committee members' objectives,

4) Monitoring progress toward the accomplishment of these objectives,

5) Providing the necessary motivation,

6) Preparing the agenda and reports for the Finance Committee meetings,

7) Assisting the Treasurer with the establishment of the accounting and reporting procedures,

8) Assisting with the preparation of the FEC or state reports,

9) Supervising the administrative details involved with the major and minor fund-raising events,

10) Developing and implementing the fund-raising direct mail, PAC, and out-of-district programs,

11) Assisting the Candidate, Campaign Manager, and Finance Committee Chairperson(s) with the telephone follow up program to key PACs and out-of-district contributors,

12) Establishing the procedures and supervising the Phone Bank follow up program,

13) Developing the Cash Flow schedule,

14) Implementation of the Cash Flow schedule,

15) Preparing the kits for the Finance Committee members, and

16) Developing the potential contributor lists and program for the support file.

If the campaign retains a Political Fund-raising Consultant, that person would usually do many of the above functions as a part of their contract with the campaign. If not, the person filling this role should have extensive fund-raising experience in political campaigns or in community fund-raising campaigns, such as United Way or the Red Cross.

The Finance Director is an ex-officio member of the Finance Committee.

Role The Media Secretary's primary responsibility is to assist the Candidate in obtaining the maximum amount of free media coverage possible.

The Media Secretary

In our Prototype campaign, the Campaign Manager or someone with prior media and campaign experience will fill this role. Nonetheless, I am showing the responsibilities separately in the event that the campaign is able to hire an individual for this position.

The Media or Press Secretary's primary responsibility is to assist the Candidate in obtaining the maximum amount of free media coverage possible. The two primary methods used to obtain the maximum amount of free media coverage are press releases and press conferences. A well-planned schedule based on these two methods would be as follows:

Press Release and Conference Schedule

1st Stage:

1) Leaks to the press regarding candidacy.

2) No formal press releases or conferences.

2nd Stage:

1) One press conference each month - a total of 4.
   February - Formal Announcement.
   March - Informal Issue oriented.
   April - Informal Issue oriented.
   May - Formal Guest speaker conference.

2) Issue oriented press releases every 2 weeks. Total of 9 in 2nd Stage.

3) Opposition press releases, none, unless major incident occurs.

4) Organizational releases, every 2 weeks, a full release, and every alternate week a photo release for a total of 18.

5) Spontaneous release, probable average is 1 a month for a total of 4.

3rd Stage:

1) Continue press conference each month - a total of 3.
   June - Formal - Victory conference after Primary.
   July - Informal - Issue oriented, attack.
   August - Informal - Issue oriented.

2) Issue oriented press releases. Every 2 weeks for a total 7.

3) Opposition press releases. None, unless major incident occurs.

4) Organizational releases. Every 2 weeks a full release and every alternate week a photo release - a total of 13.

5) Spontaneous release. Probably an average of 2 each month - a total of 6.

4th Stage:

1) Press conference each month - a total of 2.
   September - Formal - guest speaker conference.
   October - Formal - combine attack and poll results, if favorable. Express confidence.

2) Issue oriented press releases every 2 weeks and repeat 4 major releases with a slightly new twist - a total of 4.

3) Opposition press releases, every week for a total of 9.

4) Organizational releases:
   September - 3 + 1 photo.
   October - 4 + 2 photos - a total of 10.

5) Spontaneous releases, probably an average of 1 per month for a total of 2.

5th Stage:
1) Press conference.
Formal - day before election at headquarters to forecast victory.

2) Issue oriented press releases. None.

3) Opposition press releases - total 1.

4) Organizational releases - 1 photo, 2 progress - total 3.

5) Spontaneous releases. None.

Summary:

Stage 1:	0 conferences	0 press releases
Stage 2:	4 conferences	31 press releases
Stage 3:	3 conferences	26 press releases
Stage 4:	2 conferences	25 press releases
Stage 5:	1 conference	4 press releases
Totals:	**10 conferences**	**86 press releases**

Definition
An actuality is a summary of the message in a press release.

In addition to these, the Media Secretary would "cut" a radio actuality for all conferences and releases, except for the organizational activities.
Total actualities: 51.

The Media Secretary should also assist the Candidate in promoting drop-ins at local radio stations and newspapers for spot interviews, arrange coverage for all debates, promote talk show appearances, and arrange for local political reporters to spend a day with the Candidate on the "campaign trail."

Suggested Procedures - Press Conferences

Press conferences, like debates, can be an excellent means of generating free media coverage, if done properly.

Press conferences are usually held in two types of settings. Formal press conferences are held at the local Press Club, a conference room at a downtown hotel, or at the campaign headquarters. Informal press conferences are held "on location," such as outdoors, where the location might be used as a backdrop for the conference. The best time of day is usually 10:00 a.m., but check with the local media outlets and get their consensus on the preferred time.

The formal conference is reserved for special announcements, events, or dignitaries, while the informal conference is for issue-oriented announcements.

The formal type is normally held when the Candidate formally announces his or her candidacy, a day or two after the Primary Victory, for visiting guest speakers or dignitaries, and, if necessary, to make a serious announcement regarding the opponent or the campaign. The informal press conference should be used when the conference is issue-oriented. If the Candidate is making a major announcement about inflation, stage the conference in front or inside a supermarket. If the issue is social security, stage the conference at a senior citizen's home or club. Always select a location where the media will not need to travel too far to attend.

The campaign should arrange one press conference per month.

As a rule of thumb, the campaign should try to arrange one press conference a month. If more are attempted, the local media will normally tire of them and stop attending. After the announcement of the press conference has been sent out, a follow up telephone call should be made to key stations and newspapers to encourage attendance.

Press Releases - Types / Preparation

Press Release Types
Issue or position releases, opposition releases, organizational releases, and spontaneous, or reaction releases.

Press releases are divided into four basic types: issue or position releases, opposition releases, organizational releases, and spontaneous or reaction releases. Today, most media outlets have an e-mail address that can be used to send press releases. I do recommend that this method be used, whenever possible, but it is still a good idea to send a hard copy of the release as a back up.

Issue or position releases are essentially a regurgitation of the Candidate's position on the issues.

Issue or position releases are essentially a regurgitation of the Candidate's position on the issues (the 15 or 20 positions developed in the 1st Stage). In order to make them newsworthy, since most media outlets will not publish propaganda pieces, certain rules need to be followed. The Candidate's position must be verbalized before a group of people other than the staff or campaign volunteers to be considered news. In other words, the Candidate must integrate the position the campaign wants released into a speech before a group, usually a civic association luncheon meeting, and then "dateline" the release accordingly. For example:

Definition
The dateline indicates the date and/or time on which an event, release, speech, or statement took place.

DES MOINES, IA. (4/15/—): (Candidate's Name), (__________) Party Candidate for Congress in Iowa's 7th Congressional District, speaking before the Des Moines Grange Society at their monthly luncheon meeting today, said........

The press release should always contain the release date, who, what, where, when, why, and the contact persons telephone number.

When writing a release always state clearly at the top of the release whether the release should be held until a certain day before being published or is, "For Immediate Release." Show the Media Secretary's name as the "Contact Person," along with that person's office and home telephone numbers. The opening paragraph should always contain the five "keys," Who, What, Where, When, and Why. The following paragraphs should say briefly what the Candidate said in his or her remarks. Summarize the main points of the speech. Do not attempt to provide them with the whole speech. If they want it, they will ask for it. Type the release double-spaced and try to keep your message within one legal size page. When finished, close with "-30- or ####," thereby letting the reader know it is the end of the release.

Opposition releases are attack oriented.

Opposition releases are more attack oriented. In an issue release, the prime emphasis is on the Candidate's solution to a particular problem, with a criticism of the opponent being incidental, or inferred. In an opposition release, this is reversed. The attack might be directed toward a particular position taken or a vote recently cast by the opponent. It can also be more general in nature by accusing the opponent of a pattern, such as being a big spender, anti-defense, or unrepresentative of the district. You should always have a few specific examples to back the assertion. Close with a specific or implied statement of what the Candidate would do differently from the opponent. The intent here, of course, is to reduce the opponent's Favorability rating and to clearly define the differences between the candidates. Normally, this type of release would not start on a regular basis until the beginning of the 4th Stage. Once begun, they should be done at the rate of one a week, until the 5th Stage. If something dramatic happens in the earlier Stages, a spontaneous release, attack oriented, could be done in order to counter. However, it should not be overdone. One might be done each month during the 3rd Stage as part of a hit and run strategy designed to keep the opponent off guard. Again, it should be datelined.

Organizational releases include campaign and fund-raising progress reports, announcements of campaign and committee chairperson appointments, campaign events, and activities.

Organizational releases are usually picked up by the weekly newspapers, occasionally by the dailies, and/or electronic media. They are subdivided into several categories that include campaign and fund-raising progress reports, announcements of campaign and committee chairperson appointments, campaign events, and activities. Follow up with photo releases of the Candidate about every two weeks with different community leaders. The release should include a short caption identifying the people in the photo and what they are doing. Polling results, if the strategy calls for releasing data, and notable endorsements can also be helpful. The press releases are usually made by the campaign Chairperson(s) and datelined from the campaign headquarters. The campaign should be able to generate at least one of these releases every week.

The question always seems to come up about publishing the advance schedule of the Candidate. My experience has shown that the disadvantages (it provides the opponent with an opportunity to upstage the Candidate or, in some cases, to arrange for hecklers to disrupt the event) outweigh the advantages.

Spontaneous releases are issued in response to the opponent's voting or campaign behavior and to any occurrence of major importance taking place.

Spontaneous or reaction releases cannot be planned as to number and timing. Spontaneous releases are issued regarding the opponent's voting or campaign behavior at any given time. They are also prepared in response to some occurrence of major importance taking place either in the district, nationally, or internationally. As a political leader in the community, because of being the Party's candidate, the Candidate not only has the right but also the responsibility to give the public his or her views on these events.

Definition
A radio actuality is produced by recording the Candidate for about 45-60 seconds, summarizing the message in the press release.

Radio actualities are like press releases. The Media Secretary should always tape an actuality for dissemination to the radio stations. An actuality is a cassette tape recording by the Candidate, lasting about 45-60 seconds, that summarizes the message in the press release and is then transmitted to the station by phone, using a simple jack device available at any electronics store. Usually these are transmitted the day after the press release has been distributed. This system can also be used by the Candidate while out campaigning, simply be calling in from an outside telephone, or by the use of a special microphone attachment to the recorder. This is especially useful for spontaneous releases or a reaction to fast breaking news stories. Many radio stations do not have political news reporters and depend on this method to cover the political news stories. Radio stations will usually be cooperative and receptive to the use of actualities.

The Media Secretary should set up, as a regular part of the Candidate's campaign activity, drop-ins at local radio stations. Depending on the number of stations in the district, this can probably be done at least once a week and be repeated regularly throughout the campaign. Most stations will cut an "on the spot interview" lasting 5 to 15 minutes that they will use, either in whole or in segments, as "fill in" material to be aired throughout the day.

The Media Secretary is expected to speak on behalf of the Candidate when news stories break and the Candidate is unavailable for immediate comment. The Media Secretary, therefore, must be thoroughly aware of the Candidate's position on the issues and the total campaign operation.

The Media Secretary should assist the Campaign Manager, Campaign Secretary, and the Field Operations Director in the writing of copy for direct mail, newsletters, and tabloids. Some candidates prefer to write their own speeches while others rely, to some extent, on the Media Secretary for assistance.

The Media Secretary is also responsible for being aware of all outside media events going on in the district that the Candidate can and should attend for increased media exposure. These should be brought to the attention of the Campaign Secretary for scheduling.

Getting the media to cover a challenger Candidate, especially in the early stages of the campaign, is a very difficult undertaking. I recommend that the Media Secretary make personal contact with all the reporters in the district, print and broadcast, as soon as possible after the campaign has started. It really helps to have developed this personal relationship, especially when the campaign wants their attendance at a press conference.

Definition
Media file is a separate data file within your software, allowing the user to enter all media outlets, contact information, and activity.

Your campaign management software should have a separate Media file for entering all the media outlets in the district. This feature, in addition to being able to hold all of the pertinent data, is able to generate mailing labels for the press releases. I recommend that a Media Secretary always have at least two sets of these labels pre-printed and affixed to campaign envelopes for quick drop purposes on breaking news stories or spontaneous releases. These labels should be addressed by title instead of by contact name, e.g., Political Editor, or Assignment Editor, to insure their prompt attention.

If the Media Secretary is a hired position, the Candidate and Campaign Manager should know the distinct difference between the training and skill set of a print reporter (who is a journalist) and an electronic media reporter. In addition to the electronic media skills being sought, the electronic media reporter should have the requisite writing skills of a journalist as well.

The Media Secretary is often called upon to meet the responsibilities of the Director of Research.

Role The Director of Research is responsible for assisting the Research Chairperson and for helping to keep the Candidate informed and updated on current issues.

Director of Research

The Director of Research is responsible for assisting the Research Chairperson and for helping to keep the Candidate informed and updated on current issues. As a part of this function, the Director of Research is responsible for maintaining the "clipping" file for the campaign. In most major cities, companies will review all the newspapers within the district, on a daily basis, and clip out any articles pertaining to the Candidate or the opponent. If the campaign does not contract for this service, it becomes the daily responsibility of the Director of Research or Media Secretary.

Role The Driver/Aide is responsible for sensitivity to the personal needs of the Candidate, always trying to make the Candidate look and function, as well as possible when campaigning.

The Driver/Aide

The Driver/Aide is probably one of the hardest working in the campaign. His or her campaign day starts an hour before the Candidate's and finishes an hour or two later. Many of the duties have already been described in other sections of this chapter. Since he or she is constantly with the Candidate, his or her personal appearance is a major consideration. The Driver/Aide should develop sensitivity to the personal needs of the Candidate, always trying to make the Candidate look and function, as well as possible, when campaigning. A good Driver/Aide knows when to talk and when to listen. He or she is courteous and polite at all times, but firm when necessary.

The Driver/Aide can fill the role of advance person, checking the routes on a map for the next day's itinerary, estimating travel time, selecting alternate routes in case of traffic tie-ups or detours, and having an alternate activity planned for the Candidate if a scheduled event cancels at the last minute. At the end of each day, the Driver/Aide should write a brief objective report at the bottom of the Request for Appearance form, for each event, and return it to the Campaign Secretary when picking up the pouch for the Candidate's next day.

Twice daily, the Driver/Aide should call the Campaign Secretary to retrieve messages for the Candidate, inform the Campaign Secretary of their location, and update their schedule.

The Driver/Aide should always carry enough money to pay for routine expenses and any emergency. He or she should turn in the daily receipts to the Campaign Secretary for reimbursement. In addition, the Driver/Aide should make sure the campaign vehicle is always clean, full of gas, and well supplied with campaign materials. In effect, the campaign vehicle is a portable office.
Whenever a serious problem develops, the Driver/Aide should, if possible, immediately notify the Campaign Manager before acting. In most areas of the country, the cellular telephone systems have developed to the point of making it possible to have constant communication between the Driver/Aide and campaign headquarters. I strongly recommend that the Candidate and Driver/Aide not be without cellular communication, as it improves communications with the campaign headquarters and enables the Candidate to make necessary telephone calls while traveling between campaign stops.

A laptop computer or Palm Pilot is recommended for campaigns in larger districts that keep the Candidate and Driver/Aide away from headquarters on a daily basis.

Very early in the campaign, the Driver/Aide should develop a "control book" for use by the Candidate when campaigning. The book, a 3-ring binder, should be divided into the five Regions and should contain the following information:

1) A map of the Region, showing Areas and precincts.
2) The names, addresses, and telephone numbers of the Regional and Area Chairpersons, plus all Precinct Captains and precinct number designations.

3) The names, addresses, and telephone numbers of all elected and party officials living or working within the Regions.
4) The names, addresses, telephone numbers, and contact persons for all media outlets within the Regions.
5) Any other pertinent data the Candidate should be aware of in the Regions, like the location of senior citizen homes or clubs, major industries, and points of interest.

The above lists can be printed from the computer periodically, three-hole punched, and inserted into the binder. Many software programs have the ability to retrieve this information in this precise format.

Occasionally, the question is raised about whether the Driver/Aide could be a member of the opposite sex from the candidate. Unless the Driver/Aide is the daughter or son of the Candidate, **the answer is an emphatic NO**. Regardless of the character, reputation, and integrity of the Candidate and the Driver/Aide, there are simply too many members of the public who would challenge the character of both. It simply is not worth the risk of a scandal and the loss of votes.

The Political Campaign Consultant

Role The Political Campaign Consultant is responsible for developing the basic strategy and issues: the Political Game Plan, Budget, and Cash Flow schedule.

As has already been pointed out, the Political Campaign Consultant is responsible for developing the basic strategy and issues: the Political Game Plan, Budget, and Cash Flow schedule, analyzing the opposition research, developing all necessary manuals, writing copy for the direct mail program, and targeting it for maximum effectiveness. His or her duties also include establishing voter objectives and prioritization, coordinating, supervising, and monitoring the progress at all levels, monitoring major activities of the campaign, and supervising the activities of all the other professionals involved in the campaign to ensure complete integration with the Game Plan. Another important function of a Political Campaign Consultant is adjusting for the variables in the campaign. This person, because of education, training, and experience, is usually best able to assist the Candidate and campaign committee in developing the soundest strategy to realize the objectives in the most cost-effective manner. He also suggests the techniques that will bring in the votes.

It is a very unwise decision to attempt to manage a campaign that will have a budget of more than one million dollars without the help of a professional.

It is very unwise for an individual to attempt to manage a campaign that will have a budget of more than one million dollars without the help of a professional. There are so many variables, each with their own cost factors, that the opportunities for mistakes are simply too numerous to mention. Inevitably, a good Political Consultant will save the average campaign considerably more than the fees charged.

Unfortunately, the term “Political Consultant” is too generic to mean much today. Anyone who provides advice of a political nature to a person or organization for a fee is technically a political consultant. No certification process exists that can bring substantive meaning to this title. The only qualifying factor seems to be whether someone is willing to pay for the advice.

Based on this current reality, I suggest that what is needed in the industry when an individual is compensated as an advisor or consultant, is a more precise definition of this title or perhaps titles. For this reason, I propose the following titles and areas of expertise:

a) The Political Consultant would be any individual who provides advice of a political nature,
b) The Political Media Consultant would be any individual who provides advice of a political nature as it relates to effective use of the media,
c) The Political Fund-raising Consultant would be any individual who provides advice of a political nature as it relates to raising funds,
d) The Political Polling Consultant would be any individual who provides advice of a political nature as it relates to surveying the attitudes and preferences of the general public, and
e) The Political Campaign Consultant would be any individual who provides advice of a political nature as it relates to the process of organizing and conducting a political campaign. A generalist who is proficient in most aspects of the campaign process.

As self evident as these definitions may seem, it is surprising sometimes to see the confusion that exists in concept even among the members of the industry. Over the years, I have seen a number of Political Media Consultants profess an expertise as Fund-raising or Political Consultants, Polling Consultants who believe they are professional Media and Political Consultants, and Political Consultants who think they are Media and Polling Consultants. The only consultants who do not seem to have an identity crisis are Fund-raising Consultants.

The confused state of the professional definition only leads us to be able to define the problem, i.e. how do you find a "good" consultant, regardless of the type of individual, needed in a particular situation?

In any event, each of these fields is highly specialized and there are very few individuals who ever strive for, much less achieve, a real proficiency in more than one of them. The problem is, that it is almost impossible to learn any of these skills from a book, even one as definitive as this. Only by building on an education with actual experience, over a period of years, does anyone become truly professional, not only in this field, but also in most others.

Regrettably, every election year a large number of "consultants" seem to come out of the woodwork and the average candidate is at a loss to determine if one is better than the other. Even fees seem to vary considerably, often appearing to be based on what the traffic will bear.

It used to be that the American Association of Political Consultants (AAPC) restricted full membership to individuals who were practicing Political Consultants on a full time, year round basis, in any one of the specialized fields. This is no longer the case. Therefore, full membership status cannot be used as an indication of experience. However, membership still serves as a test of sorts and can be obtained from the AAPC at 600 Penn. Ave., SE, Suite 330, Washington, DC 20003, 202.544.9815 at www.theaapc.org. Another reference source is the National Party headquarters. Both Parties, along with their affiliated committees, maintain vendor's lists. In addition, in recent years directories have begun to appear where consultants can advertise their services. The most comprehensive one on the market is The Political Resource Directory published by Political Resources, Inc., P. O. Box 3365, Burlington, VT 05406, tel: 800.423.2677 or at www.politicalresources.com.

However, these resources tell only where these services can be obtained, or from whom. None, to the best of my knowledge, attempts to evaluate their skills. Even those that list win or loss records can be deceiving. First, no consultant wins or loses an election, only candidates do that. Second, the old saying that says, "Victory has many fathers, defeat is an orphan," is especially apropos in politics. Many in this business claim credit for wins and blame everyone else, but themselves, for the losses, given that they even acknowledge them. Finally, no two campaigns are ever exactly alike, and how a consultant does in one is not necessarily an indication of how he or she will do in another. This is especially so if the comparison is between incumbents and challengers or between different levels of campaigns, such as, Presidential and Congress, the U.S. Senate and State Senator.

In order to be able to relate to the dynamics of our Prototype campaign, an individual should have been a Campaign Manager in at least three major races and under the supervision of a Political Campaign Consultant.

So, the question remains how does a Candidate or campaign select a consultant? First, decide what kind of consultant is needed. Then focus attention on those types. Write to several asking them for a copy of their company literature and a personal biographic profile. If the campaign is going to be a combination campaign similar to the Prototype campaign presented here, one involving all three major levels of campaigning, the campaign would probably be best served by a Political Campaign Consultant. Be sure the consultant has personal experience in these areas. It is amazing how many "consultants" there are who have only managed one or two campaigns, if any, before dubbing themselves consultants. I know of several whose only real experience is in the field of journalism or research.

Watch out for references to fancy sounding titles on previous campaigns or Party activity. Most campaigns hand out titles like confetti. The only way I know of that an individual can develop in depth experience is by actually managing several campaigns. There is no substitute. Since an individual can only manage one or two campaigns in a Congressional cycle, it stands to reason it would take at least 4 to 6 years for that person to have managed at least three full campaigns. Contrary to popular opinion, it really does not make much difference whether or not they were winning campaigns. What is important is the experience gained.

The Candidate should check to see if the campaigns managed had demographics similar to the district in which he or she is running. There is a significant difference between an urban district campaign and one in a rural district, between one in the North, South, East, West, or mid-West, a "silk-stocking" district and a heavily "union" district. In my opinion, a truly "national" Political Campaign Consultant is one who has worked on campaigns throughout the country in all types of districts.

A few Political Campaign Consultants are multi-experienced and they are able to provide a high degree of expertise in the areas of media and fund-raising. Usually, their fees to provide all of these services to a campaign are considerably less than the total fees accrued by having three separate individuals perform these functions. Be sure they have actually done all of them. Otherwise, contract separately for these services. They are too important to the successful outcome of the campaign to be treated casually.

Find out how much time the Political Campaign Consultant plans to spend in the district and what type of activity he or she will do. Some Political Campaign Consultants, for example, refuse to meet with anyone other than the Candidate and Campaign Manager, if and when, they come to the district. Others believe just the opposite. They feel that it is very important to meet with the Advisory Committee, the Finance Committee, the staff, and the Candidate on each of their visits. Be sure to have a contract spelling out the fees to be charged, the number of days to be spent in the district, and the scope of services to be performed.

Costs obviously vary as widely as do skills and claims, but a multi-agency providing the aforementioned three services to a Candidate in a campaign, similar to the one in the Prototype plan, could be expected to charge as follows:

A) **Political Campaign Consulting:** This includes the development of strategy and the Political Game Plan, the Budget and Cash Flow schedule, Phone Bank and Field Operations manuals, Candidate and opponent research analysis, daily monitoring and supervision of the campaign by phone, 4 days per month in the district, establishment of vote objectives, precinct analysis, prioritization, copy writing, and targeting of direct mail. The fee would be $50,000, plus related out-of-pocket expenses.

B) **Media Creation and Placement:** This includes the research and creative work used in developing six radio and TV commercials, graphics, editing, copy writing of brochures and tabloids, analysis of cross-tabs and Arbitron ratings, personalized service with media outlets, and follow up. These functions are included in the above fee, except for actual production costs, out-of-pocket expense, and commission payable by the media outlets and not the campaign.

C) **Fund-raising:** Includes development of the Fund-raising Game Plan, supervision of its implementation, assistance with PAC and out-of-district solicitation, events, fund-raising direct mail program, copy writing, targeting, FEC assistance, and development of a support file program. The fee would be $15,000, plus 2% of the gross amount raised, excluding the Candidate's and Party's contributions, and related out-of-pocket expenses.

Total base fees: $65,000 + 2% Fund-raising commission, plus media placement commissions payable by the media outlets, plus related out-of-pocket expenses and production costs.

The best a Political Campaign Consultant can do is to improve the odds for a victory. It is up to the Candidate and the members of the campaign to execute the plan the way that it has been designed.

If the above services were contracted for separately, they would be considerably higher.

One last caveat about Political Consultants. Even the best consultant cannot do justice to more than three or four campaigns at one time. Be sure to find out how many campaigns the consultant plans on handling during the campaign year and ask his or her commitment to be part of the contract. It is not unheard of for a Candidate to negotiate with one Political Consultant only to find his or her campaign is turned over to a junior member of the firm. Also, some Political Consultants fulfill their obligations by flying into town once a month, dispensing advice, and then are difficult to reach for follow up during the rest of the month. Conversely, others literally manage the campaign by remote control staying in daily communication with the Candidate or Campaign Manager. The Political Campaign Consultant is the strategist, and in effect, the chief executive officer for the whole campaign. The Candidate should choose carefully and make sure he or she is compatible, not only in personality, but also in basic strategy and approach. Remember too, that no matter how qualified the Political Campaign Consultant, there is no guarantee of success. Unfortunately, many variable factors can influence the outcome of an election that are completely beyond the control of anyone connected with the campaign. Nonetheless, outside variables are less hazardous when internal variables are effectively controlled.

Outside variables are less hazardous when internal variables are effectively controlled.

The Political Fund-raising Consultant

Role The Political Fund-raising Consultant is responsible for the development of the Fund-raising Game Plan and the supervision of its implementation.

The duties of the Political Fund-raising Consultant include the development of the Fund-raising Game Plan, supervision of its implementation, assistance with PAC and out-of-district solicitation, events, fund-raising direct mail program, copy writing, targeting, FEC assistance, and development of a support file program. They are covered in detail in Chapter 9, The Fund-raising Game Plan.

The Political Media Consultant or Advertising Agency

Role The Political Media Consultant, or Advertising Agency is responsible for the creation, production, and placement of paid media throughout the campaign

A Political Media Consultant or Advertising Agency is responsible for the creation, production, and placement of most paid media throughout the campaign, specifically the billboards, bus signs, newspaper ads, radio and TV commercials, and sometimes graphics such as the logo, brochures, supplemental flyers, and tabloids. They do initial research, including polls, and use their creative talents to develop the ideas that will best facilitate the communication of the message desired during each stage of the campaign. After additional research of local media market conditions and polling results, they determine the targeting necessary to reach the greatest number of potential voters.

When contracted for separately, the fees can vary widely. One prominent firm averages $75,000 for the creation fee, $25,000 for research, $50,000 for production, plus placement commissions and all out-of-pocket expenses. On the average, most seem to charge around $30,000 for research and creative fees, $15,000 for production costs, plus placement commissions and related out-of-pocket expenses.

In most cases, the Political Campaign Consultant exercises supervision and final approval of the finished products and the activities of the Political Media Consultant, or Advertising Agency, as well as over the other professionals providing service to the campaign, and has final approval of the finished products. This is necessary in order to make certain the media messages are coordinated with the other levels of activity within the campaign.

The Direct Mail / Computer Company

One firm normally handles the campaign's computer activity and the direct mail activity referred to in this Manual. The political direct mail functions and potential costs have already been covered in the Campaign Manager's section of this chapter. As mentioned previously, it is imperative that the company is able to handle the campaign's requirements and that they do so in a timely fashion. Political business is sporadic and all too often it is put at the bottom of most firms' priority schedules. If possible, the campaign should include a performance bond in its contract with the direct mail/computer company. The timing of direct mail is critical to the campaign and there should be some penalty if the direct mail company misses a deadline. In addition, be sure to have a contract or price schedule spelling out precisely what the costs will be for the various services being provided.

As a point of reference, the average standard rate for basic computer services usually breaks down as follows:

a) Data entry - Transferring the names manually to magnetic tape, hard discs, or CD ROM discs. Usually the average cost is based on the number of lines per entry.

    3 lines: name, street, city/state/zip code = 25 cents
    4 lines: as above, plus telephone number = 27 cents
    5 lines: as above, plus company name = 30 cents
    6 lines: as above, plus 3 codes = 31 cents

   PAC entries usually contain 5 lines. To enter 500 would cost $150 plus a set-up charge of $50. Other Prospect File names contain 4 lines, plus a code line. To enter 10,000 records would cost $2,700 plus a set-up charge of $50.

b) Updates - Changing an entry from one category to another costs an average of 18 cents per change.

c) Transposing voter registration information - Changing voter registration data from tapes to a printout form that can be used by the Precinct Captains and Phone Bank volunteers will usually average $5,000 for the cost of the programming and the actual printouts.

d) Voter registration updates - These will usually average 12 cents per line item for deletions or changes. 50,000 changes would average about $6,000, plus $2,000 for two sets of printouts.

e) Tele-matching - Adding telephone numbers to voter registration lists will average about $25 per 1,000 names matched. To control costs, the names should be compacted by household. If more than one registered voter is shown for a household, the computer suppresses the additional names before running the tele-match program.

These average costs are based on the quote that a Candidate could expect to obtain on his or her own. Most Political Campaign Consultants should have sources for these services averaging about 10 percent lower.

The Political Polling Consultant (Polling Firm)

Role The Political Polling Consultant (Polling Firm) is responsible for developing the questionnaire, drawing the sample, supervising the polling, reading the cross-tabs, and providing a written and/or verbal analysis of the results.

Variations in prices and the timing for this activity have already been discussed.

Polls usually serve two basic purposes. First, to take a "picture" at a particular moment in time during the campaign to see where it is, and what the people in the district are thinking about the candidates, the issues, and what media outlets and programs they are watching. Second, to provide a major tool in determining where and how the Candidate must target his or her media and campaign message for maximum effectiveness.

Reading a poll and determining one's impression is relatively easy. Unless someone in the campaign knows how to interpret the cross-tabs and translate the information gained into knowledge, the campaign has wasted the most valuable part of the poll.

I was once retained to do a post election analysis on a race that was lost by less than 1 percent. After going through my normal routine, I asked to see the polls. The first and second polls showed that the campaign was on target and, given the rate of progression, should have won by a relatively comfortable margin of 5 percent. As I began to read the third poll, I immediately noticed that a dramatic shift toward the opponent had begun in a critical area of the district. The shift was unmistakable. I asked the client what corrective action had been taken to reverse the shift perhaps by a precinct blitz, direct mail, or door to door campaigning. When the client answered, "none," I was shocked.

This poll was taken 6 weeks before the election and was a clear indication that a problem had developed in one of the Candidate's base areas of support, yet nothing was done about it. The client, seeing my obvious shock and disbelief, went on to explain that no one on the campaign staff, including the Campaign Manager, knew how to read "all those numbers." Therefore, the Campaign Manager, after checking the ballot question, tossed the poll in the bottom drawer of the desk and there it lay, with its red flag waving, while the campaign went down to defeat by less than 500 votes.

Reading the cross-tabs is tedious, dull work. However, it is not difficult, at least no more difficult than cross-referencing material in a library. Is it boring? Yes. Is it necessary? Absolutely!

Most Political Polling Consultants will provide a written and/or verbal analysis of the polls. However, the larger polling companies especially are so swamped with work in September and October when those final polls are taken all over the country that they usually have a difficult time doing the kind of detailed analysis that should be done. It is up to the Campaign Manager to do this, particularly the comparisons with the two previous polls. That is one of the reasons why a campaign does at least three in order to plot trends and identify direction.

The Political Media Consultant or ad agency will do the analysis necessary to place the last media buys for maximum effectiveness. However, unless the campaign has a Political Campaign Consultant who is responsible for doing the complete analysis, only the Campaign Manager is in a position to do the final analysis.

I have worked with some of the best known Political Polling Consultants in the country, and some not so well known. Frankly, I have found the results and quality of their work to be essentially the same. Both use practically the same data accumulation methods and computation techniques. As a rule, pollsters are like CPA's. Their integrity and professional reputation mean everything to them. I have yet to meet one who would play games with the results of a poll to favor a client.

Though there might not be as much prestige involved with using a smaller firm, the campaign may find, that because their overhead is usually lower and the number of accounts fewer, that it might be able to save several thousand dollars for the same results and receive even more personalized service. Just be sure that they have experience in political polls, as there is a difference.

The question often comes up on whether the campaign should attempt to do its own polling. Developing the questionnaire, drawing the sample, and doing the interviews is not too difficult. Until recently, the development of the cross-tabs has been a major undertaking that could only be accomplished on a mainframe computer using a very sophisticated and expensive software program. Even if the campaign had a local college professor proficient in this area to help, getting time on a mainframe computer to do the calculations was difficult.

There is a company, which has developed a software program that will design the questionnaire, manipulate the data, develop the cross-tabs, and operates on most any PC on the market today. I have reviewed their program, and although I have not yet had an opportunity to use it on any campaign, it appears that the program will indeed do what its authors claim. The company is Apian Software, at 800.237.4565 or at www.apian.com. The program is called *Survey-Pro*.

For those campaigns with the ability and inclination to do their own internal polling, I would strongly recommend it. Although the results would not be that helpful as a fund-raising tool, the knowledge gained by regular polling would be an invaluable tool for developing on-going strategy. Be sure the Campaign Manager or someone on the campaign staff knows how to read the cross-tabs in a poll, then actually does read and analyze them. If there is no one available with this experience, ask a Political Polling Consultant for a detailed analysis.

The Print and Graphics Company

I have already covered a number of services supplied by these types of companies and their pricing methods. However, the campaign should be knowledgeable about a few other issues as well.

Graphics

The development of the campaign logo and the camera ready artwork used for the brochures, billboards, lawn signs, newspaper ads, stationery, and tabloids is usually done by a graphic artist and typesetter, either working for a printing company, free-lance, or at an ad agency. These individuals create the designs, determine the style of type, the size, finish, the weight of paper, and the colors. They design the layouts and do the necessary paste-ups. They do not write the copy nor, as a rule, do the photographic work. The Candidate must supply both the copy and any photographs.

Charges vary considerably. I normally set aside $5,000 in a campaign budget for this item. However, if a Candidate wants work that is more elaborate the costs can rise quickly. My suggestion is to keep it simple. Use colors to get attention, but do not go overboard with expensive paper, odd sizes, and unusual folds. These options really increase the cost of brochures, and when you need to print 500,000 of them, even an extra penny will add $5,000 to the cost.

Brochures

A campaign brochure should be printed in at least two colors. It should tell a story in pictures that illustrate that the Candidate is a decent, caring individual. It should feature the Candidate's name and the office he or she is running for, leaving the Party off, unless there is a contested Primary. It should reflect, in one or two sentences on each issue, the candidate's position on three or four issues. There should be a brief, narrative biography of the candidate. It should not be cluttered with a lot of copy. The size should be kept standard, with no more than two folds.

Tabloids

When doing the tabloids, decide what the primary function is. If its target were the above average voter, it would be issue oriented, but still broken up with several pictures in a newspaper style. If going to the average voter, it should be like the brochure, clean, with a lot of white space, telling a story more with pictures and captions rather than with lengthy descriptive text. Both should contain a narrative biography of the Candidate. I believe in using both when the campaign strategy calls for it. I have also developed a modified version that has something in it for both groups. This is a variable area and the campaign will have to make a judgment call based on the situation. There is no constant for most campaigns.

In printing a tabloid, the campaign will have to find a printer with a Web press. Most commercial printers do not have them. Usually the campaign will have to shop around for printers who do weekly or smaller daily newspapers or specialty newspapers for unions, clubs, or churches. Costs can vary considerably. Therefore, once the quantity, size, and number of pages has been determined, call around to the available printers for price quotes. Since most printers usually use newsprint, there is little or no difference in quality. To be safe however, they should be asked to send a sample copy of their publication along with their quote. A qualitative difference will usually surface when comparing the quality of printed pictures. If printing 100,000 or more, the average price for a four-page tabloid will likely be about 7 cents.

Chapter 7 - Word Index

Campaign Role Index

Chapter 8
The Finance Committee
A Means to an End

"The Gang of 20"

Definition
A campaign Finance Committee is a group of volunteers who assume the responsibility for helping a candidate raise the necessary funds to conduct his or her campaign.

A Finance Committee should be comprised of two groups. The first group consists of those who can readily afford to write a contribution check for the maximum amount allowed by law. The second group is younger professionals and business people in the community who, though unable to contribute the maximum allowed, can nonetheless usually write a check for a substantial amount and more importantly they are the type who will do most of the work when arranging fund-raising events and activities.

When soliciting members, explain your plan to take large obstacles, break them down into smaller, manageable parts, and make all your goals "doable."

How to Recruit Your Finance Committee

Ideally, a Finance Committee is comprised of two groups of individuals. Those who are successfully established professionals and business people in their community and those who are striving to become both successful and established.

The first group consists of those who can readily afford to write a contribution check for the maximum amount allowed by law and should be required to do so as a condition of serving on the committee. These individuals will also have access to other individuals who can do the same.

The second group is younger professionals and business people in the community who, though unable to contribute the maximum allowed, can nonetheless usually contribute a substantial amount. More importantly, they are the type who, when called upon, will do most of the work when arranging fund-raising events and activities.

Depending on the size of the campaign, perhaps one involving a district of up to 500,000 people, a Finance Committee should be made up of between 15 to 20 volunteers. As the size of the district increases, the size of the Finance Committee should increase proportionately. In seeking out these people, the candidate should first look to his or her own circle of friends, acquaintances, and associates. People who know you and believe in your candidacy are the best choices. Most will probably be reluctant to serve at first. On the average, people dislike asking for money, especially if they need to ask friends and relatives. You should anticipate this reluctance and realize it is not directed toward you. Have a series of small meetings in your home with three or four potential committee members each time.

Begin the meeting sharing your reasons for wanting to run for political office. Follow this with an explanation of why you believe that you can win the election. Have a copy of your political game plan for each person and guide them through the plan in a step by step presentation, much like the plan was developed, discussing the circumstances and factors that lead you to believe in your ability to win the election.

Once everyone has had an opportunity to go through the finance plan and asked any questions they may have had, give each of them a copy. Explain the process you went through to make the finance plan fiscally sound and responsive to the needs of the campaign. Continue to explain how you plan to take large obstacles, break them down into smaller, manageable parts, and make all your goals "doable." Your plan incorporates the premise that if each

Your plan incorporates the premise that if each person does his or her share, no one will be over burdened, making complete success attainable.

person does his or her share, no one will be over burdened and complete success is attainable. Ask them to serve on your committee and to set an example for others by being the first to make a contribution to your campaign.

In many cases, you will be encouraged by the positive response from your meeting. In turn, always ask your hopefuls if they know any capable candidates that might serve on the committee. Ask them, as well, to arrange a similar meeting with you for the persons they are recommending. In this manner, you should be able to recruit at least 50-75% of the members of your Finance Committee. When you have exhausted this means of recruitment, speak with your party chairperson and ask for recommendations of people who would serve and be productive members of your committee. Contact these people and go through the same process with them. If your committee is still not up to strength, contact previous candidates and elected officials in your area for their assistance and recommendations. In each meeting, follow the same procedure. It helps significantly if the person who made the recommendation attends these meetings with you.

For the chairperson(s) of your committee, I recommend asking one person from each group to serve as co-chairs. Recruit one or two prominent person(s) in your district who will allow you to list their names on your campaign stationery and name them to serve as honorary chairperson(s) on your Finance Committee.

If you follow this plan, you will have a first rate committee assembled within a month of the date you started recruiting. Half will be prominent people within the community and the other half will be young professionals and business people. Your committee should be comprised of both men and women, and through experience, I have found that insurance agents, real estate agents, and junior bank managers invariably do the best job on these committees.

How to Organize Your Finance Committee

The Finance Committee is organized around the 5 on 5 Region and Area plan and teams made up of members from both groups should be created. The number and size of the teams should be proportional to the number and size of the regions and areas.

Basing your Finance Committee needs on the 5 on 5 Region and Area plan, the committee should be divided and assigned region and area responsibilities. Teams made up of members from both groups should be created. Each team should have its own team leader either picked by you or self-chosen by a method decided upon by the team. The number and size of the teams should be proportional to the number and size of the regions and areas. That is, in some campaigns, a team responsibility would encompass a complete region, whereas in larger campaigns, there would be a need for a team to work each area, with a portion of the Finance Committee overseeing each Region.

The teams should be identified by any designation they might choose. Each team should be asked to raise a proportional share of the Finance Committee's total objective. Throughout the campaign, at all future meetings of the Finance Committee, each team leader will be expected to give a report to the whole committee on their progress toward reaching the assigned goal.

Encourage a spirit of competition by posting a huge board in the campaign headquarters listing each team's objectives and their progress toward reaching it.

Human nature being as it is, it is always a great idea to stimulate a little competition between the fund-raising teams. Before long, a spirit of competition will develop between the teams, especially, if you have encouraged it. Post a huge board in the campaign headquarters listing each team's objectives and their progress toward reaching it. You can also encourage a competitive atmosphere with minor contests along the way. If you're meeting bi-monthly, as you should be, the team with the most money raised since the last meeting could be rewarded as the guests of honor of the other teams at a local pizza parlor or some other token of appreciation. Since it is simply a friendly competition, a large prize is not necessary. It is also wise to issue a monthly campaign newsletter and distribute it to all your volunteers, keeping them current on the campaigns progress and listing each team members' name and the results of each teams' efforts since the last newsletter.

As further encouragement to them, and all of your volunteers, you should make two large "thermometers" and place them prominently in the campaign headquarters. One will illustrate the campaign's progress in its over-all fund-raising efforts and the other to illustrate your progress in acquiring positive ID voters against that objective. At least once a week, using red ink, the thermometers should be brought up-to-date. On the sides of the thermometers, put hash marks and the respective amounts that should be in place by the planned dates.

Finance Committee Objectives

The Finance Committee will raise funds through individual solicitation, major fund-raising events, direct mail appeals, PAC, Party, and OD solicitation, and personal follow-up.

The Finance Committee has several methods of fund-raising strategy to enable the campaign to realize its fund-raising potential in order to meet its goals. These goals will be attained through individual solicitation, major fund-raising events, direct mail appeals, PAC, Party, and OD solicitation, and personal follow-up.

It is a major mistake to fail to seek the "buy in" of the Finance Committee when assigning objectives to the members. Established goals must be realistic and attainable. Since the members have contributed to the establishment of the goals and committed themselves to realizing them, the chances are much greater that they will persevere under even stressful conditions.

Realistic and attainable objectives should be discussed with, and agreed to, by the members of the committee. A major mistake made by many campaigns is the arbitrary assignment of objectives to the members. Unless the members believe they are a part of the process in establishing these goals, the depth of their commitment will not be deep enough to keep pushing when the going gets tough. On the other hand, if they have contributed to the establishment of the objectives and committed themselves to realizing them, the chances are much greater that they will persevere under even stressful conditions.

The percentage of the budget to be raised by the Finance Committee depends on the status of the candidate. If the candidate is an incumbent, protecting an existing seat, the majority of the campaign funds will probably come from a combination of PAC and party contributions, assuming that the incumbent has not disavowed the acceptance of PAC money, or put any limits on it. If the incumbent candidate has restricted PAC funds, the percentage of the budget to be raised by the Finance Committee will be almost as much as for a challenger candidate. Those incumbents who do accept PAC contributions can usually raise 50-60% of their budget from PACs and their party. Some incumbents raise virtually 100% from these sources. Not politically astute, nonetheless, it is certainly expedient.

Actual percentages raised by each entity and by each fund-raising method will depend on the individual circumstances of your campaign.

The Finance Committee will be responsible for raising approximately 70% of a challenger's campaign budget. It is likely that approximately 20% will be financed with the challenger candidate's own funds. The balance, between 5% and 10%, will be raised by minor fund-raising events organized by the Field Operations Committee. Amounts raised from outside the district from such sources as the PACs or the party, on the average, will amount to only 15% for challenging candidates and that percentage will be possible only if the challenger is able to prove that his or her campaign is viable.

Be mindful of the fact that we will use average percentages based on average circumstances for the sake of our discussion. Also, to give this discussion structure, we will presume your campaign began one year before the date of the general election and that you assembled your Finance Committee during the months of December and January before the election and planned to announce your candidacy in February.

Finance Committee Methods

Individual Solicitation - Begin at the Beginning

"Ask and You Shall Receive"

In the preparation stage of your campaign, you developed lists of prospective contributors, or individual prospects. These names were put on 3 X 5 cards and into the computer in an Individual Prospect file. As they were being entered, you noted, based on an arbitrary presumption, their capability of donating over or under $150. You also indicated their occupation and title, if known.

If you have not already done this, develop your list from a variety of sources. Your personal list of friends and relatives, alumni lists, membership lists from the Chamber of Commerce, the Junior Chamber of Commerce, clubs or associations, churches, former candidates, or party contributors. These combined initial lists could number anywhere from 500 to 5,000 or more names. Regardless of how you record this data, it must be done. These names will form the basis of the starting point for your Finance Committee. In combination with other names that will be added later, this list of prospects will be the first solicited by mail and distributed to the Finance Committee for follow-up either in person or by telephone.

The Next Stage

To be cost effective and save time as well, the carrier envelope should be a #10 window envelope, enabling you to print the address once on the letter, stuffing the envelopes accordingly.

Your next step is to prepare a fund-raising letter. Ideally, a prominent person known in your district will sign this letter. If a person of this stature is not available for your campaign, then your campaign chairperson or finance chairperson could sign the letter. The letter itself should be on campaign stationery. On the left-hand side of the stationery, you should list the names of the campaign officers, your Regional Chairperson(s), and the members of your finance committee.

In the envelope, there should be a Business Return Envelope (BRE), preferably a wallet style flap envelope that gives the recipient an opportunity to volunteer as well as to record the information necessary for your financial records. You will find an example of the information that should be printed on the BRE in Appendix M. Your biographical brochure outlining your background and qualifications for office should also be included. It should feature a picture of you on the front and you with your family on the inside. You might also want to include a picture, or two, of you interacting with senior citizens or children.

The letter itself should be a one-page piece, typeset in a professional, 12-point typeface. It should be individually prepared and personalized. A sample letter can be found in Chapter 14.

If you are using a computer program, your letters can be typeset and then merged with the names and addresses in your Prospect file to produce a highly personalized letter. The letter should be mailed at first class postage

With the word processor within GOTV *Campaign Optimizer,* you are able to typeset your letters and then merge them with the names and addresses stored in your database. The program can also sort the addresses by zip code to enable you to capitalize on postage savings.

rates. If your campaign has a postal pre-sort permit, you can save 10% on your postage by sorting the letters in zip code order and stacking them in special letter trays available from the Post Office. Check with your main Post Office for the latest details. A capable campaign management program can also sort the letters while merging the addresses.

Distributing the Names

Arrange a meeting of your finance committee a few days after the fund-raising mailer has been dropped (left with the post office for delivery). On one side of the room, place 3 X 5 cards containing the pertinent information regarding the prospects who were sent the mailer on one or two long tables so that they can be easily read. In addition, display copies of both the letter and the brochure that was sent in the mailer.

The finance committee chairperson should conduct the meeting. In all probability, this will be the first opportunity for all the members of your Finance Committee to assemble at one time. It is important that you use this occasion not only to start them off on their active fund-raising, but also to motivate them to persevere throughout the entire campaign. This meeting should set the stage for the level of their activity throughout the campaign.

The campaign chairperson should address the committee first and discuss the game plan, the strategy, and the budget. The campaign chairperson then moves toward closing with a statement on why it is so important to have the candidate elected to office. He or she should introduce the candidate to rousing applause and resounding approval.

The Candidate should make welcoming remarks and thank all for coming out. The audience should be told again why the Candidate is running for this office and what it means to serve the community. The Candidate should express deep concern for the people of the District. Share specific ideas to improve their conditions, while not adding any unfair burdens on the middle class and business community. They should be told about how hard the Candidate has worked to bring the campaign this far, and how hard the Candidate plans to work in order to win. Share with them the sacrifices made by you, the Candidate, and by your family, both, personally and financially. The Candidate needs to be emphatic about his or her inability to be successful alone. Unless the Candidate, in union with the Campaign Finance Committee reach their full potential, the campaign will never be able to raise the funds necessary to communicate its message to the people. In closing, the Candidate should thank them again for making the tremendous effort on behalf of the campaign.

Now the person, known affectionately as the "hammer," rises to speak. Usually this person is the Finance Committee Chairperson. This role is called the "hammer" because it is this person's job to motivate the attendees. His purpose is to motivate them to raise funds for the campaign. This motivation can start today with their contributions.

The finance committee chairperson should begin by telling his committee members that the time for action has come. They have heard from the campaign chairperson how it can be done, and from the candidate, why it should be done. Now it is their turn to make it happen, pledging their financial support in order to get the job done.

Obviously, this is merely an example and in reality, must be tailored to the particular campaign and group being addressed.

His or her instructions should continue, *"We are going to divide the names of fund-raising prospects and contact those people to encourage them to send in a contribution. The people listed on those cards have already received a letter, paving the way for your follow-up visit or call. Before we can ask someone else to contribute, we must have the feeling of full conviction that comes only from having made our own personal sacrifice. So, right now, let us take out our checkbooks and make our personal financial commitment to the campaign. And when you get to that line that says "amount," whatever you were thinking of contributing, double it. The greater your sacrifice today, the harder you will work to convince others to equal your sacrifice. Remember we are not talking about a golf tournament or something frivolous. We are talking about our futures. Unless we have people like our Candidate in office, people who understand our concerns and are willing to fight to protect them, we are going to pay many times over in other ways. Pay me now or pay a lot more later. The choice is yours. Just remember that if you fail to act when you have the opportunity, you forfeit your true right to complain about government services, programs, or taxes again. Today, you have the opportunity; have the courage to stand up and be counted, when being counted counts."*

"Our candidate and his or her family have already made tremendous sacrifices and are willing to make many more. The least we can do is make sure they are not sacrificing alone for all our futures. Through our efforts, this campaign is winnable. Without our efforts, it will surely fail." With that or something similar being said the checks should be collected and arrangements made to collect checks from those who may have failed to bring their checkbook to the meeting.

The group should discuss the political game plan. Include a discussion and understanding of the Region and Area divisions and fund-raising team concept. Outline the team structure, pointing out that each team has a chairperson responsible for making sure that everyone has all the materials that are needed. Make certain that they realize that the Team Chairperson will be following up on the results of each team member's follow-up calling.

Direct the members to the tables on the side, and ask them to study the 3 X 5 cards, picking those individuals known, or those that one would like to follow up on. The chairperson should then collect the remaining cards and divide them up among the team chairpersons, who would then apportion them to their team members.

The members should be reminded that all the people on the cards have recently received a personal letter from the campaign. Copies of the letter should be included in the member's fund-raising kits and on the tables. Where it is available, supply the individual's telephone numbers, home, and office, on the card. Suggest that each person be contacted during the next two weeks and encourage their participation in the campaign. Instruct them that in-person contact is preferred. Face to face, one is able to discuss the political game plan intelligently and apply the greatest pressure to the fund-raising attempt. However, if this is not possible or desirable, call the prospect and speak to him or her over the telephone.

The group should agree to meet in two weeks to review the individual and team results. A petition should be made for the solicitation of any prospects for more volunteers who would serve on the committee. Encourage the members to bring them along to the next meeting. Remind them, in closing that the team chairpersons, or captains, will be calling periodically to see how everything is progressing.

The chairperson should always close the meeting with a gracious thank you and adjourn the meeting.

The Follow Up

The team captains must call their members and record the names that each member has for follow up. A duplicate list is made and sent to the Finance Committee Chairperson who transfers this information to a duplicate set of 3 X 5 cards. While the team members are making their follow up calls, the team captains should continue to follow up and insist on progress reports every two or three days. It is very important that these names receive contact within the first two weeks of receiving their solicitation letter.

Consider involving the team captain, Finance Chairperson, or even the Candidate, if this assistance may secure a large contribution. Always, use the Candidate's time by appointment to avoid any waste of valuable campaigning hours.

The entire Finance Committee will re-convene (in about two weeks) at a meeting scheduled at the original gathering. At this meeting, each team captain should stand and give a team report. In turn, each individual team member should also report on their progress. A brief question and answer period should be held where individuals have an opportunity to share their experiences and to ask for ideas on how to overcome any type of resistance or reluctance that they are experiencing. Consider some problem solving solutions. Sometimes the team captain or the Finance Committee Chairperson may decide to join the member on the next follow-up. Consideration should be given to the Candidate joining, if it would help in realizing an especially large contribution. Be sure this is done by appointment. Do not waste the time of either the candidate or the potential contributor.

With the exception of the first full Finance Committee meeting, finance meetings should be kept on a tight time line, not lasting for more than one hour, excluding time for refreshments.

The members should be asked to return the cards on those individuals who have contributed, or flatly refused to contribute. Those cards remaining would include the ones requiring a further follow-up or people who have not yet been contacted. The date should be set for the next meeting, in two or three weeks, beforre adjourning.

By the time the Finance Committee meets for the third time, a spirit of camaraderie should be developing. It is at this meeting that a spirit of competition should be added to the atmosphere among the teams. The methods used to accomplish this should be decided upon at a meeting held among the Finance Committee Chairperson and the team captains before the scheduled meeting with the whole committee. The team captains should plan for one of them to issue a challenge to the other teams at the next meeting. The challenge could be that the team raising the most money by the next meeting would be the guests of honor for pizza and beer, compliments of the losing teams. It could be a sporting event or other popular activity that is not too expensive and will be socially acceptable to team members. At the event, the winning team should issue a new challenge to the others and wager their position at the top against another outing.

You will find most team members will be caught up in this spirit of competition. As with most challenges, the pride of winning is the important thing, not the size of the prize.

The campaign newsletter should be a regular feature throughout the campaign. A major feature in the newsletter should be continuing updates and encouragement regarding fund-raising efforts, including a listing of the teams and each of their members and a story about the latest challenge. The teams will become serious about the competition aspect, insisting that their team receive proper credit for every contribution that is a result of their efforts and look forward to their team's notoriety in the campaign newsletter.

The campaign should distribute a monthly newsletter to all of the volunteers keeping them "in the loop" and updating the volunteers on all of the campaign's activities and progress.

At the fourth meeting, which should occur three to four months into the campaign, the follow up program should end and all remaining 3 X 5 cards should be turned in. Depending on the notes on these cards, the names should be deleted from the Prospect list if repeated contact failed to obtain a positive response. If some hope remains, you might try assigning the name to someone else. If no contact has been made yet, the committee and team captain should problem solve the prospect and decide if it is worth any further investment of time and effort. The committee, as a whole, should now have its efforts directed toward a major fund-raising event to be planned for two months hence. In a normal campaign cycle, this would be scheduled in June of the campaign year.

Major Fund-raising Events

Definition
Major fund-raising events are high priced events designed to appeal to, and be afforded by, a campaign's higher middle income and higher income prospects and supporters.

A major fund-raising event is usually a dinner/dance featuring a prominent person as a guest speaker. The event is a ticketed affair, with tickets selling for at least $150.00 per person. In some cases, depending on the level of the office you are seeking and your status as an incumbent or challenger, the ticket prices could go as high as $500.00 per person.

The guest speaker could be a prominent politician, a sports figure, or an entertainment personality. Many people of this type donate their time to help candidates of their choice to raise funds. Some charge an honorarium for attending. In either case, the campaign will be responsible for paying all of their travel and related expenses.

Consider a separate contribution to arrange the opportunity for a private reception with the guest speaker prior to the dinner. The contribution should be at least equal to the price of the dinner ticket and in some cases much more depending on the prominence of the speaker.

As a rule, the more prominent the individual, the busier their schedule. Therefore, arrangements for this person usually need to be made months in advance. It is also prudent to ask two or three individuals so you have a back-up plan in case your first choice is unable to attend or fails to give a prompt answer to your invitation. If you or the members of your committees do not know anyone of this type, check with your state or national party committees. They usually maintain lists of politicians and celebrities who are willing to help in this manner.

As soon as you have a firm date confirmed by your celebrity, preferably for a Friday or Saturday evening in May or June, book the ballroom facilities at a local hotel or hall. These places are often booked far in advance, so you should have tentative reservations at several alternate places. Once all the details are brought together and a firm date is selected, have the tickets printed and begin your fund-raising activity. Remember that this should begin at least two months prior to the event.

Definition
Minor fund-raising events are low priced events designed to appeal to, and be afforded by, a campaign's lower middle income and lower income prospects and supporters.

Minor Fund-raising Events

Minor fund-raising events are usually held during the summer months and serve a three-fold purpose:

1) to raise money,
2) to involve the non-finance committee volunteers in the fund-raising process,
3) to have fun, while building enthusiasm toward the final efforts of the campaign.

Minor fund-raising events are usually priced between $20.00 and $25.00 per person, with a family discounted price offered at $30.00. They might be planed around a 4th of July picnic/rally, polka party, dance, auction, pancake breakfast, hoe-down, pizza party, spaghetti dinner, or similar event.

Minor fund-raising events fall under the auspices of the Field Operations Committee, with the assistance of the Finance Committee. Five of these events planned about two weeks apart should be held throughout the summer months. All should be held on weekends and if possible holiday weekends.

The Direct Mail Solicitation

"The Pyramid Game"

Direct mail fund-raising involves several types of activity. We discussed one type as a part of the prospect file mailings. Several other types can be equally effective if done properly. Here is a listing of several types:

1) Specialized professional mailings focus on obtaining professional membership lists and then have a prominent member of that profession send a letter to his or her colleagues appealing for their support. Doctors contact doctors, lawyers talk to lawyers and so on.
2) Political mailings cover the registered voters in your district. Another truism in this business is that the only mail you send without an appeal for funds is the final week's mailer, immediately preceding the general election, since the funds will not arrive in time to help. In this final mailer, you ask for their vote.
3) Rented list mailings involve renting names from commercial list brokers. These lists are often national in nature but the companies who manage them can usually break them out by state and/or zip codes. You are seeking names of people who are ideologically in step with your political philosophy.
4) Previous contributors list mailings to contributors of other candidates and party committees can be very successful. As these are usually very partisan contributors, the returns tend to be better than from most other lists.

There are other minor types, but coupled with your own list of prospects, these are the five major prospect-mailing categories developed in campaign fund-raising.

The Premise of Direct Mail Fund-raising

Direct mail fund-raising is one of the more scientific methods of fund-raising. We know that if X number of pieces of mail are sent out over a specific time, there will be a relatively consistent rate of return responses that will result in Y number of dollars. This premise is not a guess, but rather, is based on millions of pieces of direct mail sent over a period of many years. The premise is based on historical experience.

The rate of return is predicated on several factors including the quality of the lists, the qualities of the mailing piece, the cause involved, and the strength of the signatory. A mailer planned around concern for these characteristics will produce a return rate of about 2% and produce an average of $25.00 per return.

If your campaign mails 10,000 pieces, which result in a 2% return, you should receive 200 replies containing an average of $25.00 each or $5,000. Since the average mailing piece costs about $.50, your expense to mail the 10,000 pieces is $5,000. Obviously, this does not appear to be a very successful fund-raising program. If it costs $5,000. to solicit $5,000, you do not need a degree in economics to understand that your campaign will not get ahead very quickly at that rate. On the other hand, the campaign has gained 200 new contributors, who will now be added to your individual support file. If you mail these people four more times during the campaign, each new mailing will generate a 20% response rate at an average return of $35.00 each. If followed scientifically, each subsequent mailing will produce 200 X 20% (40) X $35.00 or $1,400, while the cost of mailing the 200 pieces via first class postage will be somewhat greater than $.50 per piece, or $100. If you solicit the original 200 names, four times during the course of the campaign, your campaign will realize $5,600 less the $400.00 cost of the mailings. This program results in a net contribution of $5,200.

The Pyramid Effect

As you continue to mail each new group of 10,000 (or any base figure that you choose for your campaign district), you will develop a pyramid effect.

To illustrate, we can label your first prospect mailing A and the subsequent support file mailings that result from it; we will label A1, A2, A3, and A4. The next group of prospect mailings we will designate as prospect mailing B and the subsequent support file mailings that will result from it as B1, B2, B3, and B4.

If you are to copy this process for each successive mailer and diagram the results with each mailing, one on top of the next, the resulting diagram would take the shape of a pyramid. Soon enough, the campaign has built a steady monthly income of X dollars.

However, understand that although this method is tried and true, it is nonetheless a slow drawn out process. Unfortunately, even if you start the day you announce your candidacy, you would barely hit stride by Election Day. For this reason, some candidates begin the process as much as two years before the election. In addition, since it requires an investment of at least the equivalent of the first two prospect mailings, many candidates are reluctant to do this type of prospect direct mail fund-raising, especially in smaller campaigns. On the other hand, if you intend to be in the political arena for the long haul, the sooner you start your direct mail campaign, the better off your position will be, and remain.

Designing the Package

A sample prospect fund-raising letter can be found in Chapter 14.

The successful prospect fund-raising letter will demonstrate the three C's - Concern, Compassion, and Common sense.

The prospect fund-raising letter is prepared on your campaign stationery and, unless you have a nationally known personality who will sign a letter for you, the letter should come directly from the Candidate.

The letter should be one or two pages in length and even though it will be a form letter, it should be made to look as personal as possible. Your campaign software is the best investment towards accomplishing personalization. In the first paragraph, introduce yourself and the office you are seeking. Then talk about why you are seeking office. Speak from the heart and not the head. Talk about your concerns and your determination to do something about them. Explain how difficult it is to campaign when you are a working person and unable to finance your own campaign out of your own resources. Ask them to search their hearts. If they are interested in good government, ask if it is worth a small sacrifice to achieve it.

Enclose your biographical brochure and a BRE flap envelope. Using a cancelled live bulk stamp, mail it at bulk rates. Most mail processing companies can handle this processing for you at very modest rates.

The Follow Up

Use of the thank you letter as your first appeal for additional funds should be incorporated into all follow up thank you letters, regardless of the source. Do not be bashful about your appeal for funds. Always ask for a specific amount for a specific purpose. Explain that suppliers will not extend credit to political campaigns, making the need immediate.

When a return response comes in, enter the new supporter into your database (assuming that you have been convinced by now of the value of a computerized campaign). Using the letter generator, send the supporter a personalized thank you letter. This letter becomes the first of your four mailings to this new Support file person. In the letter, you not only thank them for their contribution of X amount of dollars, in addition, close with an appeal for more funds. This appeal should be specific. It should relate the appeal for funds to a specific program or activity within the campaign to which the supporter can relate. For example, you are about to lose your critically needed billboards if you can not raise another $5,000 to cover next month's rental. Ask if they could please assist in the payment toward the rent of even one board at $200? Alternatively, it could be $60 for a 30-second radio spot or $10 to cover one days rent for a telephone at the phone bank.

Always be specific and relate your need to real examples. People like to believe that their dollars are going toward something singularly tangible to which they can relate. The contribution becomes their billboard or their radio spot. Subsequent follow up letters should stress your reluctance to again ask for their help, which has been so generous to date. However, the race has become even tighter than before and the expenses keep mounting. Explain how your opponent has really begun to fight back viciously and if you do not have the funds to answer the attack, the campaign effort to date will suffer. Again, be specific with your need. Enclose a sample budget regarding what the experts think will have to be spent in the final months of the campaign in order to have a better than even chance of winning. Petition them to please review it and consider a further contribution to pay for some item.

Always emphasize your regret at having to ask for support again.

Close with a together we can win theme and a God Bless you for all your help.

The fourth follow up letter is the most difficult of all. Like the others, it is a personalized letter sent first class. You are going back to the well now for the fourth time. This piece usually goes out in the first week of October.

The letter should have an emotional appeal similar to the following:

There are arguments for and against making appeals on an emotional level, no differently than there are arguments regarding religious references, such as "God Bless you". Obviously, I am in favor of the use of these types of appeals and believe it to be successful in the most general sense. Ultimately, it is up to each Candidate to decide to what extent his or her campaign will use these tactics.

You really hate having to write this final letter. All night you tossed and turned, not sure of what to do. Your anguish finally woke your spouse and the two of you discussed the cause of your concern.

After listening to my concerns and reasons for having to ask for help again, my spouse reminded me that, it was not my decision to make. Good people have supported me thus far because they believe in me and in what I am trying to do now and when elected. Ultimately, the good that I plan will benefit us all. She pointed out that my supporters know that both my family and I have made tremendous sacrifices in order to help all of us realize our dreams.

On the other hand, she continued, how upset do you think they would be if they knew the outcome of this election depended on just a few more dollars and I did not tell them. What if I did not give them the opportunity to help if they could? She wanted to remind me that this is their campaign too. They have already made many sacrifices to assist in the campaign effort. Those that are able to help further will not abandon the effort now.

I realized that my spouse was right and how self-centered I was thinking that my sacrifices were any greater than theirs were. A campaign is not just a battle between two individuals. It is a struggle between two different philosophies about the role of government in our lives.

Give your supporters a frank assessment of where the campaign is situated and the costs that need to be incurred in order to win. Let the choice be theirs.

I have asked for the chance to be a leader in that struggle and the responsibility of a leader is to be frank and honest with the people, at all times. The choice of whether to continue the fight is as much yours as it is mine. I am here to assure you that I am ready, willing, and able to continue the fight.

It is for these reasons that I am not ashamed to ask for your help again.

At this point in the letter, give them a frank assessment of where the campaign is situated and the costs that need to be incurred in order to win. Let the choice be theirs. The polls and your honest assessment of the situation say you can win. However, there are still a sizable number of undecided voters in the district who are waiting until the last minute before they will make up their mind. Our campaign's message must continue to be communicated until the last hour. This takes money!

Express how we must finish with an intensive drive to get all of our supporters to the polls on Election Day. Based on the enclosed budget for the final weeks of the campaign, we must raise X amount of dollars for the final effort.

Together, shoulder to shoulder, let's go forward into this final battle. Together, we can win.

Thank them in advance for their staunch commitment to better government and the willingness to press on to the end. Close with God Bless you.

Powerful emotional appeals are powerful because, to paraphrase, "The heart does many things, the head knows not the reason why."

These are very powerful emotional appeals. Many candidates, especially attorneys, are reluctant to use this type of appeal, believing that it is too emotional. People, after all, should be motivated to contribute based on each candidate's stand on the issues. This argument certainly has a point, but the operative word is *should*. In truth, most of us only become involved in political activity when our emotions are involved. The single person who could not care less about school board issues becomes a dedicated advocate when he or she has become the parent of a 6 year old. The 30 year old really does not focus on Social Security issues. Once past 55, consider the attitude change that takes place if anyone tries to mess with Social Security. Childless persons can be very intellectual about solving our country's drug problem, and frankly, be more concerned about the rights of the individual, but you will get a very different response from the parents of a 17 year old who is an addict resorting to crime to support their habit. It is human to respond when our emotions are involved.

8

After 30 years of fund-raising, I should be as hard-hearted as anyone could be to a fund-raising letter. However, I still find myself responding to a well-written appeal to my emotions.

I once composed a fund-raising letter for a charitable organization. To make it unique, I wrote it in long hand on a yellow tablet and reproduced it that way. The impression was given that the letter was being written by a missionary in the heart of Africa, writing by the light of a kerosene lamp late at night, while listening to the crying sounds of hungry children in his orphanage who couldn't sleep. The orphanage desperately needed a new water pump to provide fresh drinking water for the children. The letter was highly emotional and as one person said, "it could produce tears from a stone." The response rate from that letter was over 7%, against the norm of 2%. I do not believe that anyone receiving that letter actually believed it was written by a missionary next to a kerosene lamp in the middle of Africa. But, the letter delivered an image that brought home a message about the terrible problems afflicting our fellow human beings in that part of the world. It is the image that they responded to when they sent their donations.

A well-written letter can add a graphic image to the appeal. The graphic image makes the appeal more understandable and meaningful. It is no different than becoming emotionally involved with a good book, movie, or television show. A strong emotional appeal will strike a responsive chord in our emotions that we are able to identify with, and relate to, in spite of what our head knows.

PAC and Party Solicitation

Always keep in mind that your party committees and the PACs which lean toward you philosophically, want you to win. They really do.

If PACs and party committees who are philosophically compatible with my campaign really want me to win, you may think, "Well, if that is the case, why won't they support me? If I had their help, I could win. Obviously, they figure I cannot win so they will not help me. Sounds like a self fulfilling prophecy to me." To some extent, you would be right. Nevertheless, your argument would be based upon a weak premise. Namely, if you had their help you could win. The fact of the matter is that money by itself does not win elections. Knowing how to spend it in the most effective manner to accomplish your goals is a part of the real answer. What is the most effective manner? We could ask that question of 1,000 candidates and no more than 5 would give us a correct answer.

Money by itself does not win elections. Knowing how to spend it in the most effective manner does.

Candidates are notorious for poorly managing campaign funds and bad budgeting practices. So much so, that a number of PACs and party committees will contribute to candidates by buying goods or services for them that they know will be of some help rather than give them cash which will probably be misspent.

If you have not done the research necessary, and not just about the issues, how could you possibly know the most effective manner in which to spend your funds? For example, no reasonable person knowing little about a car would attempt to manufacture one without first hand knowledge. If they had no marketing knowledge or experience, they would need to learn everything they could about marketing the vehicle after it had been manufactured.

The PACs and party committees will find you arrogant to think that anyone can organize and manage a campaign.

Clearly, the same can be said of any undertaking that is substantially different from the one that you are presently involved in. It would be arrogant to think otherwise. This very thought is the one that PACs and party committees will be thinking if you approach them and demonstrate a lack of awareness regarding campaigning as an undertaking. These people have worked in campaigns. They have a good understanding of what is involved and they know the kinds of sacrifices you will have to make in order to learn how to run a proper campaign with a chance of success. The burden of proof is on you. You must demonstrate to them not only that you know what is involved, but also, that you know how to do it. You must prove to them that you can do it. Be assured, it is not easy. Even after learning as much as you can about how to do it, you may find you lack the particular skills necessary to translate the knowledge into action. This is why the PACs and party committees usually adopt a "wait and see" attitude. They want to have assurances that you have successfully transferred the knowledge acquired into the skills necessary to achieve your objective.

Nonetheless, remember that they do want you to win. Just as the banker wants every businessperson to succeed, since it will ultimately mean more revenue for the bank. However, they also have a fiduciary responsibility to their investors and depositors to make sure you have the ability to make your business successful. In the same manner, the PAC and party committee personnel, who ultimately make these decisions, want you to succeed. However, their investors, the people who contribute funds for them to manage, want them to make sure that every campaign they "invest" in has a reasonable chance of success.

Do not waste your time and effort on creating "smoke and mirrors" in an attempt to dazzle these people. They have seen it all.

For this reason, they will be patient and monitor your campaign. The party committees, through their network of field directors and party personnel throughout the country, and the PACs through their associates, will monitor your progress. They will also look at other tell tale signs of your campaign's progress. Poll results will be at, or near, the top of the list. The number of contributors to your campaign and the amount raised from within your district are also good indicators. Remember that all the reports filed with either the state agencies or the Federal Election Commission are public records and they can and will monitor them if they believe a campaign has potential.

Reports from other elected officials close to the scene also influence their thinking. When they are really close to becoming involved, they will usually send someone to look over the campaign personally and report back to the decision-makers.

Some campaigns will try to dazzle these people with, "smoke and mirrors." However, many of these field operatives have been around for a long time and it does not take them long to see through the facade, especially if the supporting evidence does not substantiate what they are seeing and hearing.

It simply makes good sense having representatives of PAC related professions on your finance committee.

I referred earlier to the associates of PACs found in most districts throughout the country. Many of the larger, better funded PACs have members all over the country who have the responsibility for evaluating campaigns within their communities and making recommendations for PAC support. In fact, many of these PACs cannot make a contribution unless a recommendation to do so is forthcoming from these local individuals. The medical PAC, the realtors PAC, the construction industry PAC, the auto dealers' PAC, some of the labor PACs, and the insurance industry PAC are just a few who operate in this manner.

It simply makes good sense to have a representative of these professions on your finance committee. When the time is right, they should prevail on their PAC to provide support. Their recommendation will carry more weight with the PAC than if the request comes directly from the campaign.

At the very least, you want to convince the PACs to hold back on their active support for your opponent.

Send out your PAC kit to those PACs that you believe will be the most likely supporters when you can prove that you are deserving of their support. Send them regular updates on the campaign's progress and include your campaign newsletter along with copies of favorable newspaper articles. When you have raised at least 60% of your budget through your own fund-raising efforts, then make your serious push on the PACs. If you are a state or local candidate, go to your state capitol for a few days and make the rounds of the PACs armed with your poll results, game plan, and the statistics on your political and financial progress to date. If a federal candidate, plan to spend a few days in Washington, DC. Your party will usually help arrange your schedule after they see your results. In fact, with the right kind of statistics they will start pushing the PACs with whom they have influence to come on board. No one can guarantee a win. They know that. They want to know that your campaign is viable and has a reasonable chance of winning. At the very least, your trip will be successful if you can convince them to hold back on active support for your opponent.

Candidate Fund-raising Activity

The candidate is the single most effective "tool" in the fund-raising process.

The candidate is the single most effective "tool" in the fund-raising process, both in terms of providing a personal contribution to the campaign and regarding the solicitation of contributions. Without a candidate who has the resources to provide enough "seed money" to effect confidence from other prospects, the overall fund-raising process is flawed from the beginning. In other words, it will be expected that the Candidate be prepared and able to, "put his or her money where his or her mouth is!"

Secondly, it is essential that the Candidate be ready, willing, and able to hold his or her hand out at every opportunity, and with head held high, be prepared to solicit, or in other words, beg for funds from every prospect available.

We will investigate these concepts in the next chapter in more detail.

Chapter 8 - Word Index

Chapter 9
The Fund-raising Game Plan

"We have the tools! Now make them work!"

The Fund-raising Campaign

In every Political Campaign, two campaigns operate simultaneously: the political campaign and the fund-raising campaign.

Just as there are two strategies operative within the Political Game Plan, there are two campaigns simultaneously operative, i.e., the political campaign and the fund-raising campaign. The following sections will complement and reinforce some of the material previously covered.

As has been pointed out several times in *The Campaign Manual*, money supports communications, while information and motivation stimulated by hard work, results in votes. In some ways, money can replace hard work, but if you remove money from the equation, the Candidate will lose.

How *effectively* money is utilized is far more advantageous than how *much* money is available. However, it is crucial that a Candidate be able to raise the money necessary to implement the strategy.

Those who still charge that money buys votes are naive about the political process, behind the times, or trying to create a smokescreen issue. This is not to say that a candidate with an unlimited budget does not in some ways have an advantage. However, more important than how *much* money is available, is how *effectively* the money is utilized. In fact, it is very possible to overspend in a campaign. Nevertheless, it is critical that a Candidate be able to raise the money necessary to implement the strategy required by the particular circumstances of his or her campaign.

9

No matter how skillful the Political Fund-raising Consultant is, the objectives will not be reached unless the Candidate has an active Finance Committee that is willing and able to implement the Fund-raising Game Plan.

It is, therefore, of paramount importance for the Candidate to develop a Fund-raising Game Plan with as much care and concern as is used in the development of the Political Game Plan. The Political Fund-raising Consultant or adviser is invaluable to the Candidate in this regard. The methodology used, though not a precise science, is definitive enough to require a high degree of knowledge and experience. A Political Fund-raising Consultant does not actually solicit contributions for the Candidate. He or she will develop the Fund-raising Game Plan, supervise its implementation, and instruct the staff and Finance Committee on proven methods to be used for events, individual solicitation, and PACs. He or she will also write the copy for fund-raising direct mail and use extensive research to target the solicitations for maximum return. Most Political Fund-raising Consultants are experts on the FEC and state campaign finance regulations and will provide valuable guidance on proper compliance.

Previously, I outlined the design of a potentially first rate Finance Committee. Within that structure, there are two basic types of individuals; the individuals in the upper range of the economic scale who could personally write a check for $1,000/$2,000, and the individuals in the middle range who, though personally unable to contribute that amount, are willing and able to actively solicit contributions in the $100+ range. In this campaign, both types are of equal importance when it comes to implementing the plan.

Organization of the Finance Committee

The Finance Committee ideally would have at least 15 persons of the upper income group and 15 from the middle income group, plus any others who wish to serve on this committee. The Candidate, the Political Fund-raising Consultant, the Campaign Manager, the Treasurer, and the Secretary/ Bookkeeper are also members of this committee. There should be two co-chairpersons, preferably a man and woman, and an honorary chairperson, who is usually a former major officeholder or highly respected person in the community.

As the Candidate begins recruiting those individuals, keep in mind the groups they should represent. They must be dedicated to the Candidate and the campaign and be willing to make the personal sacrifices of time, money, and effort that will be required in the months ahead. They should be willing to make an immediate personal contribution and commit themselves to raising the funds necessary to satisfy their individual objectives.

Finance Committee Objectives

We all need goals. Experience has proven that this is especially true in political campaigns that have few "natural" devices to measure progress.

Based on the sources of income projection, the Finance Committee's individual objectives might be as follows:

a) Higher Income Group - Individual solicitations of $5,000 plus a personal contribution of $1,000, dinner and private social hour ticket sales of $5,000, totals a projection of $11,000 each x 15 members = $165,000.

b) Middle Income Group - Individual solicitations of $3,000 plus a personal contribution of $500, dinner and private social hour ticket sales of $2,500, totals a projection of $6,000 each x 15 members = $90,000.

Over a 10 to 12 month period these objectives are reasonable if the Candidate has recruited an active and energetic group. It is important that all members commit themselves to these objectives. At the Finance Committee meetings a progress report should be distributed showing each member's objective, the amount raised to date, plus a summary of current campaign income and expenditures.

Naturally, the objectives for each source are projections only. No one would object, however, if an upper level type, in addition to a personal contribution, wished to meet the objective by asking his or her spouse to contribute $2,000; $1,000 in the Primary period and $1,000 in the General period. Presently, this is the maximum amount a person is legally allowed to give a Federal Candidate. In addition, I do not believe that anyone would object if an individual's personal objectives were exceeded.

Timeline and Fund-raising Schedule

When the money is raised, is almost as important as how much is raised. The fund-raising portion of the campaign is keyed to the demands of the political Timeline. Note the tight coordination. Naturally, the further ahead of the schedule that the campaign is, the more likely are its chances for success.

It should also be noted that all money raised before April is projected to come from within the district. This is not an accident. Most of the PACs, national parties, and any potential out of district (OD) contributors will want proof that enough people in the district believe in the viability of the campaign before they will make their contributions. Regardless of how much they might want the opponent to lose or believe in the efficacy of the Political Game Plan, they know that a Candidate's campaign is difficult to win without adequate financing; it is virtually impossible to raise all of the funds needed from outside the district. They also need proof that the Candidate's supporters are solidly behind him or her and that they are willing to finance the campaign in a meaningful way.

Initial Procedures and Methodology

The first step is the establishment of fund-raising objectives and the cash flow requirements necessary to implement the Political Game Plan on schedule. When the Candidate first meets with the Finance Committee, he or she should remind them that political campaigns are notoriously poor credit risks. Few, if any, suppliers will extend credit to a campaign. Most payments must be made at the time the order is placed. It is critical, therefore, for them to understand the urgency of raising money early in the campaign and on-schedule with the timeline projections.

The members should not be expected to solicit contributions without a copy of the Political Game Plan and Budget (without the Cash Flow Schedule). Be sure to have enough copies of the required material for all the participants at the first meeting, along with the 3 x 5 cards or the computer printout of prospective contributors, and the Fund-raising Game Plan. Incidentally, some Political Fund-raising Consultants will attend the first meeting to review the plans and budget, help handle the distribution of cards, and provide the motivation to get the process started.

Exert pressure in the early stages; raising money in the later stages is relatively easy once the momentum of the campaign has developed.

During the follow up Finance Committee meetings, keep the pressure on. Review both the political and fund-raising progress, and continue to stress the urgency to raise these funds now. As distasteful as the exertion of this pressure may be, it is necessary. Raising money in the later stages is relatively easy, especially when the momentum of the campaign picks up. Nonetheless, the early money is essential if the objectives are to be met. The Finance Committee must be made to understand that there is no substitute for timing, especially in the area of building name ID rating. If the campaign falls short of its objectives in the early stages, it is more difficult to build a favorable impression among the electorate in the last months of the campaign, regardless of how much is spent.

Part of this favorable impression is created by a sense of familiarity with the Candidate, since he or she has been a part of the community, and they know him or her. This is one of the reasons why the more successful campaigns are the ones that start at least a year before the election. Later entries rarely seem to be able to make up for the lost time and are constantly playing catch up.

In addition to their responsibilities to raise their personal objectives, the Finance Committee is also responsible for overseeing the total Fund-raising Game Plan. The staff, under the supervision of the Political Fund-raising Consultant, has responsibility for the day to day implementation of the other parts of the Plan. The Finance Committee is responsible to make sure it is being done on schedule. To this end, they should receive regular and complete progress reports.

The Finance Committee should also assist in personal follow-ups when letters have been sent to the particular groups of potential contributors in the prospect file. In fact, in most cases, they should sign the letters sent to their particular group. In other words, a mailing to attorneys should be signed by the attorney(s) on the committee and those to doctors by the doctor(s). I, normally, recommend the establishment of unofficial ad hoc committees for each of the major professional groups, for example, Doctors for (Candidate's Name) (Office) Subcommittee.

Remember that all fund-raising, political letters, and political advertising on behalf of Federal and many non-Federal candidates must contain a disclaimer.

This method is legal as long as the contributions are made to the official campaign committee and are deposited in its bank account. The appeal should be made on the official campaign stationery. I should also point out that separate committees can be formed to solicit funds on behalf of a Candidate, but if managed this way, these separate committees must file separately with the FEC and the Clerk of the House for Congressional candidates and with the Secretary of State, in most states, for state candidates. This then necessitates the continuous filing of periodic FEC and state reports. Frankly that is more trouble than it is worth.

Definition
Independent Expenditures are expenditures made to "educate" the voters. They are made by a third party and must be completely independent of a Candidate's campaign.

While on the subject of independent committees, I should point out that there has been a significant rise during the last few years in what are referred to as "independent expenditures." The courts have ruled that an organization like a PAC, while limited to a $5,000 direct contribution to a Candidate, cannot be limited as to how much it wants to spend "educating" the voters in a particular district, so long as the expenditures are made independent of a Candidate's campaign. Independent means just that. There can be no communication between the Candidate's campaign and the organization making the independent expenditure.

It is hard to say what the political ramifications of this new entry into the political process are. The results so far have been mixed. From the Candidate's political point of view, it is imperative to point out to the media, if it becomes a campaign issue, that it is an independent expenditure and by law, the campaign cannot control it. If it is an extremely negative type of advertising being used, the Candidate should consider denouncing it, regardless of whether or not it is against the opponent.

The National Association of Realtors distributes a very informative pamphlet on their independent expenditures program. A copy may be obtained by writing the National Association of Realtors, Dept. of Political Communications, Political & Legislative Liaison Division, 777 14th St., N.W., Washington, DC 20005. Request Item No. 181-312.

The volume and amount of each return will be greatly improved if the aforementioned letters are followed up by a personal visit or telephone call. When a letter has gone out to attorneys for example, the attorney(s) on the Finance Committee should enlist the aid of a few other attorneys to assist as contact sources. Approximately 10 days after the letters are sent, they should all begin calling on the recipients of that letter, either in person or by telephone. If this is not possible, have the volunteers at the Phone Bank, calling on behalf of the signatories, make the follow up telephone calls. Remember, during the 2nd, 3rd, and 4th Stages, one day a week is designated at the Phone Bank for fund solicitation purposes (to follow up on direct mail letters or to help sell tickets for the special events).

Summary

The Finance Committee ideally should be made up of at least 30 people, 15 upper income level, 15 middle income level, broken down into five teams (to cover the 5 Regions), plus two chairpersons and an honorary chairperson. At the first meeting they should be given:

1) copies of the Political and Fund-raising Game Plans, including the Budget,

2) their assigned prospects on 3 x 5 cards or computer printout sheets,

3) their personal and collective objectives and responsibilities,

4) a copy of the FEC or state rules and regulations affecting their activities as solicitors for a Federal or State candidate, and

5) a strong, motivational talk stressing the urgency of raising early money and its impact on the Political Game Plan.

At subsequent meetings, Finance Committee members should receive complete progress reports on all facets of the Political and Fund-raising Game Plans.

Within 10 days, after prospective contributors in the professional and occupational groups have received direct mail fund-raising letters, committee members should make a personal or telephone follow up. The volunteers at the Phone Bank should do this follow up if the committee members are unable to do so.

Meetings of the Finance Committee should be held at least once each month during most of the campaign and twice a month during the 4th Stage. Although it will probably not be available for the first meeting, the campaign should make sure that all members receive adequate supplies of the campaign literature and position papers as early as possible.

The chairpersons of the Finance Committee are automatically members of the Advisory Committee.

The Fund-raising Direct Mail Program

There are three major areas in the Fund-raising direct mail program:

1) mass mailings developed from names supplied by a professional mailing service,
2) fund-raising through the political direct mail program, and
3) selective mailings within the district (PAC and out of district mail solicitation is discussed in the next section).

Mass Direct Mailing

There are firms located in most cities that maintain lists of area residents that include their names, addresses, telephone numbers, sex, age, occupation, and income level. These lists are rented to individuals or organizations for fund-raising purposes. This information is generally accumulated from crisscross directories, magazine subscribers, city directories, credit card holders, public information records, campaign contributor lists in states where it is legal to use them, or in a few cases, where a Candidate sells or gives away their list. The rental price for names ranges from 5 cents to 15 cents each, depending on the quality. The price is generally based on how current the data is, what information is contained, and how clean the lists are. The fewer the number of duplications, the cleaner the list is considered. The percentage of return per 1,000 pieces of mail sent and the average level of contribution per piece also greatly affect the rental price charged.

If rented, a contract is signed with the mailing list company that prohibits the duplication of the lists. You may use the list one time only. It makes no difference whether you are using labels, a magnetic tape, or 3 x 5 cards for hand addressing and telephone follow up. Only the respondents to your mailing become your "property" and may be solicited again without paying the mailing list company an additional rental charge. To insure compliance, they "salt" the list with "ringers" or "dummy" names. If a second mailing is received by the "salted" names, a breach of contract is immediately evident.

The names are available on labels that are applied by machine or pressure sensitive labels that are applied by hand, electronic file format to enable a more personalized mailing, or on 3 x 5 cards.

By carefully targeting this type of mail based on the demographics available and combining this with a well-written appeal, a good Political Fund-raising Consultant can obtain about a 3.5 percent return on the first mailing. This means that out of every 1,000 letters mailed, 35 contributions will be received. With luck, the rate of return should be enough to offset the cost of the first mailing and provide enough to "seed" the cost of subsequent mailings. In this way, contrary to some claims made, the real profit in this program is realized during the second, third, and fourth mailings to the contributors from the original mail piece.

For example, the average initial cost per unit for 100,000 pieces of mail will be approximately:

1) 7.4 cents rental price per name, plus
2) 26.6 cents per computer letter, including a #10 window envelope, a #6 1/2 BRE, and a brochure or flyer, plus mail processing, plus
3) 24 cents for bulk rate postage, equals
4) 58 cents x 100,000 mail pieces = $58,000, not counting any fees and commissions for a fund-raising consultant, if one is involved.

The return should be about 2 percent, or 2,000 contributions averaging about $25 per contribution. This is a total of $50,000, or roughly break-even. Apparently, not worth the effort. However, a thank you should be sent to the 2000 contributors, also including a diplomatic appeal for funds, which will result in further contributions from some. About 2 months after the first mailing, a second letter should be sent to the 2,000 who responded the first time. The cost of this mailing is approximately 50 cents per letter, for a total of $1,000. Approximately 30 percent, or 600, will respond and the amount per return should increase to $30 per contribution for a total of $18,000, for a "net profit" of $16,500. The third and fourth mailings, separated by intervals of 45 to 60 days, to this same group, separated by intervals of 45 to 60 days, should each show a $12,000+ profit. Using our initial investment of $58,000 as a base, the campaign should realize total contributions of approximately $54,000, minus the fund-raiser's fees and/or commissions.

Incidentally, a professional fund-raiser would have taken the original return of $57,000, used $3,000 for the second and third mailings, and used the balance to start the cycle again with a new mailing group. The professional fund-raiser would continue this process until a list of around 25,000 contributors was developed before repaying the seed money.

Obviously, there are several problematic considerations with the direct mail approach to fund-raising:

1) It requires an experienced person to orchestrate the program for maximum effectiveness, adding additional cost to the unit price,
2) A campaign must have the seed money to finance the original mailings. Unless the campaign has a very powerful list to begin with, or a very strong signatory for the solicitation letter, the campaign must depend on high volume, or mass mailings of 100,000 pieces and up to make the program viable.
3) It is a long-term project, requiring at least 6 months to reach full potential.
4) Even well planned and executed, the list could be of poor quality and the program could result in lower numbers than projected and take considerably longer than planned to show a profit. This makes it very difficult to project cash flow by these unreliable results.

In reality, the higher the name ID rating is, the more successful your direct mail program will be.

Frankly, this program is best used by an incumbent, an officeholder running for higher office, or a challenger running for the second time during the off-year before the start of the next campaign cycle, presuming he or she has enough money left over from the first campaign with which to start. In other words, the higher the name ID rating in the first place, the more successful will be the initial results.

Fund-raising Through Political Direct Mail Programs

Except for the final GOTV mailing, I recommend never sending a political letter without including an appeal for funds and volunteer assistance.

Since the cost of a #6 1/2 BRE is about 3.2 cents, I recommend that it be included in the mailing piece. Even if included in the first 300,000 pieces of political direct mail that the campaign will be sending out to Party members, independents, undecideds, and even members of the opposite Party, the added cost will be $9,600, but the strategy will increase the percentage of return.

In many cases, the campaign can avoid the cost of many names since it has already acquired them for political purposes with the registered voter lists, and the rest of the cost can be budgeted as an expense of the Political Game Plan. If the letter is well written, it should produce between $40,000 and $50,000 of the direct mail portion in the Sources of Income projections. Not only are these dollars important to help offset the cost of this part of the plan, but as stated previously, there is a rule of thumb in politics that says that each contributor, no matter how small the amount, will impact on the average, seven other people to vote for the Candidate to whom they have contributed. Even the person who sends in $1 feels they have an "investment" in the Candidate and the outcome of the campaign. As a result of their contribution, they become concerned about protecting that investment and will encourage friends and relatives to vote for the Candidate as a means for doing so.

Each contributor, no matter how small the amount, on the average will influence seven other people to vote for the Candidate to whom they have contributed. No other form of media communications guarantees this kind of response.

This is another of the reasons why I favor the use of political direct mail in a Political Game Plan. Not only does it enable the Candidate to target his or her message in a specific way that other forms of media cannot do, but it helps to develop an army of people in the district who have a vested interest in the Candidate's success. They will be motivated to come out on Election Day and vote for the Candidate and will help make sure others join them. As an added bonus, they will return at least one third of the cost of communicating with them.

No other form of media communications guarantees this kind of response. At least, not to the same degree. However, before I am misunderstood, I should point out that a large percentage of this response will be due to the other communication efforts being expended, which in effect pave the way for the direct mail appeal and cause the favorable response. Other activities are not only helpful, they are necessary, if the direct mail program is to be successful. This only serves to emphasize the importance of name ID rating one more time. Other media activities do not have the multiplier capability of the political direct mail method, but to do either one without the other is not only wasteful, it could prove to be a serious tactical mistake as well.

The advantages are obvious and the disadvantages are negligible. The added cost is more than offset by the political and financial return. Even if the campaign is not using a mail processing firm to stuff, seal, stamp, and process the letters, the extra time it takes a volunteer to stuff a BRE is hardly noticeable. There is a slight risk of irritating a percentage of people with the constant appeal for funds, but this is also negligible.

Selective Mailing Within District

Throughout *The Campaign Manual*, I have referred to the Support File. The Prototype Game Plan that we have been developing encourages the Candidate to use computer technology as a major part of the campaign strategy. This encouragement is the result of a strong understanding that I developed over the years regarding the proper use of volunteer people power.

Before becoming a Political Campaign Consultant, more than 30 years ago, I spent 10 years working as a volunteer in political campaigns, from local elections to U.S. Senate races in every position there is. In the beginning, nothing seemed more frustrating than sitting in some headquarters addressing, stuffing, and licking envelopes when I wanted to be talking to people, telling them why they should vote for my candidate. I always felt that addressing, stuffing, and licking envelopes was a major waste of my capability, and rightly so.

Few candidates know how to use the computer technology that the business community takes for granted.

When I went into politics professionally, I soon realized very few professionals and even fewer candidates at that time, knew how to use the computer technology that the business community took, even then, for granted. As a business person during those 10 years, I knew from first hand experience the cost effectiveness of computers and mail processing equipment and was determined to apply this knowledge and experience to the campaign process. Since then, I have always encouraged my clients to make maximum utilization of these techniques in their campaigns. It is a waste of human resources to have a volunteer do what a machine can do faster and cheaper. No one can communicate with another person better than another person can. Using machines to do what machines do well and using people to communicate simply makes good sense.

The average volunteer will work only 20 hours on the average campaign. The resource is by no means unlimited.

Since the average volunteer will work only 20 hours on the average campaign, it is a more efficient use of their time to be walking precincts, telephoning, being surrogate speakers, and fund-raising. A certain number of volunteers who want only to stuff envelopes will always be available to handle individualized mailings that require the use of volunteers in this manner. However, to burn out hundreds of volunteers with this type of activity, when machines are available, is counterproductive.

Support File
A database containing the personal and professional information regarding individuals that have demonstrated their support through contributions, volunteer activities, and/or endorsements for the Candidate.

At this point, I will direct my advice to the candidate who has decided that the computerized campaign *is* the only intelligent choice. That distinction being made, we will address the campaign that has the capability of mechanically processing most of its direct mail. The Support Files enable the direct mail fund-raising program to "get personal."

As mentioned previously, the Support File consists of the following data importing an electronic file or by data entry, the names, addresses, telephone numbers, occupations, and places of employment of volunteers, along with the type of activity they are willing to do, contributors, along with the dates and amounts of contributions made, and endorsers. GOTV *Campaign Optimizer* enables the campaign to sort the files by any criteria regarding the saved information, including the geopolitical demographics and the campaign's region and area designations. The same process is available with political organizations, PACs,

Parties, and associations, but will be organized in the Organization Support Files, as opposed to Individual Support Files.

Prospect File
A database containing the personal and professional information regarding those individuals that are prospects for contributions, volunteer activities, and/or endorsements.

The data for actual supporters in the Support File is obtained from the BREs, the endorsement sheets, or the volunteer cards. The Prospect File list is developed with the data found in:

1) directories of professional, occupational, or trade associations,
2) membership lists of organizations,
3) yellow page directories,
4) lists developed by other candidates, Local and/or State Party Committees,
5) lists accumulated by the Candidate and Finance Committee members, and
6) miscellaneous sources such as college alumni lists and church lists.

These lists are further broken down for transmittal to the database and clarified by profession, occupation, or primary activity.

Once this data has been entered into the software database, the campaign can begin the systematic direct mail program previously referred to throughout *The Campaign Manual.* Specific letters, personalized and targeted to members of a common grouping, signed by one of their own, and then followed up with a personal visit or telephone call, produce an unusually high rate of return in comparison to the mass mailings.

When an individual in the Prospect File contributes to the campaign, volunteers, or endorses the Candidate, their database designation should change to the Support File. It is usual for a supporter to contribute to the campaign, endorse the Candidate, and volunteer to work on the campaign. Since each designation is selectable by individual, and can be identified and sorted within the database, printouts can be developed for any designation or activity. For example, when a list is needed for volunteers who have agreed to display lawn signs, the program will sort and print a distinct listing of those people who have volunteered to do the activity specified, without including those who have contributed money, endorsed the Candidate, or volunteered to walk a precinct.

The Support File can also be used for other than fund-raising purposes. It can also provide the basis for distribution of a campaign newsletter or other type of correspondence, such as thank you letters to the contributors and to the volunteers when needed. The program can personalize the newsletter, and print the name and address labels.

The Support File is also used as the basis for promoting ticket sales to the major events. The contributors and prospective contributors can be sorted by previous or potential contribution. In this way, the campaign can restrict the mailing to those previous and prospective contributors who are the best prospects for an event requiring a certain financial commitment (for example $150+ per person). In this way, there is a major cost reduction in comparison to mass mailings, since you can target the receiver and drastically reduce the number of mailing pieces to accomplish the desired results.

Most major cities have mail processing firms that will fold, stuff, add brochures and BREs, sort by zip code if a bulk mailing, and drop the mailing off at the Post Office for about 7 to 10 cents per unit. If the campaign does not have a surplus of volunteers that will stuff envelopes, processing firms will fill this need. I have also found that most areas have community sheltered workshops that employ the handicapped to do this type of work and they do it at very favorable prices.

The Support File direct mail program is an integral part of the Fund-raising Game Plan, with benefits to the political side of the equation.

Regardless of which method the campaign uses, computerized or manual, the proper development and utilization of a Support File direct mail program should generate around $50,000 for the campaign directly, plus a portion of the income for the major events. When the program is started, it should be spread out in regular intervals. Base the program on volume as opposed to groups. The reason being that the groups will rarely be equal in size. For example, assume the total number of names in the Prospect File is 10,000 and the campaign plans on doing three mailings to them during the campaign. About the most follow up calls the Finance Committee or the Phone Bank volunteers could make in a day would be around 1,000. If mailing more than that each time, the program will overload and there will be a corresponding loss in returns.

It would be more advisable to start mailing 1,000 pieces in 1 week intervals, starting the first cycle around the third week of February and completing it by the end of April. Using this schedule, the mailings will not conflict with the solicitation program for the first major event in May. Start the second cycle around the middle of June, so it too will not conflict with the activity for the second major event in the middle of September. Normally, the campaign would send a third mailing to both the Prospect and Support Files about the first week of October. Do not however, plan on a telephone follow up using the Phone Bank volunteers. By this Stage, the Phone Bank will be too actively involved in the political program to do a fund-raising follow up.

The Support File direct mail program is an integral part of the Fund-raising Game Plan, having benefits on the political side of the equation as well. The average return for all mailings should be around $40,000, minus a cost factor of around $15,000, already factored in the budget, for a net of $25,000, plus the political advantage of keeping the campaign's message before a large segment of the community, both average and above average voters.

The PAC Solicitation Program

The anticipated income from PACs is about 30 percent of the total campaign budget.

The anticipated income from Political Action Committees is about 30 percent of the total campaign budget and obviously, a very sizeable and integral part of the plan. However, before going into the procedures and methods to use in raising funds from this source, I believe an analysis of the source itself is in order, since PAC contributions can be a political issue in themselves. PACs are the subject of much media attention, mostly negative, in every campaign cycle. Their participation is sometimes so sensitive that many candidates are either hesitant to accept any contribution from them or limit the amount they will take. Before making a decision, a Candidate should review the facts.

What Are PACs?

PACs Organizations, associations, unions, or corporations who pool their financial resources in order to contribute to candidates who share their particular political, social, religious, philosophical, or economic views.

PACs are groups of people who pool their financial resources in order to contribute to candidates who share their particular political, social, religious, philosophical, or economic views. These groups are broadly subdivided into four categories, generally based on some common interest. They are:

1) associations of lawyers, doctors, insurance agents, building industry, or real estate agents,
2) unions, such as the AFL-CIO, COPE, Teamsters, or the UAW,
3) ideological organizations, such as conservative, moderate, liberal, women's rights, pro-abortion, or anti-abortion, and
4) corporations, such as Sears, U.S. Steel, or Amoco.

The laws regulating PACs, administered by the Federal Election Commission for Federal candidates, and usually the Secretary of State for state and local candidates, are strictly defined. They are specific as to who may give to a PAC, the method of solicitation, the amount that may be contributed both to the PAC and from the PAC to the Candidate, as well as the accounting and reporting procedures used by both the PAC and the Candidate.

All financial transactions are conducted openly, above board, reported, and scrutinized. The reports are public record and a simple telephone call, e-mail, or letter to the FEC in Washington, DC, or the Secretary of State's office, will produce a complete copy of any report. Federal candidates also file a copy of their reports with the Secretary of State in each State Capitol and usually with the County Clerk's office in the major county within the district.

All PAC reports are on file with the FEC, 999 E St., NW, Washington, DC 20463. They have a toll free number, 800.424.9530 and web site at www.fec.gov, so that any person can easily obtain information. In addition, the reports contain the names, addresses, and occupations of every contributor of over $200. Every PAC contribution is itemized, regardless of size.

Few PACs have the resources to make maximum contributions and generally contribute from $300 to $1,500.

A contribution from a PAC is limited to a maximum of $5,000 in the Primary Election and $5,000 in the General period for Federal candidates, with a total maximum contribution of $10,000. Few PACs have the resources to make maximum contributions to very many candidates. Most PAC contributions are in the range of $300 to $1,500. Since the states vary widely, regarding PAC contributions to state and local candidates, each state needs to be considered separately. This information is also generally available on the State web site.

Why PACs?

Why have so many PACs been formed in recent years? Are the PACs necessary? PACs have been forming, primarily, in response to the severe limitations imposed on the amount an individual or the Party can contribute to a Federal or State Candidate. As a result, of the election reforms instituted at both the Federal and State levels after Watergate, individuals are now limited to a maximum contribution of $1,000 in the Primary period and $1,000 in the General period, for a total of $2,000. The exception is a Congressional or Senatorial Candidate, who can contribute an unlimited amount of his or her own funds to his or her own campaign.

It is a serious charge to imply that a Congressperson or Senator would risk jail or jeopardize a career and a personal reputation for a modest campaign contribution of $10,000.

The PACs have actually helped make it possible for a candidate of relatively modest means to compete with the wealthier individuals and, more importantly, with the incumbents. Ironically, the same reformers who agitated for the personal limitations on contributions are now turning against the PACs. The argument is that these single-issue groups unduly influence the Congressperson or Senator once elected. This is the same argument used to enact the reforms in the first place.

Frankly, when one looks at the size of today's campaign budget for a congressional race, though not minimizing the value of $10,000, even that maximum contribution is a relatively small percentage of the amount raised and spent. It is a serious charge to imply that a Congressperson or Senator would risk jail or jeopardize a career and a personal reputation for a modest campaign contribution. However, this is not to say that some have not been tempted or succumbed to personal offers. Even those, however, were mostly bribes involving personal funds and not campaign funds.

As for the undue advantage being brought to bear on Candidates after they have been elected, I find this, too, to be either a simplification of the facts, or perhaps a deliberate attempt to mislead the public.

Understanding PACs and Party Committees

"Make a Wish Upon a Star"

A challenger candidate has the same chance of obtaining money from a PAC as they do by "making a wish upon a star." In most cases, the same holds true for their party committees. According to the U.S. Census Bureau, there are now over 500,000 elected officials in the United States. If even half of these races were contested, consider the approximate 750,000 candidates that would be seeking funds from their party committees and PACs, every two to four years.

Even with the apparently large sums of money at their disposal, PACs and party committees do not even come close to being able to help all candidates, even if we presume that they wanted to help. When you subtract their costs of fund-raising and their administrative costs, the actual expendable dollars are closer to half the amount they report as income. In addition, many of them, both PACs and party committees, have other functions that claim a portion of those expendable dollars. Funds spent for education and research come immediately to mind.

The net result remains that for every dollar raised, only $.30 to $.35, is available for candidates. Some more, some less, but over all, based on my research over the past thirty years, this percentage is very accurate.

The problem for the PACs and party committees is not unlike the difficulty faced by most enterprises, namely the allocation of limited resources. However, since one of the responsibilities of the party committees is to encourage candidates of their party to run in all elections, the impression is often given

PACs and party committees are far more likely to assist with research, training, and advice, than with real dollars in financial assistance.

that financial assistance will be forthcoming if they carry the party's banner as a candidate. Unfortunately, it is not that simple. If a candidate were to listen carefully, what is actually being said is, *"If you put together a winning campaign, we will try to provide some financial assistance. In the meantime, we will provide you with research assistance, training, and advice, if we are able."*

The vast majority of candidates will not take the time necessary to study and learn how to develop a winning campaign. Their opponents do not defeat them, but rather, they defeat themselves.

The problem is that the vast majority of candidates will not study and take the time necessary to learn how to develop a winning campaign. As I have pointed out repeatedly, running a campaign for political office is like running a business. It requires an extensive knowledge of what you are doing, an intensive amount of research and hard work, and the active support of hundreds of people within your community. It is simply not enough to be an honorable person, have good intentions, and declare your candidacy with an expectation of winning. The opponents do not defeat the vast majority of these candidates, but rather, they defeat themselves by being naive about the campaign process.

Many PACs, party committees, and political consultants will not work with challengers running for the first time because they know from experience that most first time Candidates will have to learn the hard way before they learn to accept advice.

The PACs and party committees know this. Many of them try to educate candidates on how to run an effective campaign. In most cases, their words are ignored. Even when candidates go to the expense of hiring professional campaign consultants who, by virtue of their training and experience, know how to run campaigns, many of the candidates ignore the expertise they have paid for. They insist on running their own campaigns.

It is for all of these reasons that the PACs and party committees limit the amount of allotted resources to first time candidates. In addition to this, a party committee's first obligation is to assist its incumbent officeholders to retain their seats. Money must be kept aside for this purpose. Many PACs are affiliated with special interest groups, in business and labor, that deal with elected officials on a daily basis. They are fully aware of the excellent odds of an incumbent retaining his or her office running against the poor campaigns run by the vast majority of challengers. It is very rare for them to go against an incumbent whom they are 95% certain that they will have to deal with for another term. Many PACs will only get involved in an open seat campaign, and even then, only after they have made their assessment as to who is going to win.

Only the ideological PACs will occasionally become involved with challengers going against an incumbent. They too have a prior commitment to assist those individuals who represent their ideology to remain in office. Only when they are strongly opposed to an incumbent will they consider becoming involved with a challenger.

Approximately 5% of campaigns can expect some financial assistance from PACs and/or party committees.

In general, party committees at the national level will only target 30 congressional races for financial assitance, in any given cycle. The state and local party committees, on a percentage basis, will target even fewer. Of the 750,000 campaigns waged every election cycle in this country, approximately 5% can expect some financial assistance from PACs and/or party committees. The other 95% will have to go it alone.

How PACs Work?

The majority of PACs are highly selective when choosing the candidates that they are going to support.

First, *before they contribute,* the majority of PACs are highly selective when choosing the candidates that they are going to support. They check out the candidates' stand on the issues, send them questionnaires (sometimes referred to as "litmus tests"), interview them, and then based on input, rate them. They also do the same with the opponent. Sometimes the results are very uneven and the decision is relatively easy. They will usually support the Candidate who generally thinks the way they do about the problems and their solutions. If the comparison is considered equal, PACs will support the candidate that they feel has the best chance of winning the election.

In essence, PACs have grown because limits have been placed on the amount that individuals and the Parties can contribute to candidates. It is clear that the limits are terribly low by comparison with the current costs of communications and campaigning.

The PACs are aware of the tremendous amount of cross pressure a Congressperson or Senator experiences on virtually every vote. They realize that the majority attempt to determine that which is in the best interest of their constituents, and the country, and vote accordingly. This is also true, in most cases, at the state and local level of government. As a matter of fact, any lobbyist crass enough to even mention their affiliated PAC's contribution, or potential contribution, is usually unwelcome from that point on in the legislator's office.

I suspect that the reform agitators will not be satisfied with any system of helping a Candidate finance the campaign other than through public financing. They continue to promote the elimination of PACs by innuendo and specious attacks. They persist in spite of the fact that public financing tried in New Jersey proved to be a disaster for everyone concerned, except for the media outlets experiencing a windfall from pubic campaign funding.

My opinion remains in support of PACs. If a group of people choose to pool their resources to help a Candidate whom they believe supports their viewpoint, and therefore will best represent them in government, that should remain their right; and some would believe it is their duty as citizens.

Unless a person would deny the right of a Candidate to communicate his or her message to the people, with its subsequent denial to the people to hear that message, there really is no valid reason to attack a Candidate based on their acceptance of PAC contributions. PACs are simply people. If one group of people want to organize a PAC to support a Candidate opposed by a different group of people, they can do so by filing a simple, single page form and investing the cost of a postage stamp. This is simply an organized method for what we have been doing all along. A fundamental principle of our campaign system is for one group of people to support a Candidate who shares their point of view versus an opposing group that supports another candidate with an opposing point of view

There is a need to know how PACs function in order to solicit from them effectively, just as there is a need to know what motivates the individual contributors in the district.

It is important for a Candidate to understand what goes into the dynamics of PAC solicitation, the benefits, and the risks involved. The Candidate will probably be challenged for accepting PAC contributions, either by the opponent or by the media, and if unable to counter the implied charges, he or she could be put on the defensive and thereby give an element of credibility to the accusations.

Preparations for the Program

Note that at this writing, there are more than 4,000 PACs. Select PACs or affiliated groups that are based in your district and/or state first. Then select the PACs that have some connectivity with the Candidate.

In preparing the PAC solicitation program, the first step is to obtain a current list of active PACs from the State and National Party Headquarters. If you choose to employ one, your Political Fund-raising Consultant will have the list. Note that there are more than 4,000 PACs. If a Candidate attempted to mail all of them, he or she would be wasting resources. Instead, the list should be carefully reviewed. It should show the name, address, and telephone number of the PAC, its affiliated group, if any, the name of the treasurer and/or chairperson, the contact person, usually a director for the larger PACs, and the amount of money on hand as of the last FEC or state report. This last item can be deceiving, since many PACs do not begin to solicit funds until the election year begins. Go through the list carefully and select any PACs, or affiliated groups, that are based in your district and/or state. Many PACs limit their contributions to campaigns in their own home states, or where they have subsidiaries.

You could have a list of about 500 PACs that are your most likely prospects. If your campaign is computerized input these names into the Organization File within your database.

From this filtered list, select the PACs that have some connectivity with the Candidate either by virtue of employment, membership in the same associations, or an ideological stand on the issues. If a liberal, the Candidate can bet the American Conservative Union will pass on his or her campaign. However, a labor group like COPE would probably provide support. Look for related fields. If the Candidate is in retail sales, pick out all the PACs connected with that field, such as Sears, Ward, small businesspersons associations, and BIPAC (Business-Industrial PAC). If the Candidate is considered a fiscal conservative and strong supporter of the free enterprise system, he or she would pick out those PACs that are known to be strongly oriented in that direction, such as organizations similar to Amway Corp., Coors Co., insurance companies, and the American Medical Assn. (AMPAC). If the Candidate is considered a moderate to liberal politically, he or she might gain support from most of the union PACs, especially if a Democrat, since about 90 to 95 percent of their contributions are made to Democratic candidates. Pick major national associations and corporate PACs, as the lesser known ones are usually more parochial in their interests and with their contributions. Look for PACs that are affiliated in some way with members of the Finance and Advisory Committees. Be sure to select single interest PACs that are in agreement with the Candidates philosophy.

The First Mailing

At least a month after the formal announcement date, send PAC kits to the top 100 prospects. Send a cover letter with enclosures to the balance of your PAC prospects.

The campaign will need to prepare PAC kits for the top 100 PAC prospects. If affordable, it makes a more impressive presentation if you use customized covers. The kit itself can be loose, contained in a pocket folder, or bound in book style used for business reports.

The kit should contain the following:

a) The candidates biography,
b) a 3 x 5 glossy photo,
c) a copy of the Political Game Plan and Budget, excluding the Cash Flow schedule,

d) the position booklet or six of the major issue papers,
e) a copy of the campaign brochure,
f) a copy of two or three press clippings following the public announcement of your candidacy,
g) a copy of a recent poll, or include a reference to any recent polls taken in the district that show the vulnerability of the opponent,
h) a list of the members of the Finance and Advisory Committees, staff, and consultants, showing occupations or professions, addresses, and telephone numbers,
i) a copy of the candidacy announcement speech,
j) a cover letter soliciting their support and volunteering to provide any additional information, if needed,
k) the campaign's FEC ID number, or state number, if non-Federal candidate,
l) a report showing how much money the campaign has raised to date, the number of contributors and volunteers, and a campaign BRE.

About a month after the formal announcement date, the kits should be mailed to the top prospects in a priority mail, or at least by first class. The balance of the 500 PACs should be sent the cover letter, a copy of a press clipping, a brochure, the campaign's FEC ID number, a synopsis of the Candidate's position on the issues, and a BRE. Send the balance, at the same time, in a #10 envelope by at least first class mail. First class or priority mail is used to provide assurance that the right people have received the mailings and to enable the campaign to delete or correct the address of any mail that is returned.

The Follow Up

About two weeks after the mailing, the Candidate should begin calling the top prospects. The balance of the list is rarely called but continue to receive future mailings. The Candidate should make the initial call. Top financial committee members can make subsequent telephone follow up.

To understand why all of this is necessary, it is important to know what is happening at the other end. About this time of year, PACs are inundated with requests for assistance. A new Candidate usually resides at the bottom of their priority list. Hence, it is important for the campaign to stand out, not only as one that is different, but also one that has a plan and knows exactly what it is doing. PAC directors are politically astute people who know what the winning odds are in any given race. If the campaign cannot prove that it has its act together, the request for assistance will be filed and not considered further.

In addition to assessing prospective campaigns to contribute to, PACs are involved in other activities, such as raising money for their PAC, holding training seminars, and sending newsletters to their members. Most of them are understaffed and underpaid. To say they are "under siege" in an election year would be an understatement.

The campaign must present the burden of proof. The Candidate has to provide them with a clear picture of the campaign, the demographics of the district, and even, information on the opponent. In addition to proving that he or she can win, a case needs to be presented as to why the PAC should want the Candidate to win over the opponent. The PAC must be motivated to act now. Fortunately, unlike past PAC behavior, more and more PACs are appreciating the need for contributions earlier in the campaign and are contributing before October.

Procedures the PACs Follow

Many PACs have set procedures that must be followed. Keep in mind that most of them fully appreciate the position of trust they hold on behalf of their PAC contributors. They know they are not dispensing their own money and are very careful about its disbursement.

Many PACs will not become involved pre-Primary, for any reason. Even fewer if there is a contested Primary.

Most PACs have committees that must review and approve all requests for contributions. Normally these committees are made up of volunteers who are actively involved in their fields of work. They may meet only once a month. Occasionally, a committee member will want the Director to obtain additional information before making a decision. Another month will then pass without an answer or a contribution. A Candidate will find that "patience is a virtue" when dealing with a PAC program.

Some of the PACs, like BIPAC, AMPAC, and Associated General Contractors, work through a series of regional members or committees. Until the national PAC receives approval from the local representatives, they may be unable to act. The Candidate needs to review the published procedures for each PAC and act accordingly.

Definition
An earmarked contribution is one which the contributor directs the contribution to a candidate through an intermediary or conduit.

Some PACs act only as a conduit for individual contributions earmarked for a specific candidate. Therefore, unless some member of the PAC wishes to contribute to the campaign, the PAC is unable to contribute.

Many PACs will not become involved until they see polling results that show ballot strength and Favorability ratings. It makes no difference that the first poll will not be until June, since most PACs would not get involved before the Primary anyway. After you have campaign results in August, make your strongest appeal, making the most recent evidence of a possibie victory available.

The question might arise as to why the campaign is sending its PAC mailing so early. There are two reasons for this; to alert them to the campaign in the hope that by doing so early they will start to track the campaign's progress; secondly, to discourage any major contributions from going to the opponent.

Try to enlist third party influence; have campaign supporters write letters to PAC members on the candidate's behalf, asking for support.

Try to enlist third party influence. PAC directors might try to ignore the Candidate on occasion but they have a hard time ignoring their contributing members. Have campaign supporters write letters to their company, trade association, or union PAC urging their financial support for the campaign. If the national Party has a field director in the district's area, ask him or her, to call two or three PACs on behalf of the campaign. Many of the Party field directors know the PAC directors and they can help obtain favorable consideration for your request.

The Second PAC Mailing

Be honest with PACs, they are getting information from a number of sources.

In the second PAC mailing, include one or two favorable press clippings on the campaign and update the campaign's progress in terms of active volunteers, the number of contributors, and the amount of contributions received to date. Be honest with your assessment. PACs are getting information from a number of sources, including the opponent. Whether or not they are seriously considering participating in the campaign, to attempt to deceive or mislead any PAC could have disastrous results, not only with that PAC, but also with many of the others. Washington, DC, in many ways, is a small town and the PAC Directors usually know each other well, exchanging information regularly. This is also true in most state capitols where State PACs are located.

If the campaign's Political Campaign Consultant is Washington based, refer the PAC director to him or her for additional information. Most of the PAC directors know the consultants in DC and respect their judgment.

Two weeks after the second mailing, begin the second telephone follow up. At this time, others, including the Campaign Manager should help. Continue this process until each PAC has either contributed, or given a definite "No." Remove the definite "No's" from your prospect list. The contributing PACs should have automatically been placed on your Support File list for continuing follow up. Send the campaign newsletters and updates regularly. Remember that they now have a stake in the outcome of the election. Not only might they be able to give further, but they might also encourage other PACs to join them in supporting the campaign.

Other PAC Activities the Candidate Should Do

A Candidate should do two other activities regarding PACs. At some point, shortly after the Primary, he or she should plan a 3 day trip to DC, if a Federal Candidate, or to the State Capitol, if a non-Federal Candidate, personally visiting with as many PAC directors on the preferred list as possible. If the Political Fund-raising Consultant is DC based, he or she will usually help arrange the itinerary. If not, the Candidate should see if the National Party Headquarters is able to lend assistance. If no other help is available, ask the PAC Director of a PAC already supporting the campaign for assistance.

The second activity requires even more planning. Some PACs in the DC area will not contribute money directly to a campaign, but will buy tickets to an event. In all honesty, I have never fully understood the reason for this. Arrange for the campaign's consultant, national party, or a supporting PAC to sponsor a cocktail party for the Candidate during his or her visit. There are a couple of facilities used regularly in DC for these events and they have standard procedures. Usually the campaign can raise several thousand dollars from this activity. This is money that would not be available by any other means.

One last comment about the PAC program. The Candidate should not overlook the help of any officeholder he or she might know personally. They can be very helpful in opening doors for the Candidate with PACs. In addition, party leaders are more than willing to help. Be sure to visit with them while in DC or your State Capitol.

Out of District Fund-raising Program

The out of district (OD) program involves two basic activities:

1) a program similar in approach to the PAC program, such as, a combination of direct mail with a telephone follow up and a broad based direct mail program, and
2) sponsorship by solicitation of important individuals connected to a particular industry or association.

Both of these are predicated on the fact that there are people outside of the district, who, like the PACs have an interest in the outcome. This interest will be based on an agreement with the Candidate's views, or perhaps in opposition to the opponent's viewpoint, or because of an opportunity to add a vote in the legislature to their party total (helping gain or retain a majority). In effect, they are single people PACs, sometimes-wealthy individuals, who prefer to be autonomous rather than pooling their resources with a group.

Direct Mail and Telephone Follow up

In the 1st Stage, the Candidate obtained lists of party and state candidate contributors, from around the state, from the state Party Committee or the records at the Secretary of State's office. If possible, add the names of contributors with over $500 potential from the National Party Headquarters to this list. If the party is unwilling or unable to help, check the resources available from a reputable mailing list firm.

Prepare a kit for OD contributors, as you did for the PACs, and send it to the top 100 - 200 individuals, while sending only the cover letter with enclosures to the remainder of the list.

Between these two sources, it should be possible to develop a list of about 5,000 names. Ask the state Party chairperson, executive director, or county chairperson to help select about 100 to 200 of the most likely contributors in the state. Prepare a kit for OD contributors, as you did for the PACs, and send it to the individuals. Be sure to change the cover letter to conform to this solicitation.

Send the cover letter, a brochure, a one-page synopsis of the Candidate's position on the issues, a two page outline on why the campaign is winnable and how it is going to be won, and a BRE to the remainder of the list. If the 5,000 names can be added to the prospect database, the use of a mail merge capabilities will simplify this process.

About two weeks after the PAC mailing has been dropped, drop the entire OD mailing. Two weeks later, the Candidate should personally begin to call the potential major contributors from around the state. Mail to this OD group two more times during the course of the campaign. Have staff and committee assist on 2nd and 3rd telephone follow-ups.

Depending on the campaign's success in putting together a quality list, the campaign should net approximately $40,000 from these three mailings, including the second and third appeals to first-time contributors. The follow up appeals will take place automatically when the campaign again solicits the Support File. The Political Fund-raising Consultant can be of invaluable assistance with this program, in copy writing, list selection, and targeting.

"Sponsorship" Solicitation by Key Individuals

The second activity involves the assistance of third parties, either persons or groups. Certain individuals and organizations around the country maintain regular communications with associates or members via newsletters or subscription magazines. During the campaign year, they use these communication resources to advise their associates or members of campaigns around the country that need and deserve their personal and financial assistance, and suggest that they send contributions directly to a specific campaign.

I do not feel at liberty to disclose the names of the third parties in this Manual without their permission. However, I would suggest that inquiries, while making the PAC and OD follow up calls, or while speaking with the National Party field staff, would produce the necessary information. I can say that if these individuals or organizations will act as advocates on the Candidate's behalf, this activity could net as much as $50,000 in campaign contributions. Most Political Fund-raising Consultants should be familiar with these resources and how to approach them.

Major Events

Another primary source of income for the campaign is the major event, usually a dinner featuring a prominent individual as a guest speaker with tickets averaging $150 or more per person. Despite being somewhat overdone in recent years, these events done properly and sparingly, can be very successful.

In the Prototype Game Plan, I have projected two major events, one in May and one in September. The timing for these events is very important, since they also serve as political rallies and media events to generate momentum at critical points in the campaign.

Arranging for a Guest Speaker

Do not wait until a month before the event and expect a major "headliner" to be available. The competition with other candidates around the country may be fierce, since May and September are among the most popular months for these events.

The first problem to be solved in arranging these events is obtaining a "headliner" as your guest speaker. You need a featured guest speaker who will help draw contributors. The speaker will also maximize the media attention given to the campaign.

The two months used in the Prototype plan, May and September, are among the most popular months for these events. The competition with other candidates around the country will be fierce. First, determine who would be the best draw in the district. If the President, or a former President, as the case may be depending on the Candidate's Party, would be the best, try for him or her, but do so early. Do not wait until a month before the event and expect a major "headliner" to be available. You must make contact with the political scheduler by mail and telephone at least 5 to 6 months before the event.

The first inquiry will be met with the usual, "We'll consider your request and get back with you." This is not simply "a stall." Both the President and former Presidents will allocate a very limited number of days for political activity during the campaign year. Being limited in the number of visits they can make, they rely on their own political advisers and the national parties to assist them in the selection process. This is normally a drawn out process with final decisions coming about a month before the event.

As a back up plan, the campaign should select at least five other persons, such as the Vice-President, Cabinet members, House leaders, Senate leaders, or former ranking officials who might be helpful. Make an appeal to them at the same time that the campaign requests assistance from the President, or former President. The campaign can always cancel the unneeded invitations if it receives an acceptance. Those solicited will understand. This is a relatively routine procedure during the campaign year.

After extending the invitation, ask National Party or legislative leaders to make calls on behalf of the campaign to the people being sought. As a backup to this first list, the campaign should send the same letter to the U.S. Senator in your state, Governor, or a well-known Representative, if they are members of the Candidate's Party. It should first be determined that they would not be a liability in the district. When writing, give them an option of at least two proposed dates for the spring event and two for the fall event, preferably a Friday or Saturday. However, some would draw well on any night.

The campaign should not overlook the possibility of a national figure in another field, like sports or entertainment.

Many sports and entertainment celebrities contribute a certain amount of their time for political appearances on behalf of the candidates of their party during the campaign year. Some, including former elected officials, are also available for an honorarium. Check with the national party headquarters to obtain a list regarding who has volunteered to help this year. Do not overlook the possibility that someone on the committee knows someone personally to whom you can appeal directly. The important thing is to make these appeals early.

Secure the Location

At the same time, reserve a location such as, a hotel, country club, or major restaurant that can handle 300 or more people. They usually have their dates booked months in advance. To be safe, it is a good idea to make a tentative booking when the initial letters are sent to the prospective speakers. A reservation can usually be canceled or altered. Thoroughly understand the policies of any establishment considered regarding cancellations, etc. Be sure the location selected is centrally located, has adequate facilities, and is reasonably priced. Some places will not charge for the dining room, if a certain number of meals are guaranteed.

The Event (major fund-raising)

It is essential that media cameras are unable to avoid campaign signs while filming the speakers.

This is not a rally, but nonetheless, the campaign banner should be placed right behind the podium and a campaign sign should be placed in front of the podium. Hopefully, the media will provide coverage of the event. If promoted properly, there is an excellent chance that they will.

The program should call for an ecumenical benediction (grace), the pledge of allegiance, dinner if it is a dinner, a short speech by the candidate followed by the guest speaker. After the program, the music should be appropriate dance music selections. The Candidate and other members of the campaign should circulate among the guests. The entire event should last about four to five hours and end at midnight.

Personalized pictures should be sent to contributors as a memento of the event.

If you are having a private reception earlier in the evening, it should be held in a separate room. There should be an open bar and hors d'oeuvres served throughout the private reception. You and the guest of honor should circulate and give all the attendees an opportunity to visit. A photographer should be there to take pictures of the Candidate, the guest of honor, and the attendees together.

The sample event timetable would look similar to the following:

6:30 PM - 7:30 PM	Private Reception
7:30 PM - 8:00 PM	Public Reception
8:00 PM - 8:45 PM	Dinner
8:45 PM - 9:30 PM	Speeches
9:30 PM - 12:00 PM	Dance

The Finance Committee should focus on assisting with the minor fund-raising events and the PAC solicitation program during the summer months.

A second major fund-raising event similar to the first event should be planned for the end of September or the first weekend in October. The advance and follow-up procedures should be the same. If the campaign is going exceptionally well and you are leading in the polls, raise the ticket prices at least 25%, and as high as 50%, depending on the circumstances.

Cost Factors

If possible, the cost of the event should never exceed 25% of the price of the ticket. This includes all of the costs involved from the mailings to the event itself. The room for the event should be decorated professionally, look impressive, but not ostentatious. Do not be extravagant with decorations or on the meal itself. The audience attending is aware of the primary reason that they are invited, to make a campaign contribution. If a dinner, for example, they will not expect filet mignon. Try to make the menu interesting, but keep it modestly priced. Always cater to the beef, fowl, and vegetarian eaters with appropriate entrée choices. Never offer an open bar unless the ticket prices are over $500, and even then, drinks should be limited to two per person by a tasteful coupon system. The campaign should establish a maximum allowance per person for everything connected with the event, except the "host" costs for the guest speaker. A figure in the area of $50 should include the invitations, floral arrangements and decorations, a band, if used, and the cost of meals and the room.

Never offer an open bar unless the ticket prices are over $500, and even then, drinks should be limited to two per person by a tasteful coupon system.

The costs of a presidential visit are considerably higher than the cost of most other guest speakers, but they are offset by other considerations.

The host costs for the guest speaker will vary considerably. A President usually does not charge a fee, although former presidents often do (charge). However, the campaign is normally responsible for covering the cost of accommodations while in town, including accomodations for the official entourage and the Secret Service. Usually, they will want at least one whole floor of the hotel. Sometimes the hotel will provide this benefit free as an advertising and public relations write off, especially, if the campaign is having its dinner at the same establishment. Incidentally, the total costs of a Presidential visit are considerably higher than the cost of most other guest speakers. There are, however, off setting considerations:

1) the charge for a dinner like this is usually at least $250 per person,
2) the private social hour that precedes the dinner usually will draw at least $500 per person, and
3) the ensuing publicity for the campaign is invaluable.

Other guest speakers may or may not charge a fee but the campaign is always responsible for their expenses. If they are on a circuit, the campaign will be expected to pay for its share of the plane costs from his or her last location to the event.

The treatment of the guest speaker is subject to certain rules of etiquette.

There are certain rules of etiquette to be followed regarding the treatment of the guest speaker. From the time they arrive until they depart, the campaign is totally responsible for their reasonable needs and comfort. A car and driver/aide should be assigned to them with the responsibility of picking them up at the airport and attending to them while in the district. The guest is not expected to make any expenditure for meals, room, and transportation during his or her stay. They should be made as comfortable as possible and their visit should be made an enjoyable one. Be sure that they are briefed on any local issues and on the Candidate's stand on the major issues before any meeting with the press. If they have not been sent this information in advance, the driver/aide should have it available for the guest speaker on arrival at the airport, along with a copy of the itinerary.

Operations and Promotion

The tickets to the private social hour are usually priced between $250 and $500. Normally, any person who has already contributed $1,000 is invited to attend these private social meetings without cost.

After firming the date and the guest speaker, have the tickets printed and call a meeting of the Finance Committee. It will be advantageous to establish an ad hoc Dinner Committee made up of a ticket chairperson(s), a host chairperson(s), and a dinner chairperson(s) to be responsible for the event. Tickets should be given to members of the Finance Committee and each person should be asked to sell at least one table, ten people to a table, within a definite timeframe, usually, two weeks. In addition, they should be asked to sell tickets for the private social hour, which is a private meeting with the guest speaker. This event is usually held in a separate room at the same location as the dinner and is priced between $250 and $500. Normally, any person who has already contributed $1,000 is invited to attend these private social meetings without cost.

The upper level income members of the committee should sell at least two tickets each to this pre-dinner event. They should collect the funds and the names should be placed on a special list to be used by an usher at the door. As mentioned before, this event is usually held in the hour just prior to the public social hour before the dinner. Remember that the press conference should be held prior to the private social hour.

At the same time these arrangements with the Finance Committee are being made, the staff should be sending an invitation letter, including two to four tickets to be bought or sold, and a BRE to all previous contributors and prospective contributors of over $150.

Include all elected district and committee officials of the Candidate's Party. If it is the President or a former President, include higher level state elected officers and officials. Send out a press release with the formal announcement of the dinner and the guest speaker and be sure to include the names of the Dinner Committee chairpersons so that they are suitably recognized.

How To Sell Tickets

In larger campaign situations, each Region should assume the responsibility of holding one or two major fund-raising events.

Initially, develop a major fund-raising event letter to be sent to all the people in your prospect and support files. This letter should contain the invitation letter itself, a RSVP reservation card, and an addressed, stamped return envelope. The style of this invitation can be either a formal one, similar to a wedding invitation, or sized to fit in a #10 envelope. I prefer the latter. In either case, it should be done on quality stationery in a formal style. It should be very professional and look very impressive, but not ostentatious. It is preferable for the envelopes to be personalized individually by your software application. In the alternative, if you have enough volunteers, you could address them by hand in a neat, legible style. In any case, do not use labels.

Remember that you can save 10% on postage rates by pre-sorting and metering in zip code sequences.

Two months before the event, mail the invitations at first class postage rates. To save on postage rates, you need a pre-sort permit and the metered imprint must indicate that they are pre-sorted. Frankly, for this type of mailer, I recommend foregoing the slight savings and using a regular stamp. A meter imprint looks very commercial.

At the same time that you drop the invitation mailer, the campaign should send out a press release announcing the details of the upcoming event, including a feature paragraph regarding the guest speaker. The campaign should also generate a fresh set of 3 X 5 cards indicating which are from the prospect files and which are from the support files, i.e., those who have already contributed to the campaign.

The Follow Up

At the regularly scheduled meeting of your Finance Committee, approximately the fifth meeting, repeat the format of your first committee meeting. The campaign chairperson should bring the members up-to-date on the progress of the campaign. Cite the results of any polling that has been done and the results of the Field Operations (the phone bank and precinct operation activities). Discuss the progress of the media portion of the campaign and those plans as well.

Sharing the Candidate's campaign experiences and the public's reaction to the Candidate should not be overlooked as an important aspect of campaign team meetings.

The Candidate should share campaigning experiences during the past three months and the reaction that has been witnessed from the people that have been met along the campaign trail. In addition, discuss the results of any joint appearances you may have had with your opponent. Express appreciation for their efforts and share your feelings regarding what it all means to you knowing they are working so hard on your behalf.

The Finance Committee chairperson should then explain the details of new fund-raising activity and bring the members abreast on the financial position of the campaign. Discuss the comparative regarding where the campaign finance plan is, in relation to where it should be. Review the major expenditures coming up in the near future. Cite and congratulate those teams and individuals that are in first and second place in achieving their goals.

Similar meetings of the Finance Committee should be scheduled at least every two weeks leading to the event and at the beginning of the final week before the event to repeat the procedures outlined.

State the ticket sales objectives of the major fund-raising event. The objectives need to be difficult, yet reasonable and achievable Each team is then assigned a proportionate share of the ticket sales objective. As in the first meeting, members should select from the 3 X 5 cards, or this time they might be pre-selected and distributed based on experience. Each member should have a proportionate share of prospect and support file cards. An award of some kind should be announced for the first team to sell its quota of tickets. In addition, there should be a follow up award for each succeeding team.

Always remind the members that they are not limited to the names on their cards and that they can contact anyone they believe might be willing to contribute or attend a fund-raising event. Be sure that your administrative system will credit mailed contributions toward the deserving team and member, just as though they picked up the contribution personally. Be sure to record the names assigned to each team member so they can be tracked and recorded. This is another way in which a capable, campaign software can reduce the workload and increase the likelihood of your success.

To back up the efforts of the Finance Committee, beginning one month before the event, the phone bank should call everyone who has not RSVP'd. They should verify receipt of the invitation, remind the people the event is only one month away, and ask them if they plan to attend. If they are, they should be asked to mail their card a.s.a.p. Alternatively, arrange for someone to pick it up.

At this time send out the second press release and include a biography and a photo of the guest speaker, usually available from their offices, the time and location of the press conference, and a progress report on ticket sales, if the sales are impressive. Make final arrangements for meals, decorations, hosts and hostesses, ticket takers and sellers at the door, and suitable transportation requirements.

If the guest speaker is the President, Vice-President, or other major personage, there will usually be a traveling press corps with them. Though not absolutely required, it is good public relations to have several vans with drivers at the airport to provide transportation for them and their equipment. As a matter of courtesy, they may be offered free tickets to the public social hour and dinner.

Most are not allowed to accept gifts and will insist on paying the actual cost portion of the ticket price. This same arrangement should be offered to members of the local media.

A large banner is used as a backdrop behind the speaker's podium.

Make sure that the room used for the press conference is large enough to accommodate all of their equipment. In arranging the room, a large banner, usually a reproduction of the first billboard poster, on heavy paper or oilcloth, is used as a backdrop behind the speaker's podium, both here and in the dining room. Use flat paint so the TV lights do not reflect off the banner. Arrange a window or lawn sign on the podium. The Candidate should be on the right hand side of the guest speaker throughout the press conference. Have press kits available for members of the visiting press corps.

Other Possible Activities

As circumstances dictate, the campaign may have to shift to a luncheon or some other type of event that would not be as financially successful for the campaign. It is hard to tell the President's scheduler that if the campaign cannot have him for a dinner, it does not want him to come. If this happens, the campaign will have to provide for a second event to make up the difference in cash flow.

If time permits, and the guest speaker is willing, try to arrange a political rally at a local college auditorium or other public place where all the supporters and the public can attend and have an opportunity to see and hear the Candidate and the guest speaker. If it is an enclosed place, consider charging a $5 admission fee to offset the costs of rental, security, and sound equipment.

An Airport Rally

If the guest speaker is the President, Vice-President, a former President, or a major dignitary, and if the guest and time permit, the campaign should arrange for an airport rally.

Organize as many people as possible to meet the plane at the airport on arrival, and to return on departure. To build the crowd, invitations should be sent to all volunteers, endorsers, local schools, senior citizen clubs (providing buses if necessary), political organizations, and scout troops. Arrange for a local high school band to be on hand. Sometimes a contribution to the band uniforms or traveling fund, and a motorcade with police escorts is stipulated. If you incur any problems building a crowd, have the Phone Bank make notification calls.

Initiate a series of 30-second spot radio commercials announcing the arrival time of the guest speaker.

A week before the event, initiate a series of 30-second spot radio commercials announcing the arrival time. Make the public feel welcome to attend. In the ticket letter to the contributors and prospective contributors, be sure to include the same information, encouraging attendance. Remember that this is both a major media event as well as a fund-raising event. If handled properly, the campaign should dominate the local political news for at least 10 days.

The day after the event, send out the final press release. Give an update on the success of the event, in terms of people participating and express appreciation to the guest speaker, the guests, and everyone who helped make it such a huge success. Do not mention any fund-raising considerations.

Finally, send out special thank you letters containing the same message to that same group of people. Include their photo with the Candidate, if available.

Minor Fund-raising Events

Minor fund-raising events are not difficult to plan and in fact can be fun to arrange.

During the months of March, April, June, July, and August, each team on the Finance Committee, working with one of the Regional Committees, should put on a minor event in their Region, designed as much for morale and political purposes, as for fund-raising. Low priced ticket events, ranging from $25 for an individual to $35 for a family, are reasonable. The intent is to involve as much of the public as possible. Spaghetti and/or chicken dinners, picnics, period (50/60's) dances, fashion shows, river cruises, pancake breakfasts, pizza parties, auctions, and potluck dinners are all popular ideas that work well. They are not difficult to plan and in fact can be fun to arrange.

FEC guidelines are subject to change and need to be verified for your campaign and your timeframe. Visit www.fec.gov up-to-date regulations.

Presently, the FEC law allows a contributor, even if they have already contributed the maximum $1,000, to pay for the expenses of an event up to another $1,000 or $2,000 if the spouse hosts the event as well. This is legal as long as the event is held in their home, a church hall, or a community room not normally used for commercial purposes.

The two committees should do promotion and sales, with campaign headquarters providing logistical support and arranging for press releases before and after the event.

Minor Fund-raising - The Details

Each Region should assume the responsibility of hosting at least one minor fund-raising event.

A team captain from the Finance Committee should be assigned to provide technical assistance to each Region. However, the primary responsibility belongs to each Regional Chairperson and their respective Area Chairpersons.

It is the Regional Chairperson and their respective Area Chairpersons that should plan the event, generate the promotional materials, tickets, and letters. Ultimately, the success of the event falls on their shoulders. These events are not expected to net a major number of direct contributions to the campaign. In fact, if the campaign realizes $1,000 after all expenses are paid, it should be considered a financial success. The main purpose is to get voters to participate, to commit volunteers to the campaigning effort, and to benefit from the multiplier effect.

Definition
The political fund-raising multiplier effect has determined that for every campaign contributor of even one dollar, the contributor will attempt to influence no less than seven additional voters to support the candidate represented by the campaign that they have supported.

In political fund-raising there is a multiplier effect. We know that everyone who contributes even one dollar to the campaign will attempt to influence at least seven other people to vote for their candidate. Since the contributor has made a commitment, he or she will work to defend their judgement. From this political perspective, minor fund-raising events can have major significance in the outcome of the campaign.

Because there is not a lot of lead-time involved in setting up these events, invitational letters usually are not practical. Since the primary thrust is within the specific Region hosting the event, flyers are the best communication choice to announce the event and distribute the information throughout the Region.

If possible, the Campaign Committee Chairperson and Candidate should attend the planning meeting in order to stress its importance and help build enthusiasm.

While planning the event, the Regional Chairperson should call a meeting of all precinct captains and other volunteers to announce the event, assemble an ad hoc committee to handle the details, and allocate tickets to each of the volunteers to sell.

Do not miss the opportunity to announce the event in the other Regions. Invite them to participate, especially in the 4th of July picnic and rally. The campaign should generate press releases for all events as they occur, with special emphasis given to the weekly newspapers that have a high circulation within the specific Region hosting the event.

Do not miss the opportunity to announce the event in the other Regions.

These events should be opportunities to have fun, as well as to raise some campaign contributions. There is also a possibility that you will be able to recruit more volunteers. Do not structure the program too tightly and keep the speeches to a minimum. A few words from the Campaign Chairperson, followed by a few from the Regional Chairperson, leaving the Candidate to close with a 10 or 15 minute speech. The whole presentation should not last more than 30 minutes.

The Event (minor fund-raising)

If the event itself involves an outdoor activity, hold it on a Saturday or Sunday afternoon. Reserve a park or similar facility. Decorate the surrounding area so there is no mistaking its political characteristics, especially as it relates to your campaign. Extend an invitation to local elected officials who are supporting your candidacy. Many of them will come since it also gives them an opportunity to do some campaigning as well.

Dress casually for the event and take advantage of the situation. Participate in the activities and relax, since these are your supporters. As a candidate, you will have few opportunities to do this during the campaign.

Have some of your volunteers assigned to handle a variety of structured activities for the younger children. Depending on the nature of the event, there should also be some form of professional entertainment. Make sure that there is plenty to eat and drink. While the festivities are going on, the Candidate should circulate among the guests offering them appreciation for coming and a word of encouragement for the hard work that lies ahead.

If the event were an indoor type, it would normally be held on a Friday or Saturday evening so that school aged children can participate. Starting time is usually around 7:00 PM and the event should finish by 11:00 PM. Many of the children, possibly your own, are feeling a bit neglected by all the time their parents are spending on the campaign. These events give them an opportunity to share in the campaign and feel like they are a part of it. This makes coping easier for them. Spend some time with the children and let them know how proud you are of them for letting their parents help on the campaign. Share with them how important their parents work is to the campaign.

During the event itself, set aside some time to hold an auction. Auctions are not only fun; they can be very productive as a fund-raiser. It is amazing how people are caught up in auctions. Where they would not contribute another dime to the campaign, they would spend $35.00 bidding on a free haircut or shampoo donated by a local hairdresser. Many of the merchants and restaurants in your district will be happy to donate to these events as part of their public relations efforts. Likewise, you can write to prominent politicians of your party and celebrities for auction items; they will normally respond with some memorabilia of interest.

Intermingle items that you think will draw the most interest. Keep the auction to no more than one hour. Attempt to have the Candidate personalize items with a dated signature. Items that are left over can be used at another similar event, given to staff and volunteers as a reward for hard work, or donated to a local charity.

Make every effort to obtain and record the names and addresses of the attendees. All of the people who attend should have their names entered into your support file for future fund-raising appeals. Remember that these people have made an investment in your campaign. Not only will they vote for you, but they will influence at least seven others to join them in their support for you as well. In the final month of the campaign, when you send out your last appeal for funds to pay for the final media blitz, at least 20% of them will respond with an additional contribution.

There is also a significant political advantage in listing all of these contributors on your financial report forms, though you are not usually legally required to do so for small amounts. This list of minor contributors indicates broad-based support from the community. This can often influence major contributors, PACs, and your political party to participate with their financial support, now and in the future.

The Candidate's Role

The Candidate's Contribution

Except in rare cases, most candidates have to provide a major portion of the seed money in the 1st Stage of the campaign.

The last source of income to be discussed is usually the first contribution made. Except in rare cases, most candidates have to provide a major portion of the seed money in the 1st Stage of the campaign. Usually this is done in the form of a loan to the Campaign Committee so that, if a surplus remains at the conclusion of the campaign, the Candidate can recover a portion of this initial investment. If not, he or she writes it off as a direct contribution on the year-end FEC report or carries it forward to the next campaign, if running again.

The average Congressional Candidate can expect to invest between $75,000 and $100,000 in the campaign effort.

In addition to this direct contribution, the Candidate, if he or she is a challenger, will be contributing time, energy, and effort, in addition to a loss of salary during the 6 months of full-time campaigning. There will also be a considerable investment in clothes, meals, transportation, and incidental expenses. In many cases, the average Congressional Candidate can expect to invest between $75,000 and $100,000 in the campaign effort.

Since few candidates have the money readily available, most borrow during the campaign and usually end up with a personal debt. Normally, a fund-raising dinner party will be held shortly after the election in an attempt to retire as much of this debt as possible. As might be expected, this is much easier to do if the Candidate is the winner. Whatever debt remains, can usually be deferred until the next campaign period by paying interest only, if the lender or creditors agree. Normally, an early fund-raising effort combining direct mail and a dinner is held in the spring or fall of the following year to complete this debt retirement and provide the seed money for the next campaign.

Although the odds of a challenger Candidate losing the first time are very high, the chances of winning the next time improve considerably. Major contributors are very aware of this and will usually provide the support necessary for the second opportunity.

Although the odds of a challenger Candidate losing the first time are very high, the chances of winning the next time improve considerably. The voter ID data accumulated, including the Support File, plus the improved name ID provide an excellent base on which to build the next campaign. The major contributors, PACs, and Party officials are very aware of this and will usually provide the support necessary. In fact, it is usual for major contributors, PACs, and Party officials to insist on a commitment from the Candidate to run again, win or lose, before they make their initial contribution. In rare cases, they will even support a third try, depending on the circumstances and an analysis of the first two losses.

Candidate Fund-raising Activity

"The Lonesome Trail"

Many candidates have the attitude that the campaign is not for them personally, but for all the people who share their feelings about how the government and the country should be run. They see themselves as merely the catalyst to make this happen. Within this framework, they have no problem making the necessary requests for funds, time, and effort from those who share those beliefs and want to effect a change. As long as this is the operative framework, the candidate is able to believe others will respond in a positive manner. If a candidate does not have this attitude, the resulting problems can be insurmountable.

The Problem

The Candidate is the single most effective "tool" in the fund-raising process. Any elimination of this activity seriously affects the campaign's ability to meet its objectives.

Most candidates find raising campaign funds personally the most difficult activity to do in the campaign process. They will usually find every excuse imaginable to avoid doing it. The *problem* is that the Candidate is the single most effective "tool" in the fund-raising process. Any level of eliminating this activity from the campaign seriously affects the campaign's ability to meet its objectives.

Many candidates are unable to distinguish between raising funds for themselves personally and raising funds for the campaign. They must force themselves to make the distinction.

The Candidate's involvement in the types of fund-raising already discussed is relatively easy to do. They are somewhat detached from the actual process thus most candidates can handle those activities. It is when they must sit face to face with a potential contributor and ask for money that the problems arise. Candidates, by their very nature, tend to have strong egos. They are usually self-sufficient, independent personalities who have reached their levels in life mainly through their own efforts. Whatever financial help they may have received through the years, has usually come from family or close friends. The thought of asking strangers for financial assistance goes against their basic instincts and, in fact, is seen as distasteful. The stress caused by this dilemma can be very serious. It not only can affect the campaign's ability to meet its financial objectives; it can also spill over and affect the quality of the Candidate's political activity.

Essentially, the problem is one of attitude and therefore psychological by nature. The candidates with this problem have a strong tendency to internalize this activity. That is, they are unable to distinguish between raising funds for themselves personally and raising funds for the campaign. They personalize the campaign to such a degree that they become inseparable. In effect, they are the campaign.

The Solution

The problem is one of attitude.

The truth is, only your relatives, friends, and close supporters know you personally. Consequently, the vast majority of voters could not possibly be voting for you personally, or against you personally.

We all want to be liked and well thought of, but giving up this need is just one of the prices you pay when you become a candidate for public office.

If raising campaign contributions personally is the most difficult activity in the campaign process, you must force yourself to make the necessary distinction between *"you, the person,"* and *"you, the Candidate."* In order to make the distinction; you must understand the distinction. Consider, in reality, which candidate the electorate is voting for when they go to the polls. *"You, the person," or "you, the Candidate?"* The truth is, only your relatives, friends, and close supporters know you personally. Consequently, the vast majority of voters could not possibly be voting for you personally, or against you personally. After all, they know only your representation of yourself through your campaign media and candidate activities, in conjunction with what they have heard from your opponent and your opponent's supporters. Surely, this would be a mixed message of the totally positive and the totally negative. In addition, many voters consider you *"the enemy"* simply by virtue of daring to challenge their candidate. For all they know, you could be a *"Mother Theresa."* Notwithstanding, you are challenging their candidate, and for this reason alone, they will reject you. It is by making the distinction between *"you, the person"* asking for campaign contributions, and *"you, the Candidate"* asking for campaign contributions, that you will find the solution to the problem. In other words, by understanding this distinction, *"you, the person"* will be more comfortable with *"you, the Candidate"* soliciting campaign contributions.

After consideration, you will realize that many, if not most, who contribute to your campaign and ultimately vote for you, will do so for reasons which have literally nothing to do with you personally. A sizable percentage will support you simply because of your party affiliation. Many will support you because they can identify with you by the ethnic *"sound"* of your name or by virtue of your gender. In some cases, sounding Hispanic or being female is all the reason that they will need. Many of them will support you simply because you are the incumbent, or because you are not. A few will even support you because they prefer your stand on the issues or because your campaign's activities actually made the effort to ask them to support you. Only a relatively insignificant percentage will support you, or will not support you, because you are you. You must understand this distinction, because it is true.

Only a relatively insignificant percentage will support you, or will not support you, because you are you. You must understand this distinction, because it is true.

In my career, I have even seen campaigns won by "ghost" candidates. A real person was running, but the image created of that person in the campaign was, to all intents and purposes, a total fabrication. I even recall one campaign where the candidate was sent out of the country for the duration of the campaign so he could not contradict the image created by his consultants. He won. Lest you chuckle too hard at the gullibility of that particular electorate, I should mention it was a state representative race in one of the most affluent and best educated counties in the country.

Think about the hundreds of votes you have cast over your adult lifetime. Except for the presidential campaigns and high media campaigns at the statewide level, how well did you know the candidate for whom you voted? The fact is most candidates are decent, caring, educated individuals who would make great neighbors or friends. Even their goals and objectives are usually very similar. Their primary disagreements come in how to achieve those goals and objectives.

A Candidate is not asking their prospects for personal support. A Candidate is asking supporters to contribute to their own campaign to have their view or philosophy prevail in meeting the election objectives.

Essentially, this is what the voters decide in most campaigns. Which candidate most closely agrees with their own views on how the stated objectives should be realized, and at what price. When you ask someone to contribute to your campaign, you are not asking him or her for personal support. You are asking them to contribute to their own campaign in order to have their view or philosophy prevail in meeting the election objectives. You are simply the "spear carrier" or the focal point for their campaign. If they will not support their campaign, then they have in effect, conceded their position to the opposition. You have nothing to be embarrassed about by asking them to support the campaign. It is those who fail to "put their money where their mouth is," who should be embarrassed. Even if you haven't put a single dollar of your own into the campaign, which is highly unlikely, the personal sacrifices you and your family are making by being the "spear carrier" far exceeds their monetary sacrifice.

It is those who fail to "put their money where their mouth is," who should be embarrassed, not the Candidate for asking.

Voters know that campaigns cannot be waged without the funds to communicate to the electorate, just as battles cannot be won without the funds to purchase or manufacture weapons.

9

How to Make it Happen

Not unlike the party and the PAC leaders, the voters want you to win; they just are not convinced that you can.

The bottom line is that most campaigns rarely have anything to do with personalities. They are really battles between ideas. However, if this is the case, why do these potential contributors not recognize this and support the campaign, especially when they have so much money it could not possibly be a case of their inability to make a contribution?

The reasons by now should be obvious. Like the party and the PAC leaders, they want you to win. They are just not convinced that you can. In addition, they are concerned that they will need to get along with your opponent long after the election is over.

It is not enough simply to be willing to undertake the rigors of a campaign; it takes certain skills and hard work to make it happen.

Most of these potential contributors have been around long enough to see many candidates fail to win because they were not serious enough about winning to do what was necessary to develop a winning campaign. Many of these potential major contributors are business people who know how difficult it is to start a new business. They realize a campaign is even more difficult. Unless you are an incumbent, the silent question being asked in their mind is "what makes you think you have the ability to win?"

They know it is not enough simply to be willing to undertake the rigors of a campaign. As the old proverb goes, "The road to Hell is paved with good intentions." It takes certain skills and hard work to make it happen. Try putting yourself in their place. Here is a relatively young person who comes to you seeking your financial help. You do not know this person, but you have heard positive things about their personality and character, so you are willing

If you cannot convince an individual that you are deserving of their support, it is unlikely that the chances are good that you will be able to convince the PAC and party committee leaders that you are deserving of their support.

to listen. The person shares with you his or her concerns and eagerness to do something *"Okay, that's fine,"* you think, *"but how are you going to do it? What are your qualifications? Have you properly researched the market? Do you even know how to properly research the market? What about your competition? How much do you know about them and their current market penetration? What do you know about marketing techniques and technology? How much do you know about managing and administering a business this size? What are the qualifications of the support personnel you have on board, especially your management team? Have you developed a reasonable budget to help meet your objectives? Are you under capitalized? If I give you this limited amount, what are your plans for obtaining the remainder that you say you need?"*

Remember that most of the people you have selected to ask to contribute really do want you to win. Nonetheless, they are not fools and are not about to put a wager "on a last place horse."

Truly, the list does not end here. What do you know about the issues? How would you evaluate the ramifications of those potential solutions? Are you able to work out a compromise with other legislators and settle for half of the pie if you cannot have the whole pie? These are, or should be, the kinds of questions you would ask if you were on the other side of the desk being asked to do the giving. So, now I ask you, *"why should it be any different for the potential contributor to your campaign?"*

The burden of proof will always rest on you and it has little to do with your personality or character. You can presume that your prospect has heard positive things about you or you would not even have the opportunity to make your appeal. In the final analysis, it is no different than campaigning for another vote.

The Right Way

The wrong way to approach a prospect is to go into the meeting poorly prepared and bad mouthing your opponent.

The person that you are speaking to probably has a fair idea of your opponent already and if they don't, they would prefer to find out on their own. Anything coming from you is immediately suspect because of your own self-interests.

The right way is to approach a prospect, introduce yourself, and give them a brief idea of your background. Explain to them why you are running for this particular office and what you hope to accomplish if elected.

The right way involves an introduction of yourself and a brief outline of your background, why you are running for this particular office, and what you hope to accomplish if elected. That was the easy part. Then comes the difficult part: *Explain to them how you plan to win the campaign. Start off by admitting that when you first considered running for this office, you realized you knew next to nothing about where to begin. You realized much research needed to be done before you could start. So you obtained and studied everything you could lay your hands on about how to be a candidate, develop strategy, raise funds, and manage a campaign. You talked to party personnel and former candidates. Then you studied the demographic characteristics of the people in your district and developed a plan to market your campaign among the various groupings.*

Express how you recruited some of the finest talent you could find to serve on your executive or steering committee, as well as on the Finance and Field operations committees. Finally, you did a poll in the district to assess your opponent's strengths and weaknesses among the electorate and to discern the primary issues of concern to them. Then you developed a detailed game

You must convince them that you have the willingness, determination, and ability to be successful, to win the campaign.

plan, fund-raising plan, budget, and timeline. You began to organize your campaign. You purchased a computer and began to accumulate the database that you would need to get started. You obtained a map of the district and began to divide it into manageable regions and areas. You selected a headquarters site and have begun the task of assembling an operations staff. As you discuss this, you lay out brief overviews of these accomplishments. The whole presentation should not take more than twenty minutes.

Have the right attitude, then go for the close.

Then go for the close. If you have done your presentation properly and it is complete, the potential contributor cannot help but be impressed. Say to that person, you have done your part and you intend to continue doing so throughout the campaign. Now it is his or her turn to do their part. If he or she can, ask that they contribute their fair share of X dollars to the campaign and speak to at least five of their associates about supporting you as a Candidate. Suggest a breakfast or lunch meeting between you, your supporter, and his or her associates in order to help convince them to do their fair share as well.

You would use the same approach with PAC and party committee leaders.

This is the type of "no nonsense," professional approach that many people will respond to when asked to contribute. Its success is conditioned on (you) having done the work necessary to convince them that you are prepared, that you are serious, and that you have a chance of winning.

Candidate Summary

It is not *your* campaign. You are simply one of the essential players.

You must have the right attitude. This is not your campaign, you are simply one of the essential players, albeit the key one. This is everyone's campaign that shares the same approach to solving the problems that government can address. All of the people, especially in your district have a responsibility to do their fair share. First, however, you must convince them that you have the willingness, determination, and ability to be successful, i.e. to win the campaign. Apply this attitude to all of your fund-raising activities.

You, the Candidate, are the essential fund-raiser in the campaign, especially in the early stages. Many of the potential major contributors are going to insist on meeting you face to face and sizing up your chances before they will consider a contribution. As a point of interest, if you cannot convince an individual that you are deserving of their support, it is unlikely the chances are good that you will be able to convince the PAC and party committee leaders, that you are deserving of their support.

Fund-Raising Game Plan Summary

The outcome of the political campaign is directly related to the success of the fund-raising campaign.

The fund-raising game plan should contain the following:

1) Description of the Finance Committee, its purpose, structure, goals, objectives, and methodology,
2) Budget and sources of income,
3) Brief analysis of each source of income and the procedures the campaign plans to use to tap them,
4) Modified copy of the Timeline, showing the dates involving fund-raising activity, and a

The Fund-raising Game Plan is only as good as the people responsible for implementing the plan. Select the committee with great care.

I recommend that specific activity dates in the public version of the fund-raising plan be deleted, showing months only. This precaution will minimize the chances that the opponent will schedule similar activity at the same time in an attempt to upstage the campaign.

Be sure the members of the Finance Committee are thoroughly familiar with the FEC or the state regulations regarding soliciting contributions and accounting.

5) Copy of the FEC or appropriate state rules regarding federal or state campaign solicitation.

All Finance Committee members should receive a copy of this plan at their first meeting, along with a copy of the Political Game Plan, minus the Cash Flow schedule. Finance Committee members should become thoroughly familiar with both.

In most cases, the National Party, some major PACs, and major prospective contributors will want to review a copy of the fund-raising plan before considering their contribution. Since the assumption is made that one of these copies will end up in the opponent's hands, I recommend that specific activity dates in the public version of the fund-raising plan be deleted, showing months only. This precaution will minimize the chances that the opponent will schedule similar activity at the same time in an attempt to upstage the campaign.

Always keep fund-raising activity uppermost in everyone's mind. The Finance Committee and the staff must be reminded constantly that the outcome of the political campaign is directly related to the success of the fund-raising campaign.

Consider the pros of securing the services of a Political Fund-raising Consultant. This service is usually less expensive if provided as part of a total contract with a multi-agency. If unable to obtain a multi-agency, a separate contract will more than pay for itself by helping to insure the success of the fund-raising campaign.

A plan is only as good as the people responsible for implementing it. Select the committee with great care. Make sure it is well balanced and representative of a broad cross section of the business, industrial, professional, labor, and trade communities. They must believe in the Candidate and be committed to attaining the campaign's objectives.

The fund-raising campaign must be as well organized and strictly implemented as the political campaign. It will be usual for several activities to be going on at the same time. Only organization and discipline will prevent chaos, confusion, and collapse. A well prepared Timeline, strictly adhered to, will help considerably in keeping all activities on track.

Remember that all events are opportunities for additional media exposure, as well as fund-raising. Be sure to maximize this aspect of the activity. When releasing fund-raising progress press releases, (not to be confused with individual event releases) format information in terms of the number of contributors and the average contribution per person, as well as the total amount raised.

Stick to the budget and cash flow schedule. If a surplus develops, there is a strong tendency to spend for items or activities not originally called for in the Political Game Plan. Do not succumb to this temptation. Either put the money aside in an interest-bearing account or in the media trust account being maintained by the ad agency for the campaign and hold it in reserve to deal with the unforeseen.

Since the Candidate is legally responsible to insure that the campaign complies with every regulation, it is then his or her responsibility to research laws and regulations that affect his or her campaign and to be knowledgeable regarding not only the laws and regulations as written, but also their possible interpretations.

The specific figures used in this Chapter were illustrative only and were based on the Prototype Game Plan. Each campaign's figures should be based on its own situation and game plan.

A scandal involving illegal campaign contributions is always a disastrous event for any campaign to deal with, at any time. The Treasurer or Political Fund-raising Consultant should establish a sound accounting procedure for the campaign. The staff must adhere to it no matter how rushed they might be or feel. Call the FEC, Secretary of State, or the national or state party's legal department if there is a question before proceeding with a questionable transaction.

Violations of these regulations are usually criminal offenses subject to fines and/or jail terms.

Chapter 9 - Word Index

9

Chapter 10
What the Opponent Will Be Doing

"It Takes Two to Tango"

Whatever event takes place, even one that scores major points for the opponent, the ensuing panic in the ranks of the Challenger is the worst case scenario.

It would be nice if the campaign were operating in a vacuum. Obviously, that is not the case. The opponent will be campaigning as intensely as he or she knows how, with everything at his or her disposal. If the opponent is an incumbent, that can be a formidable obstacle to victory.

A major problem in many campaigns is the overreaction that occurs, either by the Candidate or the volunteers, when the opponent scores points. It will happen! Expect it! Anticipate how and when it will happen! Be prepared to counteract point by point, as soon as possible. Whatever happens, your panic is more damaging than the points they are bound to score.

First Stage - Strategy and Activity

The franking privilege is a routine activity. The Challenger should not make the mistake, as many candidates do, by crying "foul." Those candidates only embarrass themselves.

Initially, the opponent will take the high road, ignoring the Challenger Candidate, concentrating on the maximum utilization of free media coverage through conferences, releases, and actualities. If an incumbent, he or she will take full advantage of the franking privilege and the usual election year dispensation for grants to various agencies within the district. If the Candidate is a challenger, he or she should not make the mistake, as many candidates do, by crying "foul." Those candidates only embarrass themselves. These activities are routine and the news media knows it. If the charge is justified, it is proper to chide the incumbent for his or her new found election year interest in the district. Gradually, the opponent may begin to acknowledge the Candidate's existence, but only in a backhanded sort of way, designed to put the challenger down by pointing out his or her lack of experience and expertise.

An opponent with a low name ID rating is usually a very strong sign of vulnerability.

The opponent, if an incumbent, already has, or should have, a high name ID rating. Therefore, the primary emphasis in this early activity will be on what an excellent job he or she is doing for the district and how hard working he or she is. Incidentally, if an incumbent, after three terms, does not have a name ID rating of at least 65 to 70 percent, something is wrong. This low rating is usually a very strong sign of vulnerability.

Constituent service will show a marked improvement. Telephone calls and letters will be returned promptly. Flags that have flown over the Capitol will be passed out to every school, American Legion Post, and VFW chapter in the district. Graduates in the district will receive a congratulatory letter from the incumbent. Constituent surveys, showing the incumbent's desire to know what the people are thinking, and that he or she is listening will abound. The district staff will begin appearing at every function and meeting that they can to imprint on the people's consciousness the incumbent's concerned and desire to do everything possible to be helpful. The incumbent will significantly increase the number of visits to the district and decrease the "junkets" around the country and overseas. A number of "right" bills, courtesy of the Party leader, will start being co-sponsored by the incumbent. The media will find the incumbent much more accessible for interviews. Town Hall meetings will be held so the incumbent can show how accessible he or she is to the public.

Most of this effort will be expended to help create a positive feeling about the incumbent, increasing the Favorability rating, and to establish that he or she is different from the rest of the people's representatives on Capitol Hill. He or she will convey the image of a caring, experienced, trustworthy, honest representative that is doing a great job and must be returned to finish the job that has been started.

The incumbent will have had professional polls done to determine the major issues and concerns of the people in the district. Staff and national party research services will be developing every statistic and fact they can come up with to prove he or she is on the right side of these issues and voting the way the constituents want. Even the doubtful votes will have a perfectly sound explanation prepared for them.

A theme or slogan will be developed to help communicate the positive feeling. The names, addresses, and telephone numbers of every person who received any kind of personal correspondence from the incumbent during the last few years will be melded in his or her political mailing list, i.e., the incumbent's Support File. Campaign stationery might be developed to give the appearance of the incumbent's official stationery. The photo files will be searched for photos showing the incumbent receiving an award or interacting with people on a personal level. It is a sure bet that every type of humanitarian activity will be featured, whether it is the Scouts, Easter Seals, March of Dimes, Diabetes, or the Cancer Research Foundation.

Second Stage - Campaigning

Around mid-summer, more overt political campaigning will begin. Rare is the incumbent who will walk precincts, but most will do a few plant gates or shopping center visits. They will usually be at all the fairs, festivals, and parades. Almost every civic association or club will have the incumbent at their monthly luncheon or breakfast meeting. The final franking mail stressing the incumbent's voting record will be sent out to all households in late August.

About the last thing an incumbent will want to do is provide the challenger with an opportunity for additional free media coverage. Therefore, as a rule, they will find every excuse imaginable to avoid joint appearances and/or debates. However, eventually, they will have to engage in some public forum or risk public and media disapproval. "The later, the better" is usually the motto. Only if polls show slippage will the reverse hold true.

Third Stage - High Gear

It is usual for the incumbent to move into high gear after Labor Day.

On or about Labor Day, the average incumbent will swing into high gear. The billboards and bus signs will go up. Political direct mail will begin, first to Party members, then to previous supporters who are listed in the constituent file and then to the independents. The Phone Banks will spring into action, either with volunteers or paid telemarketers. A major event with a "heavy hitting" guest speaker in attendance will normally take place in both September and October. At least one major rally will usually take place in late September. It is usual for the incumbent to run a short blitz, lasting 7 to 10 days, on radio

It is usual for the incumbent to organize a blitz for late September or early October. The Candidate's campaign must be prepared to neutralize this thrust.

and TV in the second or third week in September. Expect a heavy 10-day run just before the election. Much, however, will depend on what the polls are saying about the challenger's progress.

Yard, window, and corner signs will flower during the month of October. A tabloid can be expected around the first week of October, followed shortly thereafter by a series of well-designed endorsement and issue type newspaper ads.

A second mailing, coordinated with the media blitz, will go out during the final week of October. A major GOTV effort, tied into the local Party's program, will be made in the last days of the campaign. Most local candidates are anxious to attach themselves to the incumbent's coattails and will tie him or her into their grass roots programs. I would also expect key supporting organizations to provide large numbers of volunteers for the GOTV effort.

Opposition Strategy and Tactics

It would be unusual for an incumbent to attack a challenger directly, appearing weak or defensive.

It would be unusual for an incumbent to attack a challenger directly. If they do, they run the risk of appearing weak or defensive. However, if their polls indicate they are in serious trouble, expect almost anything. Even personal attacks, though usually handled by a third party, are possible. Most incumbents, or their more avid supporters, will have done an intensive background check on the challenger early in the campaign. If there is anything there to exploit, it will be exploited, if necessary.

Experts will appear to prove the challenger's positions are unrealistic at best, or damaging to the country, at worst. If the incumbent can get a copy of the challenger's speaking schedule, individuals or "truth squads" can be expected to be there to sandbag the challenger with loaded questions. Every effort will be made to stack the audience with supporters whenever a joint appearance or debate is on the schedule, especially, if the media is there. The incumbent might try to upstage any event or activity a challenger has planned. An incumbent is usually more newsworthy and can, therefore, draw the media away.

The incumbent might try to prove the challenger is an extremist, representative of only a small segment of the district. The tone of the attack will be that the majority of the people in the district must rally together behind the incumbent in order to prevent that group from taking power. Just as the challenger will be trying to lower the Favorability rating of the incumbent, the incumbent will be trying to lower the Favorability of the challenger. Since the challenger does not have a voting record to prove where he or she is in the political spectrum, the incumbent will use the challenger's position papers, contributors, and public statements to make a case against him or her.

A third party, such as the Campaign Manager or a Chairperson will make these attacks and/or counterattacks. This tactic usually achieves the desired result, while keeping the incumbent above the fray. In the absence of a strong objection from the challenger, it will continue.

Summary

The basic strategy of the incumbent is to usually capitalize on the high name ID, reserving the campaign funds to build a higher Favorability rating and concentrating on the above average voting group. As long as he or she can, every effort will be made to avoid media opportunities that will be helpful to the challenger. Covert campaigning can be expected right after the first of the year, plus extensive fund-raising activities. Overt campaigning will usually begin midsummer, gradually increasing in intensity until Labor Day, at which point it will go into high gear.

The incumbent will try hard for the center ground on the issues and will take the "high road" politically by having third parties mount the attack against the challenger, personally, politically, or philosophically, as necessary.

Since incumbents usually do not have as strong a volunteer force, they will rely more heavily on paid personnel to do the telephoning and the GOTV program. They will also tap heavily into precinct organizations of the local Party, key organizations, and other candidates.

In a debate or joint appearance, an incumbent can be expected to rely heavily on statistical data and less on demagoguery, creating the impression he or she knows what he or she is talking about.

Within the District, every favor owed for favors done will be called in, especially if it appears to be a close election. The incumbent will usually do a limited amount of broad based campaigning just for cosmetic or media purposes. The greater concentration will be on Centers of Influence, essential groups, and the media.

Since campaign funds are relatively easier to come by and significant expenditures are unnecessary before Labor Day, an intensive media program in September and October can be expected and the Candidate's campaign must be prepared to neutralize this thrust.

Rarely, can or will an incumbent do a voter ID program on the scale a challenger will attempt. An incumbent's Phone Bank will be geared primarily toward advocacy calls to ticket-splitters, independents, and Party members during the GOTV effort. An incumbent will usually rely more heavily on free and paid catch all media spots to campaign for the average voter group and personal campaign activity in addition to the targeted use of the media for the above average voter group.

The incumbent knows he or she usually has the advantage over the challenger. Expect the incumbent to maintain that advantage by not allowing the challenger to accelerate campaign activity. In other words, if the incumbent's campaign proceeds at a rate equal to the challenger's, the incumbent is usually assured of victory. That being the case, an astute incumbent can be expected to carefully monitor the challenger's progress against his or her own through extensive polling, and to adjust the campaign plan accordingly.

A normal campaign budget for an incumbent to accomplish this will average $750,000.

Chapter 10 - Word Index

Chapter 11
The Campaign Plan

In Retrospect

In the previous chapters, I have pointed out many of the basic procedures that must be planned and implemented to manage a successful campaign, i.e., those activities that are fundamental and basic to most candidates' campaigns, regardless of the type or location of the district. Except for those sections where we specifically referred to a congressional campaign, or an incumbent's strategy, everything presented is applicable to all other campaign levels.

If it were possible to quantify these constants in terms of a percentage of the whole campaign, I would estimate that they would represent an average of 85 to 90 percent of the activity. Yet, so often, many consultants, advisers, or strategists will concentrate on the 10 to 15 percent that make up the variables. The assumption is that the Candidate is already aware of the constants or can figure them out, and therefore, does not need this kind of detailed assistance. In some cases, it may be a result of the lack of campaign experience on the part of the adviser.

My own experience has shown almost the opposite. The candidates I have studied over the years, no matter what their other skills might be, usually have had to spend an inordinate amount of precious campaign time learning the peculiarities of campaign management and techniques. Eventually, by trial and error, they are able to understand the majority of the issues. More often than not, however, this understanding through experience manifests itself with only about 60 days to go before the election. Many opportunities for potential votes are lost in the process.

11

The Campaign Manual has been written to speed up this learning process. As any professional will point out, there are at least a dozen different ways to solve the same problem. The methods presented in the Manual cover only a few. My primary intent has been to help the reader to understand the problems, to define objectives, to suggest basic methods that will work, and procedures to be followed.

When managing a campaign, the constants or basics are of fundamental importance. That you use Direct Mail is the issue, not how you use it.

For example, further reading on the subject of how direct mail letters should be written will sometimes suggest apparently contradictory methods. Frankly, I do not believe there is a "best" way. At different times, I have used one-page letters and three-page letters, short paragraphs and long paragraphs, straight margins and indents, letters signed by "heavies" and some that were signed by "nobodies". They all seem to work equally well. As long as they are sincere, straightforward, and well targeted, they will produce positive results. What is important is the constant, the use of direct mail in the campaign.

Another example is the activity in the Pre-Announcement or 1st Stage. How the tasks are accomplished. Whether done by the Candidate personally, by a committee, or by someone else, is not the constant. The accumulation of this data and the preparation activity is the important factor and the task that must be accomplished.

In developing the strategy and game plan, the Candidate must develop a realistic awareness of the problems being faced. He or she must provide reasonable solutions and a viable plan to implement them. The methodology used in this Manual is one example of how someone might go through this systematic procedure. It is by no means the only way to accomplish the goals. It is, however, one of the surest ways.

After taking stock, a Candidate must weigh his or her resources, including an objective self-appraisal as a candidate. He or she needs to know what kind and how much support the Candidate can really expect from the Party, friends, and acquaintances. Does the Candidate really have the caliber of staff and committee people needed? Are those who are willing to devote the required time and energy to the campaign actually available? Is the family and the Candidate really prepared and committed to what lies ahead? Can he or she realistically raise the seed money that will be required to initiate the campaign successfully? Do the members of the Finance Committee have the ability and willingness to raise the money expected of them?

Is the opponent, if an incumbent, vulnerable or is this simply a wishful thought on the part of the Candidate? Is the Candidate really committed to serving the people in the district, or is this idea born from ego, arrogance, or a means of building name ID for commercial purposes? Is the media availability in the district such that it can be used effectively to communicate the Candidate's message? If not, are there realistic alternatives available that will accomplish essentially the same results? For example, if the district is in the New York City media market, the cost of TV would probably be prohibitive, or at best, the buy would be considerably weakened in comparison with the program called for in the Prototype Plan. There would then have to be a viable alternative to accomplish the objectives that would otherwise be realized on TV.

The Candidate's plan, regardless of its final form, must also accomplish these objectives. If it fails in any one of the six areas, the campaign will almost surely fail as well.

In review, the important objectives are:

1) the Candidate must have a method which will build up his or her name ID rating equal to the opponent's, if an incumbent,

2) the Favorability rating must be greater,

3) there must be a secondary Political Game Plan that will effectively deliver the Candidate's message to the above average voters,

4) a program is needed that will identify the voters,

5) the campaign must have a communication method and program that will help motivate the electorate to come out and vote for the Candidate, and

6) a program must be in place that will maximize the vote potential on Election Day.

The programs and systems outlined in the Prototype Plan address all of these objectives. It is the refined version of a plan that has been used in a number of campaigns, and when implemented properly, has resulted in a high degree of success. It is not based on theory alone and each step is achievable. The Candidate's plan, regardless of its final form, must also accomplish the above objectives. If it fails in any one of the six areas, the campaign will almost surely fail as well.

It would be a rare situation where an incumbent does not appear to have a sizable lead over a challenger at the outset.

It would be a rare situation where an incumbent does not appear to have a sizable lead over a challenger at the outset. Given that an incumbent is not going to concede just because a challenger is in the race, the Candidate must devise a strategy that presumes an active campaign on the incumbent's part. If the best the Candidate could hope to do is neutralize the incumbent in the media level of the campaign, the needed gains have to be made in the other two levels, i.e., field operations and Candidate activities. As mentioned earlier, the challenger usually has a decided advantage in these two levels, if he or she capitalizes on them. If the incumbent were to maintain as strong a program as this, he or she would be virtually unbeatable.

Many candidates do not realize that the cost factors involved in an extensive field operations program actually exceed the cost of the electronic media.

What so many candidates do not seem to realize, or fully appreciate, are the cost factors involved in an extensive field operations program. A careful analysis of the Prototype Budget will show that the field operations costs for staff, materials, telephones, and logistical support services actually exceed the cost of the electronic media portion of the budget. However, without those support materials and services, the field operations volunteers could not possibly accomplish their objectives.

A challenger/candidate reduces the ability to make gains over an incumbent if unable to make the "candidate's expenditure," i.e., cash outlay, lost wages, and time.

The same holds true of the Candidate's level of operation within the campaign. Although not as expensive in direct cash outlays, the value of lost income and time involved while campaigning full-time, can be substantial. Unless this "expenditure" is made, a challenger/candidate has reduced considerably one of the only two methods he or she has to make gains over an incumbent.

The Candidate's Media advantage is hidden in the finite limit to the amount of communication that any candidate can do, regardless of financial ability.

In the media level, there is a hidden advantage in that there is a finite limit to the amount of communication that any candidate can do, regardless of how much money he or she has to spend. Although it is no easy task, it is possible to neutralize the opponent by matching his or her media expenditures, at least to the degree that it is prudent, and the candidate does not risk overexposure.

Because of the existing TV advertising atmosphere, the Candidate has an opportunity to communicate his or her message through this medium as effectively as the opponent.

Based on present legislated restrictions, TV stations must offer (to any candidate) an equal amount of advertising time, both in terms of quantity and quality, to that sold to any opponent. In addition, they must also make the schedule of the opponent's "advertising time purchases" available to the Candidate. This legislation, gives the Candidate an equal opportunity to communicate his or her message through this medium as effectively as the opponent. These same rules are usually followed by radio stations, newspapers, and billboard companies.

Direct mail is the only area of paid media communications where there are no limits or restrictions. However, logic dictates that the maximum number of mailings an opponent can do in a 2-month period is three. More than that risks overexposure.

I have deliberately avoided spelling out the number of TV and radio spots necessary to achieve the campaign's objectives. Too many factors must be considered when making this determination to provide the reader with a constant that would be meaningful. This decision can be made successfully only after studying the targeting needs, polling results, the Arbitron ratings, media availability, and cost factors. If the campaign has not taken advantage of professional assistance in any other area of the campaign, it should do so for this one.

Most candidates lose as a result of their failure to plan and implement a sound campaign, not because the opponent beats them.

In the Prototype Plan, these limitations on the opponent's media capabilities are anticipated, matched, and effectively neutralized. By maximizing the results of the field operations program and Candidate activities, it is possible for a challenger/candidate to actually erode the incumbent's normally favored position. In fact, I am convinced that at any given time, if exploited properly regardless of prevailing ideological shifts, 70 percent of all campaigns are winnable by the challenger because of these advantages. As mentioned before, most candidates lose as a result of their failure to plan and implement a sound campaign, not because the opponent beats them.

Since the implementation is conditional on adequate financing, it is imperative that a viable Finance Committee be formed and made operational early in the campaign. Remember that a campaign is similar to a business. If it is undercapitalized at the outset, the chances for success are reduced proportionally.

There are those campaigns (four or less "fluke" wins in any given year), which will occasionally be successful in spite of themselves or their lack of planning. However, for a Candidate to base his or her campaign hopes on this unlikely occurrence could only be described as foolish. A Congressional Candidate's campaign often represents a capital, time, and labor investment of over one million dollars over a 12 month period. This is far too much to be ventured on an exercise in futility, especially when substantial sacrifices are being asked of so many. Remember that even if a Candidate can assemble a very talented, energetic group of individuals within his or her Campaign, there is still a need for an experienced coach to help the Candidate and his or her campaign group perform as a unit with maximum effectiveness. Someone must assess the situation critically, develop the strategy, call the plays, and motivate the members to perform according to the plan, or change tactics if a certain development was not anticipated. This is most important when the team falls behind and time is running short. An old adage reminds us that, "A doctor who treats himself has a fool for a patient." That can easily be applied to the Candidate who tries to run his or her own campaign.

Similar to that old adage about doctors, "The Candidate who manages his or her own campaign, has a fool for a campaign manager."

Since an opponent's votes reach beyond the district and can affect individuals and/or groups throughout the state or country, there are many sources of assistance available to a candidate. These potential allies usually will not become enthusiastically involved unless they believe the Candidate has the knowledge and expertise to take maximum advantage of the opportunities. The telltale signs are the Political Game Plan and Budget, in addition to the results of early fund-raising efforts, both in terms of amount and the number of contributors. They are accustomed to hearing all the possible arguments about why they should help. They usually know the opponent's voting record, if an incumbent, or his or her position on the issues, if a challenger. They are also aware of the opponent's vulnerability. However, unless the Candidate can prove to them that he or she has at least an even chance of winning, they will be reluctant to commit a portion of their limited resources to the campaign. There is rarely anything personal in this decision. It is simply pragmatic. The most tangible proof the campaign can give is to show the first $150,000 of campaign funds being raised by the Finance Committee within the district.

The purpose of political communications is to inform and to motivate. The cost of the campaign is a direct function of that need to communicate.

The purpose of political communications is to inform and to motivate. The cost of the campaign is a direct function of that need to communicate. In recent years, the cost factors for paid communications have increased at an astronomical rate in comparison with most other areas of the economy. It is rather hypocritical, therefore, when the opponent or members of the media question the size of a Candidate's campaign budget. This claim is usually a smokescreen that is designed to divert public attention from the real issues in a campaign. Fortunately, the more objective and informed media reporters do not fall for this tactic, as they often did in the past, and refuse to be used by the opponent in this manner.

Almost any negative attack can be turned around.

Remember that almost any negative attack can be turned around by the Candidate and used to his or her advantage, if the attack is anticipated, the responses are prepared in advance, and a mechanism is put in place to deliver the response quickly. It is when a candidate reacts in panic that mistakes are made and the opponent is able to score points at the Candidates expense. Build measuring devices into the campaign that will enable the campaign to assess positive or negative impact and evaluate progress. Reinforce those measuring devices with professional polls that help to confirm or deny the results of the internal methodology. If the field program is realizing its objectives on schedule, but a poll indicates the Candidate is trailing badly, then in all probability the initial objectives were understated and the campaign should take immediate corrective action

Be certain that the poll is taken and results are broken down by the Regional alignments. This will help to adjust strategy, if necessary, on a more localized basis.

The campaign must do extensive research before establishing its Region, Area, and precinct objectives. They should be realistically attainable and adequate to guarantee victory.

Plot the campaign's targets on a graph to reduce the chances of oversight and/or mistakes being made.

Remember that the three main types of political targeting are direct mail, demographics, and media. One type is applicable to each level of the campaign, field operations, media, and candidate activity, and the calculations for each type have their own methodology. Avoid confusing them or attempting to apply one to the other. The method of implementation used is then subdivided and dependent on the stages of the campaign.

The safety net concept relies on one level of activity below another. Each level is a planned safety net or activity to make up the objective shortfall of the level above.

As the analysis and planning for each level is done, determine whether an activity's primary purpose in a given stage is to build name ID and a favorable impression of the Candidate or a negative impression of the opponent. Then, sub-categorize the activity as to its primary respondent grouping, the average voter or the above average voter. Keep the safety net concept in mind. If one activity partially misses its objective, what activity has been planned to make up the differential? Is there a third net beneath the second one? A fourth net within a given level is usually unnecessary and inefficient.

Tracking surveys through polls taken weekly in campaigns using the safety net system have shown that it is 90 percent effective in realizing its objective.

To review briefly how this strategy works, look at the field operations and media programs in the 4th Stage, as an example. The primary objective of this stage's activity is to inform the above average voter group about the Candidate and his or her differences with the opponent. By Negative Advocacy, provide them with a reason to vote for the Candidate and/or to vote against the opponent. Since the campaign does not know specifically who the above average voters are, this will be a partial catchall program directed to undecided voters and designed to insure communication with them. The number, however, is substantially reduced by 2nd and 3rd Stage activities.

The first net is the Precinct Captain's program, backed up by the second net, the Phone Bank volunteer program. The third net is provided by the media level programs, i.e., the free media generated by debates and attack press releases, the first 3 weeks' run of TV and radio commercials, and the direct mail program to the unidentified members of the opposition party that accomplishes a secondary objective of this Stage.

Tracking surveys through polls taken weekly in campaigns using this system have shown that it is 90 percent effective in realizing its objective. The targeted group received the required additional information needed to reach a decision on how to vote. On the average, over 60 percent of those who were previously in the undecided category decide to vote for the Candidate because of this contact and the message received.

In each stage, the personal political activity of the Candidate is designed to either supplement or capitalize on the activities taking place at the other two levels in the campaign. While others are concentrating on a higher name ID by identifying and informing in the 2nd Stage, the Candidate is concentrating on Centers of Influence and selective groups, which will help increase public awareness of the campaign.

Keep in mind the emphasis has been on primary objectives in each stage and there will always be a certain amount of activity, at all levels, that will help realize other objectives. This activity will usually be concurrent, e.g., the billboards through all stages are designed primarily for building name ID, a primary activity in the 2nd Stage, but in this case a secondary activity during the remainder of the stages. In addition, the primary activity in the 3rd Stage is positive advocacy. However, if the opponent is an incumbent who, for example, votes contrarily to a majority of the people in the district, the stage in which the event happens should not preclude the Candidate from taking issue with the opponent to create an advantageous edge. However, these departures should be chosen carefully and be done infrequently.

The Candidate should be cautious about adopting well-intentioned advice, regardless of the source, especially if it is not compatible with the Game Plan. No matter how experienced the individual, or what source they represent, unless they have taken the time to study in detail the campaign's particular situation, the advice, even if positive in some way, could adversely impact another area of the campaign.

If hiring a consultant, regardless of the type, be assured that he or she is one that is experienced in the level and type of the campaign being run. Many of the better known names in the business developed their reputation on presidential campaigns where there is a considerable amount of national publicity. There is about as much similarity between running a Presidential and congressional race as there is between a football and a baseball game. Actually, most political consultants shy away from publicity as much as possible to avoid taking any media attention away from their client or causing the media to tag the Candidate based on the philosophical leanings of their previous clients.

If possible, consider using multi-agencies for congressional and smaller races. They are usually the most cost efficient. Check prices carefully when negotiating with all potential suppliers since the differences can be substantial. Remember even a 2-cent differential on a direct mail piece equals $10,000 when mailing 500,000 pieces. Most reputable multi-agencies can save the cost of their fee to the campaign in discounted rates alone.

When negotiating contracts, the Candidate should be sure he or she knows what the campaign is receiving. There is a significant difference between a managing consultant and one who simply dispenses advice during a monthly visit to the district, with little or no follow through on the days in between. Once selected, do not second-guess or question loyalty. The vast majority of Political Campaign Consultants, especially those, who are full members of the American Association of Political Consultants, are full-time professionals. Once retained, like an attorney or doctor, they must put the campaign's interests above all other considerations. The Candidate's campaign becomes their campaign and, frankly, in 30 years I have never heard of a Political Campaign Consultant violating that position of trust. If they did, they would be expelled from the industry. With only a few hundred full-time Political Campaign Consultants in the country, it would not take long for the word of their indiscretion to be known.

A Candidate should be sensitive to the campaign's internal morale and avoid becoming so busy campaigning that it is overlooked. Remember that for most volunteers a campaign is a social experience. There is no rule, which says they should not have some fun. Make sure the staff receives the recognition and appreciation they deserve. Some Political Campaign Consultants believe an adversary relationship should exist between the Candidate and the Campaign Manager. I do not. I believe they are partners in the effort. The activity of each should complement the other's efforts. The same holds true for the consultant.

The Candidate's spouse and family are participating in the campaign, either directly by working on it or indirectly by doing without the Candidate for the next 12 months, covering his or her share of the household functions and responsibilities. The Candidate should let them know continuously how much their support is appreciated and share the campaign experiences with them. Let them feel that they are a part of what is happening.

The Candidate should never forget he or she is asking the people of the district to accept him or her as their leader in the U.S. House of Representatives, the legislature, or the city council. Regardless of the specific office, the position carries a great responsibility. They should always conduct and project themselves as a leader should. Show respect for the office and the person serving in it. Do not engage in gutter politics or dirty tricks no matter what the provocation. When they resort to this type of campaigning, candidates only demean their own integrity and the integrity of all the people who have placed their trust in them. That is not to say they should not play hardball when necessary, but always play fair ball.

Finally, remember that the overall strategy must be to neutralize the opponent by matching him or her in the media level of the campaign and to use the volunteers and the candidate to maximum advantage to a greater degree than the opponent can or does.

If the Candidate develops a sound Political Game Plan with a realistic Budget, raises the funds necessary to implement it effectively, organizes a comprehensive dynamic precinct and phone bank program, and organizes a capable staff to administer it, he or she can win.

Chapter 11 - Word Index

Chapter 12
The Computerization of the Campaign

Let's Talk Tools

In today's world, technology has soared, those who remain technologically current have a decisive advantage over those that are not. You may consider this to be sad, but make no mistake about its truth.

The truism for the 21st Century will be, *"the candidate having the best campaign strategy in conjunction with the most current technology, will win, almost every election."*

In other words, waging the battle of a campaign from a technologically backward position will likely doom you, no matter how well you plan your campaign strategy. Telephone systems, fax phones, cell phones, pagers, telemarketing, computers, networks, servers, printers, copiers, high speed modems, palm pilots, the Internet, voice mail, e-mail, snail mail, direct mail, some mail, no mail, too much mail. We are really sure of only one thing; despite having no idea where the technology train will take us, we had better get on board, if winning is our goal.

Am I really saying that you can not win without today's current technological advances? Well, I suppose not. I could refine the statement and say, if you do not have today's current technology in your campaign arsenal, you had better have a veritable army of volunteers in order to keep pace. Unfortunately, in today's hustle and bustle world, an army of volunteers is near impossible to assemble, no matter how loved you and/or your policies are.

The work of one computer will eliminate the need for literally thousands of volunteer person hours. If you have any experience with today's technology, you will be unable to remember what we did before we had VCRs, microwaves, and faxes. I have purposely used examples of electronic gadgetry that are far from the crest of today's technological advances. In fact, they can not even be considered a part of 21st Century technology. If you need further proof, let us be determined not to communicate with anyone, in any electronic form, for a single day. That would mean we can not use any telephone (landline or cellular), fax, pager, palm pilot, voice mail, e-mail, radio, television, or the fastest growing link to the world, the Internet. Since I am presently communicating to you using an electronic word processor, I am first to be eliminated from our test. You can continue and ascertain how long it will be before you need to communicate through electronic means.

Despite having no idea where the technology train will take us, we had better get on board, if winning is our goal.

Regardless of the configuration of hardware or which software program the campaign uses, **there is an undeniably critical need in today's environment to computerize the campaign.**

Political Campaign Management Software

The next consideration in the computerization of the campaign is the software that makes use of the computer and directs the computer to carry out the campaign needs as defined by the user. There are a number of companies that have developed computer software to assist in the management of the campaign and/or the campaign data. Not unlike most software topics, campaign management software applications are available in different shapes and sizes and I am sure that each company distributes a fine product. Nonetheless, based on my research, they have several drawbacks in common. I know of none that have been designed by an experienced Political Consultant. I know of none that are based on the strategic content of a campaign manual as comprehensive as *The Campaign Manual.* Many are too expensive. Many are adaptations of applications that not only were not originally designed for political campaigns, they were never intended for political campaigns. GOTV *Campaign Optimizer* is based solely on the logic and goals of *The Campaign Manual*. It is available from AmeriCan GOTV Enterprises, LLC. GOTV *Campaign Optimizer* is reasonably priced. It was designed with political campaign needs specifically in mind. Its logic and goals are based on *The Campaign Manual* written by an educated and experienced Political Campaign Consultant.

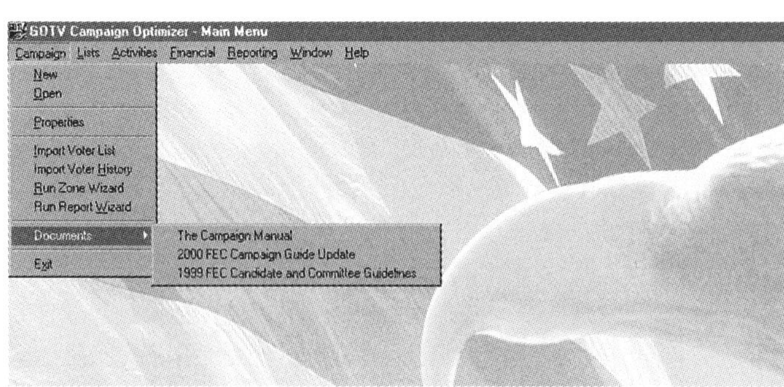

GOTV *Campaign Optimizer*

I have stressed the advantages of having a computer or computer network to assist the campaign. In fact, I am convinced that it is an indispensable tool for any campaign, regardless of its size.

We have talked extensively throughout *The Campaign Manual* about collecting contact information from literally every contact made with every registered voter, tracking their development from identification to enlisting their support by Election Day. What better way to manage contacts than with a database, accumulating information regarding all of your contacts before, during, and after the votes are counted. Registered voters, prospects and supporters, both individuals and organizations, media and vendor contacts; all lists of valuable contacts made, and cultivated throughout your political aspirations.

Voter Registration File

The Secretary of State or State Board of Elections maintains an electronic file containing registered voter data. Most County Board of Election offices will also maintain this information. For a fee, the Board of Elections will transfer all or specific data that you request in an electronic data file for your use. The manual for GOTV *Campaign Optimizer* will identify the exact format that is required for this file and direct you through the import process with its Voter List Wizard. When you have completed this task, you will have a listing of all of the registered voters in your district in an electronic database. You will be able to search, sort, identify, and categorize voters for any reason deemed necessary. You will be able to create campaign literature and target your message specifically to any group sorted from the voter list.

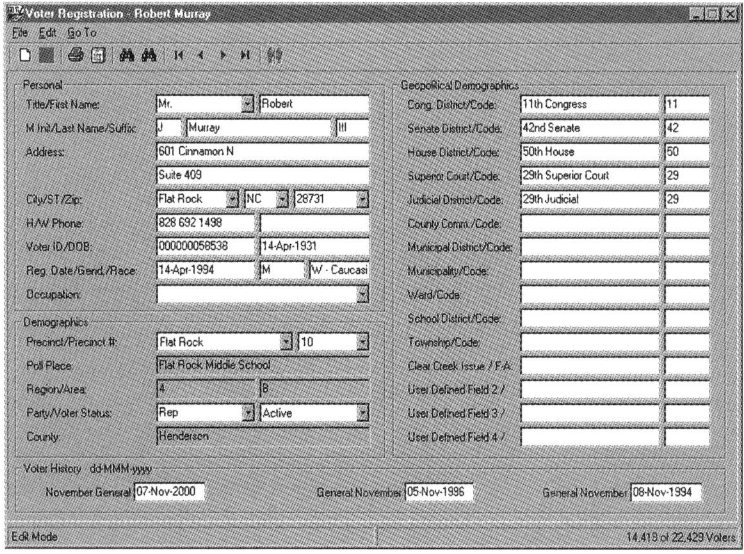

In addition to the general and geopolitical information that can be managed on each registered voter, corresponding voter history data can be downloaded in order to analyze voter trends in your district.

GOTV Campaign Optimizer will be both your first, and your last campaign management software application.

To attempt to do all of this manually, even in the smallest electoral district, is a very inefficient use of time and resources. Today, it is possible to purchase an excellent computer system for any size campaign, with an upgrade capability. GOTV *Campaign Optimizer* is reasonably priced to enable the smaller campaign to take full advantage of its power. Whether one is transferring from one period to another or from one office to another, the valuable information accumulated and stored will never need to be reentered.

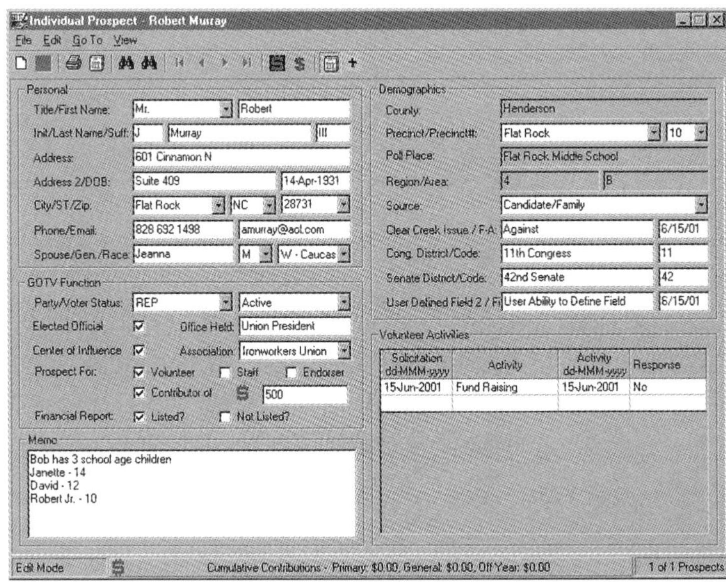

Individual Prospect File

Once you have access to the registered voter files, you can begin to identify them as either For, Against, or Undecided regarding your candidacy, as outlined in this manual. Each voter contact can be recorded and tracked. Through direct mail, Precinct activity, and Phone Bank Operations each voter's intention is identified. After contact with the voter has been established, each voter's status (for, against, undecided, or even declined to say) and all associated information can be collected, verified, and recorded. If the voter is identified as a prospect or supporter, the file is copied to the prospect or supporter database. Voters identified as "against" the Candidate are "marked" within the database to avoid the needless waste of resources associated with direct mail, and other campaigning costs. All with the click of a button! Within the prospect files, you are able to identify essential information regarding each voter. Voters can be qualified as prospects for contributions, volunteering, and endorsements. Prospective contribution information is transferred to the Projected Income Statement in order to assist and validate the Finance Plan. Solicitations for volunteer work are recorded and tracked.

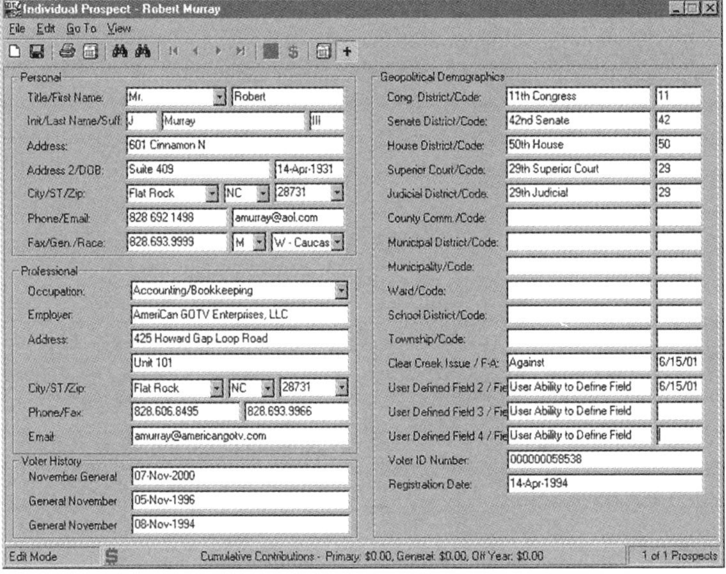

Additional Information is retained on a second prospect file form and remains attached to the prospect record.

All with the click of a button!

Note also the availability of four optional, user defined fields to enable the user to record and track specific issues that may be essential to their individual electoral race.

Individual Support File

After recording a support function, the program identifies a Prospect as a supporter and automatically transfers the file to the Support designation. A support function can be a contribution, a volunteer activity or an endorement.

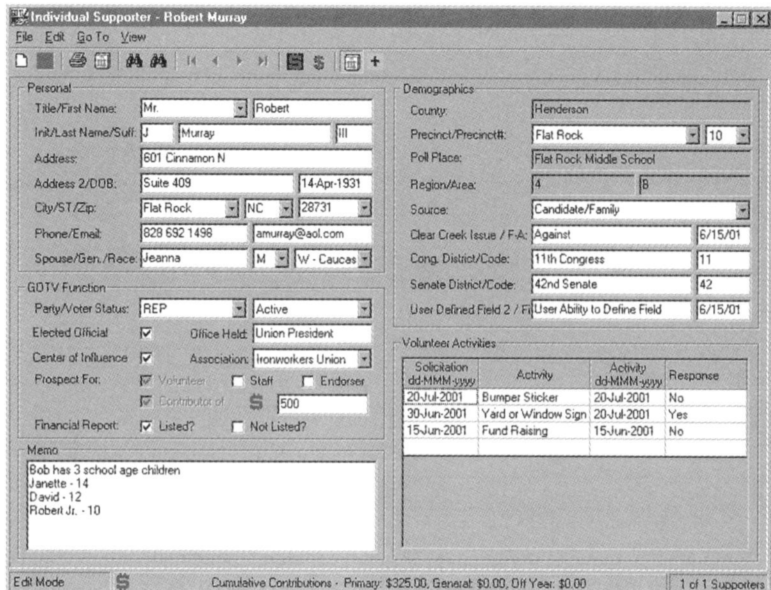

Contributions are tracked by record, in real time, on-screen.

The Support File records the amount contributed, the Precinct, Polling Place, the Region, and Area designations. If a volunteer, the file tracks the type of activity agreed to or not interested in, the supporter's response, and the dates regarding the commitment. The file also contains the person's name, address, telephone number, occupation, employment information, contributor, volunteer, or endorser detail, any center of influence or elected office held by the supporter, the original source of the support, and much more.

Organization Prospect and Support Files

Records should be kept on every organizational prospect for support. This list includes the Party, PACs, and associations. Campaign reports require a separate accounting for organizations. Records should also be available on every prospective organizational source of support, such as PACs and associations from which the campaign hopes to obtain contributions, research support, or endorsements.

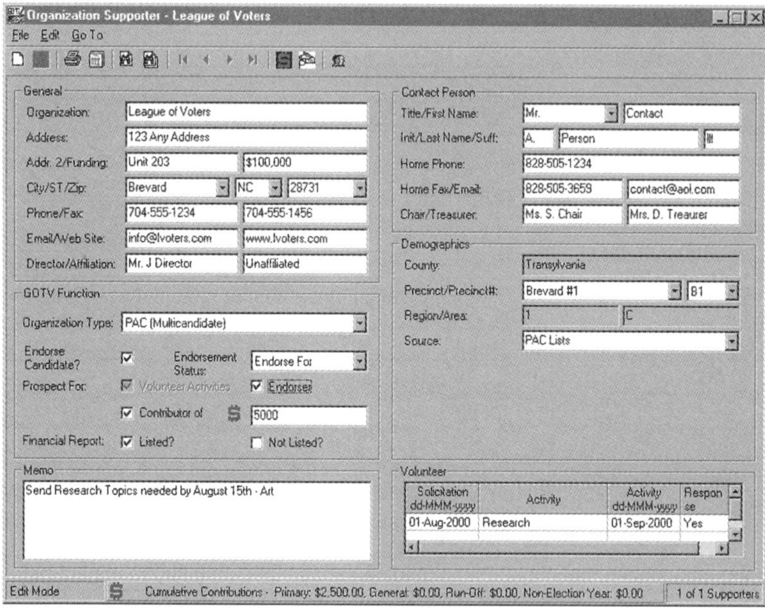

The relationship and functions of the Organization files mirror the flexibility and capability of the Individual Prospect and Support files. This enables the user to track the differences between the designations, but reduces the learning curve of the program, as functional aspects are identical.

Contribution information is automatically transferred to the financial records and tracked against regulations.

Note that contributions are tracked by record, in real time, on-screen. This information is also automatically transferred to the financial records contained within the program.

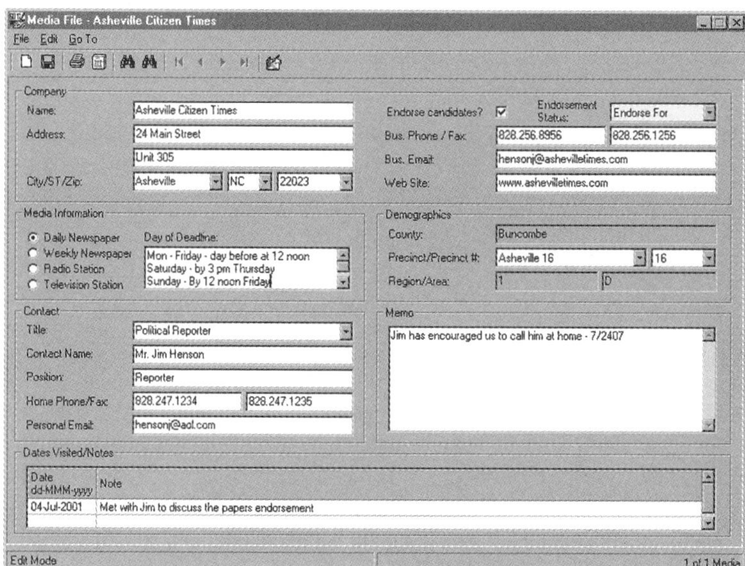

Media File

Naturally, due to the major role that the media plays in every campaign today, records should be maintained on all media outlets affecting the district, including the name of the contact persons for each outlet. Depending on the district, they could number in the 100s of records. These records need to be maintained separately to prevent accidental solicitation.

Records should be maintained on all media outlets affecting the district.

Vendor File

Campaigns need to maintain a list of vendors and track all disbursements.

The average campaign today has grown to be equivalent to the size of a small business. Of course, many have grown to be larger than most businesses. As such, there is a need to maintain a list of vendors, including vendor information, contact information, communication details, as well as the need to track purchases and payments.

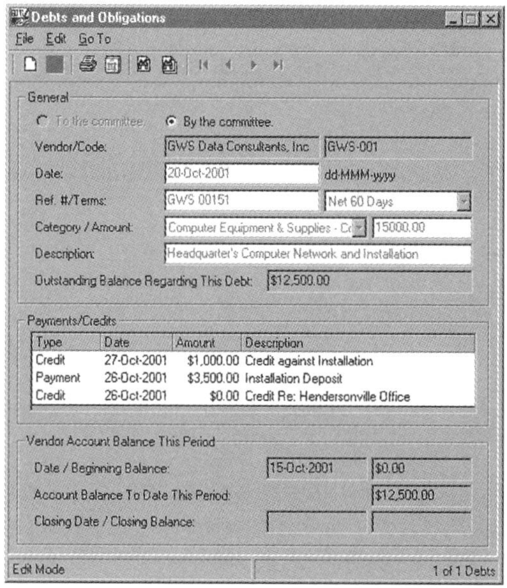

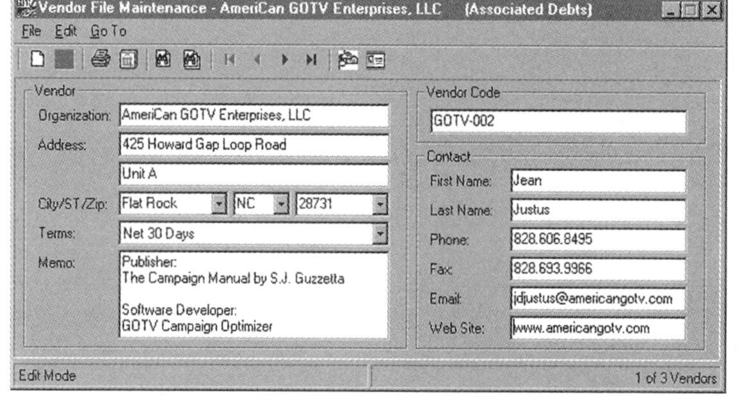

Financial reporting requirements include the tracking of all expenditures, debts, and obligations throughout the campaign, and afterwards, until they are retired. GOTV *Campaign Optimizer* was developed to include that function.

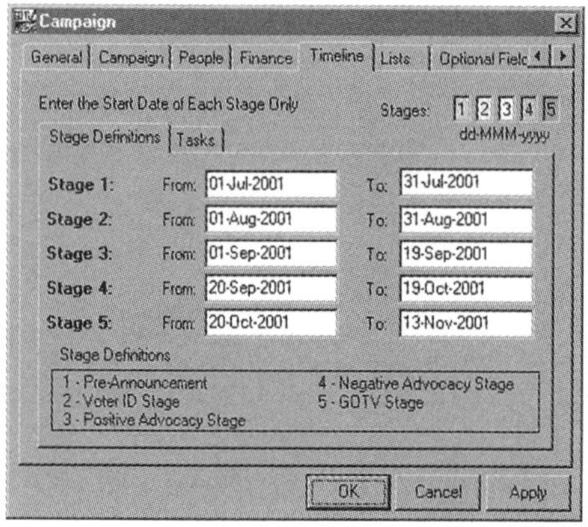

Campaign Timeline

The program generates a task reminder list to keep the campaign focused and on-time!

As discussed throughout *The Campaign Manual*, the campaign plan and strategy is developed in stages and tracked through each stage. GOTV *Campaign Optimizer* was developed to assist the campaign in defining the period devoted to each stage and to track the tasks that must be completed

Data is password protected.

within each stage. Each task can be defined and tracked until completed. In this way, the program will keep the campaign timeline both organized and visible.

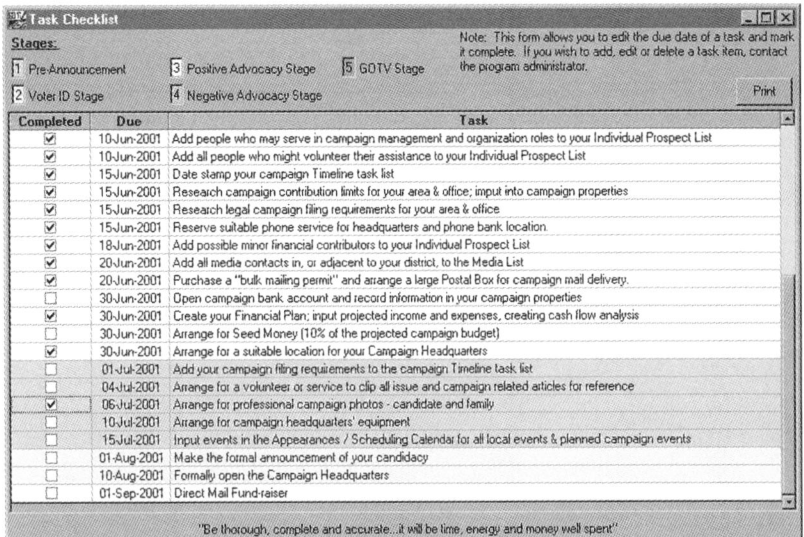

Task Checklist

Stages:
1 Pre-Announcement
2 Voter ID Stage
3 Positive Advocacy Stage
4 Negative Advocacy Stage
5 GOTV Stage

Note: This form allows you to edit the due date of a task and mark it complete. If you wish to add, edit or delete a task item, contact the program administrator.

Print

Completed	Due	Task
☑	10-Jun-2001	Add people who may serve in campaign management and organization roles to your Individual Prospect List
☑	10-Jun-2001	Add all people who might volunteer their assistance to your Individual Prospect List
☑	15-Jun-2001	Date stamp your campaign Timeline task list
☑	15-Jun-2001	Research campaign contribution limits for your area & office; imput into campaign properties
☑	15-Jun-2001	Research legal campaign filing requirements for your area & office
☑	15-Jun-2001	Reserve suitable phone service for headquarters and phone bank location
☑	18-Jun-2001	Add possible minor financial contributors to your Individual Prospect List
☑	20-Jun-2001	Add all media contacts in, or adjacent to your district, to the Media List
☑	20-Jun-2001	Purchase a "bulk mailing permit" and arrange a large Postal Box for campaign mail delivery.
☐	30-Jun-2001	Open campaign bank account and record information in your campaign properties
☑	30-Jun-2001	Create your Financial Plan; input projected income and expenses, creating cash flow analysis
☐	30-Jun-2001	Arrange for Seed Money (10% of the projected campaign budget)
☑	30-Jun-2001	Arrange for a suitable location for your Campaign Headquarters
☐	01-Jul-2001	Add your campaign filing requirements to the campaign Timeline task list
☐	04-Jul-2001	Arrange for a volunteer or service to clip all issue and campaign related articles for reference
☑	06-Jul-2001	Arrange for professional campaign photos - candidate and family
☐	10-Jul-2001	Arrange for campaign headquarters' equipment
☐	15-Jul-2001	Input events in the Appearances / Scheduling Calendar for all local events & planned campaign events
☐	01-Aug-2001	Make the formal announcement of your candidacy
☐	10-Aug-2001	Formally open the Campaign Headquarters
☐	01-Sep-2001	Direct Mail Fund-raiser

"Be thorough, complete and accurate...it will be time, energy and money well spent"

The stages of the campaign are defined from start to Election Day within Campaign Properties. This area of the program, as well as the financial data, is password protected for your campaign's security.

After the stages of the Campaign are defined, the individual tasks can be added and date stamped for completion. In this way, there is a daily tracking of all campaign task requirements from strategic inception to completion, enabling the campaign plan to stay both organized and on-track.

Request For Appearance and Scheduling

File Edit Go To

General
Entry Date/Priority: 07/13/2001 Candidate - Normal
Title/Type of Event: Interview Panel

Event Host
Organization: Asheville Citizen Times
Organization Address: 24 Main Street
City/ST/Zip: Asheville NC 22023
Phone/Fax: 828.256.8956 828.256.1256
Email/Website: hensonj@ashevilletimes.c www.ashevilletimes.com
Requested By: Jim Henson
Requested Address: 24 Howard Avenue
City/ST/Zip: Hendersonville NC 28731
H/W Phone: 828.247.1234 828.247.5269
Personal Fax/Email: 828.247.1235 hensonj@aol.com

Memo

Event Details
Date/Time From - To: 27-Jul-2001 1:00 PM 2:30 PM 00:00 am/pm
Event Scheduled For: Substitute?
Event Location: Asheville Citizen Times
Event Contact/Phone: Jo Cats 828.247.5269 Ext 21
Activity/Attendance: Panel Interview 5
Is event open to ? Public? Fundraiser?
Is event open to ? Media? Literature Distribution?
Is event open to ? Q.&A.? Speaking Engagement?
Invitee's Guest: / Other Dignitaries:

Demographics
County: Buncombe
Precinct: Asheville 16 16
Region/Area: 1 D

Event Approval
Approval Pending / Auto: After mm/dd/yyyy
Approved/Date/By: 17-Jul-2001 JDJ
Not Approved/Date/By:
Confirmation Sent/Date/By: 17-Jul-2001 JDJ

Edit Mode 1 of 1 Appearances

Appearance Scheduling

A major consideration in any campaign is appearance scheduling. Since the candidate and those substituting in candidate activities must stay both organized and on schedule, a flexible and capable appearance module is of paramount importance.

In a campaign environment, many details need to be tracked regarding appearance scheduling in order to avoid disappointment, embarrassment, confusion, and even chaos. GOTV *Campaign Optimizer* provides a scheduling form that enables the collection of all the pertinent details that the Candidate will require. In addition, the form is tied to both an event calendar and daytimer to keep all appearances organized and at one's fingertips.

Organization circumvents confusion and chaos.

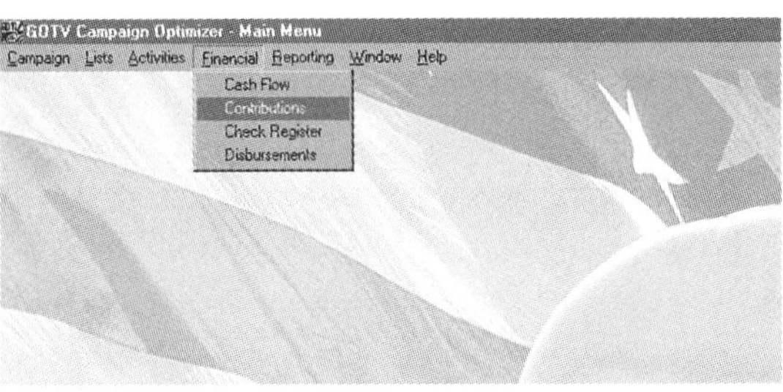

Financial Data

The financial requirements of campaigning continue to grow rapidly. Due to the rising cost of today's campaign, the need to solicit financial support from every source continues to grow as well. Correspondingly, since the Candidate is responsible for the proper use and administration of these solicited campaign funds, the restrictions and regulations regarding their tracking, use, and reporting to regulatory agencies is more

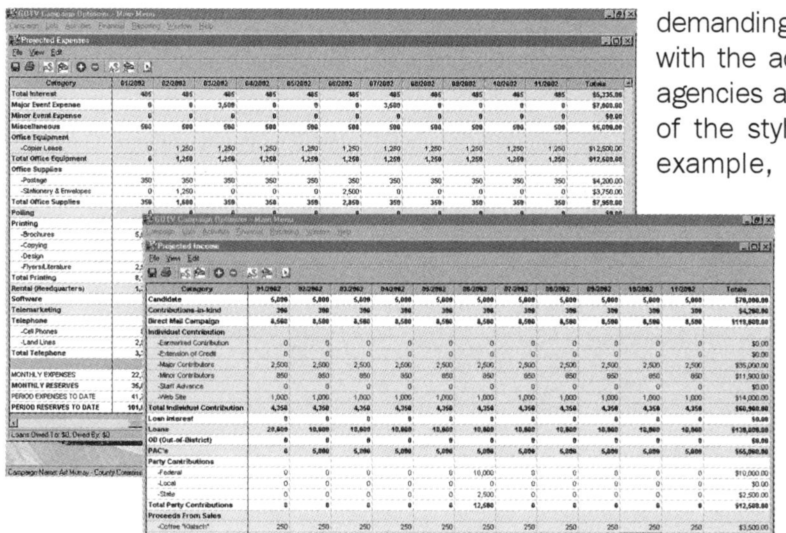

demanding with each election cycle. In addition, with the advent of the technical ability to do so, agencies are becoming more demanding in terms of the style with which reporting is done. For example, in early 2001 the Federal Election Commission made it mandatory to file all campaign finance reports electronically. Most States are following this trend. Nonetheless, although it is not presently mandatory on the State level (at this writing), many States are able to process electronic filings.

These are simply some of the reasons that GOTV *Campaign Optimizer* has been developed to efficiently track contributions, campaign expenditures, and monitor data against regulatory restrictions. As well, it is programmed to file the financial reports required for Federal, State, and local level campaigns.

A well developed campaign finance plan begins with a well organized campaign budget.

As discussed in the preceding chapters, your campaign finance plan begins with your campaign budget. The Cash Flow tools include a Projected Income and Expense spreadsheet to be used to track contributions and expenses against the Actual Income and Expense sheets.

Actual Expenses

File View Edit

Category	07/2001	08/2001
Campaign Consultant's Expenses	0.00	0.00
Candidate's Expenses	0.00	0.00
Computer Equipment & Supplies	0.00	0.00
Deposits		
-Rental	0.00	0.00
-Telephone	0.00	0.00
Total Deposits	**0.00**	**0.00**
Direct Mail	400.00	0.00
Postage	0.00	0.00
Printing		
-Brochures	0.00	0.00
-Copying	0.00	0.00
-Design	0.00	0.00
-Direct Mail Material	0.00	0.00
-Flyers/Literature	0.00	0.00
-Stationery/Envelopes	0.00	0.00
Total Printing	**0.00**	**0.00**
Rental (Headquarters)	0.00	0.00
Software	495.00	0.00
Telemarketing	0.00	0.00
Telephone		
-Cell Phones	0.00	0.00
-Land Lines	0.00	0.00
Total Telephone	**0.00**	**0.00**
Utilities		
-Heat	0.00	0.00
-Hydro	0.00	0.00
Total Utilities	**0.00**	**0.00**
MONTHLY EXPENSES	895.00	0.00
MONTHLY RESERVES	**1,355.00**	**0.00**
PERIOD EXPENSES TO DATE	895.00	895.00
PERIOD RESERVES TO DATE	**1,355.00**	**1,355.00**

Actual Income

File View Edit

Category	07/2001	08/2001
Candidate	0.00	0.00
Contributions-in-kind	0.00	0.00
Direct Mail Campaign	250.00	0.00
Individual Contribution		
-Anonymous	0.00	0.00
-Earmarked Contribution	0.00	0.00
-Endorsement / Guarantee	0.00	0.00
-Extension of Credit	0.00	0.00
-Major Contributors	1,000.00	0.00
-Minor Contributors	0.00	0.00
-Staff Advance	0.00	0.00
-Web Site	0.00	0.00
Total Individual Contribution	**1,000.00**	**0.00**
Loans	0.00	0.00
OD (Out-of-District)	0.00	0.00
PAC's	1,000.00	0.00
Party Contributions		
-Federal	0.00	0.00
-Local	0.00	0.00
-State	0.00	0.00
Total Party Contributions	**0.00**	**0.00**
Proceeds From Sales		
-Coffee "Klatsch"	0.00	0.00
-Major Events	0.00	0.00
-Minor Events	0.00	0.00
Total Proceeds From Sales	**0.00**	**0.00**
MONTHLY INCOME	2,250.00	0.00
MONTHLY RESERVES	**1,355.00**	**0.00**
PERIOD INCOME TO DATE	2,250.00	2,250.00
PERIOD RESERVES TO DATE	**1,355.00**	**1,355.00**

After the projected budget has been created, the campaign finance committee will be clear on both how much money is needed and at what time interval these contributions will be necessary in order to meet expenses.

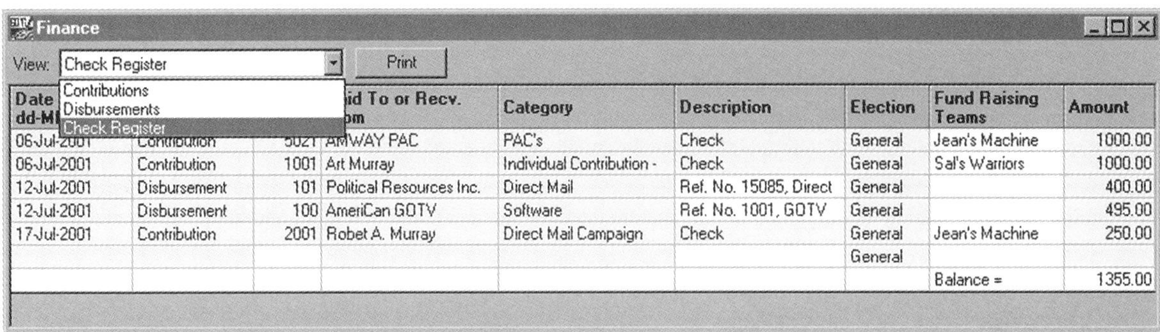

Financial tracking is accomplished through the Contribution Journal, Disbursement Journal, and Check Register, creating an Actual Income and Expense report, by month and by period.

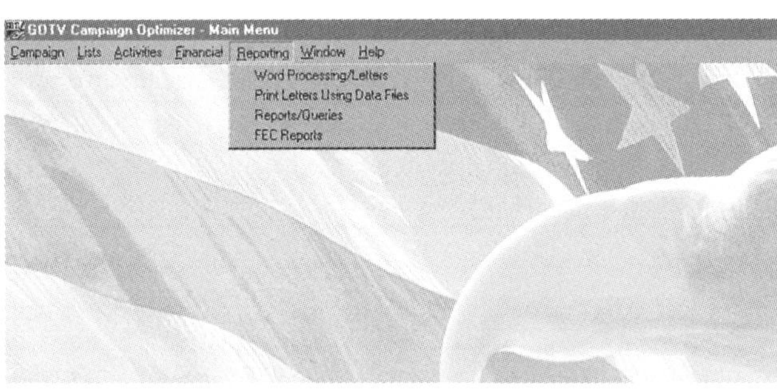

Reporting

As we have discussed, communicating with the voters is a major component of every campaign. With GOTV *Campaign Optimizer*, you have the benefit of its completely integrated word processor, which enables the user to create any number of communication documents. The processor is also compatible with today's most widely used commercial processors. In addition, through its query and merging process, the results of a search for voters can be merged with any document, personalizing the document, and targeting its delivery. Consider for a moment, mail personalization. Do you pay more attention to a mail piece addressed to you personally, or to mail addressed to "The Occupant"? With the cost of voter communication rising regularly, this process enables the campaign to focus the communication on the group that is most concerned with any given issue. In this way, major savings can be attained through targeting your message to those who care about the issue and reducing the waste of resources otherwise expended sending issue messages to those who are neither interested nor affected. In addition, you can reduce the cost of a service bureau with the ability to complete this task in-house.

Think about it!
Do you pay more attention to mail addressed to you personally, or to mail addressed to "The Occupant?"

Find: Voter
Basic | Advanced | Saved
Search: Voter — Where: DOB
on or before — 1980/01/01
Sort: Ascending
Add

Item	Criteria	Value 1	Value 2
DOB	on or before	1980/01...	
Region	equals	1	
Sex	begins with	m	
Party	begins with	UNA	

Save | Find Now | Cancel

Queries

Besides the standard query reports that are offered with the program, GOTV *Campaign Optimizer* has a superior query generator that will enable the user to search for the combination of any set of criteria that the campaign requires.

This example illustrates a search for all males, over 21 years of age, registered as Democrats, and residing in Region 1. The query process is completely flexible and the number of criteria set against the search is defined by the user and by the search requirements. Each search criteria can be saved and/or edited for a different focus. Saved search criteria can be used to create a mail merge at any time.

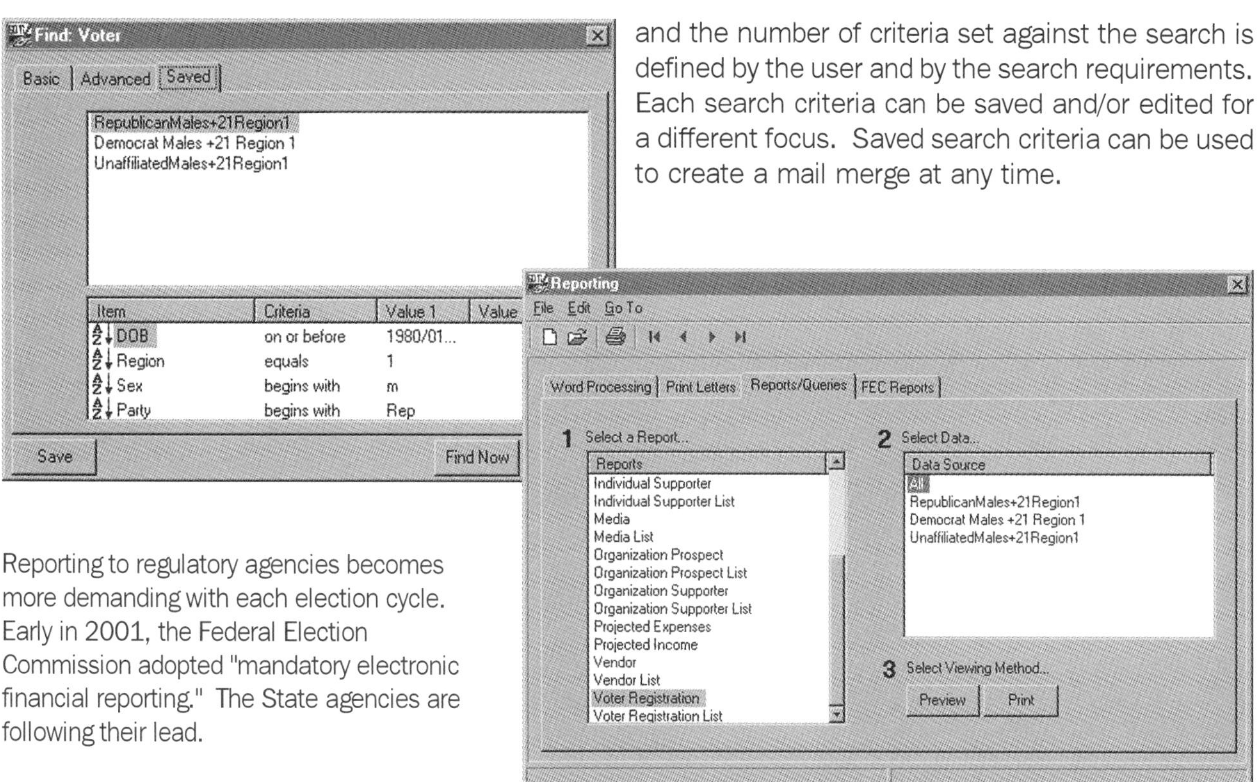

Reporting to regulatory agencies becomes more demanding with each election cycle. Early in 2001, the Federal Election Commission adopted "mandatory electronic financial reporting." The State agencies are following their lead.

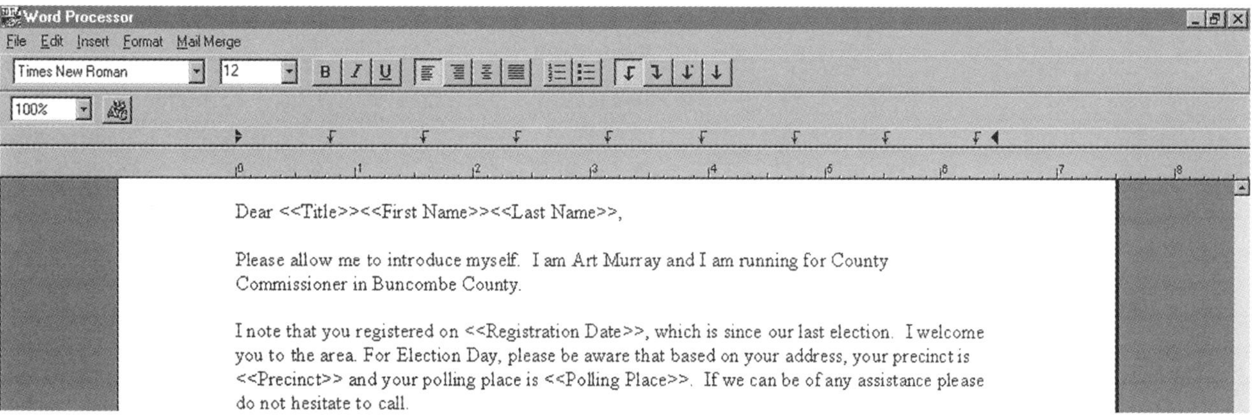

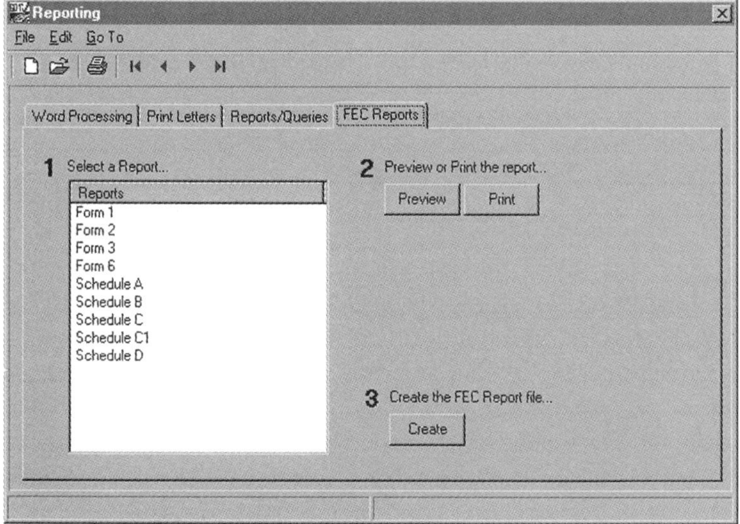

Financial Reporting

All election campaigns must comply with the rules and regulations regarding either Federal Election Commission or the State Board of Election. GOTV *Campaign Optimizer* has been programmed to record the financial data throughout the campaign and create the required campaign finance report whenever necessary.

The truism for the 21st Century will be, *"the candidate having the best campaign strategy in conjunction with the most current technology, will win, almost every election."*

In Conclusion

The average volunteer will work only 20 hours throughout the average campaign. A single computer will eliminate the need for thousands of volunteer hours.

In the first two chapters of *The Campaign Manual*, I have outlined a vast amount of work that the serious candidate needs to do in order to achieve his or her goal to be elected to office. I continue to turn your attention to a similar workload in each of the remaining chapters. Since the average volunteer will only contribute 20 hours to each campaign, a virtual army of volunteers would be required to complete the workload necessary, if all were attempted manually. In addition, time is also a major consideration. As discussed, campaigns are always constrained by a tight timeline.

Finally, and perhaps the most important factor of all is one of weaponry. We have discussed in detail the advantage of having a weapon at your disposal that your opponent does not have. I have expressed the need to match your opponent weapon for weapon, and have discussed the critical disadvantage of having fewer weapons at your disposal than does your opponent. In today's campaigning environment, the computer system in conjunction with the software used is a weapon. To have it, is an advantage over your opponent. For a manual campaign to challenge a computerized campaign, is similar to the Tortoise challenging the Hare. Of course, the Tortoise won that contest, but we all know that the victory was a fluke, and that the Tortoise should never have gained access to the winner's circle. To leave your campaign success dependent on a lucky break, or fluke, would be nothing less than foolish.

It is for these very reasons that I can not state more strongly, or more clearly, my belief that in today's campaign, you need to couple the working ability of a computer, or better yet a network of computers, with a very capable campaign management software application. I have spent a considerable amount of my time and energy, both updating this 6th Edition, and consulting on the extensive project to write a software application based on my campaign (management) knowledge and experience, and *The Campaign Manual*. We have completed this project and call the application GOTV *Campaign Optimizer*.

Forgive my bias, but GOTV *Campaign Optimizer* is the very best campaign management software application on the market today.

I will not attempt to sell you on this program other than to say, that in my opinion, and in the opinion of my colleagues, GOTV *Campaign Optimizer* is the very best campaign management software application on the market today. If you forgive my bias regarding my belief that *The Campaign Manual* is the very best campaign manual in publication, then you will accept my bias regarding its sequel software.

I have continued to reference "how" a computer and capable software program will reduce the workload and manage the information flow both during and after the campaign. Yes, after! Be mindful, that the need for this assistance does not end with your successful election to office. Your first election victory is, in fact, just the beginning. Once elected, you have set the stage for your need to either stay elected to the present office of your choosing or move on to a higher office where you will be able to serve your community on a larger scale. In either case, the *information gathering* that you have compiled from all that research that you have completed, in conjunction with the information gathering that you will continue to do, will be invaluable to you in the next campaign when you come to terms with your need to be "re-elected." In fact, the only data that may not be valuable during your future campaigns will be the specific information that you have gathered on your present opponent, unless of course, he or she challenges you next time out.

Knowledge is a weapon. Arm yourself accordingly!

I have referred to knowledge as a weapon. Make no mistake about it, it is! You will find it so much more efficient *to gather and build* your information (knowledge) base, if you have invested in a computer system and a powerful campaign management software that will make campaigning, not only more productive, but more cost effective as well. In addition, it will make you a more competitive incumbent for your present office, or challenger for your next office. GOTV *Campaign Optimizer* is that software.

GOTV *Campaign Optimizer* has all the charts that we have reviewed thus far available within its electronic document base. You need only do your research based on their guidance, posting the information that you have gathered. Consider the time and effort that this alone will save.

GOTV *Campaign Optimizer* is fully capable of downloading your local registered voter electronic file. It can sort and target your communication. It can execute all of your word processing needs and create all your mail merges. GOTV *Campaign Optimizer* enables you to link an electronic list of names and addresses to a specific letter, targeting a specific group, sorted from your registered voter list.

Regardless of which software program or configuration of hardware the campaign decides to use, the important thing is to computerize the campaign.

Throughout *The Campaign Manual*, I have discussed the needs of a capable campaign management software application and the tasks that it *should do* in order to assist you in achieving your goal. **GOTV *Campaign Optimizer* does them all.** It is that simple!

Campaigning and The Internet

The Internet's place in American Political History as a campaigning and political information tool is not yet clearly defined or decided.

Throughout *The Campaign Manual,* I have discussed campaigning in detail through technology and computerization, television, radio, newspapers, direct mail, telephones, and where it all started, door to door. I have not yet devoted time on how campaigning relates to the world's fastest growing communication tool, the Internet. The reason is simple; the Internet's place in American Political History as a campaigning and political information tool is not yet clearly defined or decided. Nonetheless, the Internet has developed a major following throughout the 90's and there is no evidence of its popularity slowing as we travel into the New Millenium. It is unlikely that political circles will ignore this trend.

Since the Internet, as a political weapon, is still in its embryo stage and changing rapidly, I will express my opinion, but wish to make it very clear that my opinion on this subject is subject to change. The Internet, as a medium, is changing far too quickly to appropriately address it in a manual such as this. The moment that a statement is made, it is dated by definition due to the rapid changing nature of both the Internet and its associated technology.

I believe that the Internet and its use in political circles is here, and here to stay.

In any event, since I am unable to predict the future, I will reserve my opinion to the present facts and trends as they relate to *The Campaign Manual*. Based

At this writing, I strongly encourage the development of a candidates web site and the use of electronic communication.

on the logic and strategies presented within the manual, at this writing, I strongly encourage the development of a candidates web site and the use of electronic communication for the following reasons:

1) It should be clear by now that I strongly believe in the need to wage the campaign battle by matching weapon against weapon. If your opponent has a web site, then *you will need one*.

2) It should also be clear that I believe strongly in attempting to use every advantage over your opponent. Therefore, you may prosper by having a web site if your opponent does not or you may prosper if your web site is better utilized than is your opponent's.

3) I believe strongly in delivering as much positive information as possible to the above average voter. Since I believe that the above average voter seeks candidate information, I make the assumption that even if the average voter spends little time searching candidate web sites, the above average voter likely does.

4) I believe that skillfully developed Candidate Web Sites will be an inexpensive and successful tool for campaign fund-raising, more and more as we move forward.

Remember that "jokes" about a "bad" site will travel far faster and far further than will news about a great site.

Having stated reasons in favor of developing a candidate web site, I caution you that I also believe that just as with every other campaigning weapon, poorly done, poorly utilized, poorly timed, or any other negative perception seen by the voting public on a candidate's web site will hurt the chances for success. Remember that "jokes" about a "bad" site will travel far faster and far further than will news about a great site.

I caution you, that although I believe that the Internet and its use in political circles is here, and here to stay, I also expect that its use will be most successful for those who use it in new and innovative ways, rather than for those who simply copy what is there at present. In addition, more so than in any other communication method, the Internet viewers expect, and even demand sites to be new and exciting. Viewers have no interest in re-reading a campaign biographical or position paper that they have already received through your direct mail program. They will want something fresh, something different, and something worth returning for. That's not to say that the biographical and position papers should not be there, but you can not afford to post those early campaign materials alone and consider the job done. They do not say a web site is "under construction" because it is finished. In fact, a great web site is always under construction. Be advised, if the content does not change the viewer will have no reason to return, or suggest that a friend or family member visit the site.

Definition
"Spam" is a funky Internet term referring to the practice of flooding the Internet with many copies of the same message.

Even those of us who are not, "Internet savvy" have probably heard of "spam." "Spam" is a funky Internet term referring to the practice of flooding the Internet with many copies of the same message in an attempt to force the message on people who would not otherwise choose to receive it. This is deemed an abuse against users of the electronic mail system and is the equivalent of uninvited flyers (junk mail) on your front porch when you return from work each evening. Junk mail annoys most of us. In the same manner, sending messages to the masses is equally annoying and a major mistake. You will simply anger the majority of Internet users, many of which are voters.

The Internet does present a communication opportunity, somewhat like electronic door to door canvassing.

On the other hand, the Internet does present a communication opportunity, somewhat like electronic door to door canvassing and its value when used in an appropriate manner should not be ignored. Your site should encourage questions and comments from viewers. Inquiries should be answered promptly and the best of the questions and answers should be posted for others to see and enable them to join in the dialogue. Your campaign newsletter should be available to any viewer who wishes a copy. The viewer should be encouraged to register to receive campaign updates, to volunteer their time, and/or contribute to the campaign. The essential element here is to give the viewer the opportunity to pick-and-choose from an assortment of opportunities. This opportunity to feel involved will be appreciated; receiving indiscriminate "spam" at their e-mail address without concern for their privacy and freedom of choice will simply annoy them. Finally, when given the "ok" to communicate with a voter through e-mail, do not inundate them with mail, but do keep them informed. While on the subject of communication, make sure that your contact information is user friendly and handy to every page. Be sure that your internal structure is able to answer each e-mail. The viewer does not necessarily expect to hear from the Candidate in each case, but will expect to hear from the campaign. The individual who answers the mail should be clearly identified.

Seriously consider a professional designer. Amateur web sites are easily spotted.

It is most important to seriously consider the expense of a professional designer. Amateur web sites are easily spotted from the professional sites. A true webmaster is knowledgeable in the ways and means of not only building a great site, but also keeping it fresh and updated. The webmaster will know what graphic is too slow to download to the average machine or too big to be viewed on the average monitor. It also takes an experienced designer to be familiar with how much animation is interesting and how much is simply too much. Miles and miles of text require the skills of a professional to break up its monotony. Since you not only want the viewer to return to your site, but also to tell friends and family to look at the site, make it different, interesting, and fun. This will likely necessitate the use of a professional web designer.

There are some facts about the Internet that we can not afford to ignore. One such fact is the growing pool of Internet connected households, now 40 million strong and growing stronger each day. The second fact, and maybe even more important than the first concerns who is using the Internet. Since surfing takes time, the young and the old dominate its use. This is most significant when attempting to predict the Internet's future political impact. The youth of today have become as devoted to the Internet as older generations are devoted to the television. I suggest then that the voters of tomorrow will not only be very "Internet savvy," they will be "glued" to the Internet, as we were "glued" to a TV. As for our Senior citizens, increasingly, they become "netizens," seeking out the new and the different offered over the Internet. As these two groups turn more and more to the Internet for their information, so to will the voters of tomorrow.

The voters of tomorrow will not only be very "Internet savvy," they will be "glued" to the Internet.

The future of fund-raising over the Internet has great potential.

The future of fund-raising over the Internet is also unclear. What is clear is that it has great potential. It is, if nothing else, efficient and inexpensive compared to traditional methods. What is clear, is that over 15 million households have made credit card purchases over the Internet in the last year and its use for commercial shopping continues to grow as shoppers continue to develop trust in its levels of security. What is also clear is that political web site fund-raising for the 2000 campaigns was in the millions of dollars, despite that amount being a very small percentage of the whole. What is unclear to me, is whether or not, these contributors would have contributed in the traditional ways, if they had been unable to contribute through a candidate's web site. In any event, the decision may be defined by whether or not the campaign can afford not to take advantage of the fund-raising opportunity offered by the Internet. It is very cost effective for the campaign and very convenient for the contributor. The best advice that I can give at this time is to rely on the advice of a professional regarding your final web site design and fund-raising decisions.

The best advice that I can give at this time is to rely on the advice of a professional regarding your final web site design and fund-raising decisions.

Web Site Facts - Campaign 2000

NetElection.org, a project of the Annenberg Public Policy Center of the University of Pennsylvania, released the following facts regarding the impact of the Internet on campaign 2000. The entire study is available through the NetElection.org web site.

1) Fifty six percent of all candidates on the general election ballots in House and Senate races operated web sites promoting their candidates.
2) The web sites were identified as paid for with campaign funds.
3) Of those web enthusiasts using the web every day, sixty-six percent used the web to follow politics on a national level. This figure dropped in half (33%) for Statewide and Congressional races and to twenty six percent for local races.
4) Over ninety percent claimed to use the Internet as a political news source due to its convenience and ability to search multiple news sources.
5) Thirty nine percent used the Internet to enable them to give their opinion on what was being read.
6) Over eighty percent posted the candidate's biography and position papers, which was desired by eighty one percent of web enthusiasts.
7) Sixty percent of the candidate sites accepted contributions, while only three percent provided the list of contributors of interest to thirty six percent of enthusiasts.
8) Sixty percent wanted to see comparative content, but few sites offered any.
9) Forty four percent were interested in an archive of candidate material, i.e. press releases, speeches (provided by 13%), and advertisements (provided by 6%).
10) Sixteen percent of the web enthusiasts indicated an interest in a moderated discussion forum, but only 3% of the sites provided such a feature.
11) Sixty eight percent of sites offered volunteer sign-up facilitation.
12) Forty four percent collected an e-mail address for continuing contact.

Steven M. Schneider authored the report from which these statistics have been drawn. Jennifer Stromer-Galley authored the survey. Schneider and Kirsten A. Foot directed the web site analysis.

Campaign 2000

• 56% of all candidates operated web sites.

• 66% of web enthusiasts use the web to follow national politics.

• 60% of candidate sites accepted contributions.

Questions and comments should be directed to the author at sschneider@asc.upenn.edu.

The Bottom Line

What is known, is that the Internet is here, and here to stay.

The use of the Internet as a tool in political campaigns continues to develop as rapidly as the technology that supports this environment. Neither its impact to date, nor exactly what impact it will have in future campaigns is known. What is known, is that the Internet is here, and here to stay.

It is clear that the Internet must be incorporated into your campaign strategy, and that you must engage professional assistance in order to take the fullest advantage of its power.

Since it is clear that the majority of campaigns are presently using the Internet as a tool to communicate to the electorate and as a tool to raise funds, it is clear that it must be incorporated into your campaign strategy. It is my advice, that since this is a new, growing, and developing opportunity, you must engage professional assistance in order to take the fullest advantage of its power. Every indication is that a well-built and well-maintained Internet web site can contribute to the campaigning process, if only to Internet enthusiasts. Enthusiasts whose numbers continue to grow exponentially.

As I have said earlier, despite having no idea where the technology train will take us, we had better get on board, since winning is our goal.

Chapter 12 - Word Index

Chapter 13
Variations for Other Type Campaigns

Size
Congressional District campaigns are usually 500,000 people or more.

Congressional Size Campaigns

The Prototype Plan used in the previous chapters is based on an urban/suburban district with a relatively compact media market. At least three other types of districts and three common situations would necessitate a fundamental change in the methodology used to achieve the campaign's objectives. They are:

A semi-rural district.
A rural district.
An urban or suburban district in a major metropolitan area.
A district without a local media market.
A district with open registration.
A contested primary.

Size
Semi-Rural
District will contain two or three medium sized cities with a population of 75,000 - 125,000

A Semi-Rural District

Normally this district will contain two or three medium sized cities with a population of 75,000 - 125,000 and be less homogeneous than an urban/ suburban district, with a smaller spread of ethnic and/or racial backgrounds. It would contain relatively equal amounts of light industry, medium industry, and agriculture, have multiple media markets, lack a dominant local daily newspaper, and will be spread over an area of around 1,000 square miles. This area is too small for the use of aircraft, too large to cover by car in a single day, and will normally cover at least four or five counties.

In the organizational structure, each county would probably be designated as a Region, regardless of individual population, and then be sub-divided into the five Areas according to the same guidelines in the Prototype Plan.

The campaign will have to analyze and develop each Region's individual objectives, as a slightly different campaign strategy will probably need to be developed for each Region. This will involve intensive precinct operations in the Regions with cities and a Phone Bank only in the more rural Regions. Without one of the field operation's safety nets in the more rural Regions, the risk will be greater that the objectives will not be fully realized. This factor will have to be taken into consideration when doing the calculations.

In addition, the campaign will probably be more dependent on local Party committees, organizations, and candidates for assistance in all stages relevant to field operations. Normally a quid pro quo arrangement can be worked out where these entities will supply volunteers in exchange for paid support services and materials, such as headquarters, slate card mailers, and computer services. The campaign must develop Regional/County Finance Committees that operate semi-autonomously. Major events will be more difficult to promote and the campaign will probably have to hold each event at two locations in different parts of the district.

Generally, these types of districts have very parochial counties, each one is like a small fiefdom presenting unique problems for the campaign. Whereas, a Candidate can operate somewhat independently of the local Party and elected officials in an urban/suburban district, if necessary, it is almost impossible to do so in this type of district. Candidates will find that many of these individuals jealously guard their territory and might work against them if they attempt to campaign independent of them and the county ticket. Regrettably, there is often deep-rooted competition between the various county bosses. The Candidate should be careful about who is appointed to the Advisory Committee. If it is loaded too heavily from one county, he or she could be asking for serious internal campaign problems because of this jealousy factor.

Greater care must be taken and more energy expended to consolidate the Candidate's base in this type of district. There will also be additional costs for extra headquarters, telephones, equipment, supplies, and staff personnel.

The free media program will also have to be based on Regional lines. The number of releases will stay constant, as in the Prototype Plan, but will be multiplied by each county's media outlets. With a few exceptions, the campaign will find most county outlets will not cover political news that has happened in another county. Drop-ins at local radio stations and newspapers are a strong must.

Since the industries are diversified, the Candidate will have to become an expert in each area's problems and solutions. In addition, the style of campaigning will vary considerably. A candidate would not arrive to tour a local dairy farm in a three-piece suit and wing tip shoes.

Ironically, the Candidate will have to campaign harder, yet will see fewer people because of the extra travel time involved. If possible, the Candidate should start to campaign full-time at the beginning of the 2nd Stage. In addition, the Candidate will have to concentrate more time on the fairs, festivals, and parades during the 3rd Stage, simply because there are more of them. To compensate, decrease activity at plant gates and shopping centers.

The campaign vehicle should be a van equipped as though it were a mobile office and a room on wheels for a place to change clothes, freshen up, and stretch out between the long runs. Make sure it has air-conditioning, automatic drive, a tape deck, and cruise control. It will also be used extensively to deliver supplies and equipment to the Regional and Area Chairpersons. Paint the campaign logo on each side of the van so that it also becomes a moving campaign advertisement.

The campaign's billboard spread will require a larger number of boards to achieve the same GRP rating. Fortunately, the rental rates are usually less in these districts. Therefore, the budget should not have to be increased substantially. Rely more heavily on unlighted corrugated 4 x 8 signs since they are less expensive. Lighted signs are unnecessary in rural areas.

Since the media market is so widespread, chances are the campaign will be unable to use TV advertising to the same extent as possible in the Prototype

Plan. Since seeing the Candidate is a necessary part of developing that very important sense of contact, I would recommend the campaign attempt some TV coverage, at least in the last 10 days of the campaign. Limit the spots to three (the biography for 3 days, the "attack" for 3 days, and the appeal for votes for 4 days). Exercise great care in placement in order to gain maximum exposure. The campaign should also use pictures of the Candidate more extensively in window signs, billboards, tabloids, and even stationery. Be sure the quality of the photo is exceptionally good.

Expand the radio coverage using the same six spots as in the Prototype Plan on a 10, 20, 30, 40 basis to partially make up for the decrease in TV exposure. The same goes for the newspaper ads. Whereas this type of media is not that important in an urban/suburban district, it is essential in this type of district. Endorsement ads are especially effective.

The direct mail will be about the same as in the Prototype Plan in both quantity and targeting. I recommend a special edition of a tabloid, heavy on pictures, for hand distribution at fairs and festivals. The use of a slide presentation or video is also recommended as a permanent feature in the campaign booth at all fairs.

In the GOTV Stage, the campaign will probably have to rely more heavily on host homes for telephoning in order to keep the long distance costs down.

The budget for this type of campaign will be about the same as in the Prototype Plan. The extra costs for billboards, signs, radio, newspaper ads, staff, and transportation should be offset by the reduced costs for TV.

Size
Primarily farm districts with a large number of small cities and towns with a population of 5,000 - 75,000.

A Rural District

These districts are primarily farm districts with a large number of small cities and towns with a population of 5,000 - 75,000. They will usually contain two or three dominant ethnic groups, have a small amount of light industry, multiple media markets, will lack a dominant daily newspaper, and will be spread over an area of several thousand square miles consisting of 20 counties, sometimes more.

In a district of this type, a Region will consist of 5 or more counties; each county will become an Area. To avoid potential conflicts with local Party county chairpersons, the campaign should designate its county chairperson the Area Chairperson.

Precinct operations are impractical, perhaps impossible, in a rural district. The Phone Bank program is the only viable means to realize the field operation's objectives. Since the cost of a Phone Bank in each county would be prohibitive, the campaign is almost totally dependent on volunteers making the necessary calls from their homes. It is usual in the 4th and 5th stages to pool resources with the local county Party committee and candidates to form organized phone banks. This system is not as effective as having the campaign's own Phone Bank, but it would be helpful. The other option is to establish a bank of ten interstate WATS lines in the base area where there should be an adequate supply of volunteers to work them and make all calls from that central location. In the end, this might be the most cost-effective method. With the constant change of telephone calling rates and services available, check with one of the major carriers and investigate the most economical arrangement.

Since one of the safety nets (precinct operations) has been eliminated, the campaign runs a greater risk of not reaching its objectives. To offset this risk, the campaign should factor this into the calculations of vote objectives increasing the safety margin by 10 percent.

The Finance Committee structure and other operations would be the same as in a semi-rural district, as is the heavier dependence on county Party organizations. The previous caveats regarding the sensitivities of county chairpersons also apply here.

The free media program and the Candidate's personal campaign activities are the same as in the semi-rural district, only multiplied even further to adequately cover all the counties. In addition to a van equipped as previously mentioned, the campaign will also need to make arrangements for the occasional rental of a twin engine aircraft with a pilot and a copilot, for use when campaigning in the farthest Regions. Arrangements should be made with the Regional or Area Chairpersons to provide ground transportation on those days.

In addition, the billboard spread will have to be even greater, though unit costs will be less. Be more selective about positioning them and place even heavier emphasis on the corrugated 4 x 8 signs.

In these districts, although the media market for TV is diversified, the rates are usually low. Unless the campaign draws from a major market area, it can accomplish the same objectives as in the Prototype Plan. If this is the case, follow the buy outlines in the Prototype Plan, 10, 20, 30, 40, and use the six basic commercials. Radio usage and newspaper ads are essentially the same as those used in a semi-rural district. The direct mail program is the same as in the Prototype Plan.

Since there will not be a corresponding reduction in the TV portion of the budget to offset the increased costs of billboards, radio, newspaper ads, and signs, the campaign will have a higher budget than the one in the Prototype Plan. Minus the savings in the precinct operations, the net increase should be around $25,000.

An Urban or Suburban District in a Major Metropolitan Area

Size
Urban or Suburban District campaigns are usually 1,000,000 people or more.

These districts are usually contained within metropolitan areas of 1,000,000 people or more. The strategy and game plan is essentially the same as in the Prototype Plan with one major difference, i.e., the electronic media.

Radio and TV costs in these districts are usually prohibitive. As in a semi-rural district, the campaign might consider a short run on very well targeted programs. Use TV but no radio during the 10 days prior to the election. In conjunction, the Candidate should use his or her picture more extensively on printed material.

However, the main substitutes are increased direct mail, at least one extra piece to undecideds, independents, and unidentified members of the opposite Party. Significantly increase precinct walking by the Candidate, especially in the top four categories of prioritized precincts, i.e., 4, 5, 3, and 2. Since there will not be the same number of fairs to attend, the time should be available.

A stronger sign and weekly newspaper ad campaign is warranted. Building name ID in this type of district is difficult due to the large size of the average voter population. Many voters here are not even sure what congressional district they reside in. To the extent that the campaign is able, flood the district with signs in windows, on lawns, poles, and fences.

Since even a short run on TV will be expensive, in addition to the added cost of extra signs and another direct mail piece, the budget will probably be higher than the Prototype Plan by $60,000.

A District without a Local Media Market

This district is essentially one that draws most of its electronic media from outside the boundaries of the district and state. Follow the appropriate guidelines already given as to the other factors regarding this type of District.

What makes this district's problem unique is the lack of interest in the race that exists on the part of the media outlets serving the district. This greatly reduces the free media coverage other candidates are able to generate and it increases whatever costs may exist for paid media.

Increase the direct mail and sign programs, as in the urban or suburban type district, and increase the TV and radio budget to enable use of the same format and amount of coverage as in the Prototype Plan. Depending on the cost factors involved, the campaign should consider using five-minute spots, strategically placed, during the month of September. The campaign's Political Media Consultant or ad agency will explain how these work technically and the specific costs involved.

Depending on the location, the budget will probably have to be increased between $60,000 and $100,000 to make up for this loss of free media coverage.

A District in a State with Open Registration

There are still a few states in the country that do not allow their residents to declare Party affiliation when registering to vote and continue to have open primaries. The voter selects the Party's primary they are going to vote in when they go to the polling place. This situation presents a unique problem to the candidate. It is solved, at least partially, by a redirection of the targeting and an increased direct mail program in the 2nd and 5th Stages.

Since the Candidate does not know who the members of his or her Party are, the campaign must follow the percentages with the direct mail pieces in the 2nd and 5th Stages. Expand those mailings to all voters in prioritized precincts 1, 2, and 3. Then change the campaigning and field operation direction from a 4, 5, 3, 2, 1, 6 priority schedule to 4, 3, 2, 1, 5, 6. Again, you will be going with the percentages.

All other factors, type of district and media situations apply, having little or no relevance to this added situation.

The differential in the budget for the extra direct mail will probably be an increase of $30,000, plus or minus $5,000 depending on the actual numbers involved.

One other possible problem exists that a Candidate should be aware of that occasionally occurs in a district with open primaries. Sometimes an opponent or a supporting organization will attempt to "sandbag" a Candidate by encouraging a person to run against him or her in the Primary. The word then goes out to that opponent's supporters to vote for the dummy candidate in the Primary who, if he or she is the winner, then "packs it in" during the General election. This guarantees a win for the opponent, or the organization that engineered the "sandbag" in the first place. As strange as this may seem, it does happen. In fact, there are some cases where several dummy candidates have been encouraged to run. What makes it so tempting is that even if the dummy Candidate does not win, the serious Candidate, whose Primary race he or she enters, is forced to spend a considerable amount of resources to beat him or her.

The only effective countermove that I have seen work is for the Candidate who is being sandbagged to make sure the opponent also has opposition in his or her Primary, so that his or her supporters are unable to cross over. This is done, of course, by encouraging someone to run against the opponent.

Other measures, like complaining to the media to counter this tactic, rarely seem to work as they require the dummy candidate to admit to being a "dummy" in public. Frankly, this tactic smacks of dirty tricks and I find it reprehensible. Unfortunately, it sometimes does happen and the campaign needs to be aware of it.

A Contested Primary

Other than the situation just discussed, a Candidate might find himself or herself in a legitimate primary race for his or her Party's nomination.

Essentially the Prototype Plan, with appropriate variations dependent on the district type and the campaign's base plan, is still applicable. However, with a contested primary, the Candidate must increase the number of stages, and in effect, superimpose another plan over it.

Chapter 13 - Variations for Other Type Campaigns

In the Prototype Plan, without a contested Primary, there are 5 Stages. Both will presume a 06/07/— Primary Election:

10/01/— 1st Stage: Pre-Announcement.
03/02/— 2nd Stage: Voter ID, all voters, build name ID.
06/08/— 3rd Stage: Positive Advocacy for undecideds and independents.
09/06/— 4th Stage: Negative Advocacy for undecideds.
10/19/— 5th Stage: GOTV - General Election.

With a Primary, there are 7 Stages:

10/01/— 1st Stage: Pre-Announcement.
02/04/— 2nd Stage: Voter ID for Party members only.
04/01/— 3rd Stage: Positive Advocacy for undecided Party members only.
05/21/— 4th Stage: GOTV - Primary Election.
06/08/— 5th Stage: Voter ID and Positive Advocacy for all voters minus Party members.
09/06/— 6th Stage: Negative Advocacy for undecideds and independents.
10/19/— 7th Stage: GOTV - General Election.

The announcement of candidacy is moved up one month to 02/01/—.

In the Primary, the field operation organization concentrates its activities among Party members only. Since this "field" is usually between one-fourth to one-third of the total electorate in an average district, the timeframes for each Stage are adequate to do the job. If the district has open registration, concentrate on the 1, 2, and 3 prioritized precincts whenever reference is made to "Party members."

In the 3rd Stage, the first direct mail piece would be similar to the Prototype Plan. A second direct mail piece would be sent to undecideds and unidentified Party members only, with a comparative flyer describing the differences between the Candidate and the closest opponent for the nomination. Remember that the Candidate is going to need the supporters of this opponent after the Primary, so stick to the issues and be factual. Instead of a letter, the campaign might consider using a tabloid since it is less expensive. Also, begin putting up lawn signs in this stage.

During the 4th Stage, a final GOTV mailer is sent to all Party members, in addition to, the contacts being made by field operations, except to those identified supporters of the opponent. On 5/28/—, the campaign should begin a 10-day run on TV and radio, carefully targeted to the demographics of the average Party members, subject to previously mentioned variations. Use three spots: a biography spot for 3 days, the issues spot for 3 days, and the appeal spot for 4 days.

The Candidate's personal campaign activity is geared almost exclusively to members of the Party. However, free media activity should be primarily directed against the presumed opponent in the General Election period, with only occasional releases directed against the Primary opponent. All the other types of releases follow the Prototype Plan.

The campaign will need additional polls. A mini-benchmark poll of 300 samples, with Party members only around 04/01/— and a follow up poll with 250 samples with Party members only should be done on 05/14/—. Both should be "weighted" by Region.

In the Prototype Plan, the increased costs would be approximately $40,000 for direct mail, $50,000 for radio and TV, $25,000 for polling, $15,000 for Administrative and Field Operations, and $20,000 for consultant fees. The total additional costs: $150,000.

This extra amount will have to be raised primarily in-district since, as mentioned before, PACs, ODs, and Party funds are rarely available to candidates in a contested Primary. The campaign will also need to add to this amount the funds that were anticipated in the Prototype Fund-raising Schedule, from outside sources before 06/07/—.

The Prototype Plan Cash Flow schedule calls for cumulative expenditures of around $300,000 as of June 7th. With the additional $150,000 needed for the Primary, the total amount would be about $450,000. Most of that would now have to be raised in-district. The Fund-raising Game Plan would have to be adjusted accordingly. The usual exception to receiving outside funds in a contested Primary is made when the perception of the experts indicate that the Primary opponent(s) are competition in name only and that the Candidate is a sure winner.

The most positive benefit of a contested Primary is the higher name ID the Candidate will realize as a result of the extra activity. A secondary benefit is the opportunity it presents to make sure the field operations program is well organized and working efficiently.

U.S. Senate, Gubernatorial, or Statewide Races

The basic strategy and Political Game Plan for a U.S. Senatorial, Gubernatorial, or other statewide campaign depends on a number of factors. Some are similar to those in a congressional race, others are quite different.

Some Similarities and Differences

The procedural and organization steps in the 1st Stage are essentially the same, as is the methodology used in calculating objectives and prioritization. Most of the activities and roles of the various players are also substantially the same, only on a different scale. There are more of them. The rules regarding voter behavioral patterns, i.e., average and above average, are about the same. Therefore, the dual campaign strategy with its programs designed for each group is also applicable. The need for safety nets to insure communications with the largest possible percentage of voters is equally important. Maximizing the use of free media is of even greater importance, but the methodology to accomplish this is essentially the same.

On all three levels of the campaign there are significant differences dependent on three basic factors, the first being the status of the Candidate. Most Senatorial or Gubernatorial candidates are existing officeholders and therefore have a voting record that can be identified and attacked, and a voter base (their present constituency) on which to build. Second, the size of the state population and/or geographic area will materially affect the budget, game plans, and the type of campaign activity done by the Candidate. Third, the availability of volunteers to do a field operations program similar to the Prototype Plan, to identify, inform, encourage support, and motivate voters to get out and vote.

1st - Status as a Previous Officeholder

The Candidate who has previously held office must essentially manage two campaign types simultaneously.

The Candidate who has previously held office, in addition to the type of research required in the 1st Stage of the Prototype Plan, must also do the type required of an incumbent. There must be a careful analysis of his or her previous voting record in conjunction with a reasonable defense of it. In effect, the specific advantage enjoyed by a non-office holding Candidate is lost. This could make the Candidate vulnerable unless the attack is anticipated and rebuttals are prepared. It is a good idea to have a committee established to play the devil's advocate and really "rake the Candidate over the coals" in mock debates to help him or her prepare for what is to come.

On the positive side, the Candidate does have a natural base of constituents on which to build. An appeal for financial and volunteer help should be made to them early in the campaign, beginning at least 6 months earlier in medium to larger states.

2nd - Size of the State Population / Geographic Area

When a state's size exceeds 6 million, the problems of size become such that adaptation from the Prototype Plan becomes very difficult.

Adaptations can readily be made from the Prototype Plan in states of up to about six million people, roughly 12 Congressional districts, but when a state's size exceeds that number, the problems of size become such that adaptation becomes very difficult. In very large states, it is very difficult to have a field operations program similar to the one in the Prototype Plan, except possibly in the Candidate's base area. Beyond that, the Candidate is almost totally dependent on a piggyback arrangement with local county Party committees and other candidates, especially those that are Congressional.

Essentially, the campaign becomes media oriented and the only valid method of checking progress is the professionally done poll.

This is one of the reasons why there is an inverse ratio regarding campaign unit costs per registered voter. In a Congressional race the campaign unit cost is about $1.50 per person. In a state with a population of, 3,000,000, the campaign unit cost is about $1.00 per person. By the time we reach a state with 10,000,000+ population, the campaign unit cost has dropped to about 75 cents per person. In effect, what is happening is the gradual reduction of the field operation's costs. Although there are increased expenses for staff, travel, administration, and paid media, there are many offsetting economies of scale. In addition, the more you buy, the lower the per unit cost.

3rd - Volunteers

In a district of this size, the volunteer scale should be at least 1000 per 500,000 of population or one for every 500 voters.

This third factor ties into the second, especially in the small to medium-sized states where a full field operations program is both feasible and necessary. If a substantial number of volunteers are available, at least 1,000 per 500,000 of population, the campaign can implement a full-scale field operations program with a reasonable percentage of the campaign budget. If volunteers are unavailable on that scale, the campaign may have to resort to paid telemarketers or a telephone system using interstate WATS lines from a central location. The program can also be modified if there are enough volunteers in the base area to use WATS lines from that geographic location to the rest of the state, whereas the campaign headquarters may be located elsewhere. Obviously, the cost of enough WATS lines to do the job properly is going to be expensive. WATS will increase cost by about 10 percent. Add the cost of paid telemarketers and it begins to equal the media budget, in effect, increasing the total budget by about 40 percent.

The number of WATS lines required will be dependent on the actual number of calls to be made and the length of time in each stage. If in a contested Primary, and most of these types of races are contested, the campaign would probably start the Phone Bank at least 6 to 9 months before the Primary Election, depending on circumstances and early fund-raising results. The formula for calculating the number of calls possible per unit, per hour of operation, can be found in Chapter 7, The Phone Bank. Remember that, in a contested Primary, the group to be called consists only of registered Party member households.

Statewide Races - The Organizational Structure

The 5 on 5 Plan is still the best method to use from both an administrative and communication point of view.

When setting up the organizational structure, the 5 on 5 Plan is still the best method to use from both an administrative and communication point of view. Following population and geographic lines, as much as possible, divide the state into five Regions, trying various combinations, e.g., all Congressional districts, all legislative districts, or all counties. Whatever method is used, try not to cross their boundaries or zip codes. Then subdivide the five Regions into five balanced Areas. This should be done regardless of whether or not a full-scale field operations program is going to be implemented. Remember that there are many other activities based on Regional and Area designations besides the precinct and Phone Bank Operations.

Increase the staff to five Field Operations Directors, one for each Region. In addition, and depending on the size of the state, the campaign will need one or two full time Media Secretaries, at least one full time Scheduler, a Finance Director, and six to eight additional secretaries. Some campaigns in medium sized states also add the position of Political Director to oversee the field operations program, scheduling, and the Candidate's campaign activities. This frees the Campaign Manager to work more on strategy, fund-raising, administration, and the paid media program. In states of this size, the campaign should also have at least two Advance Persons, working with the Scheduler, to insure maximum impact, especially for free media coverage every day the Candidate is campaigning.

Statewide Races - Candidate's Activities

Door to door campaigning and coffee "Klatsches" are usually impractical.

As for the Candidate's campaign activities, door to door campaigning and coffee "Klatsches" are usually impractical, unless they are being staged as media events. Place more emphasis on plant gates and community shopping centers. Try to cover as many of the major county fairs and festivals as possible, along with the important parades that receive media coverage. Building name ID with a favorable impression is much more difficult in a statewide race than in a congressional race. It not only takes longer, but is also much more dependent on the use of the media. Centers of Influence activity are still important but not as extensive. When scheduling, try to work in senior citizens' homes or clubs every day. It is good PR and they have the largest single voting bloc in many areas, and usually have the highest turnout. In medium to large geographic states, it is usually more cost-efficient to have a twin engine aircraft with two pilots chartered for the duration of the campaign, rather than renting the aircraft on a daily rate basis. In larger states, the campaign may need two planes, the second on stand by for use by the Campaign Manager and/or the Political Director.

Statewide Races - Paid Media Program

A series of 5-day runs in May, July, and early September, in addition to the 10, 20, 30, 40 spread 4 weeks from the General Election is recommended.

On the media level in the campaign, including the direct mail program, the same schedule and format is applicable in most states. However, if the Candidate does not have a contested Primary to generate early paid media, I would recommend a series of 5-day runs in May, July, and early September, in addition to the 10, 20, 30, 40 spread 4 weeks from the General Election.

For the May run, develop a series of at least three 5 minute biographic spots covering different segments of the Candidate's life and emphasizing his or her continuous concern and care for people. In the July run, develop three 5-minute spots concentrating on three major issues, state or national, of almost universal concern to the people of the state. In the September run, cut three 5-minute commercials critical of the opponent's record or position on those same three issues. The October run should follow the same pattern and format established in the Prototype Plan. To the extent possible, most of the 30 and 60 second spots should be drawn from the footage used in the 5-minute spots.

Commercial content remains contingent on polling results. They assume that the Candidate is not trailing by more than ten points in late August and the opponent's Favorability rating is not over 50 percent. If either of these conditions exist the campaign should consider, and I would in all probability recommend, a much more aggressive content with more emphasis on the attack, in the September and October runs. Remember that the campaign must lower the opponent's Favorability rating, if the Candidate is going to be successful.

Statewide Races - Polling

The size and number of polls are partially dependent on the size of the state and whether or not there is a contested Primary. Normally, for follow up polls, a 500-person sample is sufficient for an acceptable degree of accuracy in most states. Since the media budget is so large and dependent on poll results for accurate targeting, if the Candidate does not have a contested Primary, I would recommend the campaign do follow up polls 30 days before each run. These would take place in April, June, August, and September. Then do tracking polls every week in October. If there is a contested Primary, follow the schedule in the section on contested Primaries, plus the tracking polls. In either case, the campaign should do its benchmark poll, preferably a 500 to 800 person sample, in medium to large states, no later than February. In summary, if the Candidate has a contested Primary, the campaign should do 1 benchmark, 5 follow-ups, and 4 tracking polls.

I do not recommend using the same polling company that is being used by the congressional candidates in the state, since the campaign loses the obvious advantage of being able to cross check results effectively.

Normally, a quid pro quo is worked out with congressional districts, whereby the campaign will test their ballot strength on the portion of the poll covering their district and they reciprocate for the other campaign on their polls. I do not recommend using the same polling company that is being used by the congressional candidates in the state, if possible. If both have the same polling firm, the campaign loses the obvious advantage of being able to cross check results effectively.

Statewide Races - Fund-raising

The fund-raising methodology is essentially the same as in the Prototype Plan, except that the objectives are doubled, tripled, or quadrupled, as the individual situation might dictate. In statewide campaigns, each Region should have a separate Finance Committee and its own plan patterned after the one in the Prototype Plan. The statewide Finance Chairperson(s) and the Finance Director are responsible for coordinating all activities between the Regions.

In medium to large states, it is sometimes cost effective to use mailing lists available from firms that rent them. Most of the prospect lists the campaign will be using are available from list rental companies for 35 to 50 dollars per thousand names. This possibility should be explored with the Political Fund-raising Consultant.

Most direct mail fund-raising should emanate from central headquarters, using either the campaign's in-house computer system or a direct mail computer firm. The size of the support files in a campaign of this size will be considerably larger than in the Prototype Plan. The campaign must expand the size of the in-house computer system in order to address this situation appropriately. I do not recommend the use of an outside computer service bureau as the lead-time is generally not acceptable in order to make this program work effectively. Although this too can be addressed internally, in some cases, a service bureau can have an advantage regarding the processing of computer generated letters considerably faster than the campaign.

If a large enough system and enough capable operators are difficult to secure, I recommend a compromise. The campaign can use a computer service bureau for the prospect mailings and its in-house computer system for processing the Support File mailings. Configure the system as described in the Chapter 5 - Implementation, regarding the setup for Support File maintenance and letter generation. A separate configuration should be set up for all other computer needs of the campaign, networked through modems with each of the Regional headquarters around the state.

Statewide Races - The Use of Consultants

All of the cautions mentioned regarding the use of professional consultants in the Prototype Plan are even more important for statewide races. Unfortunately, I do not know of any multi-agencies capable of doing medium to large states effectively, which means these campaigns lose some of the economies enjoyed by smaller states (under six million persons) and Congressional campaigns. The campaign will have to retain separate firms for most of these functions, i.e., a Political Campaign Consultant, who usually oversees the whole operation, a Political Fund-raising Consultant, a Political Media Consultant or Ad Agency for production and placement, and a Political Direct Mail Consultant.

Begin with securing the Political Campaign Consultant, utilizing his or her help with the selection of the others. Most Political Campaign Consultants know how to negotiate the lowest prices commensurate with quality and with whom they can work most effectively. This is no small consideration in larger state races. You will find that there does not appear to be a uniform standard of pricing by consultants for statewide campaigns. Even my firm's fee schedule was not fixed as it was for Congressional races, but was determined after an analysis of the many factors involved, such as, the size of state, the type of campaign, and the number of days required in state.

One factor used by many consultants in setting price schedules, not often realized by candidates, is the point at which the consultant enters the campaign. The lowest rates are used when they come in at the very beginning and become progressively higher further along in the campaign. The reason is because of the extra amount of work necessary and the pressure involved to redo a whole campaign in a "crisis situation." For example, candidates will usually find that campaigns pay more for a consultant that is hired 6 months before the election than they would pay for the same consultant hired 12 months earlier. In many more ways than one, it definitely does not pay to wait.

Statewide Races - Summary

In summary, these are some of the variations on the constants in the Prototype Plan for a U.S. Senatorial, Gubernatorial, or major statewide race. Regarding these types of campaigns, the major differences are in the obvious orientation of the issues and in fund-raising. U.S. Senate candidates are subject to the same laws and limitations of the FEC as Congressional candidates. Gubernatorial and other statewide candidates are only subject to their own state's laws on campaigns. In some states, this can be a significant difference, especially regarding the limits and sources of individual contributions.

All figures and recommendations used here, as in the Prototype Plan, are for illustrative purposes only.

Keep in mind, all figures and recommendations used here, as in the Prototype Plan, are for illustrative purposes only. They are used to demonstrate the procedures, systems, or methods of calculation. The Candidate and the campaign's consultants will have to decide, after a detailed analysis, which options are right for the campaign, after considering the campaign's resources and the problems to be addressed.

Legislative Campaigns

Size
Legislative Races are generally smaller, about one-fourth to one-fifth the size in terms of population.

Where U.S. Senatorial, Gubernatorial, or major statewide races are, in most cases, much larger than our Prototype of a congressional race, Legislative races are generally smaller. The actual size of a Legislative district will vary from state to state. Generally however, they are about one-fourth to one-fifth the size in terms of population.

In spite of the fact that their basic objectives are essentially the same, legislative candidates can rarely hope to raise the kind of money, proportionately, that a congressional candidate can raise. Since the public's interest is usually not as high in legislative races, recruiting volunteers is an even greater problem. As a percentage of the campaign budget, most legislative candidates usually have to contribute a greater share of their own funds than do congressional and statewide candidates.

The electronic media costs are usually prohibitive and invariably have too much of a "spillover" beyond their district's boundaries to be cost effective.

However, because the districts are smaller, many Legislative candidates are able to walk every precinct, in some cases twice, in addition to the other types of personal campaign activities. Heavy emphasis is therefore placed on the Candidate level in the campaign.

Since budgets are severely limited, most legislative candidates have to make do with a volunteer staff, with the possible exception of a Campaign Manager, as well as an all-volunteer Field Operations and Finance Committee. The voter registration file direct mail programs are usually cost prohibitive, though more and more state Party committees are providing low cost assistance with their computers on a time sharing basis. If this is not available, the substitute has to be form letters stuffed by volunteers.

Basically there are four paid media programs that are constants for a Legislative candidate: (1) direct mail, (2) billboards (commercial and corrugated 4 x 8's), lawn, and window signs, (3) local newspaper ads, and (4) radio commercials, if they are sufficiently focused.

There are fewer above average voters the further down you go on the ballot. Many people, by the time they get to the Legislative races, simply vote the Party. About 15 percent of the vote do bother to vote the Legislative races. To offset this tendency, it is more critical than ever that the Candidate's name ID rating is higher (than the opponent's). This generally translates into a name ID rating of about 50 percent. In addition, the Favorability rating must be considerably higher with a greater percentage of the voters. Neutral is usually the highest percentage rating given most legislators by the voters when they do not know much about them.

The use of a slogan or campaign theme should be maximized in conjunction with the Candidate's picture. All literature, stationery, signs, and newspaper ads must repeat four points over and over: the Candidate's name, the office being sought, the Candidate's picture, and the slogan of no more than six or seven words. Keep it simple.

To the extent that the campaign can, the campaign should follow the field operations program outlined in the Prototype Plan with both the Precinct Captains and Phone Bank volunteers working from their homes. Few opponents expect this kind of offense and, consequently, can often be caught off guard.

Be sure to calculate the precinct objectives accurately. Keep in mind that there is usually a 15 percent drop off between the number of votes cast for the top of the ticket and the middle to bottom of the ticket. Usually, the state party headquarters or County Registrar of Voters can provide the campaign with the necessary data to determine the average percentages in the district.

Polling is generally cost prohibitive. Nevertheless, check with a local polling firm to see if a special rate might be available if the campaign and three or four adjoining Legislative district campaigns pool their resources and commission a poll together. Do not overlook the local college as a source of assistance in this area. Occasionally, a class project will conduct polls for local candidates. With the professor monitoring them and the school's computers doing the computation, they can be very accurate.

Another possible source of assistance is a quid pro quo arrangement with the congressional candidate covering the district. Normally, the Candidate would agree to share volunteers for precinct or Phone Bank activity or to do a literature drop, in return for access to the demographic and issue information plus inclusion of the Candidate as a ballot-test question. In this arrangement, the campaign is normally not allowed to release the poll information, even for its own campaign, without the consent of the congressional candidate.

In fund-raising, the Candidate is very dependent on local, in-district contributions raised through a "one on one" solicitation. Direct mail does not work very effectively. However, still insert a BRE and make an appeal with all of the mail that the campaign generates. Although many national PACs will not get involved in Legislative campaigns, nor will out-of-state contributors, do not overlook state PACs and major in-state contributors. The state party committee chairperson, treasurer, or executive director should be able to provide a considerable amount of assistance in this area.

Another source of assistance will be the Party State Legislative Caucus. Most have special committees for just this kind of help to candidates of their party. The county party committee, if active, can also be relied on to help both politically and financially. Most feel a special responsibility for legislative and local candidates within their county. Check with the national party to see what assistance is available from them. Both parties have extensive Local Elections Divisions, which focus all of their attention on these types of races. Usually, the assistance is channeled through the state party, but it does not hurt to inquire.

If the campaign sets up its Political Game Plan along the lines suggested in this section, while using the rest of the Prototype Plan as the base, the budget will probably be in the $60,000 range, based on 25,000 registered voters in the district. Of that amount, the campaign should plan to raise three-fourths within the district and could reasonably expect to raise the other one-fourth from outside sources. The budget would probably be as follows: $10,000 billboards, $4,000 yard signs, $20,000 direct mail, $6,000 brochures and stationery, $10,000 newspaper ads and radio commercials, and $12,000 for administrative and office expenses, including a computer system and software.

Local Campaigns

Size
Local Races can range from 300 to millions of voters.

The variations in these campaigns are too numerous to list. A City Council or County Supervisor campaign could be for a district seat or at-large. It could be partisan or nonpartisan. The size of the potential electorate could be from 300 to 2,500,000. In Los Angeles for example, a City Council campaign is comparable to a congressional race with a budget to match, while an LA County Supervisor has a constituency larger than many states, where the campaign there could be the equivalent of many U.S. Senatorial campaigns, with a similar budget.

The Prototype Plan, with the appropriate variations matching it with the size and makeup of a specific electorate and district, will be just as operational for the local election effort. The objectives and limitations are virtually the same. It is for this reason that throughout *The Campaign Manual,* I have constantly referred to districts in terms of numbers of people.

The primary differences regarding local campaigns relate to fund-raising. Since many of these local campaigns are nonpartisan, the parties do not become overtly involved, nor do national PACs and OD contributors. Where races are partisan, only the county and state committees usually offer party help. However, to offset this handicap, most local elections have the least restrictive campaign laws regarding the source and amount of contributions.

In the medium to larger cities and counties, there are many individuals, organizations, and companies with significant personal stakes at issue in city and county level decisions or votes. It is through these individuals and groups that most city and county candidates draw financial and volunteer support. In many cases, the local candidate is often labeled in the media by the group that each represents. He or she may be labeled the PTA Candidate, the homeowner's association Candidate, or the Chamber of Commerce Candidate. Unless an individual is able and willing to finance the bulk of his or her campaign personally, he or she invariably has to be aligned with one or more of the major organized groups within the community. The budget, as with the appropriate game plan, will also be dependent on the population and type of district.

Chapter 13 - Word Index

Chapter 14
Sample Plans That Work

In this Chapter, you may review actual plans and procedural manuals that were developed and used during actual campaigns. They have been edited to remove all references to party, dates, and the actual candidates involved. Some figures are dated, but are included to illustrate how the calculations were developed.

Keep in mind that these are adaptations of the Prototype Plan presented in this Manual. In some areas, the Prototype Plan is a more updated, improved version of these plans and procedural manuals as a result of my constant effort to improve the process after the experiences of each campaign cycle.

Sample Political Game Plan

A campaign plan prepared for internal use by the campaign and for inclusion in press and PAC kits. The cover page and biography of the Candidate have been removed.

March Miller Congressional Committee
P. O. Box 4927
Springfield, VA 20522-4927
123-555-5555

POLITICAL GAME PLAN

Prepared By:
Sal Guzzetta
S. J. Guzzetta & Associates

TABLE OF CONTENTS

Analysis and Strategy

During the last primary election in the 10th Congressional District, the total number of votes cast was 47,000. Allowing for a more intensive campaign, we estimate that the total number of votes that will be cast in a ---- primary election, covering this same approximate area, to be no greater than 53,000. Our objective therefore, is to obtain at least 26,500 votes in this election.

Since we are uncertain at this time as to what the district's boundaries will be, or for that matter who our potential opponent(s) will be, we intend to create an imaginary district (District X) by using March's home as the center and drawing a circle with a radius of approximately 20 miles. The radius will be only 10 miles east of the center.

Our signs, both billboards and yard, will be focused in this area during Stage 1. Stage 1 will be identified as the ID stage. Most of the campaign's activity will be devoted to building up March's name ID throughout District X. Our free media campaign will focus on the media outlets contained within District X and our first political/fund-raising mailer will be sent to all Republican households meeting our prioritization schedule and falling within this area.

When the actual district boundary lines are finally established by the state legislature or the courts, probably by late November, ----, we will re-focus our sign and mailing program in this area. Our paid direct communications program will also be re-directed to this new district.

During Stage 2, we will focus on identifying positive supporters and convincing those who are undecided, through our Advocacy Program to vote for March. Stage 3 will focus on the GOTV (Get Out The Vote) program. This means making sure all positive Miller supporters go to the polls and vote.

Since this will be a new district, because of re-apportionment, there will not be an incumbent. However, in all likelihood any one of three existing Representatives could become our opponent. Although they will try to claim incumbency, the fact is none will actually be the incumbent of this new district. Should our eventual opponent try this maneuver we should call them on it immediately and continuously until they desist.

Our basic strategy will be to build-up March's name ID to 90%+, i.e., 90% or more of the registered voters in the district recognize his name, with a Favorability rating of at least 50%, which means they know him and like him, or his stands on the issues. We will stress repeatedly his qualifications for this position and the special expertise that he alone can bring to the elected office.

Stage 1: 7/15/---- - 12/15/----

A - MEDIA OPERATIONS

During this stage, our media will consist of yard signs, billboards, and bus signs. Every effort will be made to saturate District X with at least 2,000 yard signs beginning in September. In October, we will place 15 billboards on strategic highways coming in and out of the District. In addition, those bus routes that traverse the District will be used extensively. In the event that we are unable to secure the billboards desired, we will alternate with 4 x 8 signs at selected locations. All signs will feature the campaign logo.

During this stage, we will begin production on a 12 - 15 minute video. This video will then be reproduced in sufficient quantity to mail to all Republican targeted households within the District. Since the actual mailing will be to those households which fall within the new District, and since we do not know when that District's boundaries will be decided, we will have to be sure that the videos are ready for distribution anytime after 11/1/----.

Beginning around October 1st the campaign will begin to disseminate press releases to all media outlets covering District X. The releases will focus on March's positions on the issues, organizational information, and topical releases. Special emphasis will be placed on the weekly newspapers.

B - FUND-RAISING OPERATIONS

The Finance Committee will be organized during this stage. Members will be asked to bring into campaign headquarters lists of potential contributors to whom they want the campaign to mail fund-raising letters. They will then follow up these mailings with personal telephone calls and personal meetings with March, if necessary.

On September 18th, a fund-raising letter will be dropped to all targeted Republican households within District X. This letter will contain a bio brochure, a BRE, and a personal appeal from March. Additionally, at this time we will send out the first of our PAC kits to selected PACs.

On October 19th, the first of two major fund-raising events sponsored by the Finance Committee will be held. The second event is scheduled for December 13th. Both of these events should be priced at $100 per person and the over all objective for each will be 500 attendees. The Finance Committee will determine the actual nature of these events.

Throughout this stage, every effort will be made to have as many minor fund-raising events as the campaign can schedule. Usually, these events are held on Friday, Saturday, or Sunday and can be cocktail parties, coffees, lunches, or lawn parties.

Since fund-raising is of paramount importance to the success of the campaign, fund-raising events will always receive the highest priority in scheduling March's time during the campaign.

C - FIELD OPERATIONS

The Field Operations committee will focus on recruiting and training members during this stage in anticipation of an intensive program during Stage 2. They will also be responsible for the placement of yard signs throughout the District and the distribution of bumper stickers.

Every effort should be made during this stage to use March to help with recruiting efforts. One of the best methods for doing this is to have Coffee "Klatsches" in their homes and invite as many of their neighbors and friends to attend the "meet and greet" with March.

D - RESEARCH ACTIVITIES

By October 1st, the Research Committee should have developed March's position papers on all major issues. These papers will then be printed in a Position Booklet, which will become a part of March's Media Kit and PAC Kit. A synopsis of each of these positions (2 or 3 sentences) should also be prepared for inclusion in the Precinct Captains' kits.

During October, mock debates should be held with March to prepare him for actual debates that will take place during Stage 2.

E - MARCH AND ELEANOR'S ACTIVITIES

March and Eleanor should focus their activities on individual and PAC fund-raising, attending fund-raising, political activities, meeting with Centers of Influence throughout the District, and visiting the media outlets and civic groups impacting the District. Actual door-to-door campaigning will not begin until Stage 2.

F - CAMPAIGN OPERATIONS

It is anticipated that the campaign staff will eventually be made up of a campaign administrator, campaign secretary, field operations director, driver/aide, and a media/research secretary. During July and August, the paid staff will consist of the campaign administrator only. The campaign secretary will come on-board in September, the media/research secretary in October, the field operations director in November, and the driver/aide in December.

During Stage 1, the campaign headquarters can operate in two or three rooms sub-rented from the Trimester Co. However, by Stage 2 it is anticipated that a separate headquarters will be needed. This headquarters will be a ground floor office within the same area so the existing telephone numbers can be retained.

Staff act in a support role for the candidate and the campaign committees. They are responsible for making sure that whatever administrative services are required by the committees are provided. To enhance these operations, all staff members should be trained thoroughly on the computer, its use, and its capabilities.

By mid-August, the electronic files containing a list of the registered voters within District X should be obtained from the Registrar of Voters Office. Republican households will be selected to meet our targeting criteria and a set of labels prepared, in ZIP order for the September mailing.

As soon as the new district boundary lines are established, Republican households meeting our targeting criteria will be converted to our computer format and loaded into our computer database. A set of labels, in ZIP order should then be created for the video mailing.

Throughout this stage, staff should work with Field Operations Committee to ensure that at least 2000 Patriot yard signs are strategically placed throughout the District.

Stage 2: 12/15/---- - 2/28/----

A - MEDIA OPERATIONS

By now, we should know the exact boundaries of the new district and who will be our primary opponent(s). Whatever adjustments need to be made in the placement of all signs will be made during the first two weeks of this stage. During the first four weeks another 2,000 Patriot yard signs should be placed within these new boundaries in addition to those already in place. By Jan. 15th, the remaining videos should be mailed to any new targeted Republican households acquired as a result of the re-districting.

On Jan. 27th, we will drop a Campaign Tabloid to all targeted households in the new District. This Tabloid will be issue-oriented and contain March's position papers. Feb. 10th will be the start date of our radio ads. These will continue at a graduated pace until Election Day. The schedule of press releases will increase to three a week beginning Jan. 15th and continue until the final stage.

B - FUND-RAISING OPERATIONS

There will be a final major fund-raising event on Jan. 18th. The objectives will be the same as for the first two. The Finance Committee will decide on the type of event. Individual and PAC solicitation and minor events will continue as in the previous stage.

A second fund-raising letter will be sent to all prospects previously mailed who did not respond to the first mailer by Jan. 10th. By Feb. 10th, we will drop another fund-raising letter to all previous contributors.

The Field Operations committee will be sponsoring a fund-raising event in each of their five regions during the month of February. Although the Finance Committee is not directly responsible for the successful outcome of these events, they will be asked to provide support assistance.

C - FIELD OPERATIONS

On January 6th, the Field Operations Committee swings into action. Because of the short amount of time involved, they will have only four weeks to complete a canvass of the District. During this canvass, they will contact every targeted Republican household, pass out literature, and attempt to determine whether or not the voter is FOR March, AGAINST March, or UNDECIDED (F, A, U).

As this determination is made, their precinct sheets will be marked accordingly, by circling the appropriate "F, U, A" codes on the sheets. As these sheets are completed, they will be turned into headquarters for database update. Given the time constraints, it is critical that this phase of the campaign be accomplished with the highest degree of precision possible.

Those individuals identified as Undecideds will then receive a specific letter encouraging them to vote for March. During the month of February, they will be re-visited by the precinct captains and ID'd again. As they commit to vote for March their status will be changed to F (For) in the database.

Concurrent with this operation, the same program will be conducted by a professional telemarketing firm. Their results will also be keyed into the database and follow up mail will again be sent to the undecideds. Where there is a conflict between the results of the precinct captains and the telemarketers, the voter will be carried as an undecided in the database until a third contact is made, which might resolve the difference.

During the first week of February, all voters identified as FOR in the database will be re-contacted to determine if they will need an absentee ballot application for the election. Details for this program will be in the Field Operations Manual and the Phone Bank Manual.

It is imperative that we complete the identification of the 26,500 voters that we must have in order to win at least two weeks before the election, i.e., before the beginning of Stage 3.

During February, each Region within the Field Operations Committee will be responsible for promoting a minor fund-raising event. There are two objectives for these events: (1) to raise money, and (2) to promote morale within our ranks. These should be fun events. Dances, auctions, or parties, whatever will bring together large groups of our supporters within the Region. Ideally, each event will draw at least 500 supporters at $20 each.

D - RESEARCH ACTIVITIES

As soon as our opponent(s) is identified, the Research Committee will develop a complete profile of that person(s). This profile should include their voting records, if a previously elected officeholder, disclosure reports, and previous campaign information. Briefings should be given to March regarding this information.

On January 8th, a benchmark poll will be conducted by a professional polling firm. The size of the sample will be 300 persons.

Beginning the first week of February, the Research Committee will conduct weekly tracking polls to determine the direction of the campaign's efforts. The size of the sample will be 150 persons and will be randomly drawn from our list of targeted households. The campaign will use the *Survey-Pro* program to develop the cross-tabs. In effect, these polls will act as a third safety net. They should confirm the results being achieved by the precinct and telephone operations. If there is a discrepancy, it will alert us in time to take corrective action.

Challenges will be made to our opponent(s) to publicly debate. A member of the Research Committee should meet with the sponsors of the debate to ensure that the ground rules are fair and equitable and to facilitate agreement on the format. Insist on the standard rule, whosoever opens first, closes first. A member of the Research Committee will also attend at all debates and critique March as soon as possible thereafter.

E - MARCH AND ELEANOR'S ACTIVITIES

During the first three weeks of this stage, most of their activities, in addition to fund-raising, should be oriented around holiday parties. Actual precinct walking would not be appropriate. However, some campaign activity, if allowed, could be done on Saturday mornings at local malls.

After the first of the year, March should plan to walk targeted precincts, especially on Saturdays and Sunday afternoons. These targeted precincts will be identified during the holiday period.

Visits with editors and Centers of Influence should continue, with special emphasis given to those who were uncertain of their support during the first round of visits in Stage 1.

Wherever possible, special emphasis in March's schedule will be given to high-profile media events. During this stage, March should attempt to attend at least two different churches every Sunday morning. If allowed to speak from the pulpit, he should plan to do so. At a minimum, he should attempt to have the Pastor introduce him to the congregation from the pulpit, or as they leave the church.

Schedules of local events will be assembled by campaign headquarters and whenever possible, March or Eleanor should attend. The level of profile should be in keeping with the type of event and other circumstances. All Republican Clubs and Organizations within the District must be visited during this stage, as well as all Republican elected officials.

F - CAMPAIGN OPERATIONS

After the first wave of the name ID program is completed in the last week of January, the database will be updated, i.e., purged of those voters positively identified as being AGAINST (A) March. The records should be deleted from the prospect files. Staff will then be responsible for the Tabloid mailing to the targeted households on Jan. 27th. This procedure must be repeated on Feb. 19th, to prevent our final mailings from going to negative households, wasting resources.

In addition to the regular and on-going support work for the various committees, the staff will begin to assemble the materials necessary for Stage 3 during the final two weeks of Stage 2. Final printouts should be prepared for the Precinct Captains and a final set of labels drawn for those receiving the GOTV mailing. Arrangements should be made for the Election Day Victory Party.

Stage 3: 2/28/---- - 3/10/----

A - MEDIA OPERATIONS

In the final Get Out The Vote (GOTV) Stage, the media will be directed toward encouraging the voters to get out and vote for March on Election Day. The radio ads will be geared to this objective and in addition, a limited number of newspaper ads will be used.

All remaining yard signs will be posted, except for those reserved for polling places. Billboards and bus signs will continue as in Stages 1 and 2.

B - FUND-RAISING OPERATIONS

Except for some final individual solicitation and telephone follow-ups during this stage, the Finance Committee has little else to do. If so inclined however, they will be encouraged to help the Field Operations Committee with their GOTV efforts.

C - FIELD OPERATIONS

A final mailing to all known supporters will be mailed on March 5th, reminding all that Tuesday is Election Day and encouraging them to get out and vote. Precinct Captains should also be calling on all of March's supporters in their precinct and emphasizing this message. Inquiries should be made to see if any need assistance getting to the polls or baby-sitting services on Election Day. The names of those that do need help should be sent to headquarters where they will be marked as such in the database and assistance coordinated.

The telemarketing firm will be duplicating these efforts over the telephone.

On Election Day, all of these households should be telephoned by the Field Operations Committee to remind them that it is Election Day and urge them to get out and vote. The polls will be checked at mid-day and the names of those known supporters will be checked against the lists of those who have voted. Those supporters who have not yet voted will be re-called during the afternoon. Repeat this procedure around 5:00 PM and continue until all know supporters have been re-called.

To the extent that the numbers of volunteers on election day allows, at least one volunteer will be stationed at each polling place with a yard sign and literature, encouraging voters to vote for March as they approach the polling place. Local election laws must be followed in this regard.

D - RESEARCH ACTIVITIES

The Research Committee will closely monitor election "news" emanating from March's opponent(s) during this stage and be prepared to respond rapidly if any last minute negative campaigning takes place.

Those members not assigned to this final task will be asked to assist the Field Operations Committee in their efforts.

E - MARCH AND ELEANOR'S ACTIVITIES

In addition to meeting the scheduled demands of the campaign, which are routine during this stage, March and Eleanor will meet with as many of the campaign volunteers as possible in order to boost morale and ask them to expend maximum effort during this period.

On Election Day, they will separate in order to visit as many of the Precinct's polling places as possible, especially the highly targeted precincts.

F - CAMPAIGN OPERATIONS

Staff will be responsible for dropping the final GOTV mailer on March 5th. They will be heavily involved in working with the Field Operations Committee during this entire stage. Extra care will be given to ensure that volunteers who come on-board during this stage are immediately keyed into the computer so that the appropriate Thank-You Letters from March can be sent to them on March 11th.

Since campaign headquarters will literally become the campaigns center during this stage, the staff will be expected to work straight through all ten days of this stage.

Conclusion

The Timeline, Flow-Chart, and Budget attached to this plan form a part hereof and detail more closely the items and activities listed above.

As stated at the outset, this plan is designed to raise March's name ID in the District to 90%+ and his Favorability rating to at least 50%. If executed properly, and in a timely manner, it will accomplish these minimum objectives.

All components of this plan are necessary to realize these objectives. The objectives and time constraints dictate the demands. If March is to be successful, all the participants must be successful in their efforts. Although it is true that only March wins or loses, it is also true that March cannot win or lose without the cooperation, or lack thereof, of everyone involved in this campaign.

There are two elements of a campaign, which have not been addressed in this plan, i.e., timing and luck. Although not stated, the plan is designed to control the timing or momentum of the campaign. If adhered to, it should discourage "peaking too soon," a common and disastrous problem in many campaigns. It also is designed to handle the "luck" factor. There will always be outside factors or incidents during a campaign, which will be totally beyond the control of our plan. Nonetheless, if our plan is followed, the campaign will be able to take advantage of these situations, if they occur. That is one of the "secrets" of well-organized, well-run campaigns. This type of campaign has the ability to exploit positive situations that occur, rolling quickly over any possible negatives, which might also occur.

The opposition is going to score points. They are just as determined to win as we are, and just as convinced that their candidate is the best person for the job. We must be extremely careful not to over-react when they do score points, and avoid needlessly changing our basic strategy.

Pivotal to the success of this plan is fund-raising. Unless the required amounts of money are raised when needed, we will be unable to implement the precise targeting of our message outlined herein. Contingency plans should be made to cover shortfalls in the fund-raising schedule if they occur and be implemented if necessary.

The campaign game plan for the general election period will be drawn up by April 1, ----. Fund-raising should not be a major problem since the national party committees will become actively involved at that point and provide the bulk of the necessary funds. During this period from 3/11/---- to 4/1/----, the campaign staff, volunteers, and March and Eleanor will take time off for R&R and prepare for the general election period.

We recommend that this plan be treated with maximum security and shared only with those persons on a "need to know" basis.

Sample Field Operations Manual

Field Operations Manual
March Miller Congressional Campaign

The task you are undertaking as a Precinct Captain for the March Miller Congressional Campaign is probably the most important single effort in the entire campaign. Every other function in the campaign is either directly or indirectly supportive of your efforts. Without your complete cooperation and effort, this campaign will not result in victory on November --, ----. The decision was made many months ago that only an intensive "grass roots" type campaign would be successful here in the 10th district. Because of this decision, all of the media efforts, radio, TV, and newspapers will be subordinated to the Field Operations.

As you study this guide, please be mindful of what you are reading. The success of this campaign depends on YOU! Outlined in this guide are systematic procedures for each of the five stages during the course of the Campaign. Please study them carefully and accomplish the tasks as completely as possible. Every step is important and has relevance to the other elements and programs within the campaign. If you have any questions, please do not hesitate to call your Area or Regional Chairperson for assistance.

Thank you for all of your assistance and cooperation in this effort.

REGION: ______________________ AREA: ____________________

PRECINCT: ____

REGIONAL CHAIRPERSON: ____________________ TEL.: __________

AREA CHAIRPERSON: ________________________ TEL.: __________

FIELD OPERATIONS GUIDE

Stage Two - Voter ID
February 2, ---- through May 5, ----

During this stage, we would like you to make an intensive effort to contact every household in your precinct that has a registered voter. If possible, this contact should be attempted in person first, and only by telephone if personal contact fails. Our primary objective during this stage is to identify and record the definite Miller voters (Votes For), the definite Baker voters (Votes Against), and the undecideds. In your kit, you will find endorsement sheets. Please take a moment to fill in the information at the top. So often, we receive these sheets at Central Headquarters without this information and a considerable amount of time is wasted identifying the sender. Remember that there are hundreds of precincts in the 10th Congressional District. Without accurate record keeping, the logistics will be impossible to handle.

When you contact these homes in your precinct, simply identify yourself as their Precinct Captain, and inform them of your survey in order to identify whom they are planning to support in the upcoming election. If they plan on voting for March tell them you think that's great and ask them to do two things: (1) please sign your endorsement sheet (actually, they should PRINT their name and then initial it) and, (2) show them the return envelope and ask them what type of activity listed there they would like to volunteer for, if any. Have them complete the envelope. If appropriate, take back the completed envelope and mail it to Central Headquarters.

You should, in every case, mark your Precinct Sheet with an " F " next to their name if they intend to vote FOR Miller. If they say they are undecided, place a "U" next to their name, and if they indicate that they intend to vote AGAINST Miller, put an "A " next to their name. If they decline to state put a "DS." Somewhere on their line, you should also record their telephone number if it is not already listed. This will make your work in the later stages considerably easier.

You should not put any other markings on these Precinct Sheets. The coding on the sheets must remain consistent and the set you have has to transmit accurate information through the entire campaign. When an Endorsement Sheet is filled, please send it directly to Central Headquarters, P. O. Box 7954, Springfield, VA. When these sheets are received by Central, a copy will be made and sent back to your Regional Chairperson. The name may be used at some point in the future for an Endorsement Ad in your local newspapers. We will also make an Endorsement Card on each one for our central file and enter the name and corresponding information into our database. As you will see in the later stages, these names will also become crucial in the successful completion of your efforts in getting out the vote on Election Day.

In summary, then for Stage 1, our primary objective is to identify and record our known Miller supporters and secondly to recruit additional volunteers for the campaign. Each person is to be surveyed, regardless of party designation. We do not expect you to spend a significant amount of time in trying to educate the undecided(s) or to make "conversions." This will be accomplished in the later stages of the campaign.

Stage Three - The Positive Advocacy Stage
May 6, ---- through September 10, ----

In this stage, we would like you to again canvas your precincts, calling only on those people who indicated in Stage 1 that they were undecided (U). The primary objective will be to convince as many of them as possible to vote for Miller in November. To assist you in this effort, we will provide you with a synopsis of March's position on the issues sometime during the month of May. We suggest you call on these people in person, identifying yourself as their precinct captain for the March Miller Congressional Campaign and that you would like to help them to become better informed on the issues and the candidates. In your kits, you have a "biographical" sheet that shows a background we can all be proud of. March Miller has been accurately described as a political moderate and a fiscal conservative, the very kind of person most of us can identify with and trust. He is one of the people of the 10th district, he knows the problems and issues facing us, and even more importantly, he knows how to get the job done in Washington. He is strongly opposed to the growing bureaucracy in Washington and the outrageous increase in taxes legislated year after year. He is also a strong advocate of equal rights and opportunity for every person in our Country.

As you talk with these people, if they indicate they would like to support Miller, do not hesitate, ask them to sign the Endorsement Sheets and fill out the return envelope if they would like to be a volunteer, just as in Stage 1.

As an alternative to individual contact, some Precinct Captains prefer to have a series of "Coffee Hours" in their home to which they invite only the known undecideds. They then ask their area or regional chairperson to come by and talk to the group about our candidate. Sometimes this "third" person influence can be very effective.

Incidentally, during Stages One and Two, March and his wife Eleanor, will be walking many of the precincts throughout the district. Naturally, you will be advised when they are going to be in your precinct and you will be asked to help plan their activity while there. Your area chairperson will advise you regarding this activity.

In addition, during Stage 2, if our budget permits, we are going to try to open storefront headquarters in each of the regions. Your area chairperson will let you know about this sometime in June.

To summarize, Stage 2 efforts are directed toward educating the undecideds about March. If you have already reached your basic goal of 100 known supporters, keep going. There are bound to be a certain number of precincts that will not make their objectives. Your extra effort could make the difference.

Stage Four - The Negative Advocacy Stage

September 4, ---- through October 5, ----

Bristol Screen, Inc., 200 Delaware Ave., Bristol, TN 37620, manufactures a static cling, vinyl window decal that can be removed without leaving any residue. Telephone 423.968.5871. Web site: www.BSI-america.com.

Study your precinct sheets. Are you satisfied that you have all the information you need on our known supporters? Call them and ask, (1) if they will be unable to get to the polls on Election Day, Tuesday, November 4th, for any reason, and do they need an absentee voter application, and (2) if they would like to have a bumper sticker for their car, or a yard sign. This gives you a chance to get back in touch with them to make sure there has not been any softening of support. We recommend that you carry a roll of scotch tape with you and show them how to place the bumper sticker on the bottom center section of their rear window, inside. This gives maximum visibility, lasts longer, and does not mess their bumper. They will appreciate the option.

14

After you are satisfied that our known supporters are firm, review your list of undecideds. It is imperative that you contact all of them during this stage. The choice at this point will be clear and well defined. We will send you a biographic profile of our opponent, along with his position on the issues. With this information, you should be able to point out to the known undecideds the differences between him and March. You should be able to make a strong appeal at this time for their commitment to March, unless they want a continuation of the policies of the last twenty-five years. If you are successful in your efforts to get them to endorse March, continue sending the names to Central Headquarters until October 15th, so they can receive our final mailing.

Names obtained after October 15th should be designated on your sheets in such a way that you will be certain to give them a top priority on Election Day. During this stage, you should also develop a list of people who had previously indicated they would be willing to put up a yard or widow sign for Miller. On the weekend of October 28th, you should organize a sign "planting" effort in your precinct and see that everyone who requested a sign has one put up in his or her yard. This is usually a fun project for some of the teenagers associated with the campaign.

The media campaign will be especially intensive during this stage and the 4th Stage. Newspaper ads, radio and TV commercials, billboards, and direct mailings will support your efforts. Notice that we said, "support." The primary effort is YOURS! March and Eleanor will be concentrating their campaign activities in those precincts which our analysis shows need the most help, and which have the best chance of being won over.

Remember this is our last chance to "sell" those people who remain uncommitted to vote for March Miller. Plan your schedules far enough in advance, so that you will be able to give it your very best effort.

Stage Five - Get Out The Vote (GOTV), General Election
October 15, ---- through November 4, ----

This is the climax. If you have done your job properly during the last nine months, you should have a minimum of 100 names on your precinct sheets of people who have said they will go out and vote for March Miller on November 4th. Hopefully, you will have 120 names to contact, just to be safe. You should contact all of these people by telephone to see if they need any special assistance on Election Day, and to remind them that it is coming up very quickly. After doing this, if time permits, you should give one last call to any undecideds still on your list. If our budget permits, we will try to send them one last mailer in this stage, but in all probability, the final contact will be yours.

Again, the phone banks will be in operation to provide back-up assistance. In the seminar preceding this stage, you will be given detailed instructions on how to coordinate their activities with yours. You will also receive instructions on the way that you can help on Election Day.

If you have any problems during any of these stages, please do not hesitate to contact your area or regional chairperson. They are there to help you. If you feel you cannot do the job, try to recruit your own replacement and let your area chairperson know what is happening.

All supplies will come to you from your area chairperson. If you encounter any problems along these lines, please call Campaign Central Headquarters for assistance.

SOME SUGGESTED DO'S AND DON'TS:

Do keep in contact with your Area Chairperson.

Do keep a smile on your face and a very positive attitude when talking with your fellow voters.

Do try to give a positive impression of yourself and the campaign at all times.

Do develop the attitude that what you are doing is an integral part of the American political process. It Is!

Do conserve brochures and supplies. Costs for these items have increased tremendously in the last few years. Use everything effectively.

Do not ever belittle, or personally attack our opponents, regardless of how much "mud" they might sling. We are going to run a positive campaign based on the issues.

Do not do anything to interfere with our opponents' signs or other advertising programs.

Do not spread rumors about our opponents and do not believe any you might hear about March Miller and the campaign. If in doubt, call Headquarters. You will always get a straight answer.

Do not give up. We have a tough fight ahead of us, but an excellent opportunity to win solidly and have our voices heard in Washington, loud and clear.

THANK YOU!

Sample Fund-raising Letters

Fund-raising Letter No. 1

Date
Address Block

Dear ,

On Tuesday, November (date), (year), we will have an opportunity to vote for one of the most qualified persons running for political office that I have ever met.

(Name), an outstanding leader in our community for many years has agreed to enter the race for (office), in the (#) District. It is indeed an honor and a pleasure for me to be serving as the (title) Chairperson of (name)'s campaign.

When several of us discussed with (name) the possibility of entering this race to represent us as our candidate, we assured (name) that many members of the community would be proud to endorse and support (his or her) candidacy.

We did extensive research on the requirements to facilitate a winning campaign. We developed the strategy, a sound game plan, and a budget that is adequate to implement it properly. Several of us then agreed to serve on (name)'s Finance Committee and work to raise the funds necessary to communicate our message to the electorate. As you well know, the cost of communications has increased considerably in the past few years.

I am writing to you now to ask for your financial support. Although it is (Name), who is running, it is truly our campaign. If (Name) wins, (he or she) will be our representative in (electoral district) and we could not ask for a more capable individual to serve on our behalf.

Enclosed please find a brochure detailing (name)'s background and a return envelope. Please send as much as you can for your share in this effort, $50, $100, $200, or more. Be assured it will be put to good use.

Sincerely,

(your name)
(title)

Sample Fund-raising Letters

Fund-raising Letter No. 2 - Major Event

Date
Address Block

Dear ,

On Saturday, May (date), (year), we are planning a major fund-raising event for our candidate, (name)'s campaign for (office) in the (#) District. You are cordially invited to attend. The event will be a dinner/dance, held at (location), beginning at 7:30 PM, and lasting until 12:00 PM. Dinner will be served at 8:15 PM. Dress is semi-formal.

We are pleased to announce our guest of honor for the evening will be (name), one of the most popular personalities (whatever).

Tickets for this event will be $150.00 per person. A table for eight is $1,200.00. Prior to the dinner, we will host a private reception for our guest of honor and (candidate's name). Tickets for the reception are $250.00 per person. The reception will be limited to 50 guests.

As you know, (name)'s campaign for (office) has been going very well. The polls indicate that the race is tightening with the momentum going in our favor.

Nonetheless, if we are to keep the momentum building, we must proceed with the next stage of our game plan on schedule. Two tickets for this event will pay for one month's rental for one of (name)'s billboards. Buying a table will pay the rent through the end of the campaign. If you would like, we can arrange for you to choose the billboard that you would like to sponsor.

Please use the enclosed envelope to send in your reservations now. It promises to be a fun evening, and a great way to support our campaign.

Sincerely yours,

(your name)
(your title)

Enclosures

Sample Finance Committee Operations Manual

Finance Committee Manual
March Miller Congressional Committee

The function of the Finance Committee is to help raise the funds necessary for the successful completion of March Miller's campaign for U. S. Congress.

That this accomplishment is possible is beyond question.

1) Our research indicates that the maximum number of voters who will turn out in the March Primary Election will be no greater than 53,000. Allowing for a close election with whoever our opponent(s) are, leads us to believe that no more than 26,500 votes will be necessary for a victory.

2) Any reasonable re-apportionment of the existing District will follow the same demographic breakdown. The new District will still be heavily Republican, which means that the winner of the Primary is almost certain to be elected in the General Election.

3) The new district will be just that, a new District. The number designating this District will change and there will *not* be an incumbent Representative. It is therefore, an "open" race. Regardless of who our opponent(s) is, he or she will not be able to claim incumbency of the new district.

4) Every effort will be made to achieve parity with any of our potential opponents in the area of Name ID. Our strategy is designed to enable March to achieve a 90%+ Name ID Rating by March 1, ----. As this is the primary motivator behind the way people cast their ballot, we will neutralize our opponents in this area.

5) We do not underestimate the strengths of Congressmen Baker or Bell. As long-term incumbents, they have at their disposal the prestige of the office, a well-qualified staff, the franking privilege that they use with utmost effectiveness, and professional assistance with their campaigns.

In order to counter any advantages, we have retained the firm of S. J. Guzzetta & Associates of the Washington, DC area, one of the nation's leading political consulting firms. They will be responsible for our campaign operations planning and media activity.

In addition, March plans on walking many precincts in the new district between now and the election. Through this effort, we not only hope to develop a close relationship with the voters, but we will be recruiting volunteers in order to build the most intensive "grass roots" organization this area has ever seen.

We can win. In fact, we can win big. It all depends on you. With your assistance, all is possible; without it, victory would be virtually impossible

WHAT ARE THE OBJECTIVES?

The Campaign Budget has been set at $761,000.00. We intend to raise this amount from five (5) sources:

March Miller	$100,000.00
Major and Minor Fund-raising Events In-District	135,000.00
Major Contributions, Individual Solicitation	171,000.00
Direct Mail In and Out-Of-District	225,000.00
Political Action Committees	130,000.00
	$761,000.00

To accomplish this, the Finance Committee will be divided into 5 Teams. Each Team will consist of approximately 5 members. Since the Candidate is responsible for 100,000, the objective of each Team will be $132,200 ($132,200 x 5 = $661,000).

Once the new District is defined, it will be divided into 5 Geographic Regions and each Finance Committee Team will be assigned responsibility for one Region. When a contribution is received by mail from someone living in a particular Region, it is credited to the region in which the contributor lives, regardless of where or how it was raised. For example, if an event is held in Region 3 and someone attends it from Region 1, Region 1's Team would receive the credit toward their budget objective of $132,200.00. This rule also applies to any funds received as a result of our direct mail program. Contributions are automatically credited to the Region in which the contributor lives.

All fund-raising events are credited on a NET basis only. The costs of the event are deducted from the total raised and only the net amount is credited toward the Region's objectives.

Since our cash flow budget calls for an expenditure of about $234,300 by October, each Region's Team will need to raise approximately 31% of its objective by that date, i.e., $132,200 x 31% = $41,000 to be raised by each team by October or $205,000.00 in total. The Candidate will also be responsible for raising 31% or $31,000.

Since political campaigns are unable to secure credit, most of our budget items need to be paid for when ordered. In effect, this means that the Primary campaign budget must be raised by early February, in order for the campaign to stay on schedule. This in effect gives us only six months to accomplish this Herculean task.

Suggested methods follow.

THE METHOD OF OPERATION

Between now and the Primary Election we have divided the campaign fund-raising period into three stages.

Stage 1 July 16, ---- to September 15, ----

Stage 2 September 16, ---- to December 15, ----

Stage 3 December 16, ---- to March 15, ----

During these stages, it will be helpful if you keep in mind a distinction between "direct" activity and "support" activity. Direct activity is where you, as the Finance Committee, have the primary responsibility for the success of a particular fund-raising event or activity. For example, a district-wide or regional dinner and individual solicitation. Support activity would be the fund-raising event or activity that has been initiated by someone else but it is taking place within your region. For example, the political committee within your region is putting on a 60's Party to help raise funds or Central Headquarters has done a mailing to Doctors in your region, which need a follow up telephone call to solicit funds.

For your information, the political committee is in effect, your counterpart on the campaign side. This committee is referred to as The Field Operations Committee. They too are divided into 5 Regions following the 5 Regions of the Finance Committee. Their primary responsibility is canvassing their precincts, putting up signs, and getting out the vote on Election Day.

In each of the stages, at any given time, something will be happening that will require your involvement in either a direct or support role.

Stage 1: July 16, ---- to September 15, ----

During this first stage, we are asking the Finance Committee members to focus their fund-raising activities on two areas. Contact as many individuals as possible on a one on one basis and make a direct solicitation for campaign contributions. If you believe it would be helpful, especially for a potential major contribution of $1,000, do not hesitate to arrange with March to have him meet with you and the individual.

Bring into Campaign Central Headquarters lists of those individuals who are believed likely prospects for contributions. We will enter the names into the campaign database and generate a special fund-raising letter, either on campaign stationery or on your own. Each member should then personally call these people, approximately ten days after the mailing, to encourage their positive response.

Stage 2: September 16, ---- to December 15, ----

Twice during this stage, we are asking the Finance Committee to sponsor two major fund-raising events. It is considered a major event when the admission price is at least $150 per person. The NET amount to be raised from each event is $60,000, for a total of $120,000. The objective is to sell 400 tickets at $150 per person.

The first event will be a Dinner/Dance on 10/19, kicking off the Miller for Congress campaign. Campaign headquarters will handle the publicity and initial mailing but it will be up to the Finance Committee to do the actual selling. Each Finance Committee member should recruit at least 5 persons to assist them with their ticket sales.

We suggest that you organize a "prospect list" of at least 150 persons in each of your regions as potential contributors. Then call a meeting with your committee members and decide who will be personally responsible for calling at least 15 people from that prospect list. You should then reconvene your meeting ten days later to determine what progress has been made and by whom.

Remember that the above objectives are on a NET basis. Therefore, when making your plans you must take into consideration all expenses involved in the event that you are planning.

During this stage, there will be a regular and on-going direct mail program along with individual solicitation to raise funds. Our objective from these two events is $131,000. The Total Objective of Stage 2 is $285,000.

The second event during this 2nd stage will be another Dinner/Dance or alternate event, if the committee decides to do something different. May 26th is March's birthday and whatever is specifically planned should be developed around that theme. The same suggestions and objectives would apply.

Stage 3: December 16, ---- to March 15, ----

During Stage 3, we plan to have one major fund-raising event. Tentatively this too is planned as a Dinner/Dance. However, the committee can readily change the format. Nevertheless, because of budget considerations, the event should be scheduled no later than Jan. 18, ----. The previously stated suggestions and objectives would apply.

In addition to these major fund-raising events, a series of minor fund-raising events are being planned by the Finance Committee. Since we will not know the final boundaries of this new district until mid-November, or later, we will be unable to schedule these events in any organized fashion. We will have them, but more on an ad hoc basis during Stages 1 and 2. However, during Stage 3 we will schedule at least 5 of these minor events, one in each Region.

At $25 per person the NET objectives in each region are as follows:

> 5 Regions - $4,000 each
> (200 tickets @ $25 each = $5,000 - $1,000 expenses)
>
> Our objective is to raise $20,000 NET from the 5 Regions.

The Field Operations Committee will choose the event (e.g. a 60's party, a dinner, a ski party, or a fashion show). The selection of the event should be based on whatever they believe will work best in their region.

As with the major fund-raising event, a prospect list should be organized, preferably on 3 X 5 cards, and distributed to your committee members for follow up solicitation.

During this stage, our individual solicitation program will continue. Our objective from this source during this stage is $30,000. Essentially, this part of the fund-raising program will be carried on by March and members of the Finance Committee.

The direct mail and PAC solicitation programs will continue as in Stages 1 and 2.

Total objective of Stage 3 is $271,000. The cumulative total of $85,000.00 plus $186,000.00 from sources 3, 4, and 5.

NOTES:

Throughout the campaign period, the Finance Committee will be meeting on a regular basis. Headquarters will provide each Team with a complete report on their Team's accomplishments to date, including each Team member's total, as well as the Team totals.

Attached to this Manual is a copy of the campaign's cash flow budget for your review. This budget, and for that matter this Manual, are confidential. Please, respect the trust of confidentiality.

SUMMARY OF OBJECTIVES AND SOURCES:

Source:	Stage 1 7/— to 9/—	Stage 2 9/— to 12/—	Stage 3 12/— to 3/—
1. Candidate	$ 31,000	$ 40,000	$ 29,000
2. Events	$ 15,000	$ 64,000	$ 56,000
3. Major Contributions	$ 55,000	$ 61,000	$ 55,000
4. Direct Mail	$ 90,000	$ 70,000	$ 65,000
5. Political Action Comm	$ 14,000	$ 50,000	$ 66,000
Stage Totals:	$205,000	$285,000	$271,000
Cumulative Totals:	$205,000	$490,000	$761,000

Note: As mentioned previously, it is imperative to raise the projected contributions in each stage in order to fund the projected expenses of our campaign plan.

IMPORTANT CONSIDERATIONS

All Federal candidates are subject to very strict rules and regulations concerning fund-raising activities. Although some of these rules may seem foolish, the penalties for violating them can be very serious. In addition to the political damage, they involve fines and possible jail sentences.

One of the first rules is that under no circumstances can a Federal candidate accept a campaign contribution from a corporation. All contributions must be from individuals.

These FEC guidelines are subject to change and need to be researched and verified for your campaign. Visit www.fec.gov and review up-to-date regulations.

Another important rule is that the maximum a person can contribute is $1,000 during a campaign period. Keep in mind though that we are involved in two elections, the Primary and the General. Therefore, a person could contribute $1,000 for each period. Also note that it is per person. Both a husband and wife could each give $1,000 in each election period for a total of $4,000. Be aware of an important exception to this rule. An individual may host a fund-raising event in their own home or at a public hall or church and spend up to $1,000 for refreshments without charging it to the campaign or against their $1,000 limit. It is double this amount if the wife is a co-host.

All fund-raising material, including tickets, must have the following disclaimer: "AUTHORIZED AND PAID FOR BY THE MARCH MILLER CONGRESSIONAL COMMITTEE". We strongly recommend therefore that you let headquarters take care of all your printing needs in connection with any fund-raising activity, even if it is done on your own stationery.

All receipts and expenditures must be made through the Congressional Committee.

All monies received on behalf of the campaign must be deposited and recorded immediately. Please be sure to mail them to Campaign Headquarters as soon as they are received. Mail to: March Miller Congressional Comm., P.O. Box

4927, Springfield, VA 20522-4927. Be sure to include a cover note of explanation.

The campaign must have a record of the name, address, telephone number, occupation, and place of employment for all contributions over $200. The name, address, and telephone number is also required for all contributions below $200. Please, be sure to obtain this information for all contributors and submit it with the contribution.

The campaign cannot accept a cash contribution over $100. Over $100 must be made by check.

The Federal Election Commission is currently reviewing all the above rules. If any changes occur during the course of the campaign, we will notify you.

CONCLUSION

As stated at the outset, the job you have to do in the campaign is crucial to its success. The timing is equally important. As any good businessperson knows, "cash flow" is the essential phrase in any budget. Your stages of fund-raising activity are directly related to the Political Stages of the campaign. If we fail to meet objectives on schedule, the political campaign will also be unable to meet its objectives on schedule. Since timing is extremely important in the successful outcome of a political campaign we must do everything possible to succeed.

Unlike other types of "business" operations, where you can modify or adjust schedules and timetables without dire consequences, a political campaign does not have that luxury. We are dealing with a timeframe that cannot be altered. In effect, we have only one opportunity to elect an individual who is extremely well qualified to do the job and represent our interests in Washington.

When you become tired and discouraged with the monumental task before you, remind yourself of what it is all about. It is going to be difficult, but together we can do it. Campaign Headquarters will do its part with all the logistical support that you will need. March will do his part, and then some. Fund-raising events and activities will take precedence over all other events during the course of the campaign. Without these funds, we will be unable to communicate our message to the voters and after all, that is what this is all about. That is in essence what all this money buys, communication to the voters in our district. The existing representatives have been using our tax dollars for years to sell us on their programs. It is now time we sold them on ours.

Thank you for your cooperation in this worthwhile effort.

Richard L. Richardson
Finance Committee Chairman

Sample Phone Bank Operations Manual

Telephone Operations Manual
March Miller Congressional Committee

Introduction

The telephoning you are about to begin on behalf of our Congressional District Candidate, March Miller, is one of the most important jobs in the campaign. Not only will you be making the only personal contact that many of these voters have with the Miller campaign, you will also be accumulating the data essential to target our future contacts.

It is not an exaggeration to say that the outcome of this campaign will be directly related to the success or failure of this telephone program.

Please, take your time and follow the instructions carefully. Do not begin to telephone until you are certain you know what to do. If you have any questions or concerns, contact your Supervisor if you are calling from a phone bank, or Campaign Headquarters at 549-7832, if you are calling from home.

We certainly appreciate the job that you are doing, and sincerely thank you for your efforts on behalf of good government and March's Campaign for Congress.

Sincerely,

Bob Walker
Campaign Chairman

Definitions and Explanations

Take a moment to review the computer printout sheets in front of you. They may look difficult, but after your review, you will find them easy to understand. As mentioned, your Supervisor can answer any questions that you may have now, or in the future.

Starting at the top of the sheet you will notice the date of this printout is listed with the region you are calling, then the area within the region is shown. These are our campaign boundaries, which your supervisor will show you, if you are interested. Then follows the County's Ward and Precinct designations that correspond to our region and area designations. We have also listed the polling place for the precinct that you are calling.

Phone:	Where a number was available, it is listed. If time permits, when there is no number, check with the information operator to see if they have a listing and write the number in that space.
Party:	The voter lists have been consolidated where there is more than one registered voter at the address listed. Therefore RR means that there are two Republican voters in that household, I = Independent, D = Democrat. A "+" sign after the letter means that there are at least two more registered voters in that household.
Last Name:	Wherever possible we have tried to eliminate duplication of voters at the same address. Please check the sheets carefully and strike a single line through any duplication.
First Name:	Usually if there is more than one voter in the household the computer will print the male name, if it was apparent. When addressing mail where there is more than one voter in the household, address it to "The Smith Family."
Address:	Self-evident.
Sub. No.:	Indicates apartment number or special additional designation.
Zip:	The zip code number must be used on all mailings since we are mailing at bulk rates.
VRN:	(Voter Registration Number) The code number assigned to this voter for identification.
Previous ID:	Shows the results obtained during the canvas of the district earlier this year. An "F" indicates that this voter is a known Miller supporter and does not require a telephone call until Election Day. A "U" indicates that they were undecided when last contacted. When calling "U's" please use Telephone Conversation 1.
Voter ID:	U = Undecided or DS = Declined to Say or Deceased. A circle, in pencil, around one of these three letters activates certain responses from the campaign. That is, "F" will receive one type of mail and follow up messages. "U" will receive a different type. "A" will be deleted entirely and will receive no additional communications either by telephone or mail.
Will Help:	V = Volunteer. When this letter is circled the person will be contacted and asked to help on the campaign.

ABS Ballot: This response triggers the Absentee Ballot Program of the Campaign. When the voter requests assistance to vote absentee, the R is circled. When the mail person sends them a request for an absentee ballot, the date of mailing is inserted within the space following and the A is circled. One week later a follow up telephone call will be made to make certain they received the ballot. At this time, the B is circled, if they have received it. Otherwise, another request form is mailed to them.

Mailings: This code acts as a checkpoint for making sure that the mailings originating from the Headquarters are actually sent. When the voter indicates he is undecided, a tabloid (T) will be mailed and the T circled. When a voter requests an Absentee Ballot application form, a letter and form will be sent in a separate envelope and the AB will be circled.

Election Day: This section will not be used until Tuesday, November 4th. It is a control mechanism designed to help regulate the number of calls made to Get Out The Vote (GOTV) on Election Day. When the 1st call is made, circle the 1. If the person has voted, circle the + and no further calls will be made. If transportation to the polls is needed, the T should be circled and the information is given to the Supervisor. If a second call is needed later in the day to remind them to vote, then the 2 is circled following the completion of that call.

Total Households This Printout: ( ) Equals the number of households shown on this printout within the precinct. Next to this should be the number of voters in the precinct.

Total Voters: ( ) Record the final number of Miller supporters identified in this precinct prior to the election.

Precinct Voter Objective: ( ) This figure will be entered by the Campaign and compared with the total positive votes on Election Day.

Tips to Telephone Effectively

Put a smile in your voice. The easiest and surest way to do this is to have a smile on your face while telephoning.

Never argue.

Please adhere to the printed conversation. Do not ask if we can send literature.

Use only pencil markings on the voter printout sheets.

If there is no answer after five rings, please call the next number on the voter list.

Do not forget to make the appropriate mark on the voter sheet (circle F, U or A) after a completed call. Failure to do this will result in multiple calls to a home. This is irritating to voters. ONLY ONE MARK PER HOUSEHOLD. Register the response of the person with whom you are speaking and consider it the answer for the whole family.

During the conversation, repeat the name of the person with whom you are speaking as often as it is comfortable for you to do so. People like to hear their name repeated.

Do not mark the voter printout sheet if the line is "busy" or "doesn't answer." Mark the sheet only with coding indicated on conversation sheet. If number is no longer in service, draw a line through the number. Make an effort, through the information operator, to secure the new number of the voter.

Remember that it is important to ask every "yes" voter three (3) things:

(1) will he/she volunteer?
(2) would anyone in the household like to make a campaign contribution?
(3) will he/she or any member of the family need an absentee ballot?

Consult your biographic sketch of March Miller if personal information is requested. If a question is asked that you cannot answer, or if a question is posed to you regarding March's position on certain issues in the material provided, advise the voter that you cannot speak for March Miller on issues, but he or she will receive a direct communication answering the question. Verify name and address. Make note of the question, the name, and address of the voter. Give it to the Supervisor, or send it to HQ, if calling from home.

If a voter states he or she will require transportation to the polls, inform the voter that we will be happy to supply this service and that the transportation committee will be in touch with the voter closer to the election November 4th, to arrange a time mutually convenient. After hanging up, put the voter's name, address, telephone number, precinct number, and "ride to the polls" on the pad provided. Give this information to the Supervisor. Circle the T in the Election Day column on the voter printout sheet.

If irritation is encountered because of former campaign telephoning, or for other reasons, you should apologize and inform the voter that the calls are being made from the registered voter list. Add, if possible, "While I have you on the telephone may I commend you on your interest in good government evidenced by being a registered voter."

"KEEP DIALING." TELEPHONES ON HOOKS LOSE VOTES.

Telephone conversation No. 1

The Advocacy Call - Conversation to U (undecideds) and previous U's.

"Hello, Mr./Mrs. Straub, this is Ron Campbell, a volunteer with the March Miller Congressional Committee. We think that it is time for a change in government and that March Miller is unusually well qualified. He would do an excellent job for us in Congress. Mr./Mrs. Straub, may we count on your support for March Miller?

If Answer is:	Reply:	Mark Sheet
NO	Thank you for your time.	Circle A in Voter ID column. Mark a line through name.
YES	That's good to hear.	Circle F in Voter ID column

Would anyone in the household like to contribute to the Miller for Congress Campaign?

If Answer is:	Reply:	Mark Sheet
YES	Wonderful, here is the address to send your contribution.	Circle C in Will Help column.
NO	We understand, however, we do appreciate your support of Mr. Miller.	

Would you like to be part of the Miller for Congress team and work in the campaign?

If Answer is:	Reply:	Mark Sheet
YES	That's great. Our Volunteer chairman will be in touch with you. We certainly appreciate your willingness to help. After hanging up, put name, address, telephone number, and Precinct on card provided and give it to the Supervisor or send it to Campaign Headquarters.	Circle V in Will Help column.
NO	We understand; however, we do appreciate your support of Mr. Miller.	

14

Is there a possibility you or any member of your family may require an absentee ballot?

If Answer is:	Reply:	Mark Sheet
YES	We will send you a request form for an absentee ballot. This form should be completed and mailed as soon as possible. Thank you for your interest in electing March Miller.	Circle R in ABS Ballot column. (see Absentee Ballot Operating instructions)
NO	Mr./Mrs. Straub it has been a pleasure talking with you. Thanks again for your support of March Miller.	
Undecided or Non-Committal	March Miller has a remarkable record in his business and public life. Your favorable consideration and support of March on November 4th will be appreciated.	Circle U in Voter ID column. Address a tabloid to them and circle T in Mailings column on voter print out sheet.

NOTE:

1) All previously identified U's have already received a tabloid. Only the undecideds identified from this U call should be sent a tabloid following this call.

2) After you have called all the U's assigned to you please recall all previous U's (undecideds) repeating the same opening conversation and see if they have decided to vote for March. If they have, erase the circle around the "U" and circle the "F." This will insure their getting a follow up telephone call on Election Day.

If they are still undecided, address an undecided mail packet and send it to them. This applies to undecideds determined from the previous ID survey and your current call.

Telephone Conversation No. 2

Previously ID'd - Conversation to "F's" only. Begin calling Monday, 10/1/----.

"Hello, Mr./Mrs. Straub, this is Ron Campbell, a volunteer with the March Miller Congressional Committee. As you know election time is coming close and we just wanted to check with you and see if there is a possibility you or any member of your family may require an absentee ballot?"

If Answer is:	Reply:	Mark Sheet
YES	We will send you a request form for an absentee ballot. This form should be completed and mailed as soon as possible. Thank you for your interest in electing March Miller.	Circle R in ABS Ballot column.
NO	It has been a pleasure talking with you. Thanks again for your support of March Miller.	Put an X over the R in the ABS Ballot column.

Absentee Ballot Program

Step 1

All households circled with an "R" in the ABS Ballot Column should have a number ten envelope addressed to them. After the envelope is addressed, the date should be printed in the space after the R of the ABS Ballot Column and then circle the "A" in the ABS Ballot Column.

The enclosures for the envelope are:

1) Application for Absentee Ballot
2) Properly addressed and stamped plain white envelope for returning the ballot application to the County Auditor or Registrar's Office.

Step 2

Address a different envelope to the same person to whom you have just sent the ballot application. DO NOT USE THE SAME ENVELOPE CONTAINING THE BALLOT APPLICATION. Enclose the proper letter and literature from March Miller. Circle the "AB" on the voter printout sheet in the mailing column.

At the end of each day these should all be stamped, sorted by Zip code, and mailed.

During the Absentee Ballot period, approximately 10/1-10/15, it is the responsibility of the telephone volunteers to watch these dates on the voter printout sheets. Seven days after any date indicating a request for a ballot application the telephoner should call and inquire as follows:

1) was the application received, and
2) did the voter complete the form and mail it in.

The following instructions should be observed:

If an affirmative answer is received, circle "B" in the ABS Ballot column on the voter printout sheet.

If a negative response is received, the telephoner should erase the old date and write the new date on the sheet, and repeat step 1 above.

Volunteer Timetable

September	Prepare sheets for telephoning. Check telephone numbers and supplies.
September	Start Advocacy Phone Bank program with Telephone Conversation No. 1. Begin Precinct and Patriot Sign program.
October	Begin calling Previous ID's designated "F" regarding Absentee Ballot. Continue Advocacy program, concentrating on Previous ID "U" persons.
October	Begin Postcard Mail program and put up Patriot yard signs.
November	Start calling all known "F's" and remind them that Election Day is Tuesday.
November	BEGIN GOTV PROGRAM

Calling Priority:

1st All identified "F's"
2nd All households with a Party designation "R"
3rd As time permits, all households with a Party designation "D" in Regions 1, 4, and 5, unless there is also an "A" in the household.

Phone Volunteer Program Supplies

- Volunteer cards
- Information Request pads
- Ruler
- No. 10 Campaign envelopes
- Tabloids
- Single page biographic sketch
- Brochures
- Letter to Undecideds, 2nd mailing
- Transportation Request pads
- No. 2 pencils
- Absentee Ballot applications
- No. 10 Plain envelopes, with stamps
- Synopsis of Issues
- Letter to Absentee Ballot voters
- Comparison of Voting Record Sheets

Chapter 14 - Word Index

Appendix A
Physical Characteristics Check List

Characteristic	Candidate		Opponent	
Gender				
Race				
Nationality				
Age				
Marital Status				
Height				
Weight				
Color of Hair				
Color of Eyes				
Facial Hair (mustache / beard)				
Glasses	❏ Yes	❏ No	❏ Yes	❏ No
Athletic	❏ Yes	❏ No	❏ Yes	❏ No
Physically Attractive	❏ Yes	❏ No	❏ Yes	❏ No
Physical Bearing				
Condition of Health				
Physical Handicap				
Speech Impediment	❏ Yes	❏ No	❏ Yes	❏ No
Occupation				
Place of Birth				
Number of Children				
Homeowner	❏ Yes	❏ No	❏ Yes	❏ No
Make of Car Owned (foreign / domestic)				
Estimated Net Worth				
Party Affiliation				

Appendix B

Physical Characteristics Analysis

Characteristic	Code	Caucasian Male	Caucasian Female	African American Male	African American Female	Hispanic Male	Hispanic Female
Gender	+ -						
Race	+ -						
Nationality	+ -						
Age	+ -						
Marital Status	+ -						
Height	+ -						
Weight	+ -						
Hair	+ -						
Eyes	+ -						
Facial Hair	+ -						
Glasses	+ -						
Athletic	+ -						
Physical Bearing	+ -						
Attractive	+ -						
Healthy	+ -						
Occupation	+ -						
Place of Birth	+ -						
No. of Children	+ -						
Home Ownership	+ -						
Type of Car	+ -						
Net Worth	+ -						
Party Affiliation	+ -						

Appendix C
Intellectual Characteristics Check List

Characteristic	Candidate	Candidate's Spouse	Opponent	Opponent's Spouse
Estimated IQ Level				
Highest Education Level				
University Attended				
G.P.A./ SAT Scores				
Special Academic Honors				
Profession / Title				
Associations (Present)				
Associations (Past)				
Hobbies				
Alcoholic	❑ Yes ❑ No	❑ Yes ❑ No	❑ Yes ❑ No	❑ Yes ❑ No
Drug User	❑ Yes ❑ No	❑ Yes ❑ No	❑ Yes ❑ No	❑ Yes ❑ No
Neurotic	❑ Yes ❑ No	❑ Yes ❑ No	❑ Yes ❑ No	❑ Yes ❑ No
Articulate	❑ Yes ❑ No	❑ Yes ❑ No	❑ Yes ❑ No	❑ Yes ❑ No
Computer Literate	❑ Yes ❑ No	❑ Yes ❑ No	❑ Yes ❑ No	❑ Yes ❑ No
Economic Philosophy	❑ L ❑ M ❑ C	❑ L ❑ M ❑ C	❑ L ❑ M ❑ C	❑ L ❑ M ❑ C
Political Philosophy	❑ L ❑ M ❑ C	❑ L ❑ M ❑ C	❑ L ❑ M ❑ C	❑ L ❑ M ❑ C
Social Philosophy	❑ L ❑ M ❑ C	❑ L ❑ M ❑ C	❑ L ❑ M ❑ C	❑ L ❑ M ❑ C
Personal Philosophy	❑ L ❑ M ❑ C	❑ L ❑ M ❑ C	❑ L ❑ M ❑ C	❑ L ❑ M ❑ C

L = Liberal **M = Moderate** **C = Conservative**

A

Appendix D
Intellectual Characteristics Analysis

Characteristic	Values	Caucasian Male	Caucasian Female	African American Male	African American Female	Hispanic Male	Hispanic Female
Estimated I.Q.	+ -						
Education Level	+ -						
University	+ -						
G.P.A./SAT Scores	+ -						
Honors	+ -						
Profession	+ -						
Associations	+ -						
Hobbies	+ -						
Alcohol Use	+ -						
Drug Use	+ -						
Neurotic	+ -						
Articulate	+ -						
Computer Literate	+ -						
Economic Philosophy	+ -						
Political Philosophy	+ -						
Social Philosophy	+ -						
Personal Philosophy	+ -						
	+ -						
	+ -						
	+ -						
	+ -						
	+ -						

Appendix E

Emotional Characteristics Check List

Characteristic	Candidate	Candidate's Spouse	Opponent	Opponent's Spouse
Affectionate	❑ Yes ❑ No	❑ Yes ❑ No	❑ Yes ❑ No	❑ Yes ❑ No
Argumentative	❑ Yes ❑ No	❑ Yes ❑ No	❑ Yes ❑ No	❑ Yes ❑ No
Arrogant	❑ Yes ❑ No	❑ Yes ❑ No	❑ Yes ❑ No	❑ Yes ❑ No
Belligerent	❑ Yes ❑ No	❑ Yes ❑ No	❑ Yes ❑ No	❑ Yes ❑ No
Calculating	❑ Yes ❑ No	❑ Yes ❑ No	❑ Yes ❑ No	❑ Yes ❑ No
Caring	❑ Yes ❑ No	❑ Yes ❑ No	❑ Yes ❑ No	❑ Yes ❑ No
Charismatic	❑ Yes ❑ No	❑ Yes ❑ No	❑ Yes ❑ No	❑ Yes ❑ No
Compassionate	❑ Yes ❑ No	❑ Yes ❑ No	❑ Yes ❑ No	❑ Yes ❑ No
Confident	❑ Yes ❑ No	❑ Yes ❑ No	❑ Yes ❑ No	❑ Yes ❑ No
Courageous	❑ Yes ❑ No	❑ Yes ❑ No	❑ Yes ❑ No	❑ Yes ❑ No
Cruel	❑ Yes ❑ No	❑ Yes ❑ No	❑ Yes ❑ No	❑ Yes ❑ No
Cunning	❑ Yes ❑ No	❑ Yes ❑ No	❑ Yes ❑ No	❑ Yes ❑ No
Defensive	❑ Yes ❑ No	❑ Yes ❑ No	❑ Yes ❑ No	❑ Yes ❑ No
Deliberate	❑ Yes ❑ No	❑ Yes ❑ No	❑ Yes ❑ No	❑ Yes ❑ No
Demagogic	❑ Yes ❑ No	❑ Yes ❑ No	❑ Yes ❑ No	❑ Yes ❑ No
Demonstrative	❑ Yes ❑ No	❑ Yes ❑ No	❑ Yes ❑ No	❑ Yes ❑ No
Energetic	❑ Yes ❑ No	❑ Yes ❑ No	❑ Yes ❑ No	❑ Yes ❑ No
Generous	❑ Yes ❑ No	❑ Yes ❑ No	❑ Yes ❑ No	❑ Yes ❑ No
Gesticulating	❑ Yes ❑ No	❑ Yes ❑ No	❑ Yes ❑ No	❑ Yes ❑ No
Happy	❑ Yes ❑ No	❑ Yes ❑ No	❑ Yes ❑ No	❑ Yes ❑ No
Honest	❑ Yes ❑ No	❑ Yes ❑ No	❑ Yes ❑ No	❑ Yes ❑ No
Industrious	❑ Yes ❑ No	❑ Yes ❑ No	❑ Yes ❑ No	❑ Yes ❑ No
Insecure	❑ Yes ❑ No	❑ Yes ❑ No	❑ Yes ❑ No	❑ Yes ❑ No
Integrity	❑ Yes ❑ No	❑ Yes ❑ No	❑ Yes ❑ No	❑ Yes ❑ No
Introvert	❑ Yes ❑ No	❑ Yes ❑ No	❑ Yes ❑ No	❑ Yes ❑ No
Kind	❑ Yes ❑ No	❑ Yes ❑ No	❑ Yes ❑ No	❑ Yes ❑ No
Loquacious	❑ Yes ❑ No	❑ Yes ❑ No	❑ Yes ❑ No	❑ Yes ❑ No
Miserly	❑ Yes ❑ No	❑ Yes ❑ No	❑ Yes ❑ No	❑ Yes ❑ No
Modest	❑ Yes ❑ No	❑ Yes ❑ No	❑ Yes ❑ No	❑ Yes ❑ No
Moralistic	❑ Yes ❑ No	❑ Yes ❑ No	❑ Yes ❑ No	❑ Yes ❑ No
Optimistic	❑ Yes ❑ No	❑ Yes ❑ No	❑ Yes ❑ No	❑ Yes ❑ No
Patriotic	❑ Yes ❑ No	❑ Yes ❑ No	❑ Yes ❑ No	❑ Yes ❑ No
Persuasive	❑ Yes ❑ No	❑ Yes ❑ No	❑ Yes ❑ No	❑ Yes ❑ No
Pompous	❑ Yes ❑ No	❑ Yes ❑ No	❑ Yes ❑ No	❑ Yes ❑ No
Prejudicial	❑ Yes ❑ No	❑ Yes ❑ No	❑ Yes ❑ No	❑ Yes ❑ No
Reflective	❑ Yes ❑ No	❑ Yes ❑ No	❑ Yes ❑ No	❑ Yes ❑ No
Religious	❑ Yes ❑ No	❑ Yes ❑ No	❑ Yes ❑ No	❑ Yes ❑ No
Sensitive	❑ Yes ❑ No	❑ Yes ❑ No	❑ Yes ❑ No	❑ Yes ❑ No
Sentimental	❑ Yes ❑ No	❑ Yes ❑ No	❑ Yes ❑ No	❑ Yes ❑ No
Sexual Orientation				
Shy	❑ Yes ❑ No	❑ Yes ❑ No	❑ Yes ❑ No	❑ Yes ❑ No
Strong	❑ Yes ❑ No	❑ Yes ❑ No	❑ Yes ❑ No	❑ Yes ❑ No
Talkative	❑ Yes ❑ No	❑ Yes ❑ No	❑ Yes ❑ No	❑ Yes ❑ No
Temperamental	❑ Yes ❑ No	❑ Yes ❑ No	❑ Yes ❑ No	❑ Yes ❑ No
Vain	❑ Yes ❑ No	❑ Yes ❑ No	❑ Yes ❑ No	❑ Yes ❑ No
Volatile	❑ Yes ❑ No	❑ Yes ❑ No	❑ Yes ❑ No	❑ Yes ❑ No

Appendix F

Emotional Characteristics Analysis

Characteristic	Values	Caucasian Male	Caucasian Female	African American Male	African American Female	Hispanic Male	Hispanic Female
Affectionate	+ -						
Arrogant	+ -						
Caring	+ -						
Charismatic	+ -						
Confident	+ -						
Courage	+ -						
Gentle	+ -						
Happy	+ -						
Honest	+ -						
Introvert	+ -						
Industrious	+ -						
Optimistic	+ -						
Moralistic	+ -						
Patriotic	+ -						
Persuasive	+ -						
Prejudicial	+ -						
Religious	+ -						
Secure	+ -						
Sexual Orientation	+ -						
Shrewd	+ -						
Strong	+ -						
Talkative	+ -						
Vain	+ -						

Appendix G
Tabulation Work Sheet #1

Total Sample:	No.	%

Response	Totals		Male		Female	
(Q1,A)						
(Q1,B)						
(Q1,C)						
(Q1,D)						
(Q1,E)						
(Q1,F)						
(Q2,A)						
(Q2,B)						
(Q2,C)						
(Q2,D)						
(Q2,E)						
(Q2,F)						
(Q3,A1)						
(Q3,A2)						
(Q3,A3)						
(Q3,B1)						
(Q3,B2)						
(Q3,B3)						
(Q4,A)						
(Q4,B)						
(Q5,A)						
(Q5,B)						
(Q5,C)						

A

Appendix H
Tabulation Work Sheet #2

Total Sample:	No.	%

Response	Totals	Caucasian Male	Caucasian Female	African American Male	African American Female	Hispanic Male	Hispanic Female
(Q1,A)							
(Q1,B)							
(Q1,C)							
(Q1,D)							
(Q1,E)							
(Q1,F)							
(Q2,A)							
(Q2,B)							
(Q2,C)							
(Q2,D)							
(Q2,E)							
(Q2,F)							
(Q3,A1)							
(Q3,A2)							
(Q3,A3)							
(Q3,B1)							
(Q3,B2)							
(Q3,B3)							
(Q4,A)							
(Q4,B)							
(Q5,A)							
(Q5,B)							
(Q5,C)							

Appendix I

Personal History Check List

Personal History	Candidate		Candidate's Spouse		Opponent		Opponent's Spouse	
Place of Birth - City, State								
Date of Birth								
Father's Name								
Mother's Maiden Name								
Father's Occupation								
Mother's Occupation								
Number of Brothers								
Number of Sisters								
Ranking in Family								
Raised - City, State								
Junior High School								
High School								
College								
Occupation								
Childhood Religion								
Current Religion								
Hobbies								
Military / Branch / Rank								
Physical Impairments								
Wife's Maiden Name								
Date Married								
Ever Divorced	❑ Yes	❑ No	❑ Yes	❑ No	❑ Yes	❑ No	❑ Yes	❑ No
Number of Marriages								
Number of Children								
Number of Grandchildren								
Social Organizations								
Religious Organizations								
Ethnic Origin / Ancestry								
Date Moved to District								
Localities Lived In								
Fraternities / Sororities								
Athletic Activities								
Traumatic Experiences								

A

Appendix J
Personal History Analysis

Personal Items	Value	Caucasian Male	Caucasian Female	African American Male	African American Female	Hispanic Male	Hispanic Female
Place of Birth - City, State	+ -						
Date of Birth	+ -						
Father's Name	+ -						
Mother's Maiden Name	+ -						
Father's Occupation	+ -						
Mother's Occupation	+ -						
Number of Brothers	+ -						
Number of Sisters	+ -						
Ranking in Family	+ -						
Raised - City, State	+ -						
Junior High School	+ -						
High School	+ -						
College	+ -						
Occupation	+ -						
Childhood Religion	+ -						
Current Religion	+ -						
Hobbies	+ -						
Military/Branch/Rank	+ -						
Physical Impairments	+ -						
Wife's Maiden Name	+ -						
Date Married	+ -						
Ever Divorced	+ -						
Number of Marriages	+ -						
Number of Children	+ -						
No. of Grandchildren	+ -						
Social Organizations	+ -						
Religious Organizations	+ -						
Ethnic Origin/Ancestry	+ -						
Date Moved to District	+ -						
Localities Lived In	+ -						
Fraternities/Sororities	+ -						
Athletic Activities	+ -						
Traumatic Experiences	+ -						
	+ -						
	+ -						
	+ -						
	+ -						
	+ -						
	+ -						
	+ -						
	+ -						
	+ -						
	+ -						
	+ -						

Appendix K

Career History Check List

Career History	Candidate	Candidate's Spouse	Opponent	Opponent's Spouse
Present Employer Date of Employment Recent Position or Title Approximate Annual Earnings Type of Work Performed Number of People Supervised Noteworthy Accomplishments				
Past Employer Period of Employment Position or Title Approximate Annual Earnings Type of Work Performed Number of People Supervised Noteworthy Accomplishments Reason/s for Leaving				
Previous Employer Period of Employment Position or Title Approximate Annual Earnings Type of Work Performed Number of People Supervised Noteworthy Accomplishments Reason/s for Leaving				
Next Previous Employer Period of Employment Position or Title Approximate Annual Earnings Type of Work Performed Number of People Supervised Noteworthy Accomplishments Reason/s for Leaving				
Next Previous Employer Period of Employment Position or Title Approximate Annual Earnings Type of Work Performed Number of People Supervised Noteworthy Accomplishments Reason/s for Leaving				

A

Appendix L
Civic History Check List

Civic History	Candidate	Candidate's Spouse	Opponent	Opponent's Spouse
Boy/Girl Scout Leader				
Little League Coach				
PTA Activist				
Benevolent Organization				
United Way Fund Activity				
Parks & Recreation				
Bond Committees				
Homeowners Association				
Youth Activity				
Altar Society				
Choir				
Deacon				
Veteran's Activities				
Organization Visiting Sick				
Organization Helping Homeless				
Foster Care				
Hospice				
Sr. Citizen Activities				
Organized Charities				
Other				

Appendix M
Sample Forms - Inside Flap / BRE

Dear

I hereby publicly endorse and support your candidacy for ______________(office) from ________________________(district). I would also like to volunteer my services on your behalf. I can do the following:

- ❏ Be a Precinct Worker
- ❏ Help Distribute Literature
- ❏ Put Up a Yard Sign
- ❏ Help Raise Funds
- ❏ Do Telephone Work
- ❏ Do Office Work

____
Signature

The Campaign Reporting Laws prohibit accepting contributions which do not accompany the following information. **Please Print Clearly.**

Name: ____________________ Occupation: ____________________

Address: ____________________ Employer: ____________________

____________________ Address: ____________________

Home Phone: ____________________ ____________________

Amount of Contribution: ____________ Work Phone: ____________________

Inside Flap of 6.5" BRE (wallet style)

Appendix M

Sample Forms - Pledge Card / Contributor's Card

Pledge Card

I hereby pledge to the ______________________________ (Committee)

the sum of $ ______________, to help ____________________ in his/her efforts to

win the ____________________ (office) race in ____________________ (district).

❑ Please bill me immediately.

❑ Please bill me in equal installments on the 1st of each month for the next 4 weeks.

Date: ____________________ Signed: ____________________

Name: ____________________ Occupation: ____________________

Address: ____________________ Employer: ____________________

____________________ Address: ____________________

Home Phone: ____________________ ____________________

A copy of our report is filed with the Federal Election Commission and is available for purchase from the Federal Election Commission, Washington, D.C. ______________ Treasurer ____________________ (Committee), P.O. Box ____________________

Contributors Card

Name: ____________________ Region: ____________________

Salutation: ____________________

Address: ____________________ Area: ____________________

____________________ PCT.: ____________________

Phone: (H) ______________ (W) ______________ Non-District: ____________________

Occupation: ______________ Code: ______________ Transmitted: ____________________

Employer: ____________________ Volunteer? ____________________

____________________ Endorsement? ____________________

Amount: $ ________ Date: ________ YTD: $ ________ TYL: ________ By: ________

Amount: $ ________ Date: ________ YTD: $ ________ TYL: ________ By: ________

Amount: $ ________ Date: ________ YTD: $ ________ TYL: ________ By: ________

Amount: $ ________ Date: ________ YTD: $ ________ TYL: ________ By: ________

Comments: ____________________

____

Appendix M

Sample Forms - Volunteer's Card / Endorsement Cards

Volunteer's Card (Blue)

Name: ______________________ Region: __________

Address: ______________________ Area: __________

______________________ PCT.: __________

Occupation: ______________________ Letter Sent: __________

Phone: (H) __________ (W) __________ Transmitted: __________

Source: ______________________ Date: __________

Type of activity willing to do: ______________________

Comments: ______________________

____

____

____

Endorser's File Card (Pink)

Name: ______________________ Region: __________

Address: ______________________ Area: __________

______________________ PCT.: __________

Occupation: ______________________ Volunteer? __________

Phone: (H) __________ (W) __________ Contributor? __________

Source: ______________________ Date: __________

Verified By: ______________________ Date: __________

Comments: ______________________

____

____

____

Endorsement Card (White)

I do hereby publicly endorse and support the candidacy of ______________________

for ______________________ in __________, ______

____

Signature

Name: ______________________

Address: ______________________

____

Occupation: ______________________

Phone: (H) __________ (W) __________

A

Appendix M
Sample Forms - Request For Appearance Form

Event Details

Name of Event: ____________________
Location of Event: ____________________
Type of Event: ____________________
City: __________ State: __________ Zip: __________
Date: __________ Time: __________
Event Scheduled for: Event Contact: __________
❑ Candidate ❑ Substitute__________ Event Contact Phone: __________
Event open to: ❑ Public ❑ Fundraiser Invitee's Guest/Dignitaries: __________
❑ Media ❑ Q. and A. __________
❑ Literature Distribution __________
❑ Speaking Engagement __________
Attendance: __________ Activity: __________

General

Entry Date: __________ Entry Priority: __________
County: __________ Precinct: __________
Precinct No.: __________ Region/Area: __________/__________
Title: ____________________

Event Host

Host Organization: ____________________
Address: ____________________
City: __________ State: __________ Zip: __________
Phone: __________ Fax: __________
E-mail: __________ Web Site: __________
Requested by: ____________________
Requested Address: ____________________
Phone: __________ Fax: __________
E-mail: ____________________

Event Approval

Approval: ❑ Pending ❑ After: __________ Approval Date: __________
❑ Not Approved: Date: __________ By: __________
❑ Confirmation Sent Date: __________ By: __________
Special Instructions: ____________________
____
____
____
Candidate/Campaign Manager Approval: __________

Appendix M

Sample Forms - Endorsement and Support Signature Sheet

Region:____________________ Area: ________________ PCT: ________________

Date received at Central:____________________Circulator's Name:________________

When completed, please return to: Phone:________________

We the undersigned, do hereby publicly endorse and support the candidacy of ________________
for____, in________________

PLEASE PRINT CLEARLY.

Date:	Name:	Address:	Phone:	Occupation:

Appendix M

Sample Forms - Daily Schedule Form

Time:	Appointment
6:00 am	
6:30 am	
7:00 am	
7:30 am	
8:00 am	
8:30 am	
9:00 am	
9:30 am	
10:00 am	
10:30 am	
11:00 am	
11:30 am	
12:00 pm	
12:30 pm	
1:00 pm	
1:30 pm	
2:00 pm	
2:30 pm	
3:00 pm	
3:30 pm	
4:00 pm	
4:30 pm	
5:00 pm	
5:30 pm	
6:00 pm	
6:30 pm	
7:00 pm	
7:30 pm	
8:00 pm	
8:30 pm	
9:00 pm	
9:30 pm	
10:00 pm	
10:30 pm	
11:00 pm	

Campaign Organization Roles

Campaign Stage References

Campaign Organizational Flow Chart

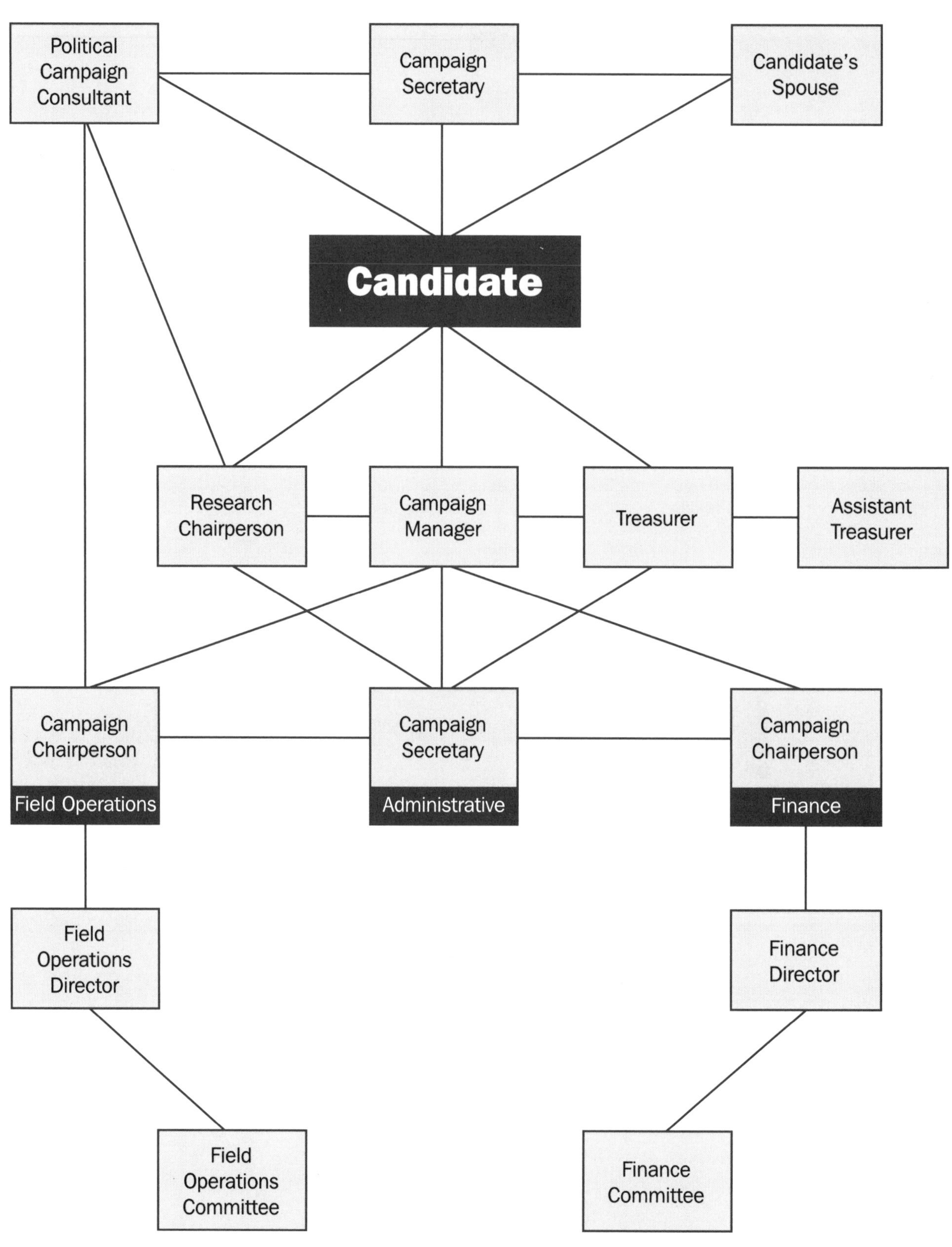

Finance Organizational Flow Chart

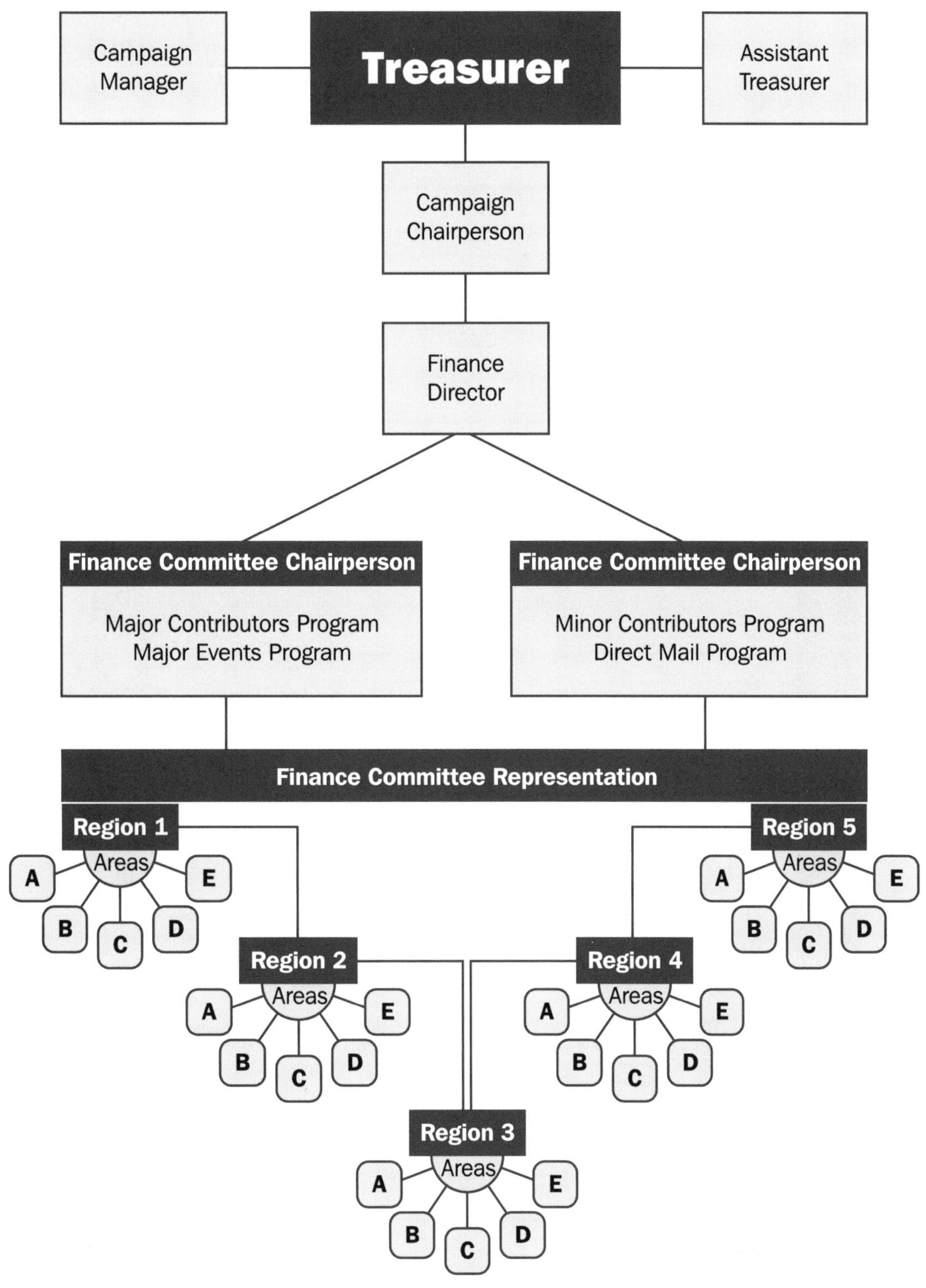

C

Field Operations Organizational Flow Chart

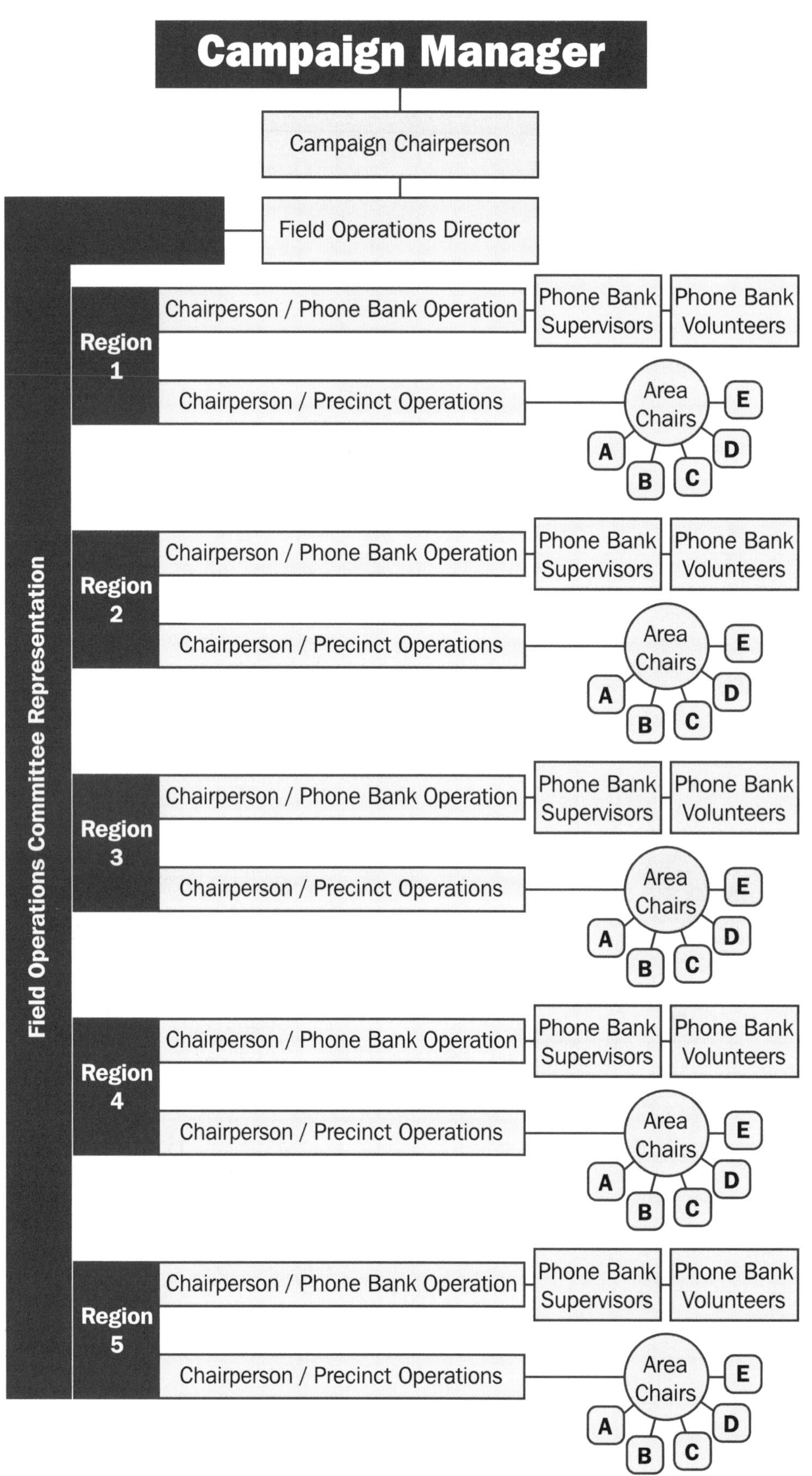

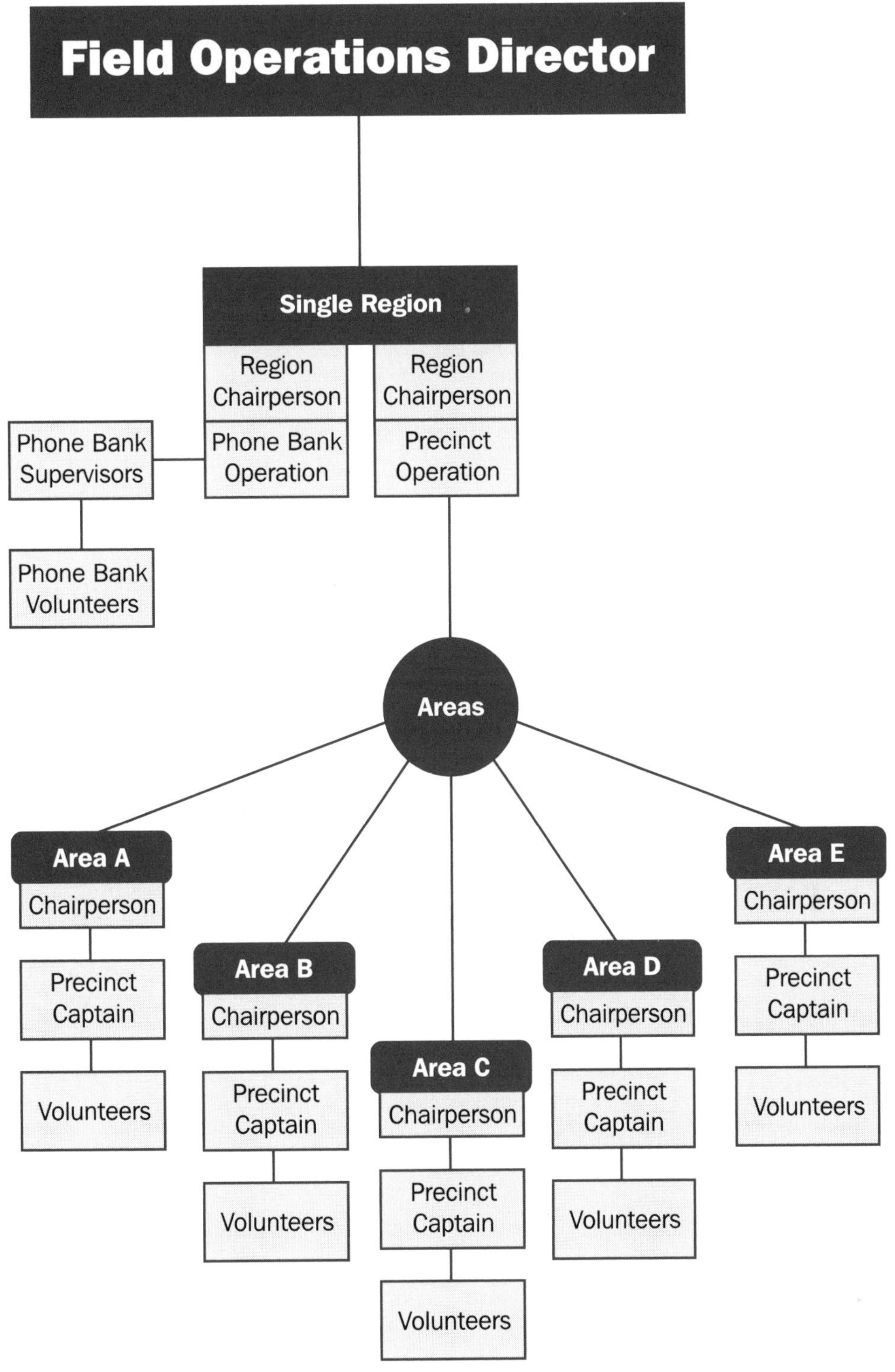
Field Operations Director
Single Region
Region Chairperson
Region Chairperson
Phone Bank Supervisors
Phone Bank Operation
Precinct Operation
Phone Bank Volunteers
Areas
Area A
Chairperson
Precinct Captain
Volunteers
Area B
Chairperson
Precinct Captain
Volunteers
Area C
Chairperson
Precinct Captain
Volunteers
Area D
Chairperson
Precinct Captain
Volunteers
Area E
Chairperson
Precinct Captain
Volunteers

C

Definitions

Definitions

D

Directory of Political Resources

Publisher's Note: On the following pages, you will find a directory listing of political resources and possible sources of assistance.

These pages contain the addresses and telephone numbers of the National Parties, government agencies, and others that might be helpful to political candidates seeking information and assistance.

Possible Sources of Assistance

American Association of Political Consultants
The Association For Political & Public Affairs Professionals
600 Penn. Ave., SE, Suite 330, Washington, DC 20003
Tel.: 202.544.9815 • Fax: 202.544.9816
E-mail: aapcmail@aol.com • Web: www.theaapc.org

Apian Software, Inc.
400 N. 34th St., Suite 310, Seattle, WA 98103
Tel.: 206.547.5321 • 800.237.4565 • Fax: 206.547.8493
E-mail: sales@apian.com • Web: www.apian.com

Bristol Screen, inc.
200 Delaware Ave., Bristol, TN 37620
Tel.: 423.968.5871 • Fax: 423.968.9247
E-mail: greg@bsi-america.com • Web: www.bsi-america.com

Campaigns & Elections, Inc.
1414 22nd St. NW, Washington, D.C. 20037
Tel.: 202.887.8530 • Toll Free: 800.888.5767 • Fax: 202.463.7085
E-mail: campaignline@cq.com • Web: www.campaignline.com
Web Buyers Guide: www.campaignline.com/buyers

Clerk of the House
H-154, U.S. Capitol, Washington, DC 20515
Tel.: 202.225.7000
Web: www.clerkweb.house.gov

CSS Direct, Inc.
313 North 30th Street, Omaha, NE 68131
Tel.: 402.341.3537 • Fax: 402.341.3647
E-mail: sales@cssdirect.com • Web: www.cssdirect.com

Democratic Congressional Committee
430 S. Capitol St., SE, Washington, DC 20003
Tel.: 202.863.1500 • Fax: 202.485.3522
Web: www.takebackthehouse.com

Democratic National Committee
430 S. Capitol St., SE, Washington, DC 20003
Tel.: 202.863.8000 • Fax: 202.863.8063
E-mail: mail@dnc.democrats.org • Web: www.democrats.org

Democratic Senate Committee
430 S. Capitol St., SE, Washington, DC 20003
Tel.: 202.224.2447 • Fax: 202.485.3120
E-mail: info@dscc.org • Web: www.dscc.org

Federal Election Commission
999 E St., NW, Washington, DC 20463
Tel.: 202.694.1100 • 800.424.9530
Web: www.fec.gov

Kolker Systems, Inc.
5751 Palmer Way, Bldg. E., Carlsbad, CA 92008
Tel.: 760.431.9633 • Fax: 760.431.1866
Web: www.kolkersystems.com • E-mail: kolkersystems@mindspring.com

League of Women Voters
1730 M Street, NW, Washington, DC 20036
Tel.: 202.429.1965 • Fax: 202.429.4343
E-mail: Web Site Contact • Web: www.lwv.org

National Campaign Institute
Salvatore J. Guzzetta
6407 May Blvd., Alexandria, VA 22310
Tel.: 703.924.6612

National League of Cities
1301 Penn. Ave., NW, Washington, DC 20004
Tel.: 202.626.3000
Web: www.nlc.org/nlc_org/site

National Republican Congressional Committee
320 1st St., SE, Washington, DC 20003
Tel.: 202.479.7050 • Fax: 202.484.1154
E-mail: webmaster@nrcc.org • Web: www.nrcc.org

National Republican Senatorial Committee
425 2nd Street NE, Washington DC 20002
Tel.: 202.675.6000 • Fax: 202.675.4940
E-mail: webmaster@nrsc.org • Web: www.nrsc.org

Political Resource Directory
P. O. Box 3365, Burlington, VT 05406
Tel.: 800.423.2677 • Fax: 802.864.9502
E-mail: info@politicalresources.com • Web: www.politicalresources.com

Quality Press
14820 Countryview Place, Waldorf, MD 20601
Tel.: 301.843.3143 • Fax: 301.645.0349

Republican National Committee
310 1st St., SE, Washington, DC 20003
Tel.: 202.863.8500 • Fax: 202.863.8820
E-mail: info@rnc.org • Web: www.rnc.org

Senate Document Room
Senate Office Building, RM. B-04, Washington, DC 20510
Tel.: 202.224.7860 • Fax: 202.228.2815
E-mail: nleohr@indiana.edu • Web: www.indiana.edu/~libmps/order/sena.html

Superintendent of Documents
P.O. Box 371954, Pittsburgh, PA 15250
Tel.: 202.512.1800 • Fax: 202.512.2250
E-mail: wwwadmin@gpo.gov • Web: www.bookstore.gpo.gov • Web: www.access.gpo.gov

The Campaign Manual - Word Index

W

W